Mass Communication In Canada

ROWLAND LORIMER AND JEAN McNULTY

M&S

Canadian Cataloguing in Publication Data

Lorimer, Rowland M., 1944-
  Mass communication in Canada

Includes bibliographical references.
ISBN 0-7710-5348-7

1. Mass media – Canada.   2. Communication – Canada.
I. McNulty, Jean, 1942-   . II. Title.

P92.C3L67 1987   302.2'34   C87-093402-3

DESIGN: Brant Cowie/Artplus Limited

Printed and bound in Canada by John Deyell Company

McClelland & Stewart Inc.
The Canadian Publishers
481 University Avenue
Toronto, Ontario
M5G 2E9

61,425

Contents

PREFACE 9

CHAPTER ONE:
Communication and Culture 13

Introduction

The Range of Communication
The Social Dimension
The Political Dimension
The Economic Dimension
The Educational Dimension
The Cultural Dimension
The Technological Dimension
The Familial or Primary Social Group
Dimension
The Individual Dimension

Societies and Communication through the
Ages
Oral Society
Modern Oral Societies
Literate Society
Electronic Society

Canadian Society and Communications
A Distinctive Canadian Pattern of
Communications

Canadian Cultural Production and
Distribution
Liberal Principles in a Conservative State
A Technological High Road

Contemporary Canadian Cultural Production
and Distribution
A Cultural Low Road
Junior Partners in Our Own Cultural
Enterprise

Information Needs, Communications
Actualities, and the United Nations
Canada's Concerns and the Concerns of
UNESCO

SUMMARY
REFERENCES
STUDY QUESTIONS

CHAPTER TWO:
The Mass Media and Canadian
Society 42

Introduction: Definition

A Distinct Set of Activities
Other Forms of Mass Communication
Construction or Signification

Particular Technological Configurations
Two Crucial Elements of Technology in
Canadian Communications
Technology in the Developed and
Developing World

Formally Constituted Institutions
Private-Sector Institutions
Public and Private-Sector Institutions

Certain Laws, Rules, and Understandings
The Mass Media and the Social System
Audiences and the Public
Societal and Legislative Expectations
The Broadcasting Act
The CRTC and the Broadcasting Act
The Ideals of the Broadcasting Act and the
Realities of Canada's Broadcasting System

Persons Occupying Certain Roles
Business Influences
Government Influences

Legal Influences
Audience Influences
The Influences of Media Professionals

Information and Entertainment, Images and Symbols

The Mass Audience

A Postscript
Scenario

SUMMARY
REFERENCES
STUDY QUESTIONS

CHAPTER THREE:
The Mass Media and Government   66

Introduction

Governments and Information
Information and Democracy
Early and Modern Democratic Information
  Institutions
Perspectives on Mass Media and
  Government

Perspectives on Press Systems Around the Globe
Authoritarian and Soviet Communist
  Theories
Libertarian Theory
Social Responsibility Theory
The Mass Media, Canadian Government,
  and Democracy

Structures of Information and the Modern Nation-State
The Need, Use, and Abuse of Information
The Press in Relation to Government: The
  Parliamentary Press Gallery
The Press as a Political Information Institu-
  tion in a Controlled Environment
Unusual Political Controls on the Press
The Political Power of the Press

A Macroview of the Functioning of Press and Politics

A Microview of the Functioning of Press and Politics
The Political Effects of Institutional
  Organization

The Political Effects of the Press as Media
The Political Effects of the Press as Business
  Institutions

Government and the Politics of the Press
Political Agendas/Administrative Agendas
The Policy Development Process
The Anticipation and Manipulation of the
  Public Will

SUMMARY
REFERENCES
STUDY QUESTIONS

CHAPTER FOUR:
The Design of Information   91

Introduction
Communication as Representation

The Implications of the Indeterminacy of Representation
Signification

Methods of Study
Semiotics
An Example: A Semiotic Analysis of a CP Air
  Ad Series
Content Analysis
An Example: A Content Analysis of the
  Media Treatment of the Shooting
  Down of a Korean Airliner in Soviet
  Air Space
Comparison and Analysis

The Medium and the Message

Media Forms and Meaning Structures

The Newspaper News Story
Tabloid versus Broadsheet Treatment
Events versus Issues

The Television News Story
Thesis, Antithesis, Synthesis
The Camera versus the Reporter
The Study of News

Soaps
Soap Culture
The Soap Vehicle

Music Videos

Roots of Rock Video
Characteristics of the Form

SUMMARY

APPENDIX A: DIALOGUE ON DRINKING

REFERENCES
STUDY QUESTIONS

CHAPTER FIVE:
The Media and the Audience   126

Introduction: The Limitations of Effects Analysis

Media and Society: An Interaction of Meaning-Generating Systems
Determination versus Interaction

The Invasion of the Imagination of an Individual
Television's Pantheon of the 1950s
Hidden Culture
The Extent of the Invasion

The Invasion of the Imagination of a Culture
Cultures as Meaning-Generating Systems

The Interpenetration of Media and Culture
The Case of Annie Hall
Elvis Presley and Béla Bartók

Information and Information Programming: Media and Agendas
The Press and Prime Minister Trudeau
The Grenada Adventure
The Nicaraguan Information War

The Freedom of the Media to Create Meaning
Enoch Powell and the Consensus on Race
Carving Out and Serving Up a Monopoly

Media and Reality
Literary Devices and Real Life
Intermingling of the Media and the "Real" World
Chernobyl and Challenger
"Freeze, buddy, or you're dead!"
Research Findings
Pornography and Erotica

SUMMARY
REFERENCES
STUDY QUESTIONS

CHAPTER SIX:
The Structure and Role of Ownership   149

Introduction: People and Property
Culture and Capitalism
Private Enterprise and the Public Purpose in Media

Historical Background: Function and Ownership
Free Press, Free Market
The Public Role in Broadcasting
Media Ownership in Canada

Forms of Ownership
The Single Enterprise
The Chain: Horizontal Integration
Vertical Integration
Cross-Ownership
The Conglomerate

Forces Toward Increased Concentration of Ownership
Corporate Concentration, a Definition
Growth for Its Own Sake
Borrowing Power
Replacement of the Rich
A Small Canadian Club
Media Ownership as Status
Sunset-to-Sunrise Industries
The CRTC Contribution
Policy on Ownership

Implications of Ownership Form
Public Enterprise
The Ethic of Public Enterprise
Public versus Private
Private Enterprise: The Private, Independent Media Corporation
The Multi-enterprise Media Corporation: Horizontal and Vertical Integration
Conglomerate Relations
A Subtle Transformation in Content: Chain Journalism
Economies of Scale
Service to the Consumer
Cross-Ownership
Monopoly Control

Corporate Concentration: The Social Issue
   Participatory Capitalism
   Participatory Capitalism in the Media
   The Effects of Concentrated Ownership
      in the Media
   Monopoly Power
   Superconcentration: Beyond Monopoly
      Power
   Trends in Ownership
SUMMARY
REFERENCES
STUDY QUESTIONS

CHAPTER SEVEN:
The Functions of Media
Professionals   179

Introduction

The Ideals of Journalism
   Canadian Newspapers: The Inside Story
   Television Journalism
   Career Patterns in Journalism
   Relations between Journalists and
      Newsmakers

The Management of Information
   Editors as Gatekeepers
   The Editorial Construction Function
   Beyond the Mechanics of Construction
   A More Academic View

Other Structural Influences
   Libel
   The Media and Business
   The CBC and Its Affiliates
   Community Politics and Standards

Continuing Structural Issues in Management:
The Problem of Political Bias

SUMMARY: Professional Excellence versus Ideals
of Equal Access
REFERENCES
STUDY QUESTIONS

CHAPTER EIGHT:
Communications Policy in
Canada   200

Introduction

The Policy Environment
   The Influence of Technology on Policy
   Political Responses to Technology
   New Technologies

Policy and the Policy Field
   The Federal Department of Communications
   The Federal-Provincial Dispute

Telecommunications Policy
   The Common Carriers
   The National Telephone System
   Regulation of Telecommunications
   Satellite Communications

Broadcasting Policy
   Regulation and the CRTC
   The Canadian Broadcasting Corporation
   Canadian Content
   Towards a New National Broadcasting
      Policy
   The Broadcasting Task Force

Cultural Industries Policy
   Film and Video
   Publishing

Continuing Issues in Communications Policy
   Telecommunications Issues
   Broadcasting Issues
   Cultural Industries Issues
SUMMARY
REFERENCES
STUDY QUESTIONS

CHAPTER NINE:
The Global Geopolitics of
Information   229

Introduction: Journalism in Historical
Perspective
   Contemporary Equivalents
   Knowledge Serves the Interests of Those
      Who Collect It
   The Free Press in an Open Society

The Global News Agencies as Embodiments of
a Free Press
   A Portrait of the Globals
   Dominance by the Non-Profitable

The Colonial Roots of the Globals
The Entry of the Americans
The Performance of the News Agencies:
  The Bias of News Values

Global News Flows
  Attempts To Compensate

The Producers and Consumers of World
Cultural Products
  Consuming Exported Cultural Products
  How To Read Donald Duck
  The World Information Order: A Free
    Press in a Global Context

The New World Information Order
  The Exploitation of Dominance
  Economies of Scale and Dominance
  Who Controls the Technology
  The MacBride Report

The Continuing Debate on the New World
Information Order
  CBC Foreign Correspondents at Ryerson
  Two Other Perspectives

SUMMARY
REFERENCES
STUDY QUESTIONS

CHAPTER TEN:
The Domestic Geopolitics of
Information   250

Introduction

The Politics of Information
  Metropolis-Hinterland Theory
  The Writings of Harold Innis
  Centre-Hinterland Dynamics in Canadian
    History
  Hinterland Relations

Communications in a Cultural, Centre-
Hinterland Perspective
  The Berger Report and the Position of
    Northern Native People
  Communications and the Spiral of
    Dependency
  Magic in the Sky
  Reinforcement of the Prevailing Order

Canada as a Cultural Hinterland
  The Domestic Politics of Learning Materials:
    Textbooks and the Structure of
    Knowledge
  The Politics of Teacher Education
  The Politics of Educational Publishing
  The Domestic Politics of Canadian
    Television Services
  The CBC and Its Complement
  The Pursuit of Profit
  The Dance of the Entrepreneurs
  Profits and Hinterland Dynamics

The Canadian News and Centre-Hinterland
Relations
  CBC National Radio News (in English)
  English- versus French-Language Television
  News Services: The CRTC Study

Avoiding Hinterland Dependency: A Short
Course on Resource-Led Development

Avoiding Hinterland Dependency: Possibilities
for Communications
  Cultural Production as a Unique Resource
  Slitting Our Own Throats
  Support Programs

SUMMARY
REFERENCES
STUDY QUESTIONS

CHAPTER ELEVEN:
New Communications Technologies in
a Canadian Context   276

Introduction

A Techno-Industrial Explosion in
Communications

The Technological Foundations of Television
Broadcasting

Programming Implications of Satellite-Based
Technology

Positioning Canadian Broadcasting

Pay TV as a Key Component of Cultural
Industrial Strategy

Home Communication Components: The
Cultural Joker

Frontiers of Technology

A Canadian Response to New
Communications Technologies

New Technologies around the World: Satellites
as a Case Study
*How Is the Development of Satellite
Systems Justified?*
Implications
Legal Implications

Communications and Culture

Technology and Other Cultural Industries

SUMMARY
REFERENCES
STUDY QUESTIONS

CHAPTER TWELVE:
Canada in an Information Age 302

Introduction

Public versus Private Sector: Information as
Collective Property
Public Electronic Information
Information as a Commodity
Technological and Industrial Influences:
Print
Techno-Industrial Influences: Video
The Implications of Original Ownership
Public Involvement in Production
Public Involvement in Consumption

Foreign versus Domestic Control
Free Flows, Freely Flowing Information, and
Censorship
Alternative Information Management
Bill C-58: Sovereignty or Unfair Dealing?
Added Complications in New Technologies
Political Ramifications
Economic Considerations
Cultural Implications
A Crucial Issue: The Culture of Business
Art, Culture, Industry, and Policy
Government at Arm's Length

Culture versus Industry as a Basis for Policy
Industrial Considerations
The Consequences of an Industrially
Based Communications Policy
A Culturally Based Communications
Policy
Cultural and Industrial Support Structures
in Publishing

Participation versus Professionalization
The Modernization Paradigm of the Kent
Commission
The Participation Paradigm of the MacBride
Report

Education

SUMMARY
REFERENCES
STUDY QUESTIONS

INDEX 324

Preface

A NUMBER OF EVENTS stimulated the writing of this book. Probably the most important was, in the face of volunteering to teach introductory mass communication, the realization that a Canadian introductory textbook in communication did not exist. Second in importance was the presence of both of us at Simon Fraser University, with complementary expertise but similar basic perspectives. The prod to the side of our intent came from an unexpected source. We were approached by June Landsburg, then co-ordinating Simon Fraser's contribution to Knowledge Network television programming. She thought that if we were to commit ourselves to the production of several television programs in mass communication we might persuade the Centre for Distance Education at Simon Fraser to fund the development of print materials that could serve as a basis for a textbook. The vision of having a book to teach with, working with a valued colleague, and being given a modicum of research and writing support was enticing.

Doubtless, however, what persuaded us to proceed was the challenge and enormity of the task – the importance of creating a document that would serve as an introduction to the field of communication as seen through Canadian eyes. There is no doubt also that we felt, in some small way, that we were following in the footsteps of those giants, Marshall McLuhan and Harold Innis ("Herald," if you examine his birth certificate), whose contribution has been so immense. To produce a first textbook is to define a field in terms that have some influence on the character of that field for some time following. Our confidence in each other persuaded us to embark.

While we co-taught the introductory mass communication course at Simon Fraser we planned the book. We tried various approaches to the material and arrived approximately at the scheme you see herein. It was slightly revised with the help of William Gilsdorf. The rationale behind the ordering is as follows. We see the first three chapters all as introductory. In Chapter 1 we take a broad cultural overview, one which, following many of the ideas of McLuhan and Innis, outlines the breadth of the role of communication in human affairs. In Chapter 2 we define the mass media and mass communication in society to the degree they can be defined. Our third introductory chapter deals with the mass media and government. It is placed third and as an introductory chapter because we wish to emphasize that mass media systems are a fundamental apparatus for the development and survival of nations and cultures. To conceive of them otherwise is to challenge the legitimacy of state involvement in the fabric of culture, a challenge that Canadians and many other nationals would fight.

Chapters 4 and 5 deal with content, that which is attended to after all the housekeeping is done. Our purpose in Chapter 4 is to point out that each medium has its own structure and syntax and that the production of meaning exists within the syntactical and semantic structures that define the nature of expression. Chapter 5 is, to a degree, a rewrite of Lorimer's long-ago involvements with Jean Piaget. It combines that structuralist understanding of media and audiences with a culturalist perspective. Ideologically speaking, our intent in these two chapters was to move out of Frankfurt, to provide a simple model of how media images derive from lived culture, which incorporates media-produced images, which forms the basis of new media content, and so the circle circles.

Chapters 6, 7, and 8 examine the institutional structures that strongly influence the mass media. First, there are the constraints of ownership patterns in Canada. There are three major challenges here: the problem of excessive concentration of private ownership; the issue of the proper balance between public and private ownership; and the question of how to limit foreign ownership or indirect foreign influence through intercorporate links. In Chapter 7 we look at the dynamics of journalism. The rules on how we collect, process, and disseminate information through the mass media are no less rigid just because they are largely unwritten. The third institutional structure to be considered, in Chapter 8, is that of public policy. In Canada this has largely been an effort to balance political and cultural considerations of national sovereignty against the apparent dictates of the technology and the marketplace.

The final four chapters can be seen as applications of the ideas presented in the first eight. New information and new ideas are presented, but they are essentially derivative from the preceding material. Chapters 9 and 10 form a pair, the former on the global geopolitics and the latter on the domestic geopolitics of information. They also are parallel in conception; however, only the latter makes explicit the debt to the writings of Harold Innis.

Chapters 11 and 12 look to the future, the first paying specific attention to new communication technologies and the second focusing on the position of Canada as the expansion of industrialization encroaches on information, entertainment, culture, and art.

We have tried throughout the book to conceptualize the field from a Canadian perspective in a manner that puts the interests of Canadians at the forefront. The extent to which we have been able to achieve this objective is for the reader to determine. The degree to which we have produced something quite different from an American textbook or a British introduction can be illustrated by comparison.

We have, then, tried to be patently anti-colonial. In practice this has meant avoiding continual reference to the research produced by other nations, which defines their national realities in "as-if-universal" terms. By not following that literature closely we found it easier to avoid being drawn within their particular concerns, conceptions, ideological tricks, and so forth. To be blunt, while that literature has great value, the British is possessed by class considerations and the American by Pax Americana. A preoccupation with either of these ideologies is, to our minds, an unaffordable dalliance for Canadians.

The drawback of proceeding in this way is that perhaps we have not done our Canadian colleagues the service they deserve in citing and discussing their work. We hope that as the book comes to be known that our colleagues will bring their work to our attention for incorporation in subsequent editions. For the time being, working with others under a grant from the Secretary of State, Canadian Studies Program, we have assembled a collection of articles intended to complement this text.

As a further complement to the text, at Simon Fraser we have produced a series of five, half-hour television programs that examine the issues of five of the chapters from a fresh perspective. The five are entitled *Media Information Canada, The Fashionable Image, Video, Vinyl and Culture, Ownership and the Public Interest,* and *Canada in an Information Age.* For our own teaching purposes we also acquired rights to use other televisual material and would be happy to share information about those programs. We would also be happy to share information regarding assignments, exams, and the like for those instructors who might be interested.

An attempt to synthesize a field is a vast undertaking. Consequently, we relied on the expertise of other colleagues and students to a considerable degree. Such people included Darlene MacKinnon, who read and gave valuable editing assistance on each chapter and oversaw our authorial responsibilities in the manuscript's "distance education version." From time to time her sentences can be found tying others of ours together. Peter S. "Databank" Anderson provided a great amount of assistance and guidance for various chapters, especially the one on ownership. Elizabeth Heydon, in a course paper, provided the basis for our discussion of soap opera. Discussion with Martin Laba helped add the culturalist perspective to the structuralist base in the chapter on media and audiences.

Others who contributed included Kate Cockerill, Chris Weafer, Lianne McLarty, Marie Medeiros, Bill Richards, and Lori Walker, all of whom helped with various aspects of the research; June Landsburg, a great stimulus to the whole project, as was Colin Yerbury and his staff, including editor June Sturrock, in the Centre for Distance Education at Simon Fraser. Stan Cunningham and William Gilsdorf provided valuable advice as readers, as did Brian Scrivener, formerly of UBC Press, in soliciting their advice. Michael Harrison from McClelland and Stewart phoned at just the right time and brought with him a group who have speedily and smoothly eased this book into production. Special mention should be made of Richard Tallman for his editing skills and patience.

Personal Notes

LORIMER: For my part, I wish to make special mention of the contribution of my co-author to the organization of the book. Without that contribution we might have floundered. I was aided in a much different way through the acquisition of a personal computer, a device that has improved my ability to produce a decent manuscript, preserved my sanity, lengthened my waking and working hours, and, as a result of the latter, tested the patience of my family. It is to them and my parents that I dedicate my part of this book.

MCNULTY: When we began working on the idea of developing a Canadian book on mass communication, I was living in Vancouver and the inevitable difficulties of co-writing a book seemed to be surmountable. However, after I left Simon Fraser to teach at York University in 1984, our co-authorship became considerably more difficult. I want to thank my co-author very much for his forbearance about the priority I had to give my doctoral thesis until 1986. I consider myself fortunate to have had such a supportive and energetic co-author. Finally, I want to dedicate my part of the book to my mother and to the memory of my father.

Rowland Lorimer
Coquitlam, B.C.

Jean McNulty
Toronto, Ont.

February, 1987

CHAPTER

1

Communication and Culture

INTRODUCTION

K EN DRYDEN, in *The Game*, provides us with a deep reading of the way Canadians play hockey. By analogy, Dryden's analysis demonstrates the importance of cultural patterns of communication and the study of communication itself.

Dryden interprets the history of some of the predominant patterns of the game. For example, while hockey originally was an adaptation of lacrosse into a winter sport, its players were mostly used to English rugby. The scrum from English rugby turned into the faceoff. Also as in English rugby, in the game's original form the forward pass was not allowed. Only the puck carrier could advance the puck. He was forced to pass back to his teammates. The defenders could thus check the puck carrier with the knowledge that, given the small size of the rink and the relative speed of the skater, they would be able to regroup should he pass to another. Not only did this create a very slow game with few goals but it also meant that skating skill and stickhandling were essential. On the defensive side, body checking became a valued skill as a means of terminating the advance of the opponent. If the puck carrier were taken out the advance of the puck was set back.

The legitimation of the forward pass should have changed a great deal in the character of the game. That change in rules, designed in part to speed up the game and help sell it to American audiences, opened possibilities for team play and increased the pace of the game to the speed of the forward pass. Passing and fast skating should have become critical, stickhandling self-indulgent. With the diminished importance of the stickhandler, the importance of the body check should also have diminished.

But, as Dryden sees it, the possibilities of the forward pass were never explored. The historical patterns of the game never gave way to the potential inherent in the new rules. So other nations were provided with the chance to develop styles based on these new rules unencumbered by our history and practice. That is exactly what the Russians did. They used their experience with soccer to develop a style of play that represented a fundamental challenge to the Canadian game. This is why Canada remains the team to beat. We represent the pinnacle of one tradition; they, another.

The point of this hockey analogy is that in the same way that the historical structure of hockey determines how evolving possibilities will be responded to, so the structure and therefore the rules and patterns of communication in a society are a major determining factor of the social, economic, and political relations in that culture. Indeed, scholars such as Harold Innis and Marshall McLuhan have claimed a primary role for communication in the shaping of society and culture as a whole. Innis argued that societies in which communication takes place in an oral form, i.e., by word of mouth, differ fundamentally from societies dominated

by written communication. McLuhan advanced Innis's ideas one step further by claiming that societies dominated by electronic communication again differ fundamentally from literate societies.

The basic communications structures are analogous to the rules of the hockey game. *They evolve out of social conditions and set a backdrop for the evolution of new social forms, economic structures, and political practices.*

THE RANGE OF COMMUNICATION

Unlike hockey, communication permeates virtually every aspect of our lives. A report commissioned by UNESCO, the United Nations Educational, Scientific and Cultural Organization, often called the MacBride Report after the commission chairman, discusses how communication impinges on our lives in six spheres of activity (UNESCO, 1980).

The Social Dimension

(1) Communication fills a **social need.** How could Canadians see themselves as part of a single nation without a national communications system? While it could be argued that Sir John A. Macdonald had the CPR built primarily for the flow of goods, with the flow of goods came the flow of information – the bits of information, built into every product, about the culture in which the goods were produced. Knowing that they were ordering from Eaton's in Toronto gave Prairie catalogue users a very real connection to Toronto society. Ordering a pump organ from Berlin or Clinton, Ontario, or a wood stove from Elmira, Ontario, or Sackville, New Brunswick, gave westerners an economic link with these places and, in addition, a very real knowledge of life and a social connection to the styles of manufacturing in the

East. This they would superimpose on letters from relatives living in other parts of the country and newspapers and books that told of life in those parts.

The Political Dimension

(2) Communication is a **political instrument**. Probably the most famous English-Canadian example of how communication was used as a political instrument is William Lyon Mackenzie's *Colonial Advocate*. Mackenzie used his newspaper to politicize Upper Canadians and eventually lead them into rebellion. But communication is not connected to politics only in attempts at reform. Governments also use the press to advance their own interests. Nearly every day the federal government announces one or another initiative for the benefit of one or another group and, of course, claims the credit. In making such announcements, the government hands over to journalists the task of explaining and commenting on their programs. When they become dissatisfied with that process they attempt to go around journalistic commentary by creating media events, orchestrating the release of information, or releasing information to outlets that reproduce it rather than rewrite it or present it within a critical context (e.g., television press conferences, end-of-year interviews, or community newspapers). If that fails they can always fall back on advertising, a means of communication all Canadian federal and provincial governments use extensively. In the last analysis, however, Canadian governments rely primarily on the parliamentary press corps to inform Canadians about government policy and programs.

Another side to communication as a political instrument is usually referred to as **freedom of information**. Governments collect vast amounts of information, by surveys, census-taking, satellites, clandestine activities, and mandatory reporting mechanisms such as income-tax reporting. Concern about freedom of information usually arises over what information the government has about any one individual and whether, by virtue of that information, his or her interests might be damaged by inaccuracies or the access of others to that information. This issue involves also the principle of the right to privacy. How much right does the state have to collect information about individuals? Certainly there has been abuse. The RCMP has had access to tax records of individuals as well as to health records. However, a more general question is involved as well.

There is considerable value in all the information the government collects, whether on business, politics, the weather, or birth patterns. The government, in keeping information to itself, protects itself against political scandal or accusations of ineptitude; yet, in doing so, it also jeopardizes the ability of its citizens to use this information to advantage, whether that advantage is accumulation of wealth, political reform, or cultural development.

Communication can be a political instrument working in the interests of reform or in the interests of suppression of individuals and information. It can work for the state and the individual at the same time or it can work for one to the detriment of the other.

The Economic Dimension

(3) Communication is an **economic force**. As described above, the information a government collects has potential economic benefit for groups and individuals. The collection of information about markets or weather conditions, for example, can be used to advantage by agricultural producers. Similarly, information that allows the prediction of population trends,

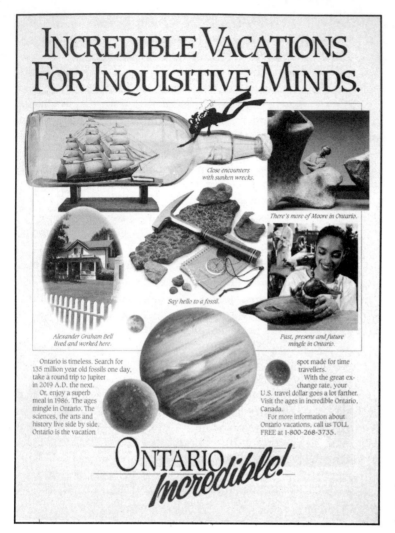

Two illustrations of government ads. Note how the content would be difficult to make into a story.

migration patterns, or birth rates is all-important in planning product development and marketing as well as social services.

The economic force of communication does not derive just from information the government collects. Because of the enhanced availability of information, nations and companies producing for export can have knowledge of market trends as sophisticated as that of domestic producers.

Distance is irrelevant. Exporters are no longer confined to basic products whose characteristics change very slowly and for which there is a steady predictable demand. They can now participate in markets where yearly fashions determine which products will sell for a premium price and which will be down-market items. Shoes and ski clothing are examples of such participation by foreign producers in volatile

1 9 8 6 — 1 9 8 7

SKI

Québec
City Region
Tourism
and Convention
Bureau
Department of the
Communauté urbaine
de Québec

Reservotel: 1-800-463-1568

QUÉBEC CITY AREA
*"Québec, the city
by the slopes!"*
SKI PASSPORT AVAILABLE

QUÉBEC WINTER CARNIVAL
FEBRUARY 5 TO 15, 1987

Canadian markets. In fact, as demonstrated by the electronics industry, such foreign producers as Sony and Technics can lead the industry in the introduction of new products and new styles of products. The near collapse of North American car production is another example not only of how a foreign producer (Japan) can participate in a market determined by style or even set the style but also, as with the game of hockey, how such a producer can use information to better advantage than can the local, traditional producer. The Japanese seized the small-car industry of North America by sound market analysis and good-quality products. From a communications perspective the information a foreign producer can have matches what any local producer has, as long as the producer can pay for the information.

The economic force of communications depends not only on the availability of information but also on the ability to analyse it, which is so important that a different section of the MacBride Report recommends that each nation achieve an informatics capability to take available information and analyse it from its own national or industrial perspective. The point is that to rely on the information and analysis generated by others for their own purposes will necessarily subordinate the independent efforts of any nation to the priorities of other more analytic, powerful nations.

The Educational Dimension

(4) Communication has an **educational potential**. New communications technologies or facilities are customarily announced in the context of the humanitarian benefits they can provide. These benefits are of two types, medical and educational. In countries such as Canada new developments in communications are described in terms of enhanced opportunities for people in outlying regions. For example, satellites currently facilitate the delivery of university-level courses anywhere in Canada. In countries with high rates of illiteracy the educational potential of communications is even more powerful. To a degree this potential circumvents the need for high levels of literacy by extensive broadcast coverage. Such a perspective, however, emphasizes the circulation or spread of information and ignores the very significant analytical capabilities that develop alongside the acquisition of literacy skills. Still, the power of electronic communication to inform should not be underrated, especially when the communications system is designed with education in mind rather than entertainment or political suppression.

A further interesting aspect of the educational potential of communication is that the professions – engineering, medicine, law – are really groups of individuals who have access to a body of information not readily accessible to others and permission to use that information in certain crucial settings, e.g., hospitals or the courts. The power of computers to store the information required by a profession and retrieve it in a selective and flexible manner could open that knowledge to a much larger group of individuals.

Telemedicine is an example of how doctors themselves are spreading their expertise within the profession, while other projects are developing diagnostic services through the use of the computer. Given the vigour of free enterprise there is no reason to believe that medical diagnostic packages will not be developed and sold to interested buyers. The possibility for enhancement of medicine in the Third World is considerable. Yet, with these packages will come the medical, institutional, and economic assumptions of developed-nation medicine. Who benefits when a Bolivian peasant learns that she needs an expensive operation and six months' convalescence? Throughout this book we will be returning to this theme: *the spread of Western information and the full implications of that increased distribution.*

The Cultural Dimension

(5) Communication is both **an impulse and a threat to culture**. The preceding example of the Bolivian peasant is exactly appropriate to the cultural implications of communication. Imagine the state of mind of the Bolivian woman as she is given the diagnosis just mentioned. In the first instance she might marvel at the advantages of living in a developed country

both for its medicine and for its ability to develop computerized diagnostics or even telemedicine. In turning to her own culture and situation she might either see the state of developed nations as an ideal to strive for or become despondent and resentful. Why aren't such services available in her country? And if they were, why is she and why are all of her class too poor to afford even the drugs manufactured by the multinational drug companies necessary for many recoveries?

As the MacBride Report phrases it, communications has the ability to distribute information or items of quality widely. Thereby, it can be an impulse to culture. At the same time it has the potential to threaten or eclipse local culture. Medical information is not usually thought of as a "cultural" item. But just as entertainment and educational programs can provide the basis for invidious comparisons of the quality of life, so medical information can do the same. In the case of cultural materials such as those used in entertainment and education, a person can easily see how a cultural impulse could be generated by the spread of items of artistic merit. The myth and the reality of rural children in Canada striving from early childhood to become as accomplished as someone heard or seen on radio or television, whether an entertainer or any other person, are powerful. So, too, is the general rejection of local culture.

The movie critic Martin Knelman reports that movies were something he, as a child growing up in Winnipeg, saw as an escape from a backwater (Knelman, 1977). If Knelman is taken as an example, we soon understand how local cultural expression is threatened by the spread of culture from such centres as Los Angeles and New York. However, it should be pointed out that much of Knelman's adult movie review work rejects the suppression of local culture.

The Technological Dimension

(6) Communication also represents a **technological dilemma**. Many people imagine that technological advance is rapid and independent of society. The usual kind of statement made about technology and society is that the latter has a difficult time keeping up with the former. However, as we point out in later chapters, technological advance does not occur as a happy side effect of the pursuance of scientific knowledge. The nuclear bomb was not developed as an "unhappy" side effect of the pursuance of research about Einstein's theory of relativity. In the case of the bomb a team of scientists were set to work whose sole purpose was to develop a nuclear device. Similarly, communications technology, from radios to videotex to satellites, is not a spin-off of the pursuit of science; rather, these developments are intentionally pursued because they are technologically feasible and because some person believes there is a market for or a value in such devices.

A good example of a technological dilemma in Canadian communications is pay television. For a number of years before CRTC (Canadian Radio-television and Telecommunications Commission, Canada's communications regulatory agency) approval, pay television was technologically feasible. The CRTC finally gave its approval when two conditions emerged. One was the development of alternative technologies, specifically videocassette recorders (VCRs) and direct broadcast satellites. Recorders meant that the distribution of programming, specifically the movie portion of programming, fell into the hands of small, unregulated video rental and sales shops. Satellites made it possible for anyone with a satellite receiving dish to have access to every sort of foreign program. Such a situation represented a direct challenge to the possibility of government control over the structure of the communication services available through other means. The second condition to emerge was that those who wished to have pay television licences were willing, as a condition of their licence, to invest a certain proportion of their profits in the development of Canadian programming.

While pay television represented a cultural threat, because of the inevitability of its distributing more foreign programming to Canadians, satellite dishes and video outlets represented a greater threat. The former provided some possibility for the development of Canadian expression, the latter none. Ironically, pay television has been so limited in its penetration of the market, partly because of the success of satellites and VCRs, that it remains to be seen whether this will ever have any beneficial effect on Canadian program production. However, as long as pay television does not collapse, the Canadian government will have maintained its ability to affect the structure of what most Canadians watch on television. It can regulate the cable companies that distribute the pay TV and other satellite services.

The MacBride Report does not discuss two other spheres of activity, perhaps because the commissioners believed these to be subcategories of the six already reviewed. We will treat them separately.

The Familial or Primary Social Group Dimension

(7) Communication influences **family or primary social group dynamics**. The penetration of communications into the family living room in developed countries and into the communities and villages of lesser developed countries changes the dynamics of the group. Children are exposed to a much wider range of information than were their parents at a comparable age. Children are also exposed to potential role models who may behave in ways quite contradictory to what the parents or community sees as desirable. Third, programs designed explicitly for children can contrast with the ability of the family or immediate community to respond to the child's desires. Just as societies must cope with communications, so must small social groups and families. The difference in the amount and the perspective of the information children and their elders have contributes to a lack of understanding between generations.

The Individual Dimension

(8) Communication constrains the development of **individual identity**. The notion that each person is psychologically distinct and should strive to use his or her special passions and talents was concurrent with the development of literacy. Written and now electronic communication open a pantheon of characters who can serve as role models. It might even be hypothesized that the diversity of role models has postponed adolescence, so much so that many people feel they have only achieved adulthood at age 40. Planners of products and programming for the "youth market" certainly see that market as including postponed adolescence. They target their products for people between the ages of 15 and 35. (In fact, they find it more useful to employ psychographics, analysis based on the psychological profile of consumers, rather than demographics, based on descriptive aspects of the population such as age, sex, and wealth.) Whatever communication has to do with developing maturity, we cannot help but see ourselves within a

world introduced to us in direct social interaction, through written materials, and by electronic means. The individual as much as the culture is a product of this information environment, both its content and its process.

SOCIETIES AND COMMUNICATION THROUGH THE AGES

B ecause communication penetrates so much of our lives it is not difficult to imagine how some theorists might see societies as having their foundations in communicational processes, or that such theorists might come from a society where, because of special factors such as population dispersion, economic wealth, and technological capability, communication plays a special role.

The theorists who do postulate a fundamental role for communications are two Canadians, Harold Innis (1950) and Marshall McLuhan (1962). They, in conjunction with others, some of whom worked out of Toronto, have developed a conception of communication that distinguishes between oral, literate, and electronic societies. Collectively they are known as the "Toronto School," and we will introduce their conceptions of the dynamics of oral, literate, and electronic societies.

One of McLuhan's followers and translators, Derrick de Kerckhove, wrote in *The Globe and Mail* of a three-part division in today's world based not on the domination of Russia, China, and the U.S. but on the domination of computers, the book, and the radio: North America, Europe, and Japan are part of Computerland; China, the Soviet Union, and Africa are in the Bookworld; and Radio City is composed of South America, the Middle East, and India. As de Kerckhove claims:

The phonetic alphabet created the Greek and Roman Empires and print led to the French Revolution and the violence of the Napoleonic Wars. But the telegraph turned the British Empire into the Commonwealth, changing the image of controlling to that of sharing.

Radio, on the other hand, wreaked havoc among literate identities, reaching back to the tribal hordes of Germany and breaking all the national boundaries. Radio has killed more people in a shorter time than any other means of communication medium ever invented by man. In its encounter with established patterns of literacy, it has proved to be the most violent and aggressive medium of all. Today, the voice of the Ayatollah (Khomeini) is sending 14-year-olds to death, the voices of Ian Paisley and others are sending terrorists into Irish streets, the voices of South American strongmen are blowing up shanties. Television and computers, however, are off-setting the potential violence of radio ... television pacifies our digestive system and our bowel movements, while computers exteriorize our nervous systems. Computers turn the most deadly weapons into toys, whereas books could turn mental play such as $e=mc^2$ into deadly weapons.

De Kerckhove follows this analysis with an interesting speculation.

> ... the nuclear bomb is both the crowning glory of the Industrial Age and the foundation stone of the Information Age.... The bomb, which is pure and total destruction, has already become pure and total information. It is the most powerful communication medium invented yet.... Respecting the bomb is probably the first step toward a responsible political attitude.

De Kerckhove's statement illustrates the central dilemma in understanding the Toronto School. Claiming that the nuclear bomb is the foundation of a new age rather than Armageddon seems to so underplay its potential destructiveness that such a claim almost appears to be a cruel joke. Two points about the value and validity of this perspective will lead us into what Innis and McLuhan themselves have to say about oral, literate, and electronic cultures.

If literate-industrial traditions and values are strong enough then there will be a rejection of the informational nature of the bomb. Not to mince words, someone or some country will decide a nuclear war is winnable. If, on the other hand, we move toward accepting an informational perspective, a perspective made possible by advances in electronic information-processing technology, then we will develop "responsible political attitudes" that will always prevent nuclear war. Who wants to test the validity of the information we have about the inevitability of total annihilation by starting a nuclear war? Presuming the acceptance of informational values, we may find ourselves a few years down the road understanding more completely what de Kerckhove meant. Indeed, it may even turn out that the statement was only part of the truth. To anticipate the future a bit and to explain a little as well, McLuhan once claimed that the electric light bulb was pure information. Its function was to expose things to our eyes. What makes the bomb a totality of information is that it contains the power to allow our continued existence or to end it.

Contemplation of de Kerckhove's statement can lead to an interesting shift in the meaning of the word "totality." Such a shift is to be expected. It is parallelled, for example, by the shift in meaning that must have occurred in the concept of "matter" as science shifted its theoretical underpinnings from Newtonian to Einsteinian physics.

Oral Society

Harold Innis's claim is that oral communication set basic parameters to the functioning of those societies in which it was predominant. For example, we as a literate people are governed by what is written in law and by the principles and statements of our constitution. In oral societies people were governed by the knowledge vested in the community and specifically preserved by certain speakers. These speakers or minstrels developed and maintained their knowledge by means of epic poems and what Innis called epic technique. Epic technique involved creating poems in hexameters with certain rigidities and elasticities. The rigidities allowed for memorization, while the elasticities permitted adaptation to local or vernacular speech. Forms, words, stock expressions, and phrases acted as aids while the local language and situation provided the basis for ornamental gloss. The development of such techniques meant epic poetry was in the hands of persons with excellent memories and poetical and linguistic abilities. And because such abilities were not innate, families of professional storytellers and minstrels developed. According to Innis, such families probably built up a system of memory aids that were privately owned and carefully guarded.

In ancient Greece mastery of words or recitation came to mean intellectual sovereignty. The epics permitted constant adaptation, as required by the oral tradition, and also allowed for the emergence of completely new content to describe conditions of social change. What was socially relevant was remembered, what was not was forgotten. Changing perspectives permitted the incorporation of sacred myths from earlier civilizations. These myths could be transformed and humanized as they were turned into content of the epic poem. The Greeks could thereby foster the development of an inclusive ideology as they expanded their empire, and this ideology could serve colonizing efforts extremely well.

The dynamics of the oral tradition in a more modern context (rural Yugoslavia from 1937 to 1959) are described by Lord (1964) in his *The Singer of Tales*. One of his many telling observations is that, for the oral bard, the recording of the words of a song is a totally foreign experience. Nor, when the recording is finally accomplished, has the bard any use for it. It exists in a dead form, a particular performance at a particular time in a particular setting; not, as we would have it, the correct or best version which is approximated by subsequent performances. The point is that the oral poet lives in an entirely different world and operates with entirely different cognitive processes than do we. They are the polar opposite to Glenn Gould's perspective (Payzant, 1984). He believed a perfect performance (especially of a composer such as Bach) could be created in the recording studio through the splicing of bits from many different performances. The concert stage merely interfered with musical perfection.

The oral tradition and its ability to preserve what past was required for present functioning, to transform that past as necessary, to base law in what a community representative saw as customary, and to see superordinate forces as part of nature point to the stability of oral societies and their tendency to preserve, extend, and adapt culture. Thus, rather than being concerned with the continued existence of formal structures and institutions, oral societies were most successful at extending the dynamics of interaction. With change came a type of adaptation that preserved ways of acting but in new circumstances. The ancient

Greeks, for example, perpetuated a stable, continuous, but adapting culture.

Modern Oral Societies

Today, the influence of oral processes has not entirely passed. In non-literate African societies there has been considerable opportunity to examine the effects of oral versus literate processes. On the literate side, in the 1900s when early British administrators attempted to record histories of certain tribes to facilitate the administration of British justice, certain origin myths of tribal structures were carefully recorded. One form of myth was that which told of the founding of the country by a particular figure who then divided the country among his sons, who became tribal chiefs of the various subsections of the country. As is readily apparent, this myth describes rather well a federation of related tribes in the midst of other "unrelated" tribes.

What amazed researchers in their return to such areas and tribes, for instance the Gonja in northern Ghana (Goody, 1975, p. 35), was the transformation of the origin myths. When asked to recount these myths in face of the further subdivision of the country, tribal narrators told the same story but with the number of sons increased. When confronted by the literate mind and the written records of yesteryear, all the oral peoples could do was profess lack of understanding of the earlier "evidence."

The point to be taken is not that members of oral societies are foolish, forgetful, naive, or even inconsistent, but that *each society has its principles for preserving knowledge* and preserving its integrity as a culture. Where literate societies emphasize the "letter of the law," as it were, oral societies emphasize its meaning. If there now exists a federated country of so many parts, given the nature of the mythical form it must have developed from a founder followed by so many sons. The myth serves and justifies present-day reality. Truth depends on whether it is oral or literate truth. The same is true of the myths of literate societies, but the relation between the present day and the past often involves a much more labyrinthine series of connections. In literate societies, out of a massive recorded history of figures and events can be drawn the heroes of the day, depending on the needs of the day.

It is not only "anthropological" societies that evidence oral processes. In the days when Bob Dylan was the spiritual leader of the youth of America and some section of the youth of the Western world, his lyrics demonstrated exactly the kind of oral process that we have been discussing in African and Greek societies. Dylan took figures and events out of American history and institutions and gave them identities within a new mythology reflecting the ideas of the youth of the day. Whether the figures were from literature, from the newspaper, or from American popular culture, all were grist for the mill.

Perceived as a set of epic poems, Dylan's early work as a whole can be seen as typical rather than unique. Indeed, it is interesting to see what musical forms arise from time to time and how they communicate the central concerns of the young adults of the time through oral/aural discourse.

The response of societies to new musical forms is also worth noting. It is a tribute to the powerful role of new musical forms and to their autonomy from central societal institutions that popular music is continually subjected to censorship. That censorship exists not only in Eastern European countries (such countries were especially frightened of jazz),

but also on a fairly continuous basis in Western countries, including the U.S. and Canada. In Western countries the absolute bans of the Eastern Bloc are replaced with strictures on the medium through which the work can be communicated. For example, AM rock stations and television broadcast channels do not play certain songs and videos respectively, although these may be available through record and video stores.

Literate Society

Greece, for Innis, represented an oral society, whereas Rome represented a literate society. It was not that Greece was unaffected by writing. On the contrary, a number of authors, notably Havelock (1976), claim that the basis of the enormous contribution Greek civilization made to modern civilization is to be found in writing, in their invention of the phonetic alphabet. Innis cites contemporary statements from the time of the emergence of writing that indicate a realization of the significance of the change from oral to written forms. For example, in Plato's *Phaedrus* Socrates reports a conversation between the Egyptian god Thoth, the inventor of letters, and the god Amon. Amon says:

> This discovery of yours will create forgetfulness in the learners' souls, because they will not use their memories; they will trust to the external written characters and not remember of themselves. The specific you have discovered is an aid not to memory, but to reminiscence, and you give your disciples not truth but only the semblance of truth; they will be bearers of many things and will have learned nothing; they will appear to be omniscient and will generally know nothing; they will be tiresome company, having the show of wisdom without the reality.

Socrates continues:

> I cannot help feeling, Phaedrus, that writing is unfortunately like painting; for the creations of the painter have the attitude of life, and yet if you ask them a question, they preserve a solemn silence, and the same may be said of speeches. You would imagine that they had intelligence, but if you want to know anything and put a question to one of them, the speaker always gives one unvarying answer.

Such statements sound like someone discussing the evils of television, and so they should, for the transformation from an oral to a literate society is as major a change as from a literate to an electronic society.

Rome and the Roman Empire represent literate society because the operating concepts and processes of Rome were derived from the written rather than the spoken word: possession of a piece of land or object became subordinated to an abstract notion of legal property, heretofore never conceived; in other legal proceedings the influence of writing could be seen in the fact that trained lawyers were responsible for defining the exact nature of a dispute within written laws (a literate function), and only then was the case handed to laymen to determine a settlement among the claimants (a community function, to gauge the significance of the crime to the community). But perhaps it was in the development of contract law where the Romans shone in their ability to invent an institution to supplant practices founded on the oral process. A contract changes an oral pact into a legal obligation. It is a precise written record of an obligation of one person to another or to others.

Such inventions allowed for both an orderly and a vast expansion of the Roman Empire. Coupled with this means of recording, the administrative power of the Roman Empire was considerable indeed. Greek-inspired teachers of rhetoric and philosophy, for example, were expelled in 168 BC and several years later (154 BC) the first school of grammar was founded. These developments reflected an attempt to rid society of the power of poetic language and to replace it with clear, ordered, unambiguous, logical prose. Less than 100 years later Julius Caesar, in 59 BC, instituted the publication of proceedings of the Senate, thus compelling senators to consider the public in their speeches. He also called for an attempt to summarize and condense written law. The written tradition was already beginning to demonstrate its excessive permanence and lack of a built-in homeostatic factor.

The writing of Cicero (106-43 BC) and other Stoic philosophers brought forward the ideas of the world state, natural justice, and universal citizenship in an ethical sense. The concept of natural law brought enlightened criticism to bear on custom (Innis, 1950, p. 98). Libraries were not only scattered throughout the empire but also became signs of conspicuous consumption. All these were characteristics of literate society. Without writing, without the ability to pursue the static representation of ideas, where by a mere eye movement two ideas could be juxtaposed and compared, they could never have existed.

Most other writings about literate societies focus on modern societies. While they discuss the nature of the influence of writing they do so within a context of an evolved technology and developed institutions (see, for example, McLuhan, 1962; Goody, 1977; Olson, 1980). The basic claim of these writers, and others who have also contributed to the tradition, is that writing has provided the means for the development of logical, linear, and sequential thinking. Literate thought is (or should be) logical because it must be presented in such a way that anyone can understand the meaning of a written passage without benefit of knowing the context within which the passage was written and without the possibility of further reference to the author. It can stand by itself as a statement that is consistent both internally and with reference to other common knowledge. Literate thought is also linear and sequential because only one idea can be presented at a time, followed by another and then another. This contrasts with what can be done on television, where a picture can be providing context while a text can provide other aspects of meaning. It also contrasts with what is available to a speaker, who can with facial or bodily gesture communicate certain aspects of a message while communicating other aspects in words. The speaker in most situations also has the benefit of monitoring his or her audience during the communication, a direct form of feedback not available with print or with electronic communication.

Electronic Society

Few scholars have taken the transformation of our society from a base in printed information to a base in electronic processes particularly seriously. Perhaps because we depend so heavily on what we associate with writing, that is, the ability to write clearly and think logically and conceptually, we cannot imagine how electronic information processes are going to replace writing. The diversionary aspect of McLuhan's work, among other things, is that his examples are from entertainment rather than information-processing media. In concentrating on broadcast television and radio he enters a domain foreign to most scholars, a domain from which they get little information of value to their scholarship. They are thus inclined to see it as a system serving needs other than their own professional needs and are therefore reluctant to consider the dynamics of electronic information-processing thoughtfully.

However, as information-processing by electronic means becomes more prevalent, that is, as computers become more pervasive in everything from cars to cameras, it is easier to see the importance of McLuhan's ideas. As scholars begin to take advantage of computers and communication technology in their own writing, information-gathering, information-monitoring, and personal and professional communications, they begin to understand new patterns of information production and consumption, which lead to new biases in the creation and dissemination of knowledge.

McLuhan himself made much of the notion of a **global village**. By that he did not mean that we would soon become members of one big happy family but that we would have the information-gathering capacity to be intimately, perhaps too intimately, aware of the goings on of all people in every kind of situation around the world. Think of the capability the world now has with its global news organizations. It is not difficult for us to find out about nearly every country and its current situation. Nightly we do find out about many countries in which "newsworthy" events have recently happened, yet most of us know that our nightly news services rarely avail themselves of news available from parts of the world that for one reason or another are not considered to be of primary interest to Canadians. In Australia, for example, an hour-long news program on that country's Special Broadcasting Service is designed to bring news from areas not covered by other stations and especially from countries that have supplied many recent immigrants to Australia. It provides a different image of the world and quite a different image of the news-gathering and presentation process than what we encounter on Canadian and U.S. television.

Our linkage with this always imperfect but steadily more inclusive global village transforms our environment, extending our realm of knowledge but also transforming our attitude to our own local environment. Various studies indicate that people who rely on television for information have a vision of the world that overestimates the violence and disorder in the world, a view derived from news and other programming that concentrates on violence (see Gerbner, 1978). At times people seem to ignore their own quiet surroundings for the more dynamic impact of the world as presented on television.

Television demands the enactment of a small drama with visual interest for the creation of a news story. Information is not collected and later transformed into a form presentable through television; rather, the event is staged and then snippets of it are used for television. The television crew must get everyone to act in a way that will make good television; people must be stage-managed so the material can be sifted through to produce what is perceived to be "good" television. Or the newsmakers can stage the event themselves. For television there is not so much a transformation by analysis as a selection. Those who can create good television are those who become newsworthy. Notice that there is a shift in newsworthiness away from what a newspaper might consider an important event to something that is visually interesting, such as a prime minister meeting some workers on an ocean-based oil-drilling rig. What is visually interesting depends on what is currently visually novel.

Numerous other examples of substantial changes to the structure and use of information echo McLuhan's concerns. In late 1984, after moving itself to plush surroundings, the Toronto Stock Exchange decided it was losing too much business to Montreal to forgo any longer the electrification of stock trading. Such electrification reduced confirmation on stock orders from two or three minutes to seconds. As one commentator, Dian Cohen, pointed out, this emphasis on speed does nothing to enhance, for example, the stabilizing value of pension-fund investment. It emphasizes quick stock market play as opposed to long-term stable investments. In another area, Martin Eslin (1980) has argued that our pattern of exposure to ways of presenting ideas has changed in electronic society. With the advent of television the predominant form of argumentation or presentation of facts has come to be dramatization. Theatricality has replaced the kind of reasoned analysis one finds in a newspaper.

Perhaps the best-known example of how information presentation has changed with electronic society is advertising. A look back at newspaper and magazine ads demonstrates how they attempted to mimic logical argument. To some degree modern survey ads, such as those for Crest toothpaste, Anacin, and Listermint, still draw on the same kind of mimicry of logical argumentation. There is no attempt in such ads to be true to the laws of logic; instead, the ad creators make claims that, though logically constructed, tell only a part of the story. The audience, however, is led to believe it is receiving the whole story.

Such ads are dated. Television lifestyle commercials, such as those used to sell beer, present an image of the beer drinker, thus targeting the beer in its market (Grady, 1983). The actual taste of the beer is such that it is indistinguishable from other beers. Bruce McCuaig, marketing vice-president for Labatt's, explains that the difference in taste of any one brand is so elusive that the customer has to keep consuming to remember that difference. The point is that the *image of the consumer is what is being sold and consumed.*

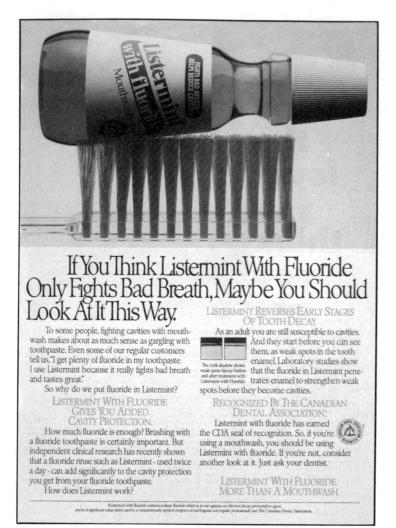

An illustration of "logical arguments" in ads. *Courtesy Warner Lambert Canada Inc.*

CANADIAN SOCIETY AND COMMUNICATIONS

Technology in general, and electronic communications technology in particular, is a significant force in modern society. Relations between society and communication are important enough, after all, to define an area of study, and indeed, a whole discipline of inquiry. The Canadian philosopher, George Grant, makes the case in *Technology and Empire* that the foundation of all modern liberal industrial and post-industrial societies, including Canada, is to be found in technique and technology:

> ... the belief that human excellence is promoted by the homogenizing and univer-

"Shall we call it a night."

BE A PART OF IT.

Canadian Club
LIGHT CRISP VERSATILE

C.C. Sunrise: 1½ ounces of Canadian Club with 5 ounces of orange juice.   C.C. Kiss: 1½ ounces of Canadian Club with 5 ounces of grapefruit juice.

An illustration of an "image" or "life-style" ad. *Courtesy Hiram Walker Brands Limited.*

salizing power of technology is the dominant doctrine of modern liberalism, and ... that doctrine must undermine all particularisms.... English-speaking Canada as a particular is wide open to that doctrine.

As we move from a consideration of the role of the broadest forms of the technologies of communication through the ages to a discussion of the role of modern technologies in con-

temporary Canada, it is important to remember Grant's perspective, its reference to a political framework, and its prediction of the implications for Canada.

Our perspective differs slightly from Grant's. This book is based on the assumption that while technology, including communications technology, may be the motive force of modern-day liberalism, a liberalism that pervades the whole of the Western world, the patterns of use of technology in any individual society go some distance in contributing to that society's distinctiveness and its very survival within that liberal mould.

A Distinctive Canadian Pattern of Communications

At the beginning of any introduction to or overview of communications in Canada we are told that Canada has a set of distinctive characteristics that are relevant to the understanding of the communications system that has evolved in the country. The first characteristic is the *vastness of the country*. This vastness is tied to a second element, the *small size of Canada's population*. Together and separately these two variables are particularly significant in the development of communications systems. On the one hand Canada's geography has required expensive per-capita transmission systems so that the country can stay in touch with itself. For example, following the establishment of a transcontinental railway in 1885 came a transatlantic radio link in 1901, a trans-Canada radio network in 1927, a trans-Canada telephone network in 1932, a transcontinental television service in 1958, a domestic geostationary communications satellite in 1972, and the first nation-wide digital data system in 1973 (*The Challenge of Communication*, DOC).

Each of these developments was cause for some rejoicing and some sense of pride. But in another sense they were comparatively insignificant. One would hardly expect major objections to a microwave link capable of bringing national television to over 70 per cent of the country. But what of a service for other Canadians, those who live beyond the ribbon of population within 100 miles of the Canada-

U.S. border? Perhaps a cause for greater celebration has been the commitment by Parliament through the CBC to provide Canadian broadcasting for all Canadians. This is such a significant achievement because the provision of broadcast services to such a widely dispersed population represents a firm national public cultural commitment – it is a commitment that can never be paid for by those who benefit from it. Whatever the problems of cultural intrusion in bringing television to northern Inuit communities, certainly no one ever expected the costs of establishing those links to be paid for entirely by the communities or by taxes generated from those communities. The same is true of the government-funded Inuit programming service, Inukshuk. No person expects the communities involved in the development and reception of Inukshuk programs to pay the costs of that development. Rather, it is a public commitment by the people of Canada, and an illustration of Canada's commitment to deal with the dispersion of its small population over the vast reaches of our land.

A third significant characteristic, derivative in part from the size of the country, is our *regionality*. Canada is not just a country of physical geographic variety; it is a country of regional cultures. It is instructive to think back to Confederation to realize that Canada is an amalgam of communities. To the original four colonies to join Confederation – Upper Canada, Lower Canada, Nova Scotia, and New Brunswick – were added in later years other distinct colonies and communities, British Columbia and Newfoundland. A national will to develop a country separate from the United States and late-nineteenth-century settlement led to other communities in Prince Edward Island and the Prairies joining Confederation.

For these disparate communities to thrive

within a nation they required means of internal communication and of initiating communication with other regions of Canada. Messages could not be generated from a central point and merely fed to outlying regions. The regions themselves needed to generate their own information for internal use and for the edification of the country as a whole.

Canada is also a nation of *two official languages*. The right to speak either English or French is now enshrined in our constitution. But Canadians have committed themselves to more than a freedom for individuals. They have committed themselves to providing various services, including broadcasting, in both official languages. As with the example of the North, in certain communities no one could ever expect that the audience would pay for the cost of service in its own official language. The criteria guiding these decisions were not economic but rather political and cultural. Bilingual government services and bilingual broadcasting channels (not just programs) are a symbol of the right of any Canadian to live and work wherever he or she may wish. They are also a continual reminder to all that we are a bilingual country.

The natural extension of the respect for plurality built into the notions of regional cultures, the extension of broadcasting services to the far reaches of our country, and bilingual services, given the extent and patterns of immigration to Canada, is a *multicultural policy*. Although it is long in coming and still severely underfunded, we are beginning to see an acceptance of the desirability of tailoring programming to various ethnic communities. While these television services are mostly distributed by cable rather than broadcast (and are therefore not available to everyone), ethnic radio services are broadcast. Together these services represent a beginning commitment to

what is accepted general government policy, a commitment to multiculturalism.

A final, never-to-be-forgotten characteristic of Canada's communications environment is its *proximity to the U.S.* Together with our acceptance of much the same basic political and economic philosophy and the resulting fairly open border, this proximity has led to a massive interpenetration between our two countries of both products and ideas. More American television programming is available to the vast majority of Canadians than is Canadian programming. On most private radio stations, more American material is available to listeners than Canadian material. On virtually all magazine racks in Canada more American magazines are available to the reader than Canadian magazines, in spite of the fact that over 200 magazines are published in Canada. More American authors are read by the average Canadian school child than Canadian authors. And on the story goes. But we are getting a little ahead of ourselves. The main point is that our proximity to the U.S. and the resultant spill-over of American cultural products comprise a major factor to be taken into account in considering Canada's communications environment.

Canadian Cultural Production and Distribution

In considering what we Canadians have produced and what we have distributed to ourselves, let us start with an historical perspective. A large part of the early history of communications in Canada focuses on newspapers and journalism. Indeed, in W.H. Kesterton's *A History of Journalism in Canada* we learn something of the role of newspapers and journalism in the formation and development of our nation. To provide an overview,

Kesterton describes press history by means of an organic metaphor that includes four stages of growth. The first period, 1752-1807, he calls the "Transplant Period," a transplant of a New England adaptation of a British activity. The second period, 1807-1858, is "Thickening Growth," the third, 1858-1900, "Western Transplant and Spreading Growth," and the fourth period, 1900-1967, "The Mutation." This last period constitutes a mutation because it was characterized by a dramatic decline in the number of newspapers although not a parallel decline in overall readership and became, essentially, a mutation into mass communications, with large-scale corporations developed on the achievements of a host of idealistic entrepreneurs yet with distributions to large populations.

It appears from Kesterton's study that the basic principles of press operation in Canada evolved from struggles fought elsewhere. These principles were not then critically re-examined for their appropriateness to the Canadian environment. Rather, it was more a case of trying to find a way of adhering to the principles in spite of the lack of journalistic evolution within Canada. The situation was most apparent in the operation of the principle of *freedom of the press*.

Freedom of the press reflects an acceptance of an underlying principle that competing elites should have access to the general audience. Viewed from the perspective of the audience, it enshrines the principle of exposure to an ideological spectrum within which individual ideas and policies can be considered. Struggles to establish freedom of the press do not arise from considered allegiance to abstract ideas. They evolve out of distinct elites, each of which feels the need for press access and access to the public. Similarly, although historically later in the development of the press, the call by journalists for the recognition of their ideals as distinct from the interests of owners springs not so much from insightful analysis but rather from the establishment of a profession independent and distinct from an owning group. What owner-editor-reporter, however philosophical, is going to call for a recognition of the distinctive set of interests for each role she or he plays?

Liberal Principles in a Conservative State

Canadian press history is distinctive because of the acceptance of liberal principles of press operation and press freedom prior to evolution of sufficient power by the relevant groups to enforce recognition of these principles. Thus, while printers were still dependent on Crown printing contracts, the principle of free comment (meaning, often, anti-government comment) by newssheet printers was, at times at least, given grudging recognition. The achievement that characterizes Canadian press history over the years is the establishment of administrative arrangements that restrain the tendency of those with power, governments especially, to act in their own interest. To be specific, there were just not enough printers to serve the various competing interests Canadians could recognize but which had yet to establish themselves. This principle of action, which runs through much of Canadian communications history, might be called a **principle of enlightened action** in that certain groups were continually having to constrain their potential power to act because of broader principles reflective of the interests of the community. Perhaps on the basis of this principle a case can be made that we Canadians have a distinctive perspective and thus a unique contribution to make within a discourse on technology (see Kroker, 1984).

A Technological High Road

A modern equivalent of this enlightened administration of principles evolved beyond our borders can be found in our continued importation of principles of operation of the communications media, for example, in the acceptance of freedom of enterprise at the point of distribution of cultural products. Canada accepts the principle that any producer who can command an audience for a message that does not run counter to basic political or social beliefs has some claim to be granted access to a channel of communication. In concrete economic terms, those who can assemble an audience have the right to sell that audience to others who wish to speak to it.

But our modern equivalent has a second element, a commitment to modern technology. The Canadian government, in co-operation with Canadian communications industries, has committed Canada to a technological high road – to remaining abreast of the most advanced communications systems available. This commitment is not entirely intended to serve the cultural needs of Canada and Canadians, in spite of rhetoric used to justify each new major expenditure. It is intended, rather, to serve industrial development interests. In keeping up with developing technologies the government has a showpiece of national unity and also a job creation program of considerable power. Jobs are created directly and numerous spin-off technologies lead to the creation of new industries, products, and hence jobs in the information sector.

However, in pursuing such technologies, Canada finds its hardware commitments and industrial and economic needs taking precedence over its cultural needs. The result is an information environment that at once keeps us abreast industrially of the most advanced nations and at the same time opens us to inundation by their cultural products. Our hardware commitments mean that we end up oversupplying ourselves with channels for other people's information.

The organization of our communications infrastructure is very much based on our acceptance of technology as an essential means of dealing with and even thinking about the world. As George Grant points out, that acceptance continually challenges our national survival. (See also Babe, 1988.)

CONTEMPORARY CANADIAN CULTURAL PRODUCTION AND DISTRIBUTION

Let us return to a consideration of the distinctive elements of Canada's communication environment now that we have seen what has been laid down historically in the way of patterns of communications. How have we chosen to reflect our distinctive national characteristics? In other words, how have the special characteristics of

- a vast country,
- a widely dispersed population,
- regional variety,
- bilingualism,
- multiculturalism,
- and the proximity of the U.S.

been instrumental in shaping our national communications system?

A Cultural Low Road

In 1983 Paul Audley wrote a report for the Canadian Institute for Economic Policy called *Canada's Cultural Industries.* In his report he provided an exhaustive analysis of the production, distribution, and consumption of cultural products in Canada. The four areas he concentrated on were publishing, film, records, and broadcasting. In his final chapter he provides an overview with recommendations. His overview is based on two summary tables of data and projections derived from the data presented in the book as a whole. Those two tables are reproduced here.

At first glance both of Audley's tables seem to be too general for our purposes. The first table, which shows the extent of expenditures Canadians make in consuming cultural products, gives us only the size of the overall market. The second table, which tells us the degree to which we produce content for our own domestic market, breaks down the data into categories of content only to a certain degree. How, therefore, can we look at regionality, bilingualism, multiculturalism, vastness, and dispersion with such gross figures?

The figures themselves provide some of the answer. While Table 1.1 gives us an estimate of the size of each medium, Table 1.2 tells us how much foreign material is to be found in each of those media. If newspapers and radio talk and information programming are excluded on the grounds that their very existence makes them Canadian, the average amount of foreign content is just over 75 per cent. This means that over three-quarters of the cultural products we consume on a daily basis are foreign produced; the remainder is information (i.e., news, commentary) we produce about ourselves and the world, although even there we rely considerably on global and U.S. news wire and television news-gathering systems, a reliance that does not appear to be reflected in Audley's data. Then, too, there is the patter of radio commentators between the playing of records, at least 70 per cent of which are foreign.

How then can we be said to have designed a communications system to respond to our distinctiveness? Our response, it would seem, has been a massive program of importation of foreign cultural products. The distinctive attributes that characterize Canadian communications are to be found within the 25 per cent margin and within information programming. Our regionality and our particular form of multiculturalism are continually underplayed, while our proximity and communality with the United States, its culture, and its regionalism and multiculturalism are continually overplayed. In addition, our dispersion is dealt with through hardware and the national broadcasting system commitments touched upon earlier, and our bilingualism has been dealt with by a dual national broadcasting system in English and French, a system that at once emphasizes our linguistic distinctiveness and separates us internally.

Even from a perspective that uses such gross figures as Audley's two tables present, we can already see how major distinctive features such as regionalism and multiculturalism are bound to be influenced by notions of these factors as they exist in foreign countries, notably the U.S. The U.S., after all, has three times as much access to Canadian audiences as we give to ourselves (i.e., 75 per cent versus our 25 per cent). Without the "system commitment" we have given to bilingualism or population dispersion, such factors as regionalism, for example, have to compete for the attention of the viewer. That competition takes us immediately into the economic reality of program production, that is, the amount of money we can afford to invest in programming, an economic reality euphemistically referred to as quality of programming.

These issues have been discussed in two papers, one by Alison Beale and the second by Robert Babe. Beale provides an overview of

TABLE 1.1

Publishing, Recording, Film, and Broadcasting: Estimated Canadian Market, 1980* ($millions)

Daily newspapers	advertising	987.3
	circulation	266.1
		1,253.4
Periodicals	advertising	276.3
	circulation**	400.0
		676.3
Books		931.7
Records/tapes		265.1
Film	NFB (net cost of operations)	37.4
	private distributors:	
	a. theatrical	115.3
	b. television	103.7
	c. non-theatrical	26.9
		283.3
Radio (private)	advertising	392.0
	production and other	5.7
		397.7
Television (private)	advertising	510.0
	production and other	52.1
		562.1
CBC (radio and television)	advertising	100.9
	net cost of operations	542.9
	production and other	3.7
		647.5
Cable television		352.2
Sub-totals by source	advertising	2,266.5
	consumption, production, and other	2,522.0
	government subsidy (film and TV only)	580.3
Total expenditure		5,368.8

*Estimates are derived as follows: Total spent by Canadian advertisers by medium plus *wholesale* revenue by medium form total sales in the Canadian market, plus government expenditure for broadcasting and NFB.
**Periodical circulation revenue is difficult to estimate. The estimate of $400 million is a cautious estimate based on reported revenue for Canadian periodicals of $121 million and imports valued for customs purposes at $277 million.
SOURCE: Paul Audley, *Canada's Cultural Industries* (Toronto: James Lorimer, 1983).

TABLE 1.2

Domestic Share By Origin of Content*
(percentages)

	Original Canadian Material	Adapted Foreign Material	Foreign Material
Newspapers			
Domestic coverage	close to 100		
Foreign coverage	0-5		95-100
Magazines	29.0	25	46.0
Books	16.1	4.4	79.5
Records	6.8		93.2
Radio**			
AM-music	30.0		70.0
talk	90-100		0-5
FM-music	10-30		70-90
talk	95-100		0-5
Film***			
Theatrical market	1.8		98.2
Televison market	7.3		92.7
Non-theatrical	41.2		58.8
Television English****			
News information, current affairs	90.5		9.5
All entertainment	11.6		88.4
Dramatic entertainment	4.0		96.0
All viewing	30.5		69.5
Television French****			
News, information, current affairs	100.0		0.0
All entertainment	39.8		60.2
All viewing	54.2		45.8

*Figures for newspapers and radio are estimates based on general industry studies.
**Based on percentages of air-time.
***Based on distributors' royalties, rentals, and commissions.
****Based on audience viewing, 1978.
SOURCE: Audley, *Canada's Cultural Industries*, which used: Statistics Canada for books, records, and film; CRTC for radio and television; Audit Bureau of Circulations for magazines (consumer only); and the Davey and Kent Commission for newspapers.

how Canadians have transformed a vast geography into a social space. Babe identifies patterns in the history of communications in Canada and concludes that the telegraph, telephone services, and broadcasting have all led not to national integration but to integration with the United States (Lorimer and Wilson, 1988).

Junior Partners in Our Own Cultural Enterprise

Audley's data point out that we are junior partners in our own cultural enterprise. Uniquely Canadian viewpoints expressed through Canadian creative artists hold a consistent minority position not just in comparison with foreign expressions but specifically with American cultural expression. Nor is there any saving grace in aspects of cultural production that Audley did not examine. In the arts themselves, such as the visual arts, dance, or theatre, the ratio of Canadian work to foreign and American work is no better (see Crean, 1976). In education (see Mathews and Steele, 1971; Symons, 1975; Symons and Page, 1984; Lorimer, 1984) the situation is again the same. The degree of commitment of all levels of government to the development and communication of social science and humanities knowledge is paltry compared to what comes into the country on purchase. One other aspect of our junior partnership needs mention. With so much cultural spill-over there is a very real problem that Canadian cultural creators cannot help but be tempted to address particular themes selected, by repetition if nothing else, as salient by foreign, i.e., American, cultural producers. Audley's data do not address that manifestation of our proximity to the U.S.

We always have been and we probably always will remain a net importer of information. We survive, as other nations survive, as a net importer because the saving grace of any community or sovereign nation is that culture and cultural sovereignty are founded to a significant degree in the day-to-day personal relations and interactions each of us has with our fellow nationals. We survive also because we have the power, in some cases in our own minds and in some cases through business and government, to transform the information we import and use it to our own advantage. Canada gains enormously from the knowledge other nations, especially the United States, collect. We have almost immediate access to much American-produced information, whether on the weather, international affairs, market projections, historical analysis, or even entertainment. As luck would have it, we also have the economic resources to set our minds and our computers to make that information work for us. But we still remain net importers of information and cultural products, products that each day influence our ideas, priorities, politics, personal ambitions, and sense of the world.

INFORMATION NEEDS, COMMUNICATIONS ACTUALITIES, AND THE UNITED NATIONS

Because of our proximity to the U.S., many Canadians equate international relations with Canadian-American relations. We tend to assume that the United States is the model of a foreign country and that it behaves in a manner consistent with its ideology of free enterprise and free trade, lumber duties notwithstanding. We tend to be surprised when other countries are similar to Canada and not surprised when they are similar to the U.S. We are often surprised to hear that other countries have stronger restrictions to the importation of cultural goods than does Canada.

Most of the time these assumptions are wrong. The United States is only one of many sovereign nations and an extremely unusual one at that. It is a leader of one way of looking at the world, a perspective that emphasizes the freedom of the individual to act as he or she pleases and specifically to engage in business enterprise of any kind without interference of the state on behalf of the general or community interest.

Because the United States is such a large and powerful nation it is in a position to benefit from the energies of its citizens as they pursue their own economic self-interest. Given a hospitable climate, a rich resource base, the freedom to pursue one's own interest without fear of interference from the state, a large home market, a place at the leading edge of technology and of consumption, it is very much in the interest of the United States and Americans as a whole to pursue an ideology of freedom of enterprise and of free trade in goods of all sorts. Basically, this allows them to sell goods developed for the American market in foreign countries. The development of the technology is already paid for. All that is required is run-on production or perhaps the shipping of manufacturing equipment to another country.

The structure of production and marketing in cultural products does not differ significantly from the production and marketing of any other product. The consumption of cultural products does. While any product has a cultural component in its very existence, but more noticeably in its style (think of Italian-designed furniture or automobile bodies), a cultural product is almost pure information or pure culture. In consuming it we consume attitudes, perceptions, ideas, a world view, and so forth. To the extent that these products are created by other cultures, they may clash with our own cultural values. In some senses, as noted earlier, they may threaten to extinguish local culture. In fact, even if they do not clash with our own visions, when they seem to fit right into our own cultural viewpoint, they may twist and pull our culture in directions that only years from now we come to understand were not in keeping with other fundamentals that we hold dear.

Such issues do not reflect merely a Canadian paranoia. We do not hear Americans crying out about the inundation of foreign ideas (unless, of course, they are Communist ideas), and therefore we might assume that people of few other nations share our concern. But virtually every other nation of the world, including the U.S.S.R. and China, is concerned by the inundation of its culture by foreign ideas, especially American ideas. This concern does not mean that they hate the Americans or even that they are anti-American, but rather that they are committed to the preservation of their own culture and nation. Their position is that if their citizens are fed a constant diet of American cultural products they will want to live like Americans; they will tend to assume that their own institutions are equivalent in function and intent to American institutions and if they are not that there is something wrong with their institutions. This perspective may be defined as pure political self-interest. But it may also be seen, more idealistically, as a commitment to a pluralistic world society in all its heterogeneity. It can readily be argued that in such heterogeneity is to be found a different level of human freedom, the freedom of communities.

Canada's Concerns and the Concerns of UNESCO

The similarity of Canada's position to that of other foreign countries (except the United States) provides any Canadian examining

United Nations research studies with a sense of recognition. (Figure 9.1 presents the results of such a study.) What those documents reflect is that every country has a distinctive cultural environment to which it can respond with the design of a particular communication system. Each country must design its communication system with elements of domestic production and elements of foreign production in mind. Accordingly, each must take into account a parallel set of distinctive qualities and production capabilities as we have put forward here in considering Canada's communication environment.

Because our fate is a common one (internationally), considerable discussion has been generated within the United Nations about communications needs, communications problems, national sovereignty, and so forth. Much of this discussion has taken place under the auspices of UNESCO and is specifically included in the MacBride Report on communications problems and prospects. As the MacBride Report indicates, *each nation needs a national informatics policy.* A nation must have the capacity to take information produced by the world community and analyse it according to national needs and priorities. While Canada has not fully committed itself to this need, along with a few other developed nations, Canada is in the happy position of being economically able to work toward an information infrastructure oriented to its national needs and the maintenance of its independence. Being already committed as we are to hardware development and hence technological sophistication in communications, being economically well-off, and being the forward shock troops for the U.S. cultural barrage, we are in a position to lead in such an endeavour for our own ends and for the benefit of other nations.

In some sense, this book will provide an understanding of the nature of that task. We will first examine in more detail the structure of the media in Canada. Then we will turn to content, management, and ownership. After that we will discuss a set of illustrative examples of major issues in mass communication. In the final two chapters we will return to the international discussion of communications issues and end the book with an assessment of Canada's place in the ever-approaching information age.

SUMMARY

We began this chapter with an analogy to hockey, pointing out that the structure of an activity, whether it be the rules of a game or the structural elements of a communication system, creates certain opportunities and suppresses others. Because communication pervades virtually every aspect of our existence, the structure within which communication processes take place have a profound effect on society spanning eight dimensions. They are:

1. the social dimension
2. the political dimension
3. the economic dimension
4. the educational dimension
5. the cultural dimension
6. the technological dimension
7. the familial dimension
8. the individual dimension

Within an historical context, according to Innis and McLuhan at least, communication has been a fundamental variable in the organization of human cultures and societies. Oral, literate, and electronic societies are fundamentally different in the manner in which they deal with information and knowledge.

Canada has developed within the sphere of

Western democratic society, applying principles imagined and tested elsewhere. Yet Canadian society has a unique set of needs for and a distinctive system of communication. The bias of our hybrid system has never matched and presently still does not quite match the nature of those needs. Modern communications technologies have made possible a distribution of content that has overcome historical barriers such as our vast geography, our low population density, and our proximity to the United States. They have also made possible the creation of content that reflects key aspects of Canadian society, such as our linguistic duality and cultural multiplicity. However, when such technologies have been combined with the economics of content production they have had a homogenizing effect that challenges our national identity and cultural sovereignty.

Canada is not alone in this position. Although Canada has a special position and distinctive needs, our needs and position are not unlike those of a great majority of other nations, something we tend to overlook when we so often regard the United States as an example of a foreign nation.

REFERENCES

Audley, P. Canada's Cultural Industries. Toronto: James Lorimer, 1983.

Babe, R. "Emergence and development of Canadian communications: technology, industry and government," in R. Lorimer and D.C. Wilson, eds., Communications Canada. Forthcoming, 1988.

Beale, A. "The question of space," in Lorimer and Wilson, eds., Communications Canada.

Canada, Department of Communication. The Challenge of Communication, videotape.

Crean, S.M. Who's Afraid of Canadian Culture? Don Mills, Ontario: General Publishing, 1976.

Dryden, Ken. The Game. Toronto: Macmillan of Canada, 1983.

Eslin, Martin. "The Exploding Stage," CBC Radio, Ideas. University of Toronto, October, 1980.

Gerbner, George. Trends in Network Television Drama and Viewer Conceptions of Social Reality. Philadelphia: Annenberg School of Communications, University of Pennsylvania, 1978.

Goody, J.R. The Domestication of the Savage Mind. Cambridge: Cambridge University Press, 1977.

Goody, J.R., ed. Changing Social Structure in Ghana. London: International African Institute, 1975.

Grady, Wayne. "The Budweiser Gamble," Saturday Night (February, 1983), pp. 28-30.

Grant, George. Technology and Empire. Toronto: Anansi, 1969.

Havelock, Eric. Origins of Western Literacy. Toronto: OISE Press, 1976.

Innis, Harold. Empire and Communications. Toronto: Oxford University Press, 1950.

Knelman, Martin. This is Where We Came In. Toronto: McClelland and Stewart, 1977.

de Kerckhove, Derrick. "McLuhan versus Orwell in 1984," The Globe and Mail, 1984.

Kesterton, W.H. A History of Journalism in Canada. Toronto: McClelland and Stewart, 1967.

Kroker, A. Technology and the Canadian Mind. Montreal: New World Perspectives, 1984.

Lord, A.B. The Singer of Tales. Cambridge: Harvard University Press, 1964.

Lorimer, R. The Nation in the Schools: Wanted – A Canadian Education. Toronto: OISE Press, 1984.

Lorimer, R., and Donald C. Wilson, eds. Communications Canada. Forthcoming, 1988.

Mathews, R., and J. Steele. The Struggle for Canadian Universities. Toronto: New Press, 1971.

McLuhan, Marshall. The Gutenberg Galaxy. Toronto: University of Toronto Press, 1962.

Olson, David R., ed. The Social Foundations of Language and Thought. New York: Norton, 1980.

Payzant, G. Glenn Gould: Music and Mind. Toronto: Key Porter, 1984.

Symons, T.H.B. To Know Ourselves: The Report of the Commission on Canadian Studies, 2 vols. Ottawa: Association of Universities and Colleges of Canada, 1975.

Symons, T.H.B., and J.E. Page. *Some Questions of Balance: Higher Education and Canadian Studies.* Ottawa: AUCC, 1984.

UNESCO, International Commission on Communications Problems (MacBride Commission). *Many Voices, One World.* Paris: Unipub, 1980.

STUDY QUESTIONS

1. The section on the range of communication deals with the breadth of influence of communications on society. Are communications all-encompassing?

2. How would you describe the structural influence of communication on society?

3. What are the defining characteristics of Canada's information environment?

4. Why is it important for Canada or for any other country to have control over its own system of communications?

5. It is often said that the mass media have made the world seem smaller and we now all live in the "global village." What do you think is meant by this label (global village)? Do you think that is where we live?

CHAPTER

2

The Mass Media and Canadian Society

INTRODUCTION: DEFINITION

CHAPTER 1 provided an analysis of the role of communication and discussed communication systems (termed in this book "communications") in a broad cultural context. We argued that the dominant modes of communication of any culture are a fundamental structuring influence on that culture. In this chapter, as a specific example of the thesis of Chapter 1, we introduce the dominant modes of communication in modern society: mass media systems in national societies. As a first example we use the mass media in Canadian society. It is our purpose here to define the key elements of the mass media and to take up issues that arise from these elements in later units.

The mass media can be said to be, following McQuail (1983):

1. *a distinct set of activities* (creating media content)

2. *involving particular technological configurations* (television, radio, videotex, newspapers, books)
3. associated with *formally constituted institutions* or media outlets (systems, stations, publications, and so on)
4. acting according to *certain laws, rules, and understandings* (professional codes and practices, audience and societal expectations and habits)
5. carried out by *persons occupying certain roles* (regulators, producers, distributors, advertisers, audience members)
6. which, together, convey *information, entertainment, images, and symbols*
7. to the *mass audience.*

The mass media are both a significant industrial activity contributing to the Gross Domestic Product and a profound cultural activity. The mass media, as noted above, are the primary institutions for the communication of the images and symbols that are central to the society of which they are a part. In playing such a role, as we have noted in Chapter 1 and as we will discuss in this and succeeding chapters, the media exert a profound influence on the ideology of society. Many observers claim that they are the most powerful controlling influence over the ideology of modern society.

1. A DISTINCT SET OF ACTIVITIES

The mass media constitute a distinct set of activities in several different ways. First, the mass media themselves are usually taken to include mass-circulation newspapers and popular magazines as well as radio and television broadcasting. With some qualifications, books, feature films, and recorded music may also be included in the definition. Book publishing, for instance, covers a wide range of printed materials, from best-seller paperback books printed by the millions to expensive limited editions. Some books may be considered part of the mass media while others are not. Feature films gain an initial distribution in theatres – but to a limited (theatre-going) segment of the population in most countries. Through later television and videocassette release, they reach a larger, mass audience. Recorded music gains its penetration of the mass market through a number of channels of communication, including radio, record sales, and the viewing of music videos.

The following table indicates the extent of media activity in Canada and the degree to which Canadians involve themselves in media-related activities.

Other Forms of Mass Communication

While the above are what are termed the modern mass media, it should not be assumed that every medium of communication to large numbers of people is considered to be part of the mass media. As Curran (in Gurevitch *et al.,* 1982, p. 202) explains:

> a variety of signifying forms apart from face-to-face interaction – buildings, pictures, statues, coins, banners, stained glass, songs, medallions, rituals of all kinds – were deployed in pre-industrial societies to express sometimes highly complex ideas. At times, these signifying forms reached vast audiences. For instance, the proportion of the adult population in Europe regularly attending mass during the middle ages was almost certainly higher than the proportion of adults in contemporary Europe regularly reading a newspaper. Since the rituals of religious worship were laid down in liturgies, the papal curia exercised a much more centralized control over the symbolic content mediated through public worship in the central middle ages than even the controllers of the highly

TABLE 2.1

Media Outlets and Industry Size (1980)[1]

Outlet	Output		Ad Revenue[2]
Newspapers[3]	No.	Circulation ('000)	Net Ad Rev. ($000)
Dailies	117	32,445	892,000
Weekend Sup.	3	4,024	17,100
Weekly, semi- tri-weekly	1,187	12,591	210,000
Periodicals		Circulation[4]	
Gen. Mags	644	36,596	152,000
Business	507	8,622	97,800
Farm	112	2,378	15,000
Directories	52	4,311	236,000
Relig., scholarly, other	48	908	11,500
Broadcast	No. of Stns.	Total Rev.	
Radio (1979)[5]			
Private	493	562,036	
CBC	65		
Total	558		391,965
Television			
Private	80	397,194	
CBC	31		
Total	111		610,334
Priv. Broad.	573	959,230	
CBC	96	647,004	
Cable		352,172	
Other Print			
Catalogue, Direct Mail		774,679	
Outdoor			
Billboards, car cards, signs			236,000
Books	Titles	Sales ($000)[6]	
Domestic	3,502	256,700	
Foreign		675,000	
Total		931,700	
Records and Tapes[7]		Rev. R&T alone $000	Total Rev. ($000)
6 largest		181,700	271,000
Total Industry		235,100	339,000
Movie Theatres[8]		Pd. Admissions ('000)	Receipts ($000)
Total		101,000	311,400

1. Unless otherwise indicated, as of 1980.
2. SOURCE: Maclean Hunter Research Bureau, *A Report on Advertising Revenues in Canada*, 1981.
3. SOURCE: *Royal Commission on Newspapers*, Research Studies, Vol. 1.
4. SOURCE: Culture Statistics: Newspapers and Periodicals #87-625. Data are incomplete to a significant degree.
5. SOURCE: CRTC Annual Report, 1978-79.
6. SOURCE: Statistics Canada #87-601.
7. The six largest are CBS, WEA, RCA, MCI, Thorn-EMI, and Polygram. SOURCE: for data: StatsCan unpublished industry survey.
8. SOURCE: *Canadian Film Digest*, 1982.

centralized and monopolistic press of contemporary Europe.

When we speak of the mass media, then, we are speaking of the modern electronic and print-based mass media. At the same time, the insights that can be gained from the study of these media can provide some valuable understandings of other "media" used to communicate to large audiences.

Construction or Signification

The mass media can be considered to be a distinct set of activities in their communicative function as well as in their form. The common-sense image of the nature of communication is that of a conduit. Some piece of information that exists at point "A" or time "A" or in the mind of person "A" is transposed largely unaffected by its mode of transmission to point "B," time "B," and/or into the mind of person "B." A predominant emphasis in socially oriented (as opposed to technically oriented) communication theory is on the *transposing* function, which is really seen as a *transforming* function.

To use the words of two different kinds of theorists to describe this transforming function, the media "construct" (see Berger and Luckmann, 1966) or "signify" reality. Their primary function as symbol- or meaning-producing agents is to construct or signify reality. Thereby they are distinguished from other non-communicative activities.

Modern communication theory also posits that this function is not a secondary or derivative activity. As Bennett (in Gurevitch *et al.,* 1982, p. 187) argues, the ideas that long held sway insisted that:

> the media can reflect only what is there.... the world of signs is granted only a shadowy, twilight existence; it 'hovers' above 'reality' as an ethereal appendage to it, deriving such

substance as it has merely from what is reflected in it.

More recent developments in the theory of language have pulled in a direction directly contrary to this, stressing not only the independent materiality of the signifier – the fleshiness of the sign – but also the activity and effectivity of signification as a process which actively constructs cognitive worlds rather than simply passively reflecting a pre-existing reality.... Sign orders world.

As the Bible says in its implicit origin myth, "in the beginning was the word."

In summary, two major components combine to make the mass media a distinct set of activities. They have a *modern technological base* and *a primary and non-derivative signifying or reality-constructing function.* This latter characteristic leads the media to play a strong ideological role, something we will take up under point 6.

2. PARTICULAR TECHNOLOGICAL CONFIGURATIONS

Considerations of the role of technology in the modern mass media are not exhausted simply by identifying them as modern as opposed to ancient. In examining the context out of which these modern technologies have developed, together with their particular properties, we gain a sense of the role of technology itself in the functioning of the various mass media.

Raymond Williams, in *Television: Technology and Cultural Form* (1974), provides a thorough account of the relationship between technology and society using television as an example. In brief, he points out that technologies do not arise from the brain of a genius working in isolation from any social context; they arise from and are incorporated into society on the basis of the structure and functioning of society. For example, television did not so much arise as an inevitable offshoot of the search for scientific knowledge but rather from the interests and conceptions of technical investigators and industrial entrepreneurs who, on the basis of their cultural background and their technical expertise, were able to imagine an electronic medium of sound and visual communication. Nor do we need to use television technology in the manner that we now do. The domination of the medium by advertisers and by certain types of programming is not necessary but the result of the interests of the persons and institutions that control content.

Two Crucial Elements of Technology in Canadian Communications

Two technical elements critical to the Canadian television environment vis-à-vis the U.S. illustrate the salience of technological configurations. The first is that, unlike that of many other countries, such as Britain, Australia, Europe, most of Africa, parts of South America, and the Soviet Union, Canadian television is *technically compatible with American television.* Simply with aerials we can receive U.S. signals. We can use our sets whether on U.S. or Canadian soil. Without that technical compatibility every American program would have to go through an expensive transformation before being received by Canadians. Some (e.g., Smythe, 1980) have argued that a technical incompatibility would have protected Canada from the inundation by U.S. programs by making them impossible to receive.

Partially as a result of the Canada-U.S. compatibility of signals, but partially also because of interstation domestic (U.S.) competition, the power of U.S. broadcasting signals has been a

second significant technical factor in structuring the Canadian television environment. Simply speaking, many U.S. signals, both radio and television, are fairly easily received in Canada. Cable companies merely erect a high-quality aerial to receive U.S. signals free of charge for redistribution to their subscribers. In addition, tapes are cheaply exported, without technical adaptation, from the U.S. to the Canadian market.

These two technical variables make it difficult for Canadians to produce affordable popular programs because they must recover their cost in a (Canadian) market one-tenth the size of the American market, and, at that, it is a diminished market because of U.S. penetration. The net result is visible in Table 2.2.

Technology in the Developed and Developing World

What are normally referred to as the developed countries are almost exclusively the source of technological innovations leading to the development of today's mass media and to the "new media" on the horizon. The economies of the developed nations have generated enormous wealth through the application of scientific research and development (R&D) for the discovery of technologies of production and distribution. The mass media are an integral part of that technological system. Indeed, some would argue that one aspect of mass media, advertising, has been essential to the continued growth of Western economies. The mass media are a creation of the industrial world and, like other aspects of industry, their origins can be traced to the Industrial Revolution of the nineteenth century.

While the mass media systems of the

TABLE 2.2

Population Coverage and Viewing Audience Share
for Canadian and U.S. Television Stations, 1967 and 1977

	Population Coverage		Audience Share	
	1967	1977	1967	1977
English-language				
CBC	90.46	94.88	34.14	18.93
CTV	68.37	92.28	18.93	24.95
Canadian independent	19.92	53.07	2.53	10.33
Canadian educational	0.00	54.05	0.00	0.74
CBS	40.99	63.66	7.20	7.27
NBC	28.87	62.27	3.78	6.41
ABC	36.55	62.30	4.94	7.25
Multi-affiliate	10.70	2.29	1.65	0.35
U.S. independent	1.47	14.82	0.17	1.34
PBS	0.00	57.05	0.00	0.83
French-language				
Radio-Canada	39.88	79.61	14.43	10.48
TVA	27.62	28.15	12.32	11.12

SOURCE: Audley, *Canada's Cultural Industries*, which used: CRTC, *Special Report on Broadcasting*, 1968-78, vol.2

developed nations have been imitated in many forms by the developing nations, modern media systems were first developed and evolved in the industrial nations and were then "transplanted," not always with similar results. The effects of mass media systems in developing countries are quite different from those in countries such as Canada. Similarly, the effects of these systems in non-industrialized regions such as the Canadian North are quite different from their effects in a region such as southern Ontario. Variations in social structures, in attitudes toward the media, in educational standards, and so on, all of which modify the effects of the media, vary not only from country to country but also from region to region.

3. FORMALLY CONSTITUTED INSTITUTIONS

The implications of technological configurations of the media cannot be discussed for long before a consideration of their associated industrial structures must be included. The mass media do not exist without industrial structures for the production and processing of content as well as the construction and maintenance of a physical plant. Media institutions have developed to provide the infrastructure needed to operate the media. These institutions may be private corporations owned by shareholders, or publicly owned corporations or state enterprises – in Canadian terms, Crown corporations.

Private-Sector Institutions

Private broadcasters may be defined as those corporations owning media enterprises for profit. Their primary purpose, obviously, is to gain the maximum revenues at minimum cost. Revenues come almost entirely from advertising charges, although some income may be generated from program sales, property leasing, and the like.

A major cost in operating a station or network is the cost of creating or purchasing content, and the economics of broadcasting show clearly that it is cheaper simply to purchase programming than to make one's own programs with an equivalent audience appeal. This is especially the case in purchasing U.S. programming for showing in the Canadian market because the costs of the original productions have usually been recouped in the U.S. market and foreign sales for the copyright holder can be made much below production cost. It is customary for Canadian broadcasters to pay the equivalent of about 10 to 20 per cent of the production cost for the national market rights for a U.S. program to show in Canada.

Clearly, domestic productions cannot possibly match these prices and still cover the production costs. Also, the economic incentive for Canadian private broadcasters to produce Canadian programming is extremely weak. Only with specific types of programs where audiences are highly interested – sports, news, and some public affairs programs – is there sufficient incentive for private broadcasters to engage in production, where production costs are considerably less than, say, for dramatic productions.

Private broadcasters produce other types of programming for non-economic reasons, primarily because they are required to maintain minimum percentages of Canadian content in their program schedules. The economic imperative tends to produce obedience to the letter of the law, as opposed to the intent of the overall broadcasting system. As Table 2.3 shows, because it is cheaper to produce game shows, for example, than it is to buy what independently produced Canadian programming manages to get made, many of the private broadcasters telecast game shows rather than entertaining or informative Canadian programs.

Public and Private-Sector Institutions

In Western nations, public media corporations are usually operated at "arm's length" from control of the government (although the length of the arm varies greatly). In socialist countries, public ownership of the mass media is achieved by means of state institutions not unlike government departments – a pattern that is also emerging in the developing countries.

The public or private ownership of media is obviously a major factor affecting the relationship between the media and the state. Thus, the political role of the mass media in a specific society, as discussed in Chapter 3, is of considerable importance. Where private ownership is dominant, considerations of profit-making and advertiser interests tend to prevail over considerations of public service. (It is, of course, possible for private ownership of a mass media system to be organized on a non-profit basis, but this is relatively rare.) Where public service prevails completely, potential advertisers complain of an inability to get information to consumers, while consumers sometimes complain of the lack of escapist

TABLE 2.3

Average Cost and Revenue of Canadian Programming by Program Category, 1978

	No. of Programs	Costs*	Revenues**	Audience † Actual	Break-even
English-Language Market					
Drama					
serials	4	$114,750	$59,536	921,500	1,776,300
short films	1	137,160	78,166	1,210,000	2,123,200
teledramas	2	112,830	46,318	717,000	1,746,000
Variety	2	115,620	74,452	1,152,500	1,789,800
Game shows	2	18,900	57,882	896,000	292,600
News	6	36,887	68,301	1,057,300	571,000
Documentaries	1	20,768	26,098	404,000	321,400
French-Language Market					
Drama					
soap operas	3	25,860	51,390	1,380,600	440,800
Variety	2	38,925	44,448	794,900	716,200
Game shows	2	21,090	42,620	708,500	193,400
News and information	2	29,730	36,025	687,500	567,400

*Costs are the average cost of a 30-minute program for a sample of programs in each category.
**The average revenue was obtained in the following manner: The minimum 30-second rate during prime time viewing for a network which had broadcast the program was multiplied by twenty time periods. This gave the revenue for a half-hour of programming for which the 15 per cent agency commission was subtracted. This income was divided by the average audience of the network during prime time, which gave the income per viewer. The average income by category of program was then obtained by multiplying the audience of each program by the revenue per viewer. The data are for rates and audiences in Fall, 1978.
†The actual audience is the audience observed for each sample program. The break-even audience is the one necessary to cover production costs.
SOURCE: Audley, *Canada's Cultural Industries*, which used: A Lapointe and J. LeGoff, *Television Programs and Their Production in Canada* (Department of Communications, May, 1980), Tables 1.25 and 1.26.

programming that allows them to forget the issues and concerns of the day.

Distinguishing state ownership from private ownership is useful in understanding major differences in media operations, but it is also too simple, especially in the case of Third World or developing countries. To appreciate fully the role of the institution as part of an industrial infrastructure one must have some understanding of the nature of the society, capitalist or socialist, within which the institution exists.

The operation of private or state-owned media in a politically stable and tolerant state such as Canada is much less encumbered than is either form of ownership in many other countries, whether capitalist, socialist, or communist. The rule of both capital and the state can be extremely harsh and intolerant. Salter (1988) has provided a useful paper on this issue within the context of how Canadians have come to conceive of the public interest in public broadcasting.

4. CERTAIN LAWS, RULES, AND UNDERSTANDINGS

The technology and institutional form of mass media systems, including the role of the industrial infrastructure and its ownership, are significant factors in the performance of these systems. However, they are far from the only factors involved. Beyond the specific political system and the industrial infrastructure, almost all media systems operate within specific societies and, as such, are subject to the patterns of control and behaviour of the society concerned. There are international media systems, such as short-wave radio broadcasting, but these represent only a small portion of the mass media overall.

Most media systems are intended to operate within one society (although significant overlaps and overflows may occur, as in the case of American media flowing into Canada). In the case of broadcasting, licensing requirements for the relatively limited number of radio frequencies available to each nation-state oblige national governments to exercise some control over the frequencies used within their borders. In the case of publishing (newspapers or magazines) most developed countries exercise little overt control. No licences are required and media content is not restricted. However, various indirect controls can be employed.

Government control exists in legislation, regulation, licensing, taxation, subsidies, and so on. It is much more difficult to observe or tabulate the indirect controls exerted by the society as a whole on the mass media. Direct subsidies, business policies, distribution subsidies, and tax breaks are several types of indirect controls.

The Mass Media and the Social System

The mass media can also be seen as a "sub-system" of the society; the sub-system has its own internal structures and interacts with the larger society on a continuous basis. From this perspective mass media systems are seen not so much as derivatives of the social system but rather as intentionally engaged in both forming social change and being formed by it.

At a more specific level of analysis, we can look at an individual mass media system as a social structure. The people working within this structure are members of the wider society and reflect at least some of the values of that society. However, they also absorb and participate in setting standards of behaviour within their own social or institutional structure. These behavioural patterns and ways of thinking within the organization are the "professional" standards toward which media workers are expected to strive. In the case of print journalists in particular, expected standards of performance in their work have evolved over a long period of time and exert a significant degree of control over how they do their work on a daily basis. Professional standards have also developed and evolved for other newer media occupations, such as television producers and radio announcers.

The extent to which these behavioural standards prevail over or interact with the social norms of the wider society is a question of continuing interest and controversy both within media professions and in the society at large. To whom, for example, is the journalist responsible? To the media organization and its expectations, to his or her professional peers, to the wider society, or to some combination of all three? This dilemma is more complex than simply pointing to the competing allegiances of journalists to their employers on the one hand and the media audiences on the other.

Audiences and the Public

The relationship between the audience and society is also complex. To many, the audience and society are virtually synonymous terms, especially in studying television. Virtually every household in a developed country such as Canada has at least one television set and most sets are turned on every day. Audiences for specific programs can number well into the millions, even in a relatively small country like Canada. The watching of television news in particular is of widespread significance because of the sheer numbers of people who view the news and who rely for information almost entirely on television news reports. Yet, watching television news and reading newspapers are series of repeated private events: there is a significant social difference between viewing something in public and viewing something in private. Even disregarding audience size, it can never be said that the whole society and the audience for a specific program are equivalent. Nor are the choices one makes as a member of an audience (to watch or not to watch a particular program) the same choices one might make as a member of the public (to have such a program available to those who may be interested).

Where, then, can we look for an indication of the societal expectations of mass media performance? Frequent references are made in debates about the mass media to the preferences of the "general public," or the "public interest," in monitoring particular media behaviour. But how does anyone know what the public wants, if by "public" we mean society at large and its interest in preserving and developing its central values?

The short answer is that, public opinion polls notwithstanding (see Chapter 3), there is no simple way of ascertaining the public inter-est. The longer answer is that many participants in the mass media – as well as audience members, government regulators, legislators, industry lobbyists, administrators, and so on – believe that they know what the public wants and, consequently, they try to influence the way the media are operated. In fact, many of the constraints within which the media operate stem from the efforts of various individuals and pressure groups to direct the media toward certain goals.

Societal and Legislative Expectations

The mass media are expected to perform various functions in society, and not all these functions can be fulfilled simultaneously or at an acceptable cost. For example, in Canada we generally expect the mass media to reflect the diversity of our society. Some of us emphasize the importance of providing media services in both official languages while others stress the importance of allowing the multicultural and multiracial character of Canadian society to be shown on our TV screens and be heard on radio and in print. Furthermore, we also expect that media will service rural and remote areas across the country regardless of the costs involved.

It is a policy of the federal government that special provisions should be made to provide media services for native people in the North in their indigenous languages. Other more general expectations that Canadians share with other societies are that media content should be provided for people of different ages and interests, and that this diversity of content should offer an acceptable balance of information and entertainment. Finally, it is expected that in any particular location, the media content should be an appropriate mixture of that which is local, regional, national, and international.

In more abstract terms, the mass media are expected to fulfil the needs of the society, particularly the needs related to the continuing existence of that society. In this view, the mass media as a social institution are required to assist in providing "continuity, order, integration, motivation, guidance, adaptation" (McQuail, 1983, p. 64). In a Canadian government interpretation of these needs, the mass media should be helping the evolution of Canadian society toward a multicultural "mosaic" and discouraging any potentially non-unifying activities such as the separatist movement in Quebec.

While the constraints placed on the mass media by society are diffuse and difficult to describe precisely, it is much easier to observe the constraints imposed through laws and corporate structures. A wide range of legislative statutes have some bearing on the operation of mass media systems; these statutes vary from those directed specifically at the mass media, such as the Broadcasting Act, to those only partly concerned with the mass media, such as the Canada Elections Act, the Official Secrets Act, the Food and Drug Act, and so on.

Most of the legislation related to the mass media in Canada is federal. All of the laws and regulations concerned with the licensing and control of broadcasting is federal for jurisdictional reasons; the right to pass such laws and regulations has been deemed by the courts to rest with the federal government. However, because of the sole right of the provinces over education, the courts have given to the provinces the right to establish and fund educational broadcasting institutions. But only the federal government can license them.

The Broadcasting Act

The pre-eminent statute in Canadian broadcasting is the Broadcasting Act (RSC 1970, c.B-11). There is no equivalent statute for Canadian newspapers, magazines, books, or recorded music. The reasons why broadcasting has received such particular attention in legislation are partly constitutional (the federal government has clear, undivided power over "radio communication," which includes broadcasting) and partly social (a widely held belief in Canada is that broadcasting is particularly important to nation-building). It is worthwhile taking a look at the Broadcasting Act as a way of finding out what this society deems broadcasting should do. The significant section of the statute for this purpose is Section 3, on policy:

a) broadcasting undertakings in Canada make use of radio frequencies that are public property and such undertakings constitute a single system, herein referred to as the Canadian broadcasting system, comprising public and private elements;

b) the Canadian broadcasting system should be effectively owned and controlled by Canadians so as to safeguard, enrich and strengthen the cultural, political, social and economic fabric of Canada;

c) all persons licensed to carry on broadcasting undertakings have a responsibility for programs they broadcast but the right to freedom of expression and the right of persons to receive programs, subject only to generally applicable statutes and regulations, is unquestioned;

d) the programming provided by the Canadian broadcasting system should be varied and comprehensive and should provide a reasonable, balanced opportunity for the expression of differing views on matters of public concern, and the programming provided by each broadcaster should be of high standard, using predominantly Canadian creative and other resources;

e) all Canadians are entitled to broadcasting service in English and French as public funds become available;

f) there should be provided, through a corporation established by Parliament for the purpose, a national broadcasting service that is predominantly Canadian in content and character;

g) the national broadcasting service should:

i) be a balanced service of information, enlightenment and entertainment for people of different ages, interests and tastes covering the whole range of programming in fair proportion,

ii) be extended to all parts of Canada, as public funds become available,

iii) be in English and French, serving the special needs of geographic regions, and actively contributing to the flow and exchange of cultural and regional information and entertainment, and

iv) contribute to the development of national unity and provide for a continuing expression of Canadian identity;

h) where any conflict arises between the objectives of the national broadcasting service and the interests of the private element of the Canadian broadcasting system, it shall be resolved in the public interest but paramount consideration shall be given to the objectives of the national broadcasting service;

i) facilities should be provided within the Canadian broadcasting system for educational broadcasting; and

j) the regulation and supervision of the Canadian broadcasting system should be flexible and readily adaptable to scientific and technical advances.

The objectives of the broadcasting policy for Canada enunciated in this section can best be achieved by providing for the regulation and supervision of the Canadian broadcasting system by a single independent public authority.

The "national broadcasting service" referred to in sub-sections f to h is to be provided by the Canadian Broadcasting Corporation (CBC).

The CBC is a Crown corporation, first established in 1932 as the Canadian Radio Broadcasting Commission. The obligations placed on the CBC are different from those placed on other broadcasters in Canada. Nevertheless, Section 3(a) indicates that public broadcasters and private broadcasters together comprise a "single system" of Canadian broadcasting that is expected to operate harmoniously.

Canadian ownership and control of the broadcasting system is required through subsection b; the "effective" ownership held by Canadians has been set by the federal cabinet (through an order-in-council) at no less than 80 per cent of licensed companies. The purpose for which this level of ownership is needed is stated to be: "to safeguard, enrich and strengthen the cultural, political, social and economic fabric of Canada." What does this mean? It appears to be an elaboration on the theme of nation-building. But to say that is to interpret the Act, something all involved with broadcasting must do. Each sub-section of this broadcasting policy has been endlessly studied and restated in the years since it was approved by Parliament in 1968. Lawyers, especially, must argue the cases of their clients within accepted interpretations of the Act.

The CRTC and the Broadcasting Act

Those most assiduous in examining the policy statement have probably been the members of the CRTC. Between 1968 and 1974 the CRTC's full name was the Canadian Radio Television Commission; it now operates under the name of the Canadian Radio-television and Telecommunications Commission, and is the "single independent public authority" referred to at the end of Section 3. It is the CRTC's task to administer the policy enunciated in the

Broadcasting Act and to examine its powers and authority as specified in other sections of this statute.

In attempting to administer the policy of the Act, it becomes apparent that many of the phrases and words are vague and require interpretation to be of use in making rejections or issuing licences. We have already raised the question of what is the "fabric" of Canada, but what about programming of a "high standard," using "predominantly Canadian resources"? How does the CBC "contribute to the development of Canadian unity" while providing for a "continuing expansion of Canadian identity"? What exactly is the public interest that shall be served in resolving conflicts between the CBC and private broadcasters? What is a "balanced" service from the CBC? What does it mean to cover a range of programming in "fair production"?

To raise these questions is not to pour scorn on the inadequacies of this Canadian broadcasting policy. Making the wording more specific and concrete risks tying the regulatory body to a series of actions that could be detrimental or counterproductive in changing circumstances. Effective regulation requires the exercise of judgement; policies spelled out in great detail leave little room for such judgement.

The Ideals of the Broadcasting Act and the Realities of Canada's Broadcasting System

However they might have been worded, the ideals expressed in the policy section are far from being realized. The practical difficulties constraining the performance of the Canadian broadcasting system are varied and deep-rooted. Probably foremost among the difficulties is the proximity to the United States and its extraordinarily powerful broadcasting industry.

Given the easy access to American programming (from both American and Canadian TV stations), the small size of the Canadian audience makes it difficult to produce affordable, popular programming that will compete effectively for audience attention.

Other difficulties stem from the increasing fragmentation of the national audience through the development of cable TV and its extension of signal coverage, the division of the Canadian audience between French-language and English-language stations, the introduction of new services such as pay TV and specialty TV that depend largely on U.S. programming inputs, and the division of the broadcasting system into public and private stations with many different, even conflicting, goals.

The various stresses and strains in the Canadian broadcasting system, arising from technology, a mixed public and private system, domestic political priorities, and Canada-U.S. relations, appear to undermine the capacity of the regulatory board and of individual broadcasting licensees to strive toward the ideals expressed in the broadcasting policy. Some, if not most, of the problem arises from the peculiar pattern of ownership that has evolved. Public corporations such as the CBC and some provincial educational communications authorities such as Radio Québec and TVOntario have mandates to provide broadcast-type programming for social and cultural purposes. They are responsible to the appropriate legislative body (Parliament or a provincial legislature) for the fulfilment of specified goals and for the expenditure of tax money allocated to them. Their audiences are made up mostly of people who are at the same time taxpayers and voters.

However, the CBC is different from the provincial broadcasters in three important ways:

1. While the CBC is publicly owned, many of the TV and radio stations that form the CBC's national network are privately owned. (The private stations are known as affiliates.)

2. The CBC's operations are much larger. No other Canadian broadcaster has TV and radio stations and networks, offers services in both English and French, and operates not only throughout Canada but also services an international audience (through Radio Canada International).

3. The political nature of the CBC's mandate differs from the educational nature of provincial enterprises.

On the other hand, as we have said, private broadcasters are in business to make a profit. Because they are dependent primarily on advertising revenues, private broadcasters must seek to maximize advertising revenues by maximizing their audience size and by attracting the kinds of viewers or listeners advertisers seek to reach. For private broadcasting stations, audiences are people whose primary role is as consumers. If audience members do not respond in sufficient numbers to advertising messages by buying the advertised products, then the commercial broadcasting system breaks down. The advertisers withdraw their advertising and may turn to other media, such as newspapers, magazines, and billboards, that can provide better consumer response.

5. PERSONS OCCUPYING CERTAIN ROLES

To some extent we have already discussed some of the ideas that might rightfully fall under this heading, such as the way in which the journalistic profession is structured, how regulation operates, members of the public as part of the public interest and as audience members, and so on. However, in our earlier discussion we have emphasized the structural role played out by these various interests. Here we will explore influences that are less built into the structure or are less "given" and thereby more subject to the control of individuals. Some of these influences – business, government, the legal system, and the audience – are outside the operating structure of the mass media. Others, the media professionals, are inside.

Business Influences

The influence of businesses on the mass media is largely exercised through advertising. Decisions by businesses on where to advertise and how much to spend collectively affect the fortunes of individual media enterprises. For example, decisions by major department stores to advertise in only one of two local daily newspapers and to favour the one with the larger circulation are likely to lead to the demise of the weaker paper. Similarly, decisions by Canadian branch-plant companies to reduce advertising budgets for television because the ads of their parent companies can reach Canadian audiences through the U.S. networks can lead to reduced revenues for Canadian TV stations and may even cause some stations to be only marginally profitable.

A less direct, but equally significant, effect of business advertising is on the non-advertising content. Media managers tend to avoid offending (or potentially offending) advertisers by ensuring that the content does not clash with the advertisers' messages. Such clashes may be specific, whereby a consumer-oriented article or program criticizes the products of a particular advertiser, or they may be more diffuse, such as descriptions of a non-consumer or anticonsumer lifestyle. Neither would fit well with the consumerism promoted in advertising.

THE 50 RICHEST

The former used-car salesman now has holdings that include supermarkets, magazine distributors, a Swiss financial company, the largest neon sign company in the world, the second-largest cannery business in the country and, of course, four car dealerships. Pattison's net worth is probably close to $390 million.

JODREY

John J. *(73). Hantsport, N.S. 1 son, 1 daughter.*

MINAS BASIN PULP & POWER CO. LTD.

David Hennigar *(47). Toronto. 1 son, 1 daughter.*

CROWNX INC.

John Jodrey is the son and David Hennigar a nephew of the late Roy Adelbert Jodrey, who built a Nova Scotia lumbering operation that has evolved into a real estate, canning, financial institution and pulp and paper empire. Jodrey continues to build through

David Hennigar

the Maritime enterprises, while Hennigar concentrates on the family's interest in Crownx, a financial services, health care and technology conglomerate controlled jointly with Toronto's Burns family.

Crownx took some flak from minority shareholders in 1986 when the families tried to consolidate power, proposing, for one thing, to split every common voting share into a voting and a nonvoting share; and eventually winning a two-for-one split of all nonvoting shares. Still, shareholders had reason to be happy: 1986 showed record revenues and a stock market eager to invest in financial institutions. Crownx became even more attractive when it set up a new merchant bank, Lancaster Financial, in midyear. The Jodrey clan is worth about $380 million.

CAMPEAU

Robert *(63). Toronto. 6 children.*

CAMPEAU CORP. LTD.

Robert Campeau sent shock waves through the North American business community in 1986 when he successfully accomplished the largest-ever takeover by a Canadian firm of an Ameri-

can company, giant Allied Stores Corp. of New York. It wasn't the first time, however, that the Sudbury-born former machinist turned real estate entrepreneur had shocked the business world. His lucrative office building contracts with the federal government, his short-lived early-'70s alliance with Paul Desmarais and especially his foiled 1980 takeover bid for Royal Trustco established Robert Campeau as a name in the news. Campeau's holding of his property company turned retail-property conglomerate makes his worth about $380 million.

SIEBENS

Harold *(81). Bahamas.*

William W. *(53). Calgary.*

CANDOR OIL & GAS LTD.

William Siebens is president of Candor, a small Calgary company that would hardly stir up notice in the big leagues. But Siebens has been an important name in the Calgary oil patch for a

generation. Father Harold made money buying and selling oil and gas lands, and son Bill, a onetime air force pilot and petroleum engineer, started Siebens Oil & Gas in 1965. When the pair sold that company to Dome Petroleum Ltd. and the CNR pension fund in 1978 for $360 million, they became personally very wealthy — their own share of the sale price amounted to $180 million.

While Siebens Sr. lives in retirement in the Bahamas, Bill Siebens is on the board of Roxy Petroleum Ltd., Sovereign Oil & Gas and Consolidated Pipe Lines as well as the Vancouver-based conservative think tank, the Fraser Institute. The family's wealth is now in the range of $375 million.

MANNIX

Frederick Charles *(73). Calgary. 2 sons, 1 daughter.*

Frederick Philip *(44). Calgary.*

Ronald Neil *(38). Calgary.*

LORAM GROUP

Commuters in Toronto and Montreal use subways constructed by a little-known Alberta family company. The Mannix empire began with a construction company, started by Frederick Charles's father, Fred, in the '20s. At one point, he sold it and Fred Jr. ran it, then later repurchased the company. The Loram Group

Frederick Charles Mannix

includes a large coal producer, pipeline and natural gas exploration, railway equipment manufacturing and real estate holdings. But with the western resource and real estate slump, its one public company, Pembina Resources Ltd., fell in value in the past year. Even so, the family is worth at least $350 million.

SOUTHAM/FISHER

St. Clair Balfour *(76). Toronto. 1 son, 1 daughter.*

John P. Fisher *(59). Toronto. 3 sons, 3 daughters.*

SOUTHAM INC.

In 1985, the widespread clan of Southams, Fishers, Balfours and other descendants of William Southam, who started a 15-newspaper chain with the purchase of one newspaper in 1877, was fighting to protect its legacy from takeover. John Fisher is the latest president and CEO representing

John P. Fisher

family interests, with a few other Southam descendants working as journalists within the newspaper-magazine chain. To put an end to the threatened takeover, family members banded together and arranged a private share swap with Torstar Corp., publishers of *The Toronto Star.*

That action placed directors of both companies in the bad books of securities regulators. For the family, however, there was another effect: During the year after the safety play for the company, the stock price was cut in half. This year, the Southam-Fisher-Balfour group is worth about $310 million.

SOUTHERN

Ronald Donald *(56). Calgary. 2 daughters.*

ATCO LTD.

In 1946, Ron Southern and his father bought 15 unassembled utility trailers and started renting them from a shack in their backyard. Today, Southern's ATCO distributes natural gas and electricity, drills for oil in North

It is no accident that this up-market Toyota Cressida ad appeared opposite an article on Canada's 50 richest businessmen. *Reprinted from The Financial Post Moneywise Magazine, February, 1987.*

Discussion of this phenomenon of avoiding offending advertisers relates to concerns that private media enterprises tailor their program content to fit with the advertisements. The mythology of the mass media suggests that the two types of material are managed quite separately and that journalists or program producers are insulated from advertiser influence. In reality, it does not seem to work that way (see, for example, the Report of the *Royal Commission on Newspapers,* 1981).

Government Influences

The influence of government, exerted from outside the mass media, has several dimensions. These will be explored in Chapter 3 and introduced briefly here. In a federal state such as Canada, more than one level of government influence is at work. Within any one government, we can also distinguish between bureaucratic (or departmental) structures and political structures.

At the bureaucratic level, the government is a major source of information for the mass media; in many instances it is the only source for specific types of information. The flow of information from government to the mass media benefits both parties but also, of course, has drawbacks. The government needs access to media outlets to inform the general public of what it is doing through government programs and expenditures. The mass media need the information supplied as a readily usable source of media content for new current affairs and public affairs materials.

Because of time constraints and limited resources, media workers rarely have the opportunity to collect this kind of information directly from government personnel, so they tend to rely heavily on news releases and handouts prepared by the government. By fail-

ing to look behind these announcements, the media outlets run the risk of acting as the propaganda arm of the government. The drawback for the government is in the sheer volume of materials pumped out by numerous departments, agencies, and ministries. The mass media cannot publish or broadcast all of it, so the selection of items can be quite arbitrary from the government's viewpoint.

The government's influence on the mass media also exists at a highly political level. Politicians are news, and daily coverage of political events is an essential part of mass media content. Rivalries between individuals and parties are extensively portrayed in the mass media and balanced coverage between the government party and opposition parties has to be handled carefully by media practitioners.

Related to both the bureaucratic and political levels of government is the phenomenon of government advertising. Advertisements can provide information on government programs, can be straightforward political campaigning, or can be in the grey area of general promotion of the federal or provincial government. Total advertising revenues from government sources form a substantial part of the revenues for mass media in Canada; the federal government outspends any one commercial advertiser.

In addition to being a source of information, the subject of "news," and the source of advertising revenues, government also has an influence on the mass media through the power to regulate and control. Both at the federal and provincial levels, government has the authority to approve legislation, to impose taxes, and in various other ways to affect the means by which mass media organizations conduct their operations. Private corporations have a strong tendency to resist or seek to reduce government controls over their operations by raising the banner of "freedom of the press." Restrictions on their freedom under legislation related to anti-combines, for example, are more apparent than real. There have been no successful prosecutions of media companies in recent history under Canada's anti-combines legislation. Nevertheless, mass media owners continue to argue that the freedom essential to a democratic press is threatened by excessive use of government power.

However, the tensions between the mass media institutions and government exist at many levels and are not likely to be resolved by allowing private corporations a free hand to operate mass media outlets. The position of public corporations and their relationships to government are also complex, although the tensions tend to focus on areas other than freedom of the press, such as public funding and accountability. The CBC in particular has a long history of difficulties in maintaining the proper balance between political freedom and public accountability.

Legal Influences

A third influence on the mass media is that of the legal system, in particular the decisions of the courts. One obligation of the courts is to interpret existing statutes in instances where specific mass media practitioners or owners are thought to have operated outside the law. A much more widespread influence on content, however, has to do with various sections of the Criminal and Civil Codes that cover such offences as sedition, promulgating obscenity, propagating hate literature, and issuing false messages. Court decisions on cases of these kinds tend to influence all mass media practitioners – particularly journalists – and are used as indicators to guide future actions taken in the selection of media content.

Audience Influences

The fourth outside influence on the mass media is the audience. The primary concern of the audience is with media content (advertising and non-advertising). Little influence is exerted on the ways mass media organizations are structured or operated. Denis McQuail (1983, pp. 168-70) has suggested that the audience can influence media content in six different ways.

1. As *critics and fans*, audience members can comment (often approvingly) on the nature of specific content pieces or content producers. Numerous publications exist to reflect critics' opinions and the preferences of fans regarding media content. Such material is now becoming more common on television and radio, not just in print. The extent to which critics or fans influence future actions is debatable; it seems more likely the value of both is to endorse the present practices of mass media operations.

2. Through *institutionalized accountability* audience members can seek to influence mass media organizations. This is often easier to do with public corporations than private corporations. In Canada, the CRTC is obliged to regulate the broadcasting system "in the public interest" and, in doing so, seeks the opinions and preferences of viewers and listeners across the country. For the printed media, press councils can act on behalf of readers who complain about specific content in newspapers, but these councils have difficulty in balancing the interests of readers against the interests of journalists and newspaper owners (all of whom are usually represented on the council).

3. Through the *market*, audience members can choose between media outlets and, through such choices, exert some influence on the mass media systems. However, any individual audience member acting simply as a

single member of the audience cannot exert much influence by this means. So far, it has proved to be impossible for audiences to organize collectively and speak with a united voice on their preferences.

4. Through *direct feedback* to mass media outlets audiences can make their views known and hope to influence future actions. "Letters to the editor" are the standard form of feedback for the press while broadcasting stations rely on phone calls. The representative character of this feedback to indicate overall audience satisfaction or dissatisfaction must be questioned, since editors select the letters to be published and radio station talk-show hosts, for example, can choose who will get on the air and who will not.

5. Through the use of *audience images* formed in the minds of content producers the audience can influence media content. However, these images are constructs formed by the producers out of what may be very limited or non-existent contact with significant numbers of audience members. Producers may construct images of audiences similar to themselves and thus take insufficient account of needs or preferences of other kinds of people.

6. Through *audience research* mass media practitioners can gain a more precise idea of audience interests and responses to specific media content. However, as McQuail points out, the type of audience most likely to be influential is that which can be delineated with statistical findings (audience size and breakdown) and conducted by the media organization itself. Qualitative research or that done by outside bodies is much less likely to affect the behaviour of mass media practitioners – especially if the research findings do not match the practitioners' own views about audience preferences.

The Influences of Media Professionals

To this point we have been looking at outside influences on the operation of mass media organizations. Of course, the internal structures of these organizations and the people who work in them also exert considerable influence on the mass media systems. Journalists and other media professionals are directly engaged in the production and processing of media content. They do this within an organizational structure, operated by media management, that may have several levels to it.

Above the managerial levels are the ultimate owners of the media corporations (or the owners' representatives). In the case of public corporations, the owners are the taxpaying public, but through Parliament and other governmental bodies responsibility lies with a governing board of some type – usually a board of directors. In the case of private corporations, the owners are shareholders or individual entrepreneurs (usually the former). Shares may be widely held among many investors or closely held by the members of a particular family. Owners may be actively involved in management of the media corporation or may rely largely or even entirely on senior managers. Internally, media corporations can be viewed as social systems with their own structures and history.

Besides these general internal role categories, many specific roles are played out, sometimes in print but more often in broadcasting organizations. The program directors, producers, executive producers, program assistants, editors, technical people, and sales managers all have at least a dual allegiance to their profession and to the company for which they work. How they play out these roles, and the social system that emerges within the corporation, can influence greatly the resulting output of the station, network, or paper. Of particular interest is the way creative people are attracted to organizations that must use, but inevitably restrict, their creativity. Gallagher (in Gurevitch *et al.*, 1982) provides an insightful account of how these individuals and their organizations negotiate in such a way that there is control and predictability over programs and at the same time room for creativity.

6. INFORMATION AND ENTERTAINMENT, IMAGES AND SYMBOLS

We cannot afford to be ambitious in an outline of what constitutes information and entertainment, images and symbols. All four terms have dozens of different meanings and usages that we might discuss. Information theory, for example, might be claimed to be the very foundation of communications as a discipline. Our discussion of these four terms therefore will be limited, providing only the simplest of outlines of their meaning.

The inclusion of the four terms is meant to distinguish the activities of the media from other industrial activities. As a group the terms tell us that the media do not distribute material goods such as washing machines, soap powders, or clothing. While they may have a materiality in the sense that they may be videocassettes, tapes, records, books, magazines, etc., their materiality is incidental to their central identity, the information (in the broad and formal sense of the word) they carry.

The words **information** and **entertainment** are to be taken in a narrow sense. On television, for instance, we are given information (news and current affairs) and entertainment (sitcoms, drama, etc.) programming. In newspapers, the same two words cover, on the one side, news, opinions found in editorials

and columns, advertisements, and even the comics, and on the other, travel, leisure, gossip, columns, and the comics. Similarly, the words can be stretched a bit to cover, say, a mixture of non-fiction and fiction articles in a magazine such as *Saturday Night*. The content of the mass media brings us direct reports on the real world in information programming and indirect reports on the warp and woof of living in entertainment programs.

To say that the mass media convey **images** and **symbols** is to look at content from a different angle. Whether through words or pictures, in print or electronically, the mass media present us with images of the world. There are two classes of images, both of which we discuss in Chapter 4. The first is denotative, i.e., those which are explicit, objective, there for anyone to see. A descriptive analysis of a photograph identifying the various elements or a rational argument presents us with denotative images. The second class of images is the connotative associations that are implied and/or that we infer from the context that surrounds the denotative images. The focus of our discussion, and the emphasis in communications literature, is on connotative images. Such images may arise from rhetorical argument. They may have a visual base and derive from the composition of a still photograph or from the timing and juxtaposition of a series of video shots, or even from the layout of a printed page. Although very different in their sources, all of these can be considered as connotative images.

Symbols can include everything from the letters of the alphabet to something as complex as an icon. Here we use the term in a general sense, stressing the interpretive tendencies of the audience. Thus, at every level of our existence from the biological through the psychological – the social, the cultural, the political, and so forth

– the meaning of a symbol is an interaction between the composition of the image and the interpretive predispositions of the audience. A death mask has a biological base; a flag has a socio-cultural as well as an aesthetic base; an appeal to democratic rights has a political base. A synonym for symbolic meaning is connotative value.

The images the media present are rich in their symbolic meaning or connotative value whether or not the media intend them to be. To some degree, the success of all media products, from movies through books to television stations and newspapers, depends on the presentation of images that are layered with symbolic meaning.

Without proceeding too far into a discussion of the significance of images and symbols, we should note that the sum of the meaning of the images and symbols presented to us by the media represents the ideological currents of society, at least those ideological currents that find their way into mass media form. Given that, the media play a fundamental role in articulating and consolidating ideological control in society.

7. THE MASS AUDIENCE

The word "mass" implies large numbers. In some sense it might be best for us to leave the meaning of the word at that. However, like information, entertainment, images, and symbols, the word carries much more with it in the many uses to which it is put. At a basic level there is a value connotation; the negative is related to the mob, the positive, to the wisdom of the aggregate.

In an early article Blumer (1939) contrasted a number of different kinds of collectivities to arrive at a meaning for "mass." Simplifying and adapting Blumer's ideas somewhat, we can say that in a **small group** all members know each other and are aware of their common membership. The **crowd** is limited to a single physical space, is temporary in its existence and composition, and if it acts, it does so non-rationally. The **public** is customarily large, widely dispersed. It is often represented by largely self-appointed "informed" people who speak publicly and in rational discourse to validate their statements and appointment. As McQuail (1983) summarizes Blumer on "mass":

> The term 'mass' captures several features of the new audience for cinema and radio which were missing or not linked together by any of these three existing concepts. It was often very large – larger than most groups, crowds or publics. It was very widely dispersed and its members were usually unknown to each other or to whoever brought the audience into existence. It lacked self-awareness and self-identity and was incapable of acting together in an organized way to secure objectives. It was marked by a shifting composition within changing boundaries. It did not act for itself, but was rather 'acted upon.' It was heterogeneous, in consisting of large numbers from all social strata and demographic groups, but homogeneous in its behaviour of choosing a particular object of interest and in the perception of those who would like to 'manipulate' it.

The above differentiations of collectivities are useful for an understanding of the mass audience, especially in an historical context. While a discussion of various schools of thought on society and culture is outside the realm of this text, one school of thought, the Frankfurt School, saw the media as weaning the mass or common folk away from their "organic" society and, in so weaning them, depriving them of their place in a rich and stable culture. Other theorists on elite culture have also seen the media as debasing culture, as pandering to the uncritical side of the common person. The Soviets, of course, see the term "mass" in a favourable way at least for public and Western consumption.

In this book we attempt to go beyond the notion of the mass audience as an amorphous collectivity while nevertheless attending to certain undeniable aspects of its identity as outlined by Blumer. This treatment falls close to the notion of mass culture as popular culture, for the activities and tastes of the mainstream of society are communicated through its dominant institutions. Media-audience relations are a particular focus in Chapter 5.

A POSTSCRIPT

It is important, especially in an introduction to a field of study, to outline the foundations of the field. In this chapter we have provided an extensive definition of the mass media. It is also important to give a sense of the cutting edge of thought in the field, not to undermine the foundations but to stimulate ideas on how those foundations may shift. The following scenario is intended to be thought-provoking. It is adapted, with the author's permission, from an essay by Umberto Eco called "The Multiplication of the Media" (1986, pp. 148-50).

Scenario

1. A firm produces polo shirts with an alligator on them and it advertises them.
2. A generation begins to wear polo shirts.
3. Each consumer of the polo shirt advertises, via the alligator on his or her chest, this brand of polo shirt (just as every owner of a Toyota is an advertiser, unpaid and paying, of the Toyota line and the model he drives).

4. A TV broadcast (program), to be faithful to reality, shows some young people wearing the alligator polo shirt.
5. The young (and the old) see the TV broadcast and buy more alligator polo shirts because they have "the young look."

Where is the mass medium? the ad? the broadcast? the shirt?

Who is sending the message? the manufacturer? the wearer? the TV director? the analyst of this phenomenon?

Who is the producer of ideology? Again, the manufacturer? the wearer (including the celebrity who may wear it in public for a fee)? the TV director who portrays the generation?

Where does the plan come from? This is not to imply that there is no plan but rather that it does not emanate from one central source.

Eco concludes:

> Once upon a time there were the mass media, and they were wicked, of course, and there was a guilty party. Then there were the virtuous voices that accused the criminals. And Art (ah, what luck!) offered alternatives, for those who were not prisoners of the mass media.
>
> Well, it's all over. We have to start again from the beginning, asking one another what's going on.

SUMMARY

The mass media and their relation to society are not simply defined. The mass media are a distinct set of activities. Other institutions, such as churches, communicate to masses of people but they are not usually considered part of the modern mass media. The primary function of the mass media is to create meaning, to construct or signify reality.

The technological configurations of the modern mass media both arise from and contribute to the maintenance of certain social relations. For example, the technological compatibility between Canadian television and U.S. television and the consequent ease of entry of American television into the Canadian market is significant. Communications technology is also a creature of the developed world applied after the fact to developing countries.

The nature of the formally constituted institutions in which modern communications reside is varied. Private- and public-sector institutions each have a range of difference and differ between each other fundamentally.

The various laws, rules, and understandings within which the mass media operate create in the media a subsystem within a larger societal totality. "Audience" and "public" mean two different things and affect the media quite differently. Key to understanding Canada's communication system is the Broadcasting Act, especially the quoted policy section.

Various persons, as paid professionals and as members of society, play out certain roles and through such roles contribute to our mass media systems. These people are not just to be found in the media themselves but also in business, government, law, and the consuming public.

All these factors combine to produce content, the information and entertainment programming and the emergent images and symbols that the mass media present for our consumption. They present not to a small group, a crowd, or a public but to the mass audience, a distinct entity in itself. It is very large and widely dispersed; its members are unknown to each other, lacking in self-awareness and self-identity, incapable of acting together but acted upon and shifting in composition: its membership spans various social strata, but it is homogeneous in its behaviour in choosing a particular object of interest.

While it is important, especially for the purpose of introducing a field of inquiry, to be systematic in outlining the basic variables of that field, the cutting edge challenges those very boundaries. As Eco argues, clear notions are not so clear when small matters are examined in great detail.

REFERENCES

Audley, Paul. *Canada's Cultural Industries.* Toronto: James Lorimer, 1983.

Bennett, Tony. "Media, 'Reality', and Signification," in M. Gurevitch *et al.*, eds., *Culture, Society and the Media.* Toronto: Methuen, 1982.

Berger, Peter, and Thomas Luckmann. *Social Construction of Reality: A Treatise on the Sociology of Knowledge.* New York: Doubleday, 1966.

Blumer, H. "The Mass, the Public, and Public Opinion," in A.M. Lee, ed., *New Outlines in the Principles of Sociology.* New York: Barnes and Noble, 1939.

Canada. *Report of the Task Force on Broadcasting Policy.* Ottawa: Ministry of Supply and Services, 1986.

Canada. *Royal Commission on Newspapers.* Hull, Quebec: Canadian Government Publishing Centre, 1981.

Curran, James. "Communications, Power, and Social Order," in Gurevitch *et al.*, eds., *Culture, Society and the Media.*

Eco, Umberto. "The Multiplication of the Media," in Eco, *Travels in Hyperreality.* New York: Harcourt Brace Jovanovich, 1986.

Gallagher, Margaret. "Negotiation of Control in Media Organizations and Occupations," in Gurevitch *et al.*, eds., *Culture, Society and the Media.*

Hall, Stuart. "The Rediscovery of 'Ideology': Return of the Repressed in Media Studies," in Gurevitch *et al.*, eds., *Culture, Society and the Media.*

McQuail, Denis. *Mass Communication Theory: An Introduction.* Beverly Hills: Sage Publications, 1983.

Salter, L. "Reconceiving the public in public broad-
casting," in R. Lorimer and D.C. Wilson, eds.,
Communications Canada. Forthcoming, 1988.
Smythe, Dallas. *Dependency Road: Communications,
Capitalism, Consciousness, and Canada*. Nor-
wood, New Jersey: Ablex Publishing, 1981.
Williams, Raymond. *Television: Technology and
Cultural Form*. New York: Schoken Books, 1975.

STUDY QUESTIONS

1. What seven elements are there to a defini-
    tion of the media? Explain them and com-
    ment on the appropriateness of such a
    definition.

2. Do you think the content of media mes-
    sages penetrates our lives to as great an ex-
    tent as Christianity or any other major
    religion does?

3. How does the Broadcasting Act impinge on
    your own television and radio watching
    and listening?

CHAPTER

3

The Mass Media and Government

INTRODUCTION

IN CHAPTERS 1 and 2 the role of communication as a political instrument was introduced, along with a number of related elements. These include:

- matters of press-initiated reform
- matters of governing and government
- setting, announcing, and implementing policy
- electoral and partisan politics
- seeking after, attaining, and maintaining public office
- government advertising
- the role of the parliamentary press corps
- freedom of information
- the general role of information in government and its relation to the people governed.

In this chapter we take up these matters. While normally we might think of government as a political institution and the media as information institutions, each can be seen as encompassing both politics and information. The two exist in the same arena when politics is viewed as information-gathering, analysis, and management. In *Politics and the News*, a basic reference for this chapter, Edwin Black (1982, p. 4) illustrates this perspective as follows:

> Significant political data, such (as) particular occurrences of political injustice, are communicated to a number of points in the circuit (citizens), dissatisfaction grows, and the system is unbalanced. Demands for change are generated and conveyed to a central accumulator or legislature. If the charge is great enough, it stimulates appropriate reactions and information flows until the system is balanced once again.

When the April 29, 1986, edition of *The Globe and Mail* hit the newsstands, the Mulroney government must have been all too well aware of the information system described by Black. *The Globe* had been searching for a case to test Brian Mulroney's conflict-of-interest code for cabinet ministers, and its reporters, David Stewart-Patterson and Michael Harris, had found one. The wife of Sinclair Stevens, the Industry Minister, had secured a $2.6 million loan, interest free for one year, from a former executive of Magna International, a company with extensive dealings with the government. The question raised was whether the loan to Stevens's wife constituted a conflict of interest.

The Canadian Press jumped on the story. Yet, Stevens and the acting Prime Minister, Erik Nielsen, made few public statements and never offered any clear justification for Stevens's position and actions in terms of the guidelines. Eventually, pressure from a heated opposition, along with public outcry, pushed the minister to resign pending the outcome of a commission of inquiry held into the matter.

The inept handling of the press-produced information in the Stevens case reduced the credibility of the Mulroney government with the electorate, especially as the Stevens affair came on the heels of press exposures of other government scandals that led to the resignation of three other cabinet ministers, a backbencher, and another charged with influence-peddling. It also made former coups in the handling of information, such as the appointment of the NDP's Stephen Lewis as Canada's ambassador to the United Nations, seem like distant memories.

The government and the press are the key players in the political information system. On the one side, government includes information production and management as part of its political functioning. It creates and manages information about itself and its society in the interests of self-preservation and the preservation of the society of which it is a part. On the other side, the media have a political role as purveyors of information in the political arena. Sometimes they are an extension of government, sometimes an unwitting ally, sometimes, as above, a critic. The media obviously differ from formal political institutions in that their central concern is with profit, entertainment, and audiences. But whatever their general motive, they are an integral part of the political process.

GOVERNMENTS AND INFORMATION

Information and Democracy

Modern democracy arose in Europe between the seventeenth and the beginning of the twentieth centuries, replacing the feudal system based on the concept of divine right of rulers. In the case of state rulers, democracies replaced feudalism both in monarchies, such as England or Denmark, and in republics, such as France. In the case of church rulers, divine right was effectively challenged by an informed individualistic or democratic ideology proposed as early as the sixteenth century by such Reformation leaders as Martin Luther (1483-1546). However, as the continuing existence of the Catholic Church attests, it was not replaced but only diminished in influence by the growth of the Protestant churches.

Democracy brought many changes to society, including an important change in the conception of who had the right, or who was fit, to rule. In more concrete words, it changed the concept of the qualifying attributes of rulers and thereby changed the qualifications necessary for membership in the ruling class.

Within feudalism the right to rule was passed on from father to son – rarely to a daughter – in a particular blood line that could be traced back to traditional rulers, who were ultimately "chosen by God" and were believed to hold the inherent ability to rule. Democratic societies, by contrast, are organized according to the belief that the people should rule and thus that a ruler should act in the name of the people. Therefore, a ruler must inspire the majority of the people with the confidence that he or she will govern in their best interests. When a leader and his/her government can no longer maintain that confidence (formally speaking, the confidence of the House of Commons or of the provincial legislatures), the government resigns and an election is called.

This change in the concept of government was brought about largely by an expanding, materialist, prosperous, and educated bourgeoisie, which also urged the separation of church and state. These changes were only a part of a massive upheaval in European society as it evolved from an agrarian to an industrial society.

The profound political change from feudalism to democracy was based on the spread of knowledge, which allowed certain citizens enough education to govern affairs in the name of their peers and enabled other citizens to make an informed decision on who ought to rule. As a consequence, information institutions became, and have remained, essential to democracies because they inform the public about the important issues of the day and the various solutions proposed by the competing elites who wish to rule.

Early and Modern Democratic Information Institutions

Early political information institutions, especially in Britain and Europe, were owned and therefore closely aligned with political parties. In Britain, various newssheets and pamphlets were published by individuals and groups who wished to inform the public on political matters. A wealth of documentation prior to and including the beginnings of copyright tells us much about the various attempts by those in power to control the output of information by their rivals. One of the more ingenious devices was a tax on cheap paper.

The alignment of information production with political interests continues in the present day. It is often assumed that a politically aligned press exists only in one-party states. That is not the case. In Italy, for example, each political party produces its own television news programming.

In Canada and the United States the history of the political alignment of information institutions, specifically the press, is slightly different in its closer association with business and more distant association with some political parties. Some of these differences from European practice can be accounted for by the development of democracy prior to mass settlement of the continent, by the lack of an entrenched ruling class in the New World, and by the quickly emerging power and ideology of the business class, especially in the United States.

Following the example of the United States, the West in general has seen control of information institutions fall into the hands of large corporations. This shift in control can be seen as (1) an evolution, a differentiation of political activities *per se* from information activities, or as (2) the bringing of information creation and distribution into the sphere of business and markets, largely for reasons of cost (see Murdock, 1982). The former view is consistent with a **liberal-pluralist** perspective; the latter is the contention of a **neo-Marxist** perspective. In either case, the range of ideas introduced to the public is constrained by the nature of ownership (see Chapter 6). But what effect has that shift of control had on the relationship between information institutions and the political realm? Before answering that question we must turn to an examination of these perspectives.

Perspectives on Mass Media and Government

A variety of perspectives might be brought to such an examination. Black, for example, notes that the media have been portrayed in a number of ways. They can be seen as civic institutions or can be distinguished by the degree to which they adhere to the journalistic ideal of **social responsibility** (see Chapter 7). The media can also be viewed from a McLuhanesque perspective, which, as we saw in Chapter 1, distinguishes between societies according to whether oral, literate, or electronic information processes predominate.

Each of these perspectives has its value. However, except for that of McLuhan (and even with him there is room for debate), they use specific models which exist within a liberal-pluralist viewpoint, one of two major perspectives common to research and writing in communications. The liberal-pluralist perspective sees the Western mass media as one set of institutions and interests within the plurality that makes up a democratic society. From this perspective, journalism is often referred to as the **fourth estate** (the first three estates being the Church, the landowners, and the bourgeoisie). Their interest is the pursuit of information in the name of the public good and this is legitimized by notions of free speech. (Note that political parties also pursue power in the name of the public good!)

From a liberal-pluralist perspective, the Western mass media function to preserve the political system within which they now exist, making it flexible enough for the changing needs of society. The media provide the information necessary for public participation in the political process and aid in the dissemination of information about public programs and services. They are also watchdogs over power, mostly political power as it is used by government rather than economic power as it is used by the private sector. In short, they provide citizens with information about matters that are part of the political and socio-economic system in which they live, yet which most citizens otherwise could not know from personal experience.

The second major perspective that characterizes much communications research is neo-Marxism. Neo-Marxists view the same activities of the media quite differently, for this perspective does not assume the preservation of the present political system of Western democracies. Neo-Marxist analysts see the mass media as promoting the dominant ideology of a society. For example, the media act as an extension of government in publicizing public programs. As watchdogs, they call for adherence to the existing system by denouncing errant individuals or institutions, or they counsel revisions to improve the basic political system rather than opting for a new, more equitable system.

In putting forward a limited range of ideas and analysis, the media, according to neo-Marxist theory, present different manifestations of the same basic ideology and, therefore, reinforce that ideology. The political alternatives they take seriously are the ideas of one of several entrenched but competing elites, all of whom are members of the same (ruling or dominant) social class. In short, they reflect the interest of their capitalist owners in maintaining a politically stable society.

The liberal-pluralist and neo-Marxist views need not be seen as contradictory, although they may be in conflict. Once their regime-constrained and counter-dominant ideological stances are understood, they can be seen as describing the same phenomena from differing points of view. The conclusion one would draw from analysis of both views is that the mass media serve to preserve particular versions of the democratic system by maintaining faith in its ideals while seeking to correct by exposure imperfections in the institutions that represent those ideals.

PERSPECTIVES ON PRESS SYSTEMS AROUND THE GLOBE

Another set of perspectives was proposed some time ago and remains in use. In representing a Western view of world press systems it highlights assumptions built into the Western view of the role of the press. In *Four*

Theories of the Press, Siebert, Peterson, and Schramm (1956, 1971) describe four different approaches to media ownership and control and the relation of these approaches to various political theories of press operation. The four theories they identify are:

- authoritarian theory
- Soviet Communist theory
- libertarian theory
- social responsibility theory.

Authoritarian and Soviet Communist Theories

The assumption of the **authoritarian theory** is that all power should rest with those who rule. Control of information can be seen as an extension of the power to rule. The government can explain how it sees things and why its policies are good ones. Such control can be exercised directly through ownership of the means of communication or indirectly through laws of various kinds, including taxes on paper or ink as well as censorship laws. Distribution channels can also be controlled through licences or quota requirements. It is interesting to know that for a considerable period of history in England the only means whereby an author could gain access to publication was through the patronage of some reputable person who also had the desire and means to underwrite the publication.

The **Soviet Communist press theory** is seen by these American theorists as an extension of the authoritarian theory. It has developed both out of Marxist-Leninist understandings of the media in combination with current understandings of the role of media in society and out of a rejection of the mode of operation of the Western media. In this theory the purpose of the media is to support the efforts of the party and hence the government to administer society. It supports society as a whole, as opposed to the individual, but more specifically it supports the ruling elite.

In the Soviet system, the media are owned by the state while individual journalists must interpret events from the point of view of the state-owners. With respect to TASS and *Isvestia*, this means the government leaders. With respect to other papers, as in Western nations, the papers examine issues from the perspective of the sponsoring body, for instance, a union of workers.

If we compare press systems on the basis of the representation of the interests of the state versus capitalist owners we do not find as large a difference as one might anticipate on the basis of the names given them in *Four Theories of the Press*. Because the interest of the state is to govern and that of the governors is to keep themselves in power, we can understand why the state-owned Soviet papers are filled with state-based and state-biased analysis of domestic and international events. For example, the failure to report troop losses in Afghanistan is understandable in this context even if such censorship seems unnecessary to a citizen of a Western democracy. It might even seem unnecessary in a more liberal Communist regime such as Yugoslavia.

Turning to the West, if we understand the interest of the owners to be capturing and maintaining audiences, which can then be sold to advertisers, as we outline in Chapter 6, and if we understand the relation of the content of the media to the general prevailing attitudes of the population, as will be discussed in the example of Enoch Powell in Chapter 5, then we can also understand why the pages of Western newspapers are filled with the extraordinary, drama, human interest, business information, and sports updates. Both the state and capitalist owners are served well by the content each produces.

In stating that the Communist press theory is authoritarian, the authors of *Four Theories* are placing one single aspect of press operations front and centre, that is, the separation of press and state powers.

Nonetheless, the differences between press operations in the Soviet Union and the West should not to be underestimated. One example may illustrate how very different are the news values in the Soviet Union as compared to here. This particular example was related by a Canadian professor of journalism, Richard Lunn.

Toward the end of a visit Lunn and a number of students from the journalism program at Carleton University were making to the Soviet Union, he was talking to the guide the Soviets had provided for the group. He asked, "If that ferry crossing the river overturned, would it be reported in the news the next day?" The guide's answer was blunt. "No," she said. "Why not?" said Lunn. "Why would it be," said the guide, "those that were involved would obviously know about it and their relatives would eventually find out, why would it be of interest to other people?"

Traditionally, the Western press interprets such lack of coverage as a coverup, as a gigantic attempt by the government of the Soviet Union to hide any imperfections in their system. But might it not also be the case, as it would appear from the remarks of the guide, that those who control the media do not deem such human interest events newsworthy? And is this really very much different from the habitual way Western news media use events for their news programming? That is, the Western media assume that any disruptive or violent event is automatically newsworthy, especially when numbers of people are killed. Many parents of young children do not appreciate the frequency with which such events are used to lead off the 6:00 p.m. television news.

Libertarian Theory

The **libertarian theory** of the press derives from concepts of liberty and the free will of individuals, which in turn derive from such liberal philosophers as John Locke (1632-1704), John Stuart Mill (1806-1873), and David Hume (1711-1766). The fundamental assumption of liberal philosophy is that individual freedom is the first and foremost goal to be sought, and that the ultimate goal of society should be to impede the freedom of the individual as little as possible. The state exists in service to individuals rather than the reverse. In serving the freedom of the individual, so the liberal philosophers maintain, the state will create the most advantageous situation for all.

It is easy to understand what role might be conceived for the media in such a theory. Rather than being arms of state enterprise, the libertarian theory sees the media as the watchdog of government, the fourth estate. The media are to be an independent voice keeping government responsible to the people by feeding information to people so that, come election time, performance can be rewarded or punished.

In striving to ensure distance between the government and the media, the libertarian concept of the press places the press in the hands of the private sector. The basic problem in this is that the private sector necessarily has its own interests – accruing profits – to consider above the interests of the people or the government of the day. As a consequence, rather than having a corporation beneficently allowing journalists to dedicate themselves to "serving the people," the privately controlled press has sought to maximize profits.

The usual example of the extreme of a libertarian press is the exploitation of sex to sell news. However, as we will see in Chapter 6, the general pursuit of profits sets quite fundamental constraints on the extent to which information is pursued and the *kind* of information that is pursued, which is of far greater importance. The seeking after profit is no guarantee whatsoever of a socially valuable press.

Social Responsibility Theory

The **social responsibility theory** arises from the failure of the libertarian arrangement to produce a press which is generally perceived to be of benefit to society. It was developed by a nongovernmental U.S. commission, the Hutchins Commission on the Freedom of the Press (1947).

A Canadian inquiry, the Kent *Royal Commission on Newspapers* (1981), explained the social responsibility theory well, pointing out that as newspaper publishing began to be taken over by big business, thereby heralding the end of a libertarian press, the notion of social responsibility was born. It was born of a need to fight against the potential of new authoritarianism brought about by big business ownership of the press. The Kent Commission (p. 235) defined the concept of social responsibility as follows:

The conjoined requirements of the press, for freedom and for legitimacy, derive from the same basic right: the right of citizens to information about their affairs. In order that people be informed, the press has a critical responsibility. In order to fulfill that responsibility it is essential that the press be free, in the traditional sense, free to report and free to publish as it thinks; it is equally essential that the press's discharge of its responsibility to inform should be untainted by other interests, that it should not be dominated by the powerful or be subverted by people with concerns other than those proper to a newspaper serving a democracy. "Comment is free," as C.P. Scott, one of the greatest English-speaking editors, wrote, "but facts are sacred." The right of information in a free society requires, in short, not only freedom of comment generally but, for its news media, the freedom of a legitimate press, doing its utmost to inform, open to all opinions and dominated by none.

The Mass Media, Canadian Government, and Democracy

The shortcoming of these various viewpoints is a lack of consideration of the press within the context of a particular democratic community. In our case this is the Canadian community. Even though such consideration may be present in the content of the media, none of the above analyses pays it much heed. The only viewpoint to consider the individual democratic community, and then only to a limited extent, is called, by McPhail (1981) and others, **developmental journalism**. In that model the specific needs of cultures and national communities have been taken into account from within an evolutionary perspective, from lesser to greater industrialization. However, the specific cultural makeup and history of a community that might call for a particular form of press and media system are not considered in these general models.

In overview, the mass media and government both have political and informational roles. At times they act in complement, at times they are in conflict, but rarely does either act in a manner inconsistent with what it sees as the common good. The perspectives used to study politics and the media reveal a great deal about the relation between the government and the mass media. Overall they demonstrate that both institutions work for the preservation of the society of which they are a part. However, they are weak in focusing on the specific needs of a culture or community.

STRUCTURES OF INFORMATION AND THE MODERN NATION-STATE

The Need, Use, and Abuse of Information

Given the notion that the modern nation-state is a sophisticated information apparatus, with government and the mass media as two of its major arms, what are some of the details of state structure and functioning? To represent the whole, the state gathers information in the name of the greatest good for the greatest number. It must seek to achieve this end but it must weigh its achievement against other communal goals and ends.

For example, the interests of the community may be very well advanced by the collection of information on every individual from birth onward. The right to individual privacy, however, is potentially in conflict with the right of the state to collect information in the interests of the community. In a greyer area, the state may design sophisticated information systems that work for government but also allow large business enterprises to have a distinct advantage over small enterprise because the former have the technology, scale of production, and monetary capability to make better use of the information. If the state fosters the creation of such information systems, it might be considered to have created a counter-obligation to small enterprise and perhaps to workers because small enterprise is a great deal more labour-intensive than large enterprise.

The Press in Relation to Government: The Parliamentary Press Gallery

Western society has created a structural response to the potential power of the state to abuse its trust not only in gathering and acting upon information but also in the general abuse of power. The response has been twofold. The first has been the institutionalization of "Her Majesty's Loyal Opposition." The second has been the development, in general terms, of an independent or free press (the word "press" is used here to encompass both electronic and print media) whose function is to gather information about all aspects of society, including government. Specifically, the parliamentary press gallery is the primary press institution with a responsibility to monitor government policy and action. (See, for example, Fletcher, 1981.)

In one sense, the parliamentary press gallery is the sum total of all journalists who are working on political stories in Ottawa or the provincial capitals who apply to become members of the Ottawa or provincial capital galleries. On the other hand, as the federal Task Force on Government Information (1969, vol. 2, pp. 115-19) noted of the Ottawa gallery, it is "the most important instrument of political communication in the country." The gallery performs two essential roles: to disseminate government information; to assess the wisdom of government policy and action by reporting and analysing House debate between government and the opposition.

The Press as a Political Information Institution in a Controlled Environment

The press, and specifically the parliamentary press gallery, makes an important contribution to modern democracy by gathering information and monitoring government. However, the press does not have free reign to carry out this role without the formal constraint of law or without informal constraints. The press exists and acts within its own political environment.

Just as the government must balance one goal with another, so must the press in pursuit of its ends. The difference between the two is that the government controls itself (subject, over the longer term, to the wishes of the electorate). The press is self-governed only to a limited extent and its self-governing mechanisms, such as professional ethics and press councils (discussed in Chapter 7), control its behaviour far less than the governmental mechanisms discussed in this chapter.

The best-known law controlling the press is **libel law**. Libel law is not a small matter used only to settle disputes between muckraking journalists and shady characters. Fundamentally, it represents an attempt to achieve a balance between two goods. On one side are the rights of individuals to such things as a good reputation or a fair trial. On the other are the rights of the press to speak freely about public affairs and to speak in such a way as to sell papers.

The trial of a Vancouver radio personality, which played in the media for approximately 18 months, is pertinent here. On the basis of press reports a reader would probably have expected a conviction on arson charges. The man was, however, acquitted, and not on a technicality. The question is, does he still enjoy a good reputation? According to Canadian libel law, the press did not overstep its bounds in this case. Were the trial held in the U.S. the press would have been even more within tolerated limits, and might have sensationalized, speculated, and implied far more than Canadian journalists did. Had the trial been in Britain, however, the press would have been far more circumspect in its coverage. The point here is that there is *no absolute interpretation of what is libelous and what is not*. It is a matter of time and place, a matter of the balance that each society considers appropriate.

A second set of constraints on the press role as monitor of society and government is that the press, like the public, traditionally has *only the right to speak or to publish but not the right to know*. The right to publish is the right of free speech. With the emergence of a greater emphasis on the press as an information institution rather than an extension of political parties, pressure has been brought to bear on governments to provide information to the press. Increasingly, in Western countries, this has led to legislation dealing with the right to know.

In the United States, for example, this pressure has resulted in freedom-of-information legislation. Under such legislation the onus is on government to demonstrate why government information should not be released. This legislation derives from the notion that government is representative of the interests of the people and has no separate interests of its own. As a result of this principle, much information has become public that heretofore was hidden. Often a Canadian reporter will seek information from the U.S. government about the Canadian operations of a company that operates in both Canada and the U.S. Indeed, the Canadian government has been known to take that very course of action itself.

In Canada and Britain, principles of confidentiality and secrecy produce almost the opposite effect. In both countries, government documents traditionally have been assumed to be only for government use unless cleared for release. In keeping with this tradition the Canadian legislation is much less powerful than American legislation and is called, significantly, the Access to Information Act (1983) rather than being legislation dealing with freedom of information.

The early experience of journalists with Canada's Access to Information Act seems to reflect this tradition. In general, restrictions on the release of information seem to be tightened up rather than loosened by the administration of the new Act. A 1986 report by the Canadian Daily Newspaper Publishers Association noted that in 1984 in the U.S., 91 per cent of requests for information under the Freedom of Information Act were granted without any deletions (McElgunn, 1986, p. 5). In the same year in Canada, the comparable figure was 42 per cent. In addition, 25 per cent of requests were granted with deletions while 33 per cent were denied or delayed. The same report noted that there were wide variations between government departments with respect to both cost and co-operation and thus recommended a variety of remedial actions.

Another aspect of this subject concerns the public's right to know (as opposed to the press right). Thus we need to look at the adequacy of journalists, and especially of the parliamentary press gallery. Fletcher (1981) has provided such an assessment in his background study for the Kent *Royal Commission on Newspapers*. He notes that the galleries have emerged in recent decades as independent from the control of government, and consequently they have become more professional than previously was the case. Some journalists still remember the retainers of the Duplessis era and the preferred access and perks federal governments conferred upon "their" reporters. However, independence from government has not created a full independence of copy. **Pack journalism** is common (just as much the result of the expectation of editors as of the herd instinct among journalists) and creating possibilities for interesting television coverage has introduced its own homogeneity and diversionary potential. Vast areas of government activities are inadequately covered, such as the courts, regulatory agencies, and policy-making and adjudication within the civil service.

The galleries have generally increased in size with the addition of the broadcast journalists and freelancers, yet the gallery perspective is now more clearly dominated by a few larger papers and services. Most noticeable is the decreased number of regional members whose sole function was to report on matters from the perspective of the region they represented.

Fletcher found also that the Canadian Press (CP) reporters played an interesting role. The large and respected CP bureau in Ottawa (to which virtually all Canadian papers now subscribe) has freed the multi-person Ottawa bureaus to specialize and investigate. However, any decrease in the size of the CP bureau, as happened with the closure of the *Ottawa Journal*, lessens the effectiveness of this CP function. In either instance, the use editors make of their press gallery copy is often limited because their surveys tell them there is limited interest in political affairs.

Fletcher's view is that the galleries are clearly understaffed and tend to vary in their effectiveness depending upon variables such as the vigour of opposition parties and the expectations of editors and publishers. Competition does not produce necessarily better coverage, but without competition the discretion of editors and publishers can be seen. The turnover rate of journalists is high, essentially because publishers are not prepared to commit sufficient resources. Finally, the range of ideological perspectives is narrow, primarily because there are too few national columnists. Such an assessment is not inclined to give one faith in the press as a fundamental instrument of democracy.

To return to access to information, the above discussion may give a false impression. The government is not consistently miserly in its provision of information to the press. At times it is positively garrulous, as when the government wishes to boast about its achievements, or when it wants the public to know about a new program or to abide by a new or old set of laws. The government then depends on the press to inform the public of such programs both in discussion and by means of government advertising.

Even here, though, the information the government releases is only of a certain type. Canadian and other British-derivative governments are extremely reluctant to release context and planning information, that is, predecision information, especially when such information is contained in cabinet documents. All governing parties seem to feel strongly about the protection of cabinet secrecy.

Society and government place a variety of other normal controls on the press. Some, which are not particularly political in their effects, will be discussed in later chapters. Those with more direct political consequences are discussed here.

Most controls could be termed performance requirements. Various statutes, taxes, and regulations attempt to keep the media within the boundaries of good taste and to prevent undue exploitation of their position of power. Requirements concerning a balanced perspective affect political commentary in the electronic media. Regulations also control certain aspects of political advertising, excluding dramatization and forbidding political ads to be broadcast within 48 hours of an election. During elections, the electronic media must be especially careful to provide equal coverage of all political parties. The print media, however, are free to cover elections as they choose. Interestingly, what has evolved in the print media, especially in big city newspapers, is editorial coverage supporting one chosen party and news coverage aimed at equality but usually slightly favouring the government. Soderlund *et al.* (1984) provide a more thorough and detailed discussion of normal press controls.

Canadian content regulations, a reflection of cultural ethnic diversity as well as regionalism, and the pursuit of Canadian identity and unity are also represented in performance requirements that apply not only to the public but also to the privately owned media in general.

In overview, the media are continually restructuring the political information environment away from one that extends from personal experience of the local through the regional and national to the international. Increasingly, we are immediately and continually in secondary or mediated touch with the centre, with the hub of the nation, while our next door neighbours are hours or days away. They only appear in our political purview at times of crisis in the local school auditorium.

As the media impress these fundamental changes on our political system, society is challenged to design a set of freedoms and constraints so that our collective interests are best served. In this section we have seen some of the constraints intended to do just that.

Unusual Political Controls on the Press

The desire, indeed the necessity, of the press to carry information between people and their government makes for extremely close relations between government and the press. The government's desire to keep the press away from certain information, such as predecision information in cabinet documents, gives to that close relationship a certain ambivalence. The desire of the press to maintain its independence and to demonstrate periodically its separate integrity transforms that ambivalence into a love-hate relationship on the part of politicians. Also, the dependence of the press on government for information makes that love-hate relationship mutual. (Two sources are particularly good for understanding this relationship, Clive Cocking's *Following the Leaders* [1980] and the proceedings of the Canadian Study of Parliament Group, *Seminar on Press and Parliament* [1980].)

As the following *Globe* article illustrates, governments and the press exist in continuous tension, as they should. Both are the focus of the most basic and broad of public trusts to act on behalf of the people in the name of the collective whole. A great deal rides on the carrying out of that public trust. As a result, mechanisms have arisen that, when they come into play, indicate a serious lack of agreement between the press and government. In Canada such mechanisms are rarely used but they are not unknown. These mechanisms are either *directed at journalism or directed at press owners.*

In recent history, these mechanisms were used most often during the Trudeau era, in part because of the times in which he was Prime Minister, in part because of his personality. During that period, specifically during the Front de Libération du Québec kidnappings, the War Measures Act was invoked along with a certain level of press and public censorship. In addition, as the CBC program *The Press and the Prime Minister* documents, Trudeau was continually engaged in matching wits with the press. On a day-to-day basis, he was neither an unsophisticated nor a mute observer of the role and failings of the press in Canadian society. At election times he was a master of media manipulation in his presentation of issues and persona.

Minister finds it 'offensive'
Erola assails newsletter art

By BRIAN MARACLE
Special to The Globe and Mail

OTTAWA — The federal minister designated to handle Ottawa's proposed newspaper legislation has criticized a Government-subsidized native publication for failing to reflect Canadian foreign policy.

Consumer and Corporate Affairs Minister Judy Erola was angered by a drawing in the newsletter published by the Native Women's Association of Canada. It depicts a massacre of Indian peasants in Guatemala by Government troops.

Gerry Gambill, a consultant to the Assembly of First Nations, said he acquired the drawing during a visit to Mexican refugee camps in the spring. It was reported to be drawn by an Indian child who survived a massacre in 1982 in western Guatemala, he said.

The military figures in the drawing wear the flag of Guatemala and their weapons and helicopters bear the letters USA, indicating U. S. aid to the military regime of Guatemala.

Last week in the Commons, Prime Minister Pierre Trudeau said Mrs. Erola would become the minister responsible for the Government's newspaper legislation at a future date. One of the provisions of the proposed legislation would provide Government subsidies to newspapers for establishing foreign or domestic news bureaus.

John Foy, general manager of the Canadian Daily Newspaper Publishers Association, refused to comment in detail on the issue but said the controversy illustrates "the very reason why newspapers would not take Government subsidies."

"I don't know of a publisher within our organization that would touch that money. They would not want to be beholden to or be dictated to by the Government," he said.

NWAC president Jane Gottfriedson said in an interview that a member of Mrs. Erola's staff telephoned the association's office in mid-August to "chastise" the organization about the drawing.

Consumer and Corporate Affairs Minister Judy Erola called the art in Native Women newsletter 'particularly offensive.'

She said the caller complained that since the NWAC is Government-financed, it has a responsibility to reflect Government foreign policy and not paint Canada's U.S. allies in a bad light.

Rebecca Butovsky, an aide in Mrs. Erola's office, confirmed making the call, which she said was done on the minister's behalf. She refused to answer further questions about it.

Interviewed outside the Commons last week, Mrs. Erola said: "The basis of my complaint must be fairly obvious to you. Is that (the drawing) Canadian foreign policy?"

She would not comment further at that time, but this week she said the proposed newspaper legislation has nothing to do with the controversy over the newsletter.

"I thought it was a particularly offensive cartoon, depicting friends of Canada in a manner that I didn't think was particularly in good taste or relevant to that particular magazine."

Pressed on the issue of Government financing, Mrs. Erola said "the issue of Government funding was not of main consideration to me. The issue of good taste and relevancy was of main concern to me."

An example of press/government tensions. *From The Globe and Mail, Toronto, September 23, 1983. Courtesy Brian Maracle.*

However, the actions of the press owners brought about a clear but contained confrontation at the end of the Trudeau years. When one major newspaper chain, Southam, shut down the *Winnipeg Tribune* on exactly the same day (August 27, 1980) as another major chain, Thomson, shut down the *Ottawa Journal*, leaving each with a monopoly in one of those two cities, the Liberal government responded in one week by setting up the Kent *Royal Commission on Newspapers*. In setting up the Commission the government subjected the chains to public examination of their operations, and by appointing Tom Kent, a former journalist, it set the journalistic community against the owners over the quality of journalism the owners were willing to pay for. The affair ended in a standoff, with ample warning given to the Thomson chain that the government would not allow it to increase its already substantial market share of newspaper holdings in Canada.

AISLIN 81.

Aislin comments on the competition between Southam and Thomson for the newspaper market. *Reprinted with permission – The Toronto Star Syndicate.*

The Political Power of the Press

The power of the press in political matters is far more constrained than one might at first think. Often the press seems to hound a good many politicians from office. Whenever governments are defeated or elected, somehow the press seems to be implicated. For example, a former leader of the British Columbia New Democratic Party, Dave Barrett, once gave a radio interview and mentioned that he would not ex-

tend wage controls to civil servants. That statement, which some have seen as costing him the election, was seen as a radio scoop rather than an extremely bad (albeit, perhaps off the cuff) policy error on the part of the former premier.

When set against the powers of government, the press has little more than the power of the pen. The power of the pen is not insignificant, but if government engages the press in a battle for supremacy, the power of words, including ridicule, embarrassment, and access to audience, pales in comparison to the arsenal of government. At its most interventionist, the press can leave behind any notion of mirroring the opinions of society and become an actor-crusader. It can mount saturation coverage, exposing and arguing, coaxing and cajoling, in the hope of changing government policy or persuading the people to change government. Not incidentally, when the media are engaged in such a power struggle, audience ratings and readership rise.

If government sees its own control and authority threatened, it can unleash a variety of devices. The most obvious is direct criticism. The authority vested in government makes its direct criticism of the press a powerful instrument, unless government can be seen to be looking after its narrow self-interest. When its self-interest is involved, it can set up arm's length bodies such as royal commissions to call the press to account. Other mechanisms include judicial harassment, setting up or encouraging others to set up competing enterprises, and withdrawing patronage. Since government is the largest advertiser in the country, the withdrawal of advertising can quickly bring the press to its knees.

The government can also exercise favouritism in its monopoly over government-created information. For example, inconsistencies in dealing with access to information can easily be exploited for political motives. Releasing news at 4:00 p.m. allows processing in time for television news but not for the evening paper. (The soft form of this sort of manipulation by government is termed "news management.")

The government can also mount, or cause to have mounted, campaigns of harassment that undermine the fundamental trust between the press and its audience. Dependent as the press is on advertisements, it need only be accused of being, in a variety of ways, in the hands of its advertisers to be put on the defensive.

Finally, the government can always invoke the national interest or censorship. In invoking the national interest, any attack on government can be construed as an attack on the national community and, in the most extreme cases, tantamount to treason. When a government feels that it can no longer tolerate a free press, it can use censorship to prevent by rule of law what is otherwise impossible to prevent.

Many of these devices may seem unrealistic, extreme, and rare. This is both a tribute to the relative harmony among the various elites in Canadian society and, if one views press ownership as far too concentrated, an indictment of the Canadian government for failing to control press owners in their search for wealth. However, these devices are used in many countries of all political stripes around the world.

A MACROVIEW OF THE FUNCTIONING OF PRESS AND POLITICS

The press can be looked at in the way it functions in relation to the overall structure of society, that is to say, other social institutions. Such a perspective is called **structural functionalism** (see, for example, Coleman, 1973). This perspective suggests seven political functions inherent in the running of society, and the press can be examined for its contribution to each. They are:

1. the articulation of various interests that span a range of the political spectrum
2. the aggregation of interests through the identification of common assumptions, values, or beliefs

3. the socialization of new members of the community into the political structure and values of the community
4. the making of rules or laws by which members of the community are meant to abide
5. the enforcement of those rules
6. the adjudication of those rules
7. political communication

The press is clearly a main agent of political communication. As such it can be seen as contributing to the prior six functions. How it contributes to the first three seems relatively obvious. By making known and discussing the political environment, it brings to the attention of its audience the various interests of groups in society and their alignment on various issues. No doubt this contributes to a certain coalescence among both new and continuing members of society. By reinforcing collective symbols, by multiple coverage of the same issues, thus giving individuals the confidence that they know which are important, and by the more usual building of consensus, recruiting people to the political process, supporting existing institutions, and casting criticism within the dominant political framework, the press plays a sizable political role.

Press contribution to making, enforcing, and adjudicating the rules of society is less direct. For example, by monitoring the behaviour of society, publicizing rules and their enforcement system, and publicizing and commenting on adjudication, the press contributes indirectly to the nature of society's rules and how they are created, observed, and amended. Given this, it should not be surprising that, whatever the role of the press with regard to the general public, it plays a key role in communication between elites in society. The most avid consumers of political news are senior civil servants and elected politicians. True, a certain amount of their consumption can be put down to egoism since the press deals in their daily affairs. But what the press reports about them, and others of their kind, is functionally necessary to their jobs.

The contribution of the press to society, and a justification for press freedoms, can be seen in the political functions outlined above. In overview, the press maintains a two-way flow of information, a multiple feedback system from a variety of communities of interest that makes government efficient and sensitive to the popular will. It aids government in assessing the adequacy of programs, first through media commentary, second, by reporting the opinions of special publics, and third, by reporting the reactions of the general public. It helps the government interpret its performance when there are few of its electorate in contact with its programs, for example, in international affairs. The press also creates a general openness that allows for messages to reach legislators, which they then may or may not act upon.

More specifically, the press and, especially, the electronic media have contributed to the nationalization of politics. The vast majority of political reporting during election campaigns (81 per cent in one instance, according to Black) deals with the activities and statements of the leaders of the political parties and their families. By following the leaders as they hopscotch across the country, the press are as much the agents of a national campaign as are the parties themselves, galvanizing local support for the party that then spills over to the local candidate.

In general, the press plays a regular and important part in the governance of society, yet it has no political coherence or unity of purpose in a narrow sense. It injects itself into the process of making public opinion and hence, over the long term, affects basic values as well as helping to shift attitudes and opinions about discrete issues. Yet its primary purpose is not to gain power for itself.

A MICROVIEW OF THE FUNCTIONING OF PRESS AND POLITICS

The above perspective of the functioning of press and politics constitutes a broad overview or macroview. Now we turn to a microview, to examine press/politics functioning in greater detail, to form a more accurate and thorough picture of the real political role of the press.

In the following section the influence of three different sets of variables on the macrosystem will be discussed:

- institutionalization
- media processes
- business dynamics

The Political Effects of Institutional Organization

The press is not composed of a great number of individual reporters covering the world whose reports are carried by one or other station or newspaper. The press has an industrialized institutional structure complete with control systems, institutional policies, occupational routines, a personnel organization, particular technologies of production and distribution, and so on. Each of these impinges on the political role the press plays.

In both the electronic and print media there are clear internal hierarchies and structures. These must be flexible enough to allow for the creativity and individuality of commentators, opinion-makers, and program creators (see Gallagher, 1982), but their presence is never-

theless forceful. For example, a reporter is given certain responsibilities by an editor. If the reporter should come across what he considers to be a great story, he must persuade that editor to allow him the time necessary to research the story.

Nor does the news organization sit on top of a world full of information, all of which gets on the air or into the paper. Slow news periods provide good examples of the way that news and commentary depend on the interests and inclinations of the editor, how he perceives his publication or program, how he perceives its audience and even the news sources to which the organization subscribes.

The politics of the press also depend on information-gathering structures. News is gathered by a fairly standardized beat system. The reporter covers certain beats or sources that customarily turn up stories. The beat might be nightclubs, city hall, the police station, or a host of other institutions, such as universities, hospitals, social service organizations, large corporations, and labour organizations. In covering these beats in search of stories, the reporter tends to identify with the source of the stories rather than with the individuals who may make the story significant: in the case of the police station, for instance, the police rather than the accused, or with a large corporation, the corporation rather than its customers or employees. This tendency has led to the creation of counter-beats, such as labour and environmental groups to balance business.

Knowing how this system of information-gathering works, politicians as well as other newsmakers can feed the system to make stories. The most obvious example is the leaking of stories to individual journalists who frequent Parliament. Politicians may wish to get an advance reading on a proposed policy or to throw another party into disarray. Or they may want to puff a story so they leak a dramatized version. By leaking a story they can issue information without responsibility and, like the arsonist who watches his own fire, anonymous in the crowd, can assess the subsequent reaction.

The press has an implicit hierarchy of coverage that differs between the electronic and print media. Pronouncements by a Prime Minister from abroad always seem to receive special attention. The perception that the Prime Minister is still thinking about the home front when touring the world may be a boost to our collective ego. (When one realizes that he has a bevy of reporters travelling with him and tracking his every move and word, the magic of his attention is diminished.)

In yet another example, a government can be assured that almost any policy announcement will be displaced by "explosions" of any sort, whether physical, political, or biological. The press is also sensitive to power in a broadly defined sense. Knowing this is to know the likelihood of the press sustaining its interest in a particular issue.

The Political Effects of the Press as Media

Each medium has its own "technique" and therefore its own bias. The print medium allows for a lot of words and a very few pictures. However, the one picture used can create the whole tone for an article. For example, during the federal election campaign of 1984, a picture of John Turner, which had in the background an insignia that looked like the devil's staff or as if Turner had horns, was printed in *The Globe and Mail*. Complaints were made charging *The Globe* with potentially creating a subliminal bias.

In contrast to the negative image in *The Globe* example is the more usual, positively biased publicity shot, such as the one presented here of B.C. Premier Bill Vander Zalm. Note the simplicity and even the purity of the image, coupled with its informality, its reaching out, and yet its beckoning, the rolled-up sleeves suggesting a willingness to be directly involved in hard work.

The more usual example of print bias derives from the form of the printed story. The story is the creation of the reporter in his or her words, and is usually built around statements by a newsmaker. The potential for inaccurate, incomplete, or wrong contexts, misquotations, and inappropriate headlines is considerable. However, one method of minimizing such problems is to issue news releases or give news conferences that lend themselves to clear and logical analysis and restatement.

The problem of context is further exacerbated by the form of newspaper stories. As we will see in Chapter 4, newspaper stories have an inverted-pyramidal structure. The basic facts of who, what, when, where, and why are outlined at the outset. The details of the story are then filled in. The necessity of this kind of structure came from fitting stories into spaces. Layout editors had to be able to lop off the ends of stories without losing any of the essentials. The top-heavy inverted-pyramidal structure was thus created. This structure has also allowed for the development of fluffy tabloids, where all one gets in the story is the basic points with little but sensational elaboration.

In a farewell comment to the press, Pierre Trudeau captured with irony the vulnerability of the politician to these and other sorts of potentially undermining inadvertencies, techniques, and tricks the press can play. He turned Richard Nixon's complaint on its head when he noted that he was sorry he would not have the press to kick around any more.

John Turner: the politician in unflattering pose.
Courtesy The Globe and Mail, Toronto.

In contrast to print, television news is dominated by the picture and few words. The words of a television newscast can fit on one newspaper page. Newsmakers oriented to television must therefore create media or television events to ensure television coverage. The contrived "photo opportunities" of Prime Minister Mulroney and of President Reagan, which have no substantive news value, are cases in point. The television stations themselves find that audiences respond well to different stimuli from those offered by print. For a newspaper, being the first with the news may be the major goal. For a television station, bringing in a set of fresh pictures may once again revive interest in an event already discussed in the print media. Visual excitement can readily replace speed of news coverage.

Most television news is planned by both the news team and the newsmakers, something which fills the needs and preferences of both the station and the politicians. During one provincial election in Quebec, so keen was he to avoid "live" coverage that Robert Bourassa ran his television campaign by issuing videotapes. In broader perspective, with television the politician is engaged primarily in political-visual image-making, in symbolic representation often devoid of the nuts and bolts of policy.

Radio deals more in sounds than in words or pictures. In its heyday and even now, the ability to recreate the actual sounds of a scene, be it a battle or a concert, drives both news reporter and creator. Sound recording is a staple for radio whether it is music, drama, reportage, or interview. The pun, alliteration, the one-line verbal quip all play very well into radio form.

All these technological biases are interwoven with press-perceived audience dynamics to form something we might call **media**

Bill Vander Zalm: the politician as hard-working friend. *Courtesy Slicko Studios, Vancouver, and the B.C. Social Credit Party. Photograph by H. Fry.*

bias. Thus a *Globe and Mail* and an *Edmonton Sun* are worlds apart in their newspaper form. The former enhances the basic bias of the printed word, milking it as best it can, while the latter attempts to match on the printed page what other media, predominantly television, offer. CBC radio uses the spoken word to extend our verbal understanding while most commercial stations are more interested in sound signatures (meaning recognizable noise patterns) in both voice and musical form. Most commercial television stations have more in common with glue companies than with attempts to reflect a culture in audiovisual form to a people.

With all this the politician must cope. What emerges is what Altheide and Snow (1979) have termed **media logic**. Events in the political realm are better understood as feed for the media than in terms of their political (in the sense of a policy) or informational ends.

The Political Effects of the Press as Business Institutions

Some might argue that, from a perspective of how the uses of information and communication ought to be situated in society, we are living with a quirk of history in having a "free press" operating clearly within the power base and dynamics of the business class. Others would contend that the basic functions of the

A cartoonist's conception of the business leanings of the press. Roy Petersen, Vancouver. *From Royal Commission on Newspapers, 1981. Reproduced with permission of the Minister of Supply and Services Canada.*

press are intimately connected to industrialized society and therefore to business dynamics. Whichever side of the debate one cares to favour, there is no doubt that the structure, functioning, and place in society of the media are all affected fundamentally by the media's placement in the business sector.

The press, whether public or private, deals in audiences. Its audiences must be of a size and type that either advertisers or Parliament deems valuable. The information it creates must be consumable and must be consumed on a regular basis. The information environment it creates must not interfere with advertiser mes-

sages, whether governmental or commercial. The press must also operate in such a way that it continues to have access to information as well as access to audiences. These and other constraints derive from the press being, essentially, a business operation.

The press might apply a number of potential levels of analysis to politics. The most abstract level is political theory, followed by ideology, policy, and then practice. It might be claimed that only with a full discussion of each of these levels are the media fully informing their audiences of their political environment. In its place we have reportage that concentrates on personalized, concrete events whose interest is further enhanced by formulas centred on simple thematics such as dichotomies, conflict, hubris, and the like.

For example, around election time the major story is winning and losing. This basic story is personalized by backgrounders on the leaders' families, their well-spent or misspent youth, their advancing age if appropriate, and so forth. Once these crude variables have been exhausted, the press moves onto only slightly more subtle themes. Fletcher and Taras (1984) use the example of a leadership cycle specifically as it was played out with regard to Trudeau's 1983 peace initiative. The press treated the initiative with considerable cynicism, a shame when the stakes in such a matter are so high. Black, in another example of the rule of theme over content, quotes Robert Stanfield, thrice-defeated national Conservative leader, as saying that if he walked on water, the press would suggest that it was because he couldn't swim.

Such topics keep ideology, policy, and, in fact, any discussion out of the abstract and within the realm of the concrete and the personal. Why? To ensure large audiences. The difficulty is that fresh thought about new phenomena becomes not only difficult but, at times, impossible. In the midst of the constitutional patriation debates the press engaged in a great deal of speculation about the exact amount of personal animosity between Prime Minister Trudeau and Premier René Lévesque. One might claim that the whole issue was, if not irrelevant, then certainly diversionary.

To consider only the level of political practice, and, consequently, the concrete and the personal, has a number of other implications. Some on the political right attempt to claim that they "are not ideological but practical,"

thus making an unsubstantiated claim to being ideologically dominant since we tend to assume practicality accepts basic givens. Because of press avoidance of discussions of ideology, it is not difficult for anyone with few ideas to make such a claim. To counter such a claim requires background context that cannot be introduced to an audience overnight, as it depends on an already existing level of sophistication.

Dwelling in established images and especially personal dramas may make for a kind of political stability: new faces, but the same old policies. But as the press, especially television, distances itself through both technique and content from all sides of the political debate, the distinctive fabric of the nation may be endangered in favour of an apparent global homogeneity. This matter will receive more attention in Chapter 9.

Keeping matters personal and concrete leads to other unfortunate consequences. Patrick Gossage (1985, p. 21), reviewing an article in *The Bulletin of the Atomic Scientists*, notes that the Canadian media have been completely unwilling to do thorough research and discuss nuclear strategy. He quotes from the article: "such reporting as there has been on strategic doctrine has largely accepted policy declarations at face value. Coverage has tended to ignore the fact that declared policy represents the facade of a complex strategic agenda."

The above biases may arguably be traced to the business orientation of the press and therefore to the necessity to deal in audiences. This is not a big-business conspiracy to gelatinize our minds in political gossip. It does, however, play to a fairly low level of political thought and calls into question the adequacy of the press as a key democratic institution.

GOVERNMENT AND THE POLITICS OF THE PRESS

Governments themselves can be seen as information systems. We discussed this notion briefly at the beginning of this chapter and must return to that discussion for this final section. To proceed with a model of the press that emphasizes the flow of information from the people and government is to impute a model of decision-making that does not bear close scrutiny. We have seen its limitations in presenting a picture of the operating realities of the press. Now we turn to government. There are three major matters to consider here: (1) the influence of the administration of governments; (2) the policy generation process; and (3) the anticipation and creation of public opinion by government.

1. Political Agendas/Administrative Agendas

Governments, when elected, have agendas upon which they have made their claims to be elected. Consistently, however, once elected a government introduces only certain planks in the platform for consideration. Part of the reason for this (other than a change of heart or a lack of intention to proceed in the first place) is that all governments must face certain administrative constraints. Programs expire, treaties come up for reconsideration, new difficulties are faced in parts of the nation, foreign governments and other sectors put pressure on fledgling governments, political crises arise for which damage control becomes a primary concern. Ultimately, one might claim that these issues originated to some extent with the will of the people, yet it is difficult for the government to prioritize such turns of events before they happen, and the public, of course, is not organized in such a way to set its government's own priorities. Thus, the press can play only a very limited role to affect this process.

2. The Policy Development Process

Similarly, the policy development process often does not take place in response to the press communicating to government the feelings of the people. Policy is developed on the basis of political theory and ideology, usually by members of the intellectual, political, and business elites (see Gandy, 1982). Economic policy is seen as the preserve of business and politicians, and even the claim to a hearing by another elite, the church (Baum and Cameron, 1984), may be greeted with disdain and shock. When not in power, political parties present policy to members to form part of the platform of the party (which then may be ignored by caucus). When in power, the policy may be developed for caucus and only have public input in terms of a reaction to a suggested policy. In each case the press is an outsider to the process.

Policy is also often developed by special publics without discussion with the general public. Thus, in the case of the military or in a particular sector of business, say the oil industry or small business, policy may be developed and then reflected in legislation with very little public debate over its principles. To take another example, certain kinds of businesses, e.g., cultural industries, were long left out in the cold by the federal government and are still in that position with some provincial governments. Essentially, this is because they were unrecognized as potential contributors to the economy. The dollars that leave the country, from the purchase of foreign novels, television shows, books, and the like, show the extent of that mistake.

3. The Anticipation and Manipulation of the Public Will

The third factor shortcutting the role of the press as a mediator between government and the people derives from the tendency on the part of government to anticipate the will of the electorate and either work around it or subvert it. A trivial example of this sort of thing occurred when the Trudeau Liberals advertised for someone to take over Canada's then new spy agency, the Canadian Security Intelligence Service (CSIS). Inadvertently, they included in the ad the size of the budget the person would administer, a fact they consistently refused to divulge in Parliament for fear of negative public reaction.

Less trivial examples are becoming more frequent with increasing use of polls by political parties. By 1986 it was rare for political parties not to be polling on all manner of issues at every stage of their consideration. Polling has placed governments at a considerable advantage in the development and casting of policy announcements, and in the whole art of maintaining themselves or displacing others from office. In contrast, the press, in spite of overall high profit levels, has been reluctant to poll to create content for these papers as opposed to attempting to increase circulation. More recently they and newsmagazines such as *Maclean's* appear to have discovered how to create interesting copy based on a poll. That they should be prepared to invest in polling only during the actual running of an election is an indication of the degree to which they see themselves as serious information institutions committed to providing for their audiences the most thorough and sophisticated information they can.

Of course, on the other side of the issue is the notion that polls create a form of pseudo-information reflective of the sophistication of the questions, not of the opinions of the people. To assume that polls reflect "true democracy" where everyone has his say is undoubtedly very wrong. And from an entirely opposite perspective, newspapers, like governments, are often remembered and respected for the ads they take that run counter to public opinion.

SUMMARY

Politics can be seen as an information enterprise and both the mass media and government can be seen as political and information institutions. Information and knowledge are foundations of the development and operation of democracy and information institutions have arisen to support those foundations.

The structures of information in modern nation-states and the place of the press in those structures are defined by a number of variables, including libel laws, the right of free speech, the right to know, government need of the press, various performance requirements, and so forth. Given those structures, the press and politicians, and their comparative power, are closely related. The considerable power of government appears to exceed that of the press, as witnessed by not only formal mechanisms but also the exercise of power by the government in recent years.

The macro political functioning of the press in a democratic society is defined by institutionalization, media processes, and business dynamics. Government processes such as administrative agendas, patterns of policy generation, and the anticipation and creation of public opinion by politicians also restrict the influence of the media on politics.

Information institutions, specifically the press,

are important in modern democracies, yet they are limited in the scope of their operation. A "free" press is something of a misnomer because the press is closely integrated with other social institutions, especially business institutions, and is constrained by real or potential controls. Still, the press does make a social contribution and is key to the operation of government through the pursuit of the public interest on the basis of a separate set of interests from those of government. (Those interests are discussed further in Chapters 6 and 7.) Essentially, the role the mass media play in the political affairs of an open democracy is substantial but imperfect.

REFERENCES

Coleman, J.S. *Power and the Structure of Society.* New York: Norton, 1973.

Altheide, D.L., and R.P. Snow. *Media Logic.* Beverly Hills: Sage, 1979.

Baum, G., and D. Cameron. *Ethics and Economics: Canada's Catholic Bishops on the Economic Crisis.* Toronto: James Lorimer, 1984.

Black, Edwin R. *Politics and the News: The Political Function of the Mass Media.* Toronto: Butterworths, 1982.

Canada. Canadian Study of Parliament Group. *Seminar on Press and Parliament: Adversaries or Accomplices?* Ottawa: Queen's Printer, 1980.

Canada. *Royal Commission on Newspapers.* Ottawa: Supply and Services, 1981.

Canadian Broadcasting Corporation. *The Press and the Prime Minister: A Story of Unrequited Love.* Directed and produced by George Robertson. Toronto: CBC, 1977.

Cocking, C. *Following the Leaders: A Media Watcher's Diary of Campaign '79.* Toronto: Doubleday, 1980.

Fletcher, F. *The Newspaper and Public Affairs.* Vol. 7, Research Publications, Canada, *Royal Commission on Newspapers.* Ottawa: Supply and Services, 1981.

Fletcher, F., and D.G. Taras. "The Mass Media and Politics: An Overview," in Whittington and Williams, eds., *Canadian Politics in the 1980's,* 2nd edition. Toronto: Methuen, 1984.

Gallagher, M. "Negotiation of Control in Media Organizations and Occupations," in Gurevitch *et al.,* eds., *Culture, Society and the Media.* Toronto: Methuen, 1982.

Gandy, O.H. *Beyond Agenda Setting: Information Subsidies and Public Policy.* Norwood, New Jersey: Ablex, 1982.

Gossage, P. "The media-government mouthpiece," *Media Magazine* (September, 1985), p. 21. The referenced article is W. Dorman, "The media: playing the government's game," *The Bulletin of the Atomic Scientists* (August, 1985).

McElgunn, J. "Publishers urging reform of the law on access to information," *Media Magazine* (May,1986), p. 5.

McPhail, T. *Electronic Colonialism: The Future of International Broadcasting and Communication.* Beverly Hills: Sage, 1981.

Murdock, G. "Large Corporations and the Control of Communications Industries," in Gurevitch *et al.,* eds., *Culture, Society and the Media.*

Siebert, F.S., T. Petersen, and W. Schramm. *Four Theories of the Press.* Urbana: University of Illinois Press, 1956, 1971.

Soderlund, W.C., *et al. Media and Elections in Canada.* Toronto: Holt, Rinehart and Winston, 1984.

STUDY QUESTIONS

1. Discuss the role the media play in affairs of state.

2. What kind of a press system is best for Canada?

3. Should Canadians have equal access to information that Americans have in their country?

4. Are there sufficient mechanisms to balance the power of the press with those of government?

CHAPTER

4

The Design of Information

INTRODUCTION

P ERHAPS THE most obvious area of study in communications is the study of **content**, that is, what is said and how it is said. At one level, that of personal interaction, we can study the content of what one person says to another and how. By examining the content of this interaction we gain some idea of the interaction and of the two individuals involved.

A concern for content is an important focus of study in material intended to have a lasting existence and a broad significance. The study of the ideas expressed in the literature of a particular epoch, by authors of a particular nation, even in one piece of writing of a particular author, provides insight into the society from which these works emanate as well as the creative process of the individuals involved in their creation.

Content is also important in material that has a large audience but which is not specifically designed to have a lasting significance. For example, the information reaching us each day via the mass media must be analysed for its content if only because we live on a steady diet of it. In it we are liable to find repeated ideas, information, and interpretations. These repetitions and their variations provide insight into the society of which they are a part and into the institutions that manufacture media programs. This content reveals the dominant themes and set of ideas or ideology of a society. It also reveals subordinate or alternative interpretations or ideology.

Communication as Representation

When we study content, we study **representation**, sometimes also called **encoding**. Representation combines the "what" and the "how" of communication. When we take up the study of representation we are by no means confined to examining the so-called truth of statements. That is, we are not limited to commenting on whether a set of statements exactly corresponds to what it purports to describe. Indeed, as researchers have focused attention on the process of representation, it has become apparent how difficult it is to adjudicate questions of accurate representation. Representation literally re-presents the matter. Different representations re-present ideas differently. They are competing forms of representation or competing interpretations. At times, some are obviously better than others. But the more interesting cases are those in which the matter is much less clear. One representation brings a certain background set of ideas or ideology to its task and draws out certain elements, while another brings other background ideas and draws out other elements.

The study of representation, especially the representation of human affairs, is a study of **indeterminate systems** that have no boundaries. In other words, there can be any number of ways of representing an object or event.

Take, for example, a political event such as the signing of a peace treaty. Each side has reasons of its own for signing the treaty. It means different things to each of the signatories. Then there are the subgroups within those bodies who sign. For some the treaty may represent a good bargain, for others a sell-out. For the people living near the centre of hostilities no doubt it will represent a return to a less violent, if not a normal, life. For those aligned with the various signatories, the treaty will also have various meanings. For political scientists and historians yet another set of meanings will be generated.

A treaty may seem like an unfair example because it is a rare event and comes from the uncertain world of politics. Perhaps something in science would seem more determinate. Let us return to an example from Chapter 1, $e=mc^2$. That seemingly innocent formula changed the whole way matter and energy were conceived and transformed our understanding of the universe. For certain groups of scientists and politicians it represented a potential military weapon. For other people it has represented a potential destruction of human life on earth. For those near nuclear energy establishments it has meant a whole new set of worries and work opportunities. For Derrick de Kerckhove it is the key to total and absolute information.

Even if we choose a less significant event, such as the utterance of a particular sentence, we can similarly discuss the various meanings that can be taken from that sentence as well as the various assumptions that went into its composition, i.e., what it represents. "John hit the ball" contains within it most profoundly an assumption basic to human understanding, the notion of causality. But it also contains less fundamental meanings: our habit of placing the agent before the verb; our tendency to speak of males more than females in abstract discourse; the popularity of "John" as an Anglo-Saxon first name; the tendency for common words to be monosyllabic. As well as the **denotative** meaning of the statement, a meaning related to a male striking a sphere, there exist a multitude of **connotative** meanings such as the ones suggested above.

The discussion of the indeterminacy of representation does not end here. In all that has been said so far we have been dealing within one system of representation – language. We might want to argue that language is a most powerful and flexible system of representation, but that does not detract from the independent nature of other systems of representation, such as music and the visual arts. And while we sometimes interpret music and art with language and rarely do the opposite, to do so is not to reduce one system of representation to the other or to encompass the full spectrum of the meaning of the one with the other. In short, as well as a multiplicity of meanings capable of being generated within one medium, meaning can be generated within further sets in the multiplicity of media. Overall, because these meanings can multiply indefinitely, we are dealing with an indeterminate system.

THE IMPLICATIONS OF THE INDETERMINACY OF REPRESENTATION

The indeterminacy of representation tends to lead the study of communication content away from what has been taken to be the foundations of philosophy, science, and social science and more toward the foundations of interpretation we find in the humanities. It leads to an emphasis of what Frye (1971) has called a truth of concern versus a truth of correspondence. More simply, it is concerned more with rhetoric than with reason. In the study of communication the importance of a statement is not limited to whether it predicts events, can be refuted by others, or generates other interesting hypotheses, all standards of science and social science. What is interesting in the study of representation is what gives a particular representation its force, its ability to persuade, or its attractiveness. Whatever makes a movie more powerful than a novel, one author or painter more popular than another, even one movie more popular than another, cannot be satisfactorily discussed by reference to the relative "truth" of each communication. They are more interestingly discussed in terms of their (rhetorical) force. In so discussing them we can compare movies with books, paintings of battles with portraits, cars with clothes, or rock music with Greek society.

Umberto Eco chose to express his accumulated knowledge of medieval society in the form of a mystery novel, *The Name of the Rose*, and the book became a best-seller. It is probably incorrect to claim that he has demonstrated the interest of vast numbers of people in medieval life; his success is perhaps rather the result of the power of the mystery-drama form to attract significant audiences. Put differently, Eco's success illustrates the degree to which the packaging of a product can supersede the attributes of the product itself. On a more metaphysical plane we can speculate as to whether the "product" remains constant with variation in packaging. Is the knowledge contained in *The Name of the Rose* equivalent to what Eco might have said in a scholarly text on medieval history?

By the time we reach such a level of discussion, we run directly into what has been a fundamental problem in the study of representation. In the history of communication studies, and to a greater degree in other social sciences, there has been a bias in favour of physical objects over verbal entities. Physical objects were seen as having a greater claim to an independent existence than representations of those objects. In fact, at times, representation has been subordinated to hypothetical entities, as in the case of language versus thought. In the same way that the physical object was seen as somehow more fundamental than its representation, thought was postulated to be something that language only partially expressed. As a result, until recently, representation was only studied as a secondary matter.

Signification

To postulate that the "real world" and the world of representations exist on different planes, with the latter having secondary importance, led early writers to assume that there were true portrayals as opposed to biased portrayals. Bennett's (1982) discussion of George Orwell's *Homage to Catalonia* is pertinent here. The more modern approach to the issue is to assume that physical objects and representations are two different but related aspects of the world. Both are seen as "real," but neither is subordinate to the other. The reality of objects has been taken as given. The reality of representation has come from the identification of systematic patterns of behaviour that are employed to collect and organize information. These patterns of media behaviour are a good example of **signification**, the articulation of a structure for determining meaning.

The beats that editors assign reporters guarantee the presence of certain information and certain perspectives in the news rather than others. That pattern of presence and absence leads to the evolution of a point of view

in the paper's overall operations. Similarly, what a television crew can obtain in the way of news is vastly different from what a single reporter writing news stories can present. Although the television equipment is invisible to the viewer and the television news seemingly puts forward a "true picture," anyone who has been the subject of a news report is well aware of the obtrusiveness of the cameras and the degree to which they interfere with, influence, and distort an event, or more accurately, how they mould an event (to what the technology and its users determine to be the demands of the medium). The work habits of communicators and the signification process that derives from these are as real as physical objects.

METHODS OF STUDY

In recent years a great deal of attention has been given to representation in the context of an indeterminate and ever-changing meaning system, especially in Britain. In an article entitled "Messages and meanings," Janet Woollacott (1982) provides an especially useful summary of such work. She notes that one school of thought, typified by Hall *et al.* (1978), is that the media inject meaning into and consequently transform events in such a way as to reproduce the ruling-class or dominant ideology. One method by which they do this is through their choice of individuals or **primary definers** to define the issue under discussion. Hall *et al.* see the media as a key terrain where social consensus is won or lost, and as such the media become a field of ideological struggle. While we will leave this literature for more advanced study, it is worth noting that because the media are in the business of producing meaning, which cannot be produced outside of some context, it would be surprising indeed if the common context of media messages was not that which reflected the dominant interests of society and the interests that allow for the existence of media institutions themselves.

Our exploration here will be oriented to a basic introduction of two methods of analysis, **semiotics** and **content analysis**. Following their introduction we will look at examples of media forms.

Semiotics

There are three basic elements to semiotics. They are: **sign, signifier, signified.** The **sign** is a concept meant to stand for a full and complete representation of an object or event or, according to Roland Barthes (1968, p. 38), the union of **signifier** and **signified.** The object or event as we conceive of it is the thing signified and the signifier is the device used to represent what is signified. The sign encompasses both. The **signifier** exists on the plane of expression whereas the **signified** can be said to exist on the plane of content. However, if we examine this distinction too closely we find a contradiction. For example, in semiology, that is, the discussion of the theory itself, signifiers (expressions) become signifieds (content) by virtue of being the objects of discussion.

Sign-signifier relations have absorbed most of the attention of researchers who apply semiotics to practical studies. In focusing on these relations researchers show a great concern for a complete accounting of the meaning contained in various signifiers. In a sense a semiotician could easily write a book on the use of one word in a particular tract. Semioticians do not usually go that far. However, one French semiotician, Barthes (1970), has written an interpretation of a work that is longer than the work itself. Other

essays he has written illustrate perspective on matters (such as wrestling, cars, etc.) we normally do not consider part of communication but which, as he points out, are profoundly communicative.

The primary focus of the semiotician is on the relations of meaning within and surrounding the piece. It is the job of the semiotician to demonstrate how his or her interpretation of a piece reverberates throughout. Nothing can show up that runs counter to the interpretation being put forward and a variety of elements must be demonstrated to be in keeping with that reading of the material.

The analytical device used to explain immediate context is the **dyad** (pair). By presenting a concept and discussing it in terms of its opposite, semioticians aim to clarify its meaning within the structure of the work in which it occurs. At the simplest level, by introducing the opposite of a term (e.g., light/heavy as opposed to light/dark), we can clarify its meaning. But, again, to emphasize the point, the semioticians are dealing with the meaning of a term, idea, or set of ideas *within the context of the piece as a whole*. They may then cast that meaning with a broader social context in a semiotics of society.

An Example: A Semiotic Analysis of a CP Air Ad Series

The following ad series appeared in two and perhaps more Canadian magazines between February and May, 1983. The first thing to note about the first version of the ad is the use of empty space. Why is it there? It does capture attention, but what would be the effect if a government ad dealing with changes to the income tax act contained a similar amount of blank space? It would have to be very cleverly done not to cause a furore. So the blank space

CPAir Royal Canadian Class to the Orient.

VERSION 1

First came Empress Class.
Now there is also Royal Canadian Class.
Another first.
And it puts you right up front in our 747s.
In first class seating. That's roomier. Two-abreast.
And limited to only 28.
You can also expect imaginative dishes. Fine wine and liqueurs. All served and poured at your table side.
There's even a SkyBar.
Also the convenience of Advance Seat Selection. And separate time-saving check-in. (Same as our First Class passengers who are now upstairs. Relaxing. In fully reclining Loungeaire sleeper seats.)

Advertisements reproduced courtesy of CP Air.

ANOTHER FIRST, IN MORE WAYS THAN ONE.

All this for slightly more than a full economy fare.
A small amount for a lot of class.

The only direct service Vancouver to Hong Kong
3 times a week.
Plus 2 more weekly flights connecting via Tokyo.
Vancouver to Tokyo: 5 wide-cabin nonstops weekly.

CP Air
Royal Canadian Class
Another First.
CP Air International.

CP and ◄ are registered trademarks of Canadian Pacific Limited.

must have more than an attention-getting function. Let us speculate.

What are the most negative aspects of a long plane trip, to the Orient or anywhere else? Surely high on anyone's list (and we can be reasonably certain that enough market research has been done on airline travel for any airline and ad agency to know this) is confinement to a rather small area. The blank space immediately contradicts that sense of a long air trip. But the blank space is just a beginning. Notice that the outline of the aircraft is a very light grey so that the boundaries of that outline easily merge into blank white space. Even in the composition of the photograph empty space is emphasized by the absence of occupants for the two front seats on the right hand side of the aircraft. Nor is there a clutter of uncleared dinners on the seat tables.

The confines of air travel are also countered by the various activities of the persons in the cabin. Part of the boredom of flying is being confined in inactivity. In the ad there is a positive panoply of activities – talking, reading, eating, drinking, standing around. Something close to a sociable party-like atmosphere has been created by the photographer. In addition, the overwhelming presence of men in business suits gives a sense of privilege. There are no hippies, grandparents, or crying babies here.

Note that these elements are images. They are neither realities nor arguments or presentations of full "facts." These visual images are then supplemented by images presented in the text. In short snappy "sentences," often phrases, sometimes mere words, privilege, space, lack of boredom, and comfort are all stressed. Words such as "first," "royal," "class," "roomier," "imaginative," and "limited" are all meant to convey the impression that there is something special, exciting, and enjoyable

about flying CP's Royal Canadian Class to the Orient. Indeed, one has to look closely to discover that there is a class above "Royal Canadian."

In addition, the layout of the text is spacious.

Partly because of short sentences and phrases.

Short paragraphs, too.

It all complements the notion of spaciousness.

Why should this be considered a valid reading of the ad? Bear in mind here that this reading was conducted without contacting CP about the ads and the possibility of using them in this book and independently of any understanding we gained of the intentions of the ad designers. The interpretation presented here is based on the notion of complementary images, an internal consistency, a system of signification. The white space works with the grey outline, which works to emphasize the space in the aircraft. The sense of privilege is conveyed by the dress and gender of the actors, which is then complemented in the text. That privilege is made attractive by the apparent activities of the actors. And so it goes.

The second version of the ad appeared in *Maclean's* in February, 1983, the same month the first version appeared in *Saturday Night*. Note that we are not discussing the frequency of the appearance of the ads nor the dynamics of placing different versions in different magazines with considerable overlap of readership. That is a whole other set of niceties that advertisers use to their advantage. But here we will restrict the discussion to ad content and presentation. In the second version of the ad white space still predominates. The print and illustration size has been reduced and a few minor textual changes have been made, but essentially it is the same ad. Consequently, it has the same power through the same

CPAir Royal Canadian Class to the Orient. Another First, in More Ways Than One.

VERSION 2

First came Empress Class.
Now there is also Royal Canadian Class.
Another First.
And it puts you right up front in our 747s.
In first class seating. Two-abreast. And limited to
only 28.
You can also expect imaginative dishes, fine
wine, liqueurs, served at your table side. There's
even a SkyBar.
All this, including the convenience of Advance
Seat Selection and separate time-saving check-in,

for slightly more than a full economy fare.
A small amount for a lot of class.

The only direct service Vancouver to Hong Kong 3 times
a week. Plus 2 more weekly flights connecting via Tokyo.
Vancouver to Tokyo: 5 wide-cabin nonstops weekly.

CPAir
Royal Canadian Class
Another First.
CPAir International.

CP and ◀ are registered trademarks of Canadian Pacific Limited.

elements as the first version. But at half size. Think of the effect it would have to the reader of both *Maclean's* and *Saturday Night*. The *Maclean's* version capitalizes on the money that was able to be spent in the *Saturday Night* version by echoing the characteristics of the more dramatic version of the ad.

This echo effect is being used in the third version of the ad, which appeared in *Maclean's* in April of 1983. Everything has been reduced by one-half once again, but the ratio of space for illustrations, text, and white space is still approximately the same. For the purposes of validating a reading of the ad, note that the empty space does not disappear, nor do any of the elements we discussed as important. Their preservation is a partial validation of the reading we have produced of the ad.

Of considerable interest is the appearance of a new version of the same ad in May of 1983. The new ad, Royal Canadian Class to the South Pacific and South America, advertises another boring, long journey that businessmen are having to make more frequently these days. The echos of the original ad are both implicit and explicit. Implicitly, they are to be found in the use of white space, the parallel naming of the class, much of the content of the text, the

CPAir Royal Canadian Class.
First to the Orient. Now Stretching Out to the South Pacific and South America.

VERSION 4

First came Empress Class.

Then came CPAir Royal Canadian Class to the Orient. Now there is also Royal Canadian Class to the South Pacific and South America.

And it puts you right up front. In your own exclusive cabin. With first class seating. Just two abreast. So every seat is an aisle or window seat.

There's room to spare. Room to stretch. Room to relax. As in fine restaurants, food is served at your table-side. There are fine wines and liqueurs.

Also the convenience of Advance Seat Selection. And separate time-saving check-in.

All this for just slightly more than full economy fare.

CPAir Royal Canadian Class. Another first. In more ways than one.

The Orient Tokyo – 5 wide-cabin nonstops weekly from Vancouver.*
Hong Kong – direct wide-cabin service 2 times a week from Vancouver.
*Effective June 9, 6 wide-cabin nonstops weekly.

South America Wide-cabin nonstop service from Vancouver or Toronto.
To Lima every Monday, continuing on to Santiago and Buenos Aires.

South Pacific Sydney – Wide-cabin service from Vancouver every Wednesday and Friday. From Toronto every Friday.

**Another First.
CPAir International.**

Royal Canadian Class to the South Pacific and South America.
Stretch out in first class seating. In a wide-cabin DC-10.

Royal Canadian Class to the Orient.
Fly with the greatest of ease. Up front in a spacious 747.

 CP and ◖ are registered trademarks of Canadian Pacific Limited.

type faces used, and so forth. Explicitly, the echo is at the bottom of the page, where we see the fusilage cut-aways.

It could be argued not only that these cut-aways are unnecessary as explicit echoes of the former ad but also that they are counterproductive. They give the viewer all the feelings the ad is designed to work against – of being cooped up in a small space surrounded by people he doesn't know and cannot talk with because of seat layout, ambient noise, and lack of space.The other innovation (which does work) is the introduction of the word "stretching" in a variety of meanings and complemented in the picture by the actor stretching out his legs into the surrounding white space.

Content Analysis

Content analysis is a quite different technique, but in some ways it is a quantified version of an incomplete form of semiotic analysis. The content analyst sets up categories that appear to be salient to a particular piece of communication. They may be salient on the basis of the focus of the author or on the basis of the interests of the analysis. With categories in place, analysts then count various types of occurrences. On the basis of frequency of occurrence they then provide a reading of the article. In providing this reading, that is, setting up and interpreting their categories, their activities approach those of the semiotician.

An Example: A Content Analysis of the Media Treatment of the Shooting Down of a Korean Airliner in Soviet Air Space

The example we will use to illustrate content analysis was conducted by Robert Hackett (1983) on *Newsweek, Time,* and *The Globe and Mail*

in the period immediately following the shooting down by the Soviets of Korean Airlines Flight 007 in Soviet air space over Sakhalin Island west of the Kamchatka Peninsula.

Hackett begins by setting the context for his analysis. He tells the story in the abstract and then informs us that his abstraction is not of the KAL incident but of a previous incident in which the Israelis shot down a Libyan airliner over the Sinai, ten years previously. Having posited a parallel between the two events and at the same time a divergence – the one involved a capitalist nation as the aggressor, the other a Communist nation – he contrasts the amount and character of coverage of the two incidents over a ten-day period: one page and some letters to the editor for *Time* and *Newsweek* for the Libyan-Israeli incident, two consecutive cover stories and 45 pages for the Russian-Korean altercation. For *The Globe and Mail,* 11 articles were devoted to the Sinai incident, 103 to KAL 007, including two weeks of front-page placement.

What explains the difference? Hackett asks. He answers: Israeli contrition versus Soviet stonewalling; the direct involvement of a superpower; ethnocentrism: "the Israelis killed only one North American passenger, the Soviets, dozens." Beyond these common-sense factors, he points to the scholarly literature on news coverage, noting that the Israeli action contradicted the pre-Lebanon media image of the Israeli David fending off the Arab Goliath. Such an inconsistency does not tend to promote extensive coverage. In contrast, the Soviet action was able to be portrayed in a manner consistent with one of the predominant media images of the Soviets, "as a brutal totalitarian threat to world peace." Building on that established media image was easy.

Hackett bolsters this interpretation of a differing amount of coverage of the two events by citing other surveys that support the notion that the Soviets are often portrayed as a "totalitarian threat to world peace." Zwicker, he notes, in carrying out a six-month, Toronto-based survey (approximately one year prior), concluded that in coverage of the U.S.S.R. "there is virtually no human face, but a dehumanized ideological abstraction." He cites Dorman's interpretation of U.S. coverage of Soviet intentions and behaviour as "in the darkest possible shades." He concludes by casting a more general statement from Chomsky and Herman to the effect that "As one of hundreds of examples two Soviet dissidents on trial gathered more press attention in 1978 than 20,000 Latin Americans tortured or killed by U.S. client states."

With the above as context, Hackett then sets the content categories of his analysis. They are three. First is the Soviets as "the evil empire." Second is "Soviet justification." Third is "a call for a reasoned response" in view of various Soviet and American realities. He then notes that credibility and ideological effectiveness demand an appearance of balance. This is a way of informing us, prior to the presentation of the data, that we ought not to look for simple-minded bias. It is certainly an interesting statement and quite open to challenge. But caveats aside, his counts support this notion: "of the *Globe*'s 129 articles in the three weeks after the KAL-007, 18 seemed directly to support the 'evil empire' frame, and 21 the 'reasoned response.' Twenty-nine articles advanced the 'Soviet justification' (mainly in the Soviet's own statements, which were the main topic of 12 articles), and 23 contained explicit refutations of the Soviet spy/provocation line."

"Yet," Hackett continues, "the 'evil empire' frame was often privileged." By "privileged" he means that he is now moving beyond quantitative categorical phenomena. For example, he notes that *Time* claimed "that the loss of 61

U.S. civilians in a military attack may have been the greatest since Pearl Harbor." Note *Time*'s speculative verb and the impossibility of comparing the two incidents. *Newsweek* cast the event as a confirmation of Ronald Reagan's warnings of the Soviet Union as the "evil empire." And so he continues with other examples.

Hackett then turns to whom the media used to "define the issues." They were government officials, politicians, and intelligence experts. *Newsweek* used one anti-nuclear activist while one *Globe* article gave the reaction of the peace movement. In contrast to the Sinai incident (where there was little coverage), victims had a prominent place. Hackett notes that victims of military action rarely receive such attention.

Hackett draws his analysis to a close by noting that both the Soviets' legal rights and how well the incident and U.S. reaction suited Reagan's scare-mongering politics had been underplayed. His conclusion is that the media treatment of the incident did not contribute to world peace and understanding.

Hackett's analysis is useful and insightful and provides a good example of both the value and shortcomings of the technique of content analysis. Hackett sets categories in the context of both common sense and scholarly literature. He proceeds through his analysis weaving reason with categories of occurrences in order to provide us with an overall picture. He introduces comparative data so that we can see the distinctiveness of the patterns. He complements his category analysis with other data, such as sources used and themes underplayed. This latter device could be seen as "negative content analysis" in that it identifies, at least from Hackett's viewpoint, what was missing. The only questionable rhetorical trick he uses is the dismissal of the balanced treatment of the themes he identifies as necessary for the maintenance of press credibility. Certainly there is a supporting literature suggesting that balance does maintain press credibility, but to dismiss its occurrence as nothing but a move to maintain credibility is probably a trifle narrow.

At the same time, his analysis opens several important questions, as must any limited content analysis. What is the common pattern of media treatment of any act of aggression or defence by the Soviets against the West and its allies? Since there is no denying the "rivalry" between the U.S. and the U.S.S.R., is there a common pattern of treatment of allies as opposed to "enemies" in the Western press, and what role do these patterns play in the governing of relations within and between the two camps? What are the temporal patterns of the themes Hackett identifies? An increasing frequency of "evil empire" stories would surely be much more alarming than an initial spate of such articles followed by the reporting of Soviet justifications and reasoned responses, even if the earlier articles do set the initial framework of understanding.

Was the story dead or did new themes emerge after Hackett completed his analysis? If memory serves, the Western press generally came to the conclusion that the KAL flight was somehow connected with U.S. spying, that a U.S. spy plane had been operating in the area that night, and that the whole incident was mired in nefarious motives and undertakings by the U.S. Given this conclusion, what then is the significance of the pattern of coverage and the credibility of sources that the media presented? It might easily be that by giving them full rein, the media revealed how untrustworthy such sources are in such cases and that we, as the audience, have seen how administrations such as Reagan's may attempt to stampede world opinion. The difficulty, as

with the little boy who cried wolf, is to know when the threat is real.

Such a set of questions almost always arises around any content analysis. A parallel set of questions arises less often in semiotic analyses because they do not seek to put forward alternative interpretations of events or to illustrate bias in media treatment as content analyses often do, and as Hackett's certainly does, although implicitly. Semiotic analyses place events and most often the media treatment in a larger context so that we can see the connection of one to the other and to prevailing sets of perspectives in society.

To be fair, Hackett is aware of at least some of the issues we have raised here and of broader concerns about the limitations of content analysis. In an article entitled "Decline of a paradigm? bias and objectivity in news media studies" (1984, pp. 241-42), he notes that:

> the growing interest in ideology and the consequent devaluation of bias have been associated with the emergence of new methods for reading ideology in media texts, notably those inspired by semiotics and structural analysis.... content analysis is limited to the manifest attributes of the text.

Comparison and Analysis

There are two basic limitations both with the semiotic approach and with content analysis.

1. As semioticians have begun to identify internal structures of media content they have found themselves in need of making reference to broader theories of society to explain the structure of the ideas embedded in the content. Very quickly their analysis comes to be a commentary on the veracity of these broader theories of social relations, commonly called ideologies. As that happens the semiotician must adopt a theory of social relations.

To put the matter slightly differently, semiotics is a **theory of structure of content**. For a reasonably thorough dealing with its subject matter it must be wedded to a theory of content. Semioticians thus take up political, sociological, or economic theories of content, which they wed to their structural analysis. These theories propose to describe the consequences of real economic or social relations in terms of basic human values. They are thus theories of the meaning of content rather than theories of the structure of that meaning, as is semiotics.

Content analysis is also oriented to the structure of content, only it is a *technique* rather than a theory. Content analyses must also, if they carry their analysis far enough, make reference to theories of the content of society. The major difference between semiotics and content analysis is that often semioticians immediately and explicitly take up theories of content before they commence their analysis. In content analysis it is often the last act, after the empirical phenomena have been fully discussed. In the example given, Hackett's analysis of the treatment of the KAL incident, his closing comments imply that the role of the press is to promote international peace. While that is an admirable ideal, it is not a realistic portrayal. Had Hackett begun his analysis with the tacit assumption that the role of the press is to consolidate social ideology, his interpretation of the sequence of the coverage would have been quite different. In short, content analysis often fails to declare its alliance with a particular social theory.

2. The second basic limitation with both theories concerns a different aspect of the content. The structural relations or frequencies of content categories (or motifs) in a piece of high-quality literature and a piece of low-quality literature may be the same. A folktale and a modern movie dealing with contemporary events may contain the same motifs, the same structural relations, and similar frequency of content. Neither a semiotic nor a content analysis, even when wedded to a broader theory of society, deals adequately with this apparent inequivalency. At the same time, as Eco (1986) points out, the notion that semiotics cannot distinguish between pulp fiction and literature is nonsense.

THE MEDIUM AND THE MESSAGE

Semiotics and content analysis provide one level of understanding of the structures and implicit meaning of content. Another level comes about through the constraints of the medium itself, which forms and carries content.

In the day-to-day world of journalism, journalists, newsmakers, and news consumers alike have realized that the various media consistently select out certain elements for emphasis. That selection leads to a bias about events that varies across each medium. The best example is the television news team as compared with the single newspaper reporter. Not only is the news team more intrusive on the event itself but also a television news story is uncompromising in demanding good visuals as part of the story. On the other hand, a newspaper story depends for its strength on various elements, including analysis. *Each medium organizes and encourages particular elements of content and particular relations between those elements.* These elements and relations are both distinct to each medium and forever shifting with the creativity of the practitioners in each: they provide the background to the effectiveness of any individual piece. For a broader discussion of this subject, see *Media Logic*, by Altheide and Snow (1979).

TABLE 4.1

Net Advertising Revenues by Media, 1966–81 ($000's)

| Year | Broadcast | | Newspapers | | | Periodicals | | | | | Other Print | Outdoor | |
	Radio	TV	Dailies	Weekend Supplement	Weeklies, Semi-Tri	General Magazines	Business Papers	Farm Papers	Phone and City Directories	Relig., School and Other	Catalogues, Direct Mail	Billboards, Car Cards, Signs, etc.	Total All Media
1966	80,048	100,392	234,915	17,457	34,457	21,872	29,650	5,714	37,155	3,650	172,340	73,975	811,559
1967	88,457	111,253	239,810	15,918	44,752	22,940	32,429	6,036	40,150	3,700	183,037	84,494	872,976
1968	95,018	114,872	260,072	17,227	49,903	23,765	28,067	5,893	43,330	3,454	186,961	86,000	914,562
1969	107,483	131,176	296,159	19,395	50,387	26,448	30,683	6,255	48,331	3,395	201,671	93,000	1,014,383
1970	113,667	139,295	301,392	19,842	52,076	26,168	30,809	5,845	53,341	3,850	217,299	96,500	1,060,084
1971	124,688	147,671	327,887	23,131	55,565	26,307	29,732	5,441	62,378	4,839	238,555	98,033	1,144,227
1972	144,703	166,025	374,465	25,938	63,848	31,431	31,899	7,216	71,390	5,714	270,999	109,271	1,302,905
1973	160,300	198,517	428,134	23,348	75,328	35,808	36,136	6,975	86,502	7,188	304,327	116,858	1,479,421
1974	182,854	225,190	496,965	23,656	84,100	47,823	44,353	7,750	99,812	7,214	368,439	132,509	1,720,665
1975	207,679	265,631	564,638	23,134	90,713	70,932	55,557	8,141	117,127	10,692	386,604	137,635	1,938,483
1976	241,800	322,598	661,422	25,790	109,267	67,938	71,003	9,280	135,947	10,009	435,702	153,000	2,243,756
1977	269,080	375,564	703,605	21,475	123,477	71,338	78,120	10,440	158,586	12,165	471,574	162,600	2,458,024
1978	305,475	441,755	762,571	21,000	146,925	105,168	82,269	10,703	176,670	12,679	543,501	182,100	2,790,815
1979	352,010	526,828	827,984	19,574	181,724	138,288	88,117	13,397	203,054	11,274	656,919	211,000	3,220,169
1980	391,985	610,334	892,000	17,100	210,000	152,000	97,800	15,000	236,000	11,500	744,679	236,000	3,614,398
1981	440,000	695,000	967,000	20,500	236,000	182,000	113,000	16,000	275,000	12,000	840,000	265,000	4,061,500

SOURCE: Audley, *Canada's Cultural Industries,* which used: Maclean Hunter Research Bureau, *A Report on Advertising Revenues in Canada, 1981* (figures for 1966–79 are Statistics Canada actuals; for 1980–81, Maclean Hunter Research Bureau estimates, except "Broadcast" data, which are actuals for 1980).

MEDIA FORMS AND MEANING STRUCTURES

The advertisement is an invention of profound significance to capitalist society. It lies at the very foundation of the commercial mass media. It is a device that allows production and distribution of information and entertainment across a wide segment of the population at very little cost to the consumer. For a surcharge paid on every other consumer product, a communications industry of immense size and power has been developed in the United States, and in other capitalist nations to a lesser extent. Table 4.1 gives an indication of the growth, size, and diversity of the advertising industry in Canada.

Did anybody need a Jolt before it hit the market? *Courtesy Jolt Beverage Co. Ltd.*

In commerce, advertising has increasingly become the means whereby producers launch products and maintain sales. In the past the performance of a product and hence consumer satisfaction were *supplemented* by advertising to increase or maintain sales, but now markets are *created* by advertisers launching new products. Consumer satisfaction is anticipated, sometimes by means of market tests. As numerous commentators have pointed out, we are either threatened or tempted by advertisers

into buying their products. The advertiser creates the need and then persuades us that this product fills that need. The accompanying photo of a billboard advertising Jolt cola illustrates how one company went about creating a market for its product.

Because so much is at stake and the constraints of space or time are so great, there is an incredible investment involved in the making of advertisements. It is not at all uncommon for a 30-second ad to have cost more to produce than the 30-minute program in conjunction with which it is shown. Millions of dollars of production investment in the advertised product hang in the balance. Nor is all the money budgeted for the ad spent on filming and production.

To summarize a general example of the process briefly, the producer first selects a target market. Some prized attribute of high-status members of this market, such as attractiveness to the opposite sex, is inextricably linked to consumption of this product. Using this process, the producer generates sales in the target audience. Sales are also made to people who envy and aspire to be like those who are part of the target market. Members of the target market essentially are presented with an idealized, supercharged image of themselves that they can consume through the purchase of a never-ending stream of products purported to be crucial to the lifestyle and values they represent. Consuming these articles not only feeds narcissism but also provides a means of gaining status.

One recent advertising phenomenon is the creation of opportunities to participate in real-life re-creations of ads. This phenomenon derives from a combination of presenting an image of an audience to itself and corporate sponsorship of various events, in this case sports. The Labatt company, for example, has sponsored something it calls "citizen races," a very American-sounding notion. In one version, for a small fee a skier can enrol at the top of a slalom run. He or she waits around for an hour or so consuming cold cuts and coffee, then runs the very easy slalom course, is timed, and is thus able to consume a "Labatt's Lite on Ice" (the phrase of the ad), or, in this case, Labatt's Lite in a snowbank. While the Labatt's Lite ads do not show these exact scenes, the ads with winter outdoor activities are aimed at

exactly the same target market as would be found on the ski slopes of Canada's ski resorts. This event brings the advertising, which purports to portray snippets of real life, full circle. Here real life mimics the advertising. Subsequent versions of this event seem to have dropped the word "citizen" and the food. However, special events are organized in such a manner to reflect current ads.

A different example of the same phenomenon has also occurred recently in a slightly different form. Again it involves beer. In the fall of 1984 Health and Welfare Canada issued an anti-drinking ad that showed a canoeist plying through peaceful waters clearly having an enjoyable workout. The canoeist is Olympic silver medal winner John Wood. The visuals draw the viewer into the picture by showing the canoeist in reflection in the water. The tone of the ad is that of a beer commercial. Then Wood says, "I like the taste of a cold beer on a hot day, but I certainly don't think you have to get the gang together with a couple of cases of beer just to celebrate the fact you've had a bit of exercise." The significance of this ad is that it addresses the ads of the beer companies as much as the drinking habits of the target audience. In addressing the drinking habits of the target audience it does so through the market research of the breweries and their discovery of that form of drinking as a valued activity of the target audience. (The background briefing materials obtained from Health and Welfare are extemely interesting. They show equal concern with the drinking habits of young people and the beer ads they see on TV; see Appendix A to this chapter.) The poster version of the ad, much less stunning in its effect, is shown here.

Yet another interesting aspect of ads, specifically beer ads, is the relation of the product to the ad. As Labatt's marketing vice-president,

Poster of canoist John Wood for Health and Welfare Canada's Dialogue on Drinking. *Courtesy Health and Welfare Canada.*

Bruce McCuaig, has pointed out (Grady, 1983), the defining attributes of the product are not distinctive and memorable attributes of the product itself, in this case, its taste. Thus, an emphasis on taste would risk alienating a significant sector of the market since there is no controlling people's taste. What is more predictable is their valued image of themselves. Product attributes that do not change the product's taste but rather change its image can then be manipulated to appeal to the target audience. For Budweiser beer the beechwood chips, though they are ostensibly elements of the brewing process that give the beer a distinctive taste, are in fact an element that appeals to the target audience's image of an ideal characteristic of the product they consume. In fact, they have no effect on the flavour.

A final note on beer: it should be apparent to any observer of the media that beer companies spend a significant amount more on their advertising campaigns than do manufacturers of other products. This, too, does not escape the notice of some consumers, nor does the surcharge aspect of advertising. These two factors have combined to create room for generic or no-name brands of beer. In objecting to consuming expensively produced images of themselves or others, certain consumers turn to non-advertised beer. But in so doing they do not avoid consuming images. Rather they consume a different and cheaper image, one that avoids advertising.

Three other types of advertising are significant. The first includes advertisements for a company rather than its products. This type is usually called a **corporate image ad**. It promotes an image of the corporation rather than a particular product or product line. In some cases, such as Gulf Canada's ads, the interests and responsible nature of the company are put forward explicitly within a Canadian context. Gulf Canada portrays itself as a company that wishes to be involved in the future of Canada's energy industry. It is interesting that a company using such an ad campaign should have been bought out by the national oil company, Petro-Canada. It is intriguing to speculate whether the corporate image was developed in anticipation of such a move.

A version of the corporate image ad is the **advocacy ad**. It can be found in the ads of United Technologies, a company that obtains a good number of contracts from the American military. Over the years it has placed ads in an American magazine, *The Atlantic*, in which UT takes a position on a variety of public and social issues ranging from the so-called governmental to the educational. As a piece of performance art, entitled *Reading Room: An Installation*, done by Bruce Barber of the Nova Scotia College of Art and Design points out, the position taken by United Technologies can be seen to be in the interests of the company, at the very least, insofar as the position taken will encourage further expansion of corporations such as United Technologies.

Finally there is the **advertorial**. This is descriptive material on, for example, the contribution of the Port of Halifax to the Maritime economy, which is prepared for print publications, apparently written by a journalist, but in fact written by an employee or agent of the company or agency that is the subject of the article. In an article on the subject Michael Enright (1984) claims that readers are confused by advertorials because they do not know whether to read them as independent commentary or as ads.

The majority of readers, however, are unlikely to be confused by the advertorial. If they are attuned to the difference in content between normal journalistic pieces and advertorials they will probably be astute enough to

An example of a corporation "advocacy" ad. *Courtesy United Technologies.*

understand how the piece came to be written as it is. Even if they are not, in every medium the relationship between what is written or produced in an advertisement is closely allied with the perspective of the advertiser. No advertiser is going to support a publication or program with content that is the adverse to the kind of values of possible advertisers. The delivery of large audiences who are alienated from advertised products is hardly going to gain the support of the advertiser.

THE NEWSPAPER NEWS STORY

The basic textbooks for print journalists inform us that the news story must have two qualities. It must be *informative* and *interesting*. To accomplish both of these goals, as we saw in the previous chapter, news stories are generally written according to a particular structure called the **inverted pyramid**. This means simply that a summary of the "important information" is put at the beginning followed by the development of the story and the context in which it happened. By "important information" journalists mean the five "w's," one "h," and one "s-w." That is to say, the story leads off with *"who, what, when, where, why, how,"* and then *"so what."* In more ways than one, that is just the beginning.

Journalists build into their stories a variety of other characteristics to try to make them both informative and interesting. First is *human interest.* A story with human actors, especially actors of some public reputation, is considered to be much more interesting than one that discusses policies or abstract ideas. A portrayal of Sylvia Ostry (former chair of the Economic Council of Canada) and Senator Michael Pitfield (former Clerk of the Privy Council) battling it out over the issue of free trade with the U.S. is much more interesting than a story listing the purported advantages and disadvantages of such a policy.

A second characteristic is *selectivity.* Information is important but only if it is relevant. No matter how hard-earned the information is, if, in the end, it turns out to be irrelevant, it must be taken out of the story.

A third characteristic is *clarity.* The language must be simple and straightforward. Clarity is achieved by the avoidance of clichés, jargon, and excessively complex phraseology, more often called gobbledygook. In addition, the writing must make specific reference to people, events, and places.

Journalistic writing must also be *concise.* Neither unnecessary words nor redundancies should appear. Conciseness is also achieved through the use of the active voice: not "It was stated by the Prime Minister ..." but "The Prime Minister stated ..." Pace and tone are crucial. Ideas must be introduced at a pace the reader can understand. The tone of the story must reflect both subject matter and treatment of the material.

Finally, *leads* are important to stories. Most often they are direct, sometimes giving the five "w's" in the first sentence. They must also serve to capture the readers' attention and orient them to the story. Delayed leads come in the second paragraph or sentence and exploit the curiosity of the reader established by an introductory delay.

Several points should be noted about the structure of a news story. The first is that, together with the headline, it allows the reader to get an idea of the news in a relatively quick fashion. With all the "important information" up front, readers can get a quick overview of the day's happenings. Given that they have some context of their own to bring to those events, they can choose to proceed through a story to its development of context and even analysis only if they so choose.

Tabloid versus Broadsheet Treatment

This story structure, as we noted earlier, has allowed the development of what are called tabloids, papers like those in the growing *Sun* chain, now in Toronto, Calgary, and Edmonton, and, to some extent, the *Vancouver Province.* In French Canada the papers owned by Pierre Peladeau (who also owns the *Winnipeg Sun*) are the equivalent. They gain their name from the half-sized format of the pages, which makes them easy to read en route to work by public transport. But the characteristics of the writing in these newspapers are the cause for the disdain usually associated with the name "tabloid."

Besides fluff, that is, pictures of pretty girls and, increasingly, handsome men, and low-level boosterism of their actual and potential advertisers, not much is to be found in any

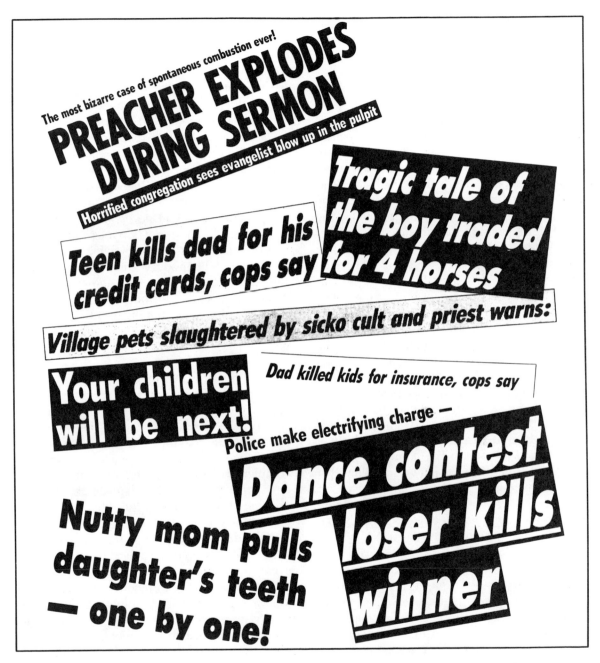

The most bizarre case of spontaneous combustion ever!

PREACHER EXPLODES DURING SERMON

Horrified congregation sees evangelist blow up in the pulpit

Teen kills dad for his credit cards, cops say

Tragic tale of the boy traded for 4 horses

Village pets slaughtered by sicko cult and priest warns:

Your children will be next!

Dad killed kids for insurance, cops say

Police make electrifying charge —

Dance contest loser kills winner

Nutty mom pulls daughter's teeth — one by one!

A collage of weekly tabloid headlines. The degree of sensationalism, which is greater than in the dailies, is readily apparent.

story besides the headline and a very quick relating of the five "w's." The format discourages lengthy analysis and detail, and little context is provided. Instead, events are over-dramatized and are interpreted as signals that things are either in control or, more often, out of control. As the accompanying collage of headlines illustrates, the unusual, unexplainable, and bizarre are often used as contexts, without analysis to make the events reported understandable both in their occurrence and with regard to measures that will be taken to control future similar happenings. The world is presented in the tabloids as somewhat out of control and quite violent. One never knows when such elements are going to invade one's own life. Consequently, the political bias of the tabloids is often right of centre and less liberal than that of the broadsheet papers.

The inverted pyramid and the medium of print mean that the journalist must tell the story, even if he or she uses liberal doses of quotations. This places the journalist and indeed the paper in a particular position in the mind of the reader. The angle taken on stories, what is brought forward and emphasized, is taken to be the perspective of the individual reporter and the paper. The discussion of context and the provision of analysis develops that implicit position taken in the opening of the story. To assume that the angle taken on a story necessarily represents the view of the reporter, the editor, or the owner of the paper is, to a degree, the old problem of blaming the messenger, a problem around which neither journalist nor reader can steer. The reporter and editor are seen to be intervenors in the construction of the news even if they might not want to be. It is they who must tell the story. And while historically the press is much less partisan than it has been in the past, the medium itself prevents the press from removing itself from this role as intervenor, interpreter, or mediator.

Events versus Issues

One further point, already mentioned in passing, must be emphasized. With the five "w's" up front, and with the constant emphasis on human interest and so on, what the news brings us is events rather than issues. As any public interest group (especially Greenpeace) knows, any amount of informed analysis about a particular issue will never bring it onto the front pages. But an event, whether putting up a tent on Parliament Hill or blowing up a hydro substation, will produce saturation coverage. Prior provision of information and analysis to a columnist is a good method of getting some of the issues discussed. But the event itself moves the issues to front and centre in the public agenda.

THE TELEVISION NEWS STORY

The most obvious difference between the newspaper news story and the television news story is the presence of visuals. These visuals are not merely moving pictures that complement a text written up much like a newspaper text and then spoken by an announcer. The visuals structure the story and a text is built around those visuals.

The nature of the video camera is that while it is extremely intrusive for the actors of an event, it is quite invisible to the viewer. It claims by its ability to record sound and picture a veracity that no other medium can match. It apparently cannot lie. In its ability to record an event, barring intentional distortion, it brings the news to us from the mouths of the participants. What we see are snippets of the actual happenings, together with interpretations by on-the-spot observers and participants.

The trick for television news producers is to edit the material in such a way that the edits also appear unobtrusive. The visual coverage of the event must be simple enough to orient the viewer, but it must not appear incomplete. The sentences and phrases that are recorded and subsequently used in the final piece must be succinct and directly relevant. The speakers' identities must be obvious and they must have an obvious validity as observers or participants.

A British Columbia television station once did a man-on-the-street interview of how Canadians felt about Pierre Trudeau's winter holidays. He was taking a few days on the beach in the South Pacific on his way to or from a diplomatic visit to the Orient. The street the news producers chose was the one on which was located the local Employment Canada office. The time was mid-February, 1982 – a year and season of high unemployment. However, in this case the plan backfired. The exception made the rule visible. The primary impression the news story gave was not of outraged people but rather of the artificial situation the news producers had created. The obtrusiveness of the news-gathering process was all too obvious.

What is primary in the television news story is not the construction of the story by the reporter out of all the information he or she can glean. Rather, it is the directing of the news crew interviewer and interviewees to create the elements of a story that can then be pieced together as a snippet of life.

Thesis, Antithesis, Synthesis

What television news presents to us is something that appears to be very direct and obviously true. But more than that, the television news story takes on a structure. In one sense it consists of two or more inverted, and many times incomplete, pyramids. First there is the visual summary of the event. Simultaneously or subsequently, one person provides his or her summary. Following this is another perspective – in a dispute, the story from the other side of the fence. The interviewer then steps back and brings these and other perspectives together not to a resolution but more to a synthesis of the various positions or perspectives. In short, what is presented is **thesis, antithesis**, and **synthesis**, and all, often, in 90 seconds.

As with the newspaper news story, a number of attributes are crucial to high-quality TV reporting. To a large extent they are equivalent to preciseness, conciseness, human interest, clarity, pace, tone, and lead. But instead of these concepts being applicable only to the text, they are applicable to both text and visuals and the relations between the two in television.

The Camera versus the Reporter

The major difference between the newspaper news story and the television news story derives from the camera, the position in which the reporter or interviewer is placed as a result of the camera's ability to present facsimiles of real events. Instead of being in a position of messenger, the interviewer and his or her crew acts as a solicitor of information from others. In presenting that information and synthesizing it in the manner noted above, television news producers are apparently removed from a primary role of interpretation. They merely provide the means whereby the story and the participants can tell what they have to tell. In synthesizing the news, producers are apparently uninvolved. They merely manage the news by placing it in an understandable format. All this is a result of the dominance of the visual element. The camera never lies, or so we are led to believe.

The Study of News

In our discussion of advertising, specifically the CP Air ads, we presented the beginnings of a semiotic analysis. A content analysis of advertising would rarely be done on a single ad or ad series but would, more often, be used with many different ads to determine the frequency of use of certain categories of images, objects, types of persons, events, and so on.

The study of news does not differ a great deal from the study of advertising. Content analyses are often performed not on the individual stories themselves but on news programs. The tables included in Chapter 10 present the data of a content analysis a group of us did on CBC national radio news from January to June, 1982. Many other content analyses of news exist (Berelson, 1972). The conclusions of such studies mostly have to do with the manner in which news is organized and what picture of the world is thereby presented to the reader, listener, or viewer. The discussion can then proceed to considering the implications of such a news structure.

Semiotic analyses of news can examine anything from a set of news programs to an individual news item, story, photograph, or visual. This type of analysis concentrates on the positioning of the various elements in the piece or the totality of pieces being considered. It works toward an articulation of the internal relations among those elements. For example, semiotic-type studies have drawn attention to the fact that labour is usually associated with on-the-street events such as strikes and the recurring disorder, while management is often used to provide analysis in the context of the controlled, peaceful, quiet environment of a plush executive office. The implications of this way of using sources is that, even in a lockout, labour is shown as the instigator of the stoppage and management the patient victim. Semiological studies thus tend to show the signification process of newsmaking: what is deemed to be important and how it is placed within a meaning system. What is the nature of the news story? How does it reproduce the dominant ideology?

There are, of course, other studies of news, the most obvious being those dealing with what gets included in the news and what does not. While content analyses can enter into these studies as a first level sorting out of what is and is not there, these studies then tend to turn away from content and toward the process of newsgathering and the influence of professional ideals and the goals of owners (see Gans, 1979; Tuchman, 1978). These issues will be taken up in Chapter 6.

SOAPS

Radio soap operas were originally developed by an ad agency for its soap company client. They were designed to socialize a home-confined female audience with disposable income into the art of consuming. In a sense, soaps represented the life of the fictitious satisfied consumer whose worldly needs were entirely taken care of by the various products she had purchased for her family. These needs satisfied, she could then turn her mind to dreaming of a richer, more fulfilling life found in the gothic and romance novels of the thirties. However, pure fantasy was not the only powerful opiate. Not long after the soaps had established themselves a kind of realistic fantasy was developed featuring professionals whose lives were made of the stuff of fiction.

So was developed an *illusion of reality* that has carried through to the present day. Our discussion of the soaps will take us through this illusion into the dominant themes of present-day soaps and then into the grammar of the medium, the devices used to achieve the realistic illusion.

Soap Culture

Perhaps the most salient characteristic of the soaps is that, in contrast to movies, novels, or night-time television, there is no obvious dramatic patterning. There is neither a beginning nor a foreseeable end. This allows for the presentation of a set of characters in continuous narrative, a narrative that follows the seasons of the year and even the various festivities of mainstream Euro-North American culture. At times, world events can enter into the dialogue. Certain issues of the time definitely do. To prevent awkward particularities from discouraging a complete identification with the characters by the viewer, generic settings, usually inside rather than outside, predominate.

The characters in a soap become like neighbours who drop by on a daily basis. What distinguishes them as visitors is they each have the power and, seemingly, the need to confide their intimate secrets and feelings to the audience without the knowledge of the other soap characters. The lives of these characters are therefore separate but continuous with the lives of the viewers. Like the lives of the viewers there is no final climax to the play but rather a series of mini-climaxes in the ongoing action. There are occasions for the utmost joy as well as jealousy, envy, frustration, greed, and so forth.

The vehicle that allows for this continuity is the family. Without the family as the centre of every soap all of the connivance, backbiting, jealousy, vengefulness, and so forth would be unbelievable. For only in the family is any individual burdened and blessed with permanent associations with other human beings. In any other social group we have the opportunity to exit, to change our circumstances, to leave behind individuals with whom we are not compatible. The family is the vehicle for continuity; but it is also the vehicle for a concentration on character, the realm of the personal and the situational psychology that emanates from it.

By putting forward the family as the central focus, the illusion of reality can be maintained with scarcely a nod in the direction of the social, economic, and political environments. In the family such realms of human striving and existence are more or less held equal. Internal family relations can, for the most part, be presented as if they were not determined or even affected by class economics and politics. Everyone is middle-class, or *nouveau riche*, or dandified middle-class. So the soaps can dwell on the personal without seeming to leave important levels of human existence out of the picture.

The Soap Vehicle

While the family is the vehicle for character continuity and a situational and character psychology, family dynamics in the sense of parent-parent, parent-child, and sibling relations are not the primary thematic content. The primary dramatic content derives from individual character relations with both family and the world. To use *Dallas* as an example, how does a greedy person like J.R. Ewing survive day-to-day life? What are the various schemes a conniving person with a lot of money, such as Pam's sister, Katherine Barnes, might invent? What are the dynamics of women in business life? Here the soaps rely on male and female stereotypes for their character and plot outlines. Women are to be found in roles of power but they are there through the efforts of some man, usually their fathers. Women who have gained position on their own merits are seen to be possessed with the curse of ambition or greed. They do not derive position from positive traits such as determination or talent.

Against a family backdrop, personal and gender politics provide primary thematic material. In both cases emancipation from a basic identity given a character, whether that of personality or gender, is forever solicited but infinitely postponed. The case is the same with body type, especially for women. Fat, thin, short, tall all contribute in a major way to the place of the character in the drama. Fat women are losers, as are women who are too short.

Nor are the themes constrained entirely by the identity of the target audience. While the target audience still remains homemakers, young love has become wildly successful as thematic material. The decision point for entry into family life (young love confirmed) could hardly be considered to be a boring subject. Its perpetual interest is confirmed by the success of Harlequin novels. Similarly, social relevancy has come to be exploited by the soaps. Prejudice, drug addiction, sexual repression, abortion, venereal disease, and so on all claim their hour upon the stage. The soaps gain a certain notoriety from airing these issues (while never contributing seriously to the debate). But their popularity is hardly surprising when one thinks that the lives of most adults are touched twice by these potentially life-determining issues: once when the adult is in adolescence and a second time as her or his children come to adolescence.

The illusion of reality and the ability to ex-ploit these themes would not be possible without a cinematic code appropriate to the genre. That cinematic code is characterized by a number of techniques. Primary is the long, peering, extreme close-up, a framing technique that allows the viewer to search the face of the actor for its expression of emotion. This technique also encourages feelings of intimacy. It contrasts to the more medium-distant shots of the news camera designed to exude authority.

The long, peering shot is enhanced by being taken from eye level. The viewer becomes the eye of the camera, intimately involved and yet quite separated and unaffected by events. Similarly, the slow pace of the drama allows the viewer time to read in a depth of emotion and thus encourages the prediction of events and interpretation of reactions.

MUSIC VIDEOS

In a fashion similar to the soap, music videos and particularly rock videos have emerged from the demands of producers to socialize an audience into an increased purchasing of their product. The difference between the soaps and music videos is that the product to be purchased is part of the promotional vehicle used to bring it to the attention of the audience. Music videos are visually enhanced versions of the records the audience is intended to purchase.

The sudden explosion of rock videos and rock video television shows is not accounted for by the fact that these manage to express something that no other medium has done quite as well. Rather, rock videos make cheap television, just as playing records makes cheap radio. As of 1987 rock videos were distributed freely to organizations that could assemble audiences, whether in pubs or through television. Suddenly, costs of a half-hour original television show dropped from $2,000-$2,500 a minute to approximately the same amount for a half hour. The beauty of the beasts was that they assembled quite sizable audiences whose attention could then be sold to advertisers.

Roots of Rock Video

As with each of the media forms discussed in this chapter, rock videos have evolved from other forms in the media. The movie featuring a rock star, for example, the Elvis Presley movies, the iconoclastic movies of Richard Lester that featured the Beatles, and filmed recordings or concerts were the precursors of the rock video. Rock videos themselves were around the industry for several years before they exploded into television (Laba and Lorimer, 1986).

Characteristics of the Form

In contrast to the soaps, rock videos are as fast-paced as any movie or television ad. They feature jump cuts, crazy juxtapositions, and an intense bombardment of images somewhat inspired by the song's rhythm and lyrics but certainly not constrained by its literal meaning. They appear to take their inspiration from the "visual effects" of movies, providing, again in contrast to the soaps, surrealistic illusion rather than realistic illusion. Their sets are often reminiscent of non-representational sculpture and appear to represent reductions of modern living to an anticipated future devolved of a clear reflection of human values and detail. They serve also to partition the rock market through easy visual identification of heavy metal, pretty-boy rock, new wave, punk, etc. Insofar as they take their leads from visual effects (which require more money than imagination), they allow the purchase of market

dominance, e.g., Michael Jackson's *Thriller*, at $14 million. They also facilitate the purchase of market presence or prominence (e.g., the direction of Sam Peckinpah and the audio production of Phil Ramone for Julian Lennon's copy of his father's style in *Valotte*).

Predominantly, rock videos are a means for a rather straightforward voyeurism of rock fans. The focus of the video is the group itself, primarily the lead singer acting as chief protagonist. The ZZTop videos are an exception, for they picture the trio as a Greek chorus, as bemused observers, or perhaps even as behind-the-scenes manipulators. The nature of the vision dominant in rock videos can best be contrasted to the literary, filmic, and choreographically based imagination apparent in Leonard Cohen's award-winning production, *I am a Hotel* (see Lorimer, 1988). There, while ample use is made of visual effects, the effects almost continually mean something in the ongoing narrative. In fact, rock videos only occasionally represent the narrative form at all.

As with other communication forms, patterns of content can be seen in current rock videos. Bondage, especially of women, and restriction of all kinds are predominant. Violence, disembodiment, chaos, explosions, destruction are also frequent. Chase scenes, or their visual metaphorical equivalent, are often used. The fragmentation and fetishization of the female body are matched by the aggressive phallic display of the male guitar players. These dominant themes serve to accentuate any different vision, such as the subtle statements of *I am a Hotel*.

It is interesting to speculate about the meaning and future of rock videos. While their sudden success is attributable to the economics of entertainment on television and in pubs, they are obviously not boring to their audience. The point to be made is that their key role in marketing, as with any promotional form, cannot help but influence the form itself.

Rock videos are similar in their structure to such movies as *Flashdance*. If we are to take seriously the words of Tom Hedley, the creator of the concept for *Flashdance*, the notion behind *Flashdance* was visual rather than narrative. Hedley sees 17- and 18-year-olds as involved in the creation of an interior musical they act out, thereby creating the style they use to live their lives. He claims that such people take their inspiration from fashion photographs and magazine illustrations. They invest in such idealizations with an individual interpretation and a dynamism (ridding the pictures of their frozenness in time) built on popular music. The personal style that results from this process is the basis for a performance, which is a style of living and hence an expression of self. It is rooted in the presentational forms basic to opera and poetry rather than narrative prose.

SUMMARY

The nature of representation or, as the semioticians would have it, signification is that it constructs meaning which refers to aspects of the real world and expresses that meaning within symbol systems such as language. It is a realm not subordinate to that of physical objects. Its study involves the study of indeterminate systems. The study of communication is thus closely aligned with interpretation, an activity more familiar to the humanities than to science or social science.

Two major methods used to study content are semiotics and content analysis. Both are oriented to the structure of content; the former is a fully developed theory, the latter a technique. The insights of semiotics lead to an understanding of the relations between a particular piece and the broader perspectives on and theories of society from which it is derived. Content analysis allows us to see repetitive patterns that suggest underlying organizing assumptions built into the material.

While semiotics and content analysis provide insight into the meaning system of any individual piece of communication in any medium, the medium within which meaning is expressed is also a determining factor in how meaning is constructed or how information is designed. Advertising emphasizes the complementarity of images. Newspaper news stories build on the standard inverted pyramid. Television news stories are organized primarily by the intrusion of the camera as opposed to the reporter. Soap operas have developed their own set of visual techniques to present an intimate, universal world. And rock videos bombard the viewer with technological gimmicks, bringing him or her back continually to the TV set and to the record store for a new hit.

APPENDIX A:
DIALOGUE ON DRINKING*

The Problem

Canadian consumption of alcohol has doubled since 1950. In Canada the annual bill for health costs and property damage directly related to excessive drinking is staggering. Fifty million dollars goes toward intensive alcohol treatment. And every year hundreds of millions of dollars are poured into paying for alcohol-related accidents.

---

*Background briefing materials from the federal Ministry of Health and Welfare, produced to accompany a government media campaign to combat overdrinking. They have been edited slightly for inclusion in this book. Reproduced with permission of Health and Welfare Canada.

Today's youth is especially vulnerable. As adolescents make the difficult transition from childhood to adulthood, they are struggling to define their own identities. As they move farther into adulthood, they face a wave of new challenges: the pressures of maturing relationships, the responsibilities of marriage and family life, and fresh uncertainties about career goals in a period of economic insecurity.

They may respond to these pressures in a variety of ways. Drinking is one. According to a May, 1982, youth Gallup Poll, the average age given for trying alcohol is twelve. Sixty per cent of the young people polled stated that alcohol consumption "can make you feel part of the group." Sixty-five per cent said that it "can make you feel less shy," and 40 per cent noted that it "can help you if you are nervous." In other words, drinking is seen as a way of easing personal stress, especially on the social scene.

Recent research studies conducted by Health and Welfare are very revealing:

- The sharpest increase in (alcohol) usage occurs between the lower and upper teens for both males and females.
- Heavy drinking among teenagers tends to involve high levels of binge drinking.
- In 1981, 169,000 persons of all ages were charged with alcohol-related traffic offences, including criminal negligence, dangerous driving, and driving while impaired. Over 40 per cent of alcohol-related traffic offences occurred among persons aged 15 to 29 years of age.

Background Research

Three major research tools were used to develop this campaign. The findings included the following:

- Young people, interviewed in Vancouver, Winnipeg, Toronto, Montreal, and Halifax, believe most moderation campaigns have been directed to older people.
- Awareness measurements of the phase one of Dialogue indicate that although the target group was 25- to 49-year-olds, 15- to 25-year-olds manifest the highest awareness.
- A Gallup youth survey, conducted in May, 1982, established that young people feel that alcohol use, like cannabis, is influenced by peer pressure.

New Program: Description

Against this background, development of the next phase of Dialogue has been undertaken. The intent is to build on the success of the media campaign and strengthen the community action strategy by:

- Focusing on *high-risk groups* and the issues associated with drinking.
- Using *advertising and promotion to give a national profile*, which will express federal government concern about hazardous alcohol use and provide an umbrella for community activity.
- Ensuring *follow-through at the community level* by working with provincial and territorial drug agencies to develop guidelines and resources to assist groups to initiate awareness and education and projects.

Objectives

To achieve a social consensus increasingly supportive of the safe consumption of alcohol.

- To stimulate self-examination of drinking behaviours in people aged 15 to 29.
- To stimulate collective examination of issues related to moderate and high-risk drinkers aged 15 to 29.

Target Group

- Males – 20 to 29 – predominantly, blue-collar workers and students.
- Females – 15 to 29 – white-collar workers and students.

Creative Strategy

Phase two of Dialogue plans to counter the beverage industry's lifestyle advertising with credible, modern messages about moderation. It should be noted that it is estimated that the beer, wine, and spirits industries spend over $100 million annually in Canada on advertising and promotion. It is vital, in order to effectively reach the target audience, to depart from the traditional and historical aspects inherent to the promotion of moderation. Therefore, a new term is proposed to describe alcohol abuse – *overdrinking*.

Since previous Dialogue ads have asked Canadians to think about it and talk about it, phase two of Dialogue will suggest the next logical step is to *take action on overdrinking*. This is in step with Canadians' growing concern on alcohol issues such as drinking and driving.

The individuals tied to this campaign will have the effect of creating, by the end of the five-year program, a new crowd of *real people who actively endorse moderation*. The people who will be selected to speak, in their own words, about moderation, will either be amateur sports champions or ordinary Canadian workers, all of the same age groups as the target audience. The visuals of these commercials will be based on the dynamics of action.

Media Strategy: Execution

Television is planned as the main vehicle of this campaign, with campaign support provided by transit/shelter and mall posters, and limited print advertising.

Purchase

Since beer advertisers concentrate their media purchases on sport properties and direct their commercials to 18- 29-year-olds, to stretch the visibility of the campaign spots on sport programs, such as baseball and football, would be purchased. The strategy is that one Dialogue ad placed with three or four beer commercials will receive more attention. The campaign would be on-air in the summer, when Canadian consumption of alcohol is at its greatest, and during the fall, when the festive season begins.

DIALOGUE ON DRINKING CREATIVE RATIONALE: ANOTHER FIVE YEARS

The advertising segment of the Dialogue II program has a difficult mandate to fulfil. It must create positive awareness for Dialogue on strict advertising terms. And it must tie in nicely with existing Dialogue materials. It should be able to fit into any specific community's ongoing alcohol abuse programs, and indeed, be complementary to it. Dialogue II must offer something more, an extension of the existing Dialogue premise; the TALK ABOUT IT: THINK ABOUT IT theme. Additionally, Dialogue II must be flexible enough to be meaningful in all regions of Canada. It should be seen to have been conceived and executed in any community. It must be broad enough in scope and potential to allow its continuity to build over a five-year period.

At the same time, and perhaps most difficult, the advertising segment must appeal across the age groups between 15 and 29 years, through the most turbulent and trying years of human development. These are just the specific program requirements.

The actual advertising of moderation in alcohol use is in itself not easy. The overdrinker is notoriously unaware of his or her habit's impingement upon performance, judgement, and the feelings of others. Teens, moving up from the smoky illegality of pot, may find alcohol a welcome legal high, endorsed weekly by parents, sipped at church, grand benefactor of baseball, hockey, and football, a high reinforced by handsome men and women after the slightest bout with sweat in TV commercials.

It's okay to drink.

It's the popular thing to do.

And alcohol has a great benefit over its running mate, tobacco. It makes you feel good.

It's fun.

It lets you forget.

Almost all present beer advertising uses beer as a reward for doing something. Whether it's "Jim and the boys getting together to launch a cottage raft, then sinking a couple of cases of Molson's" or "This Bud's for you, for all you do" or "Here's to playing hard and drinking easy," the theme of much beer advertising is that almost any activity is an excuse to party. And the set-up is not to have just one or two beers; the implication is that the beer at the end of the day is a celebration. Current beer advertising promotes the idea that if you walk, swim, crawl, or dance more than 10 feet, you deserve a beer in celebration.

The market target the breweries pitch their reward *advertising* to is similar to the one we are interested in, about 18- to 29-year-olds. Because of the high profile beer advertising receives on television, and because beer commercials appear in much sports continuity (baseball, hockey), the young end of the market scale, 18- to 29-year-olds, is particularly affected.

We believe we have an opportunity to take advantage of some of the weakness in logic of the breweries' reward appeal, to give impact and awareness to our new Dialogue II moderation campaign. As stated earlier, we have a tough job, but if we see it as *making it all right to be moderate in drinking habits*, and if we can give *visible proof* that moderation is practised by many people, especially people who are admirable, then we can make a positive statement for moderation.

But beer advertising, while capable of reinforcing a trend to partying, is not responsible for immoderate behaviour. And our advertising of moderation must try to address more basic issues of insecurity, boredom, peer pressure, etc.

Our main advertising medium should be television, with support in posters and print advertising which can be used in specific communities. Television reaches more of our market target for less than any other and does it on the same turf used by the breweries. Television imparts glamour and the aura of excitement to a message and our moderation story can take advantage of this intrinsic television benefit.

An effective television campaign must make sense when applied to specific programs in different areas of the country. If a community group has a project to help reduce drunken driving then our general advertising should be able to fit into the program, and to help give it impetus and credibility.

Flexibility is the key.

But the problem with many flexible advertising themes is that they tend to be *bland* in nature, and therefore lacking in potency and memorability. So, our strategy would include a *vehicle* capable of carrying specific theme messages in a memorable way, while offering continuity which will build awareness and stature.

This vehicle should be able to operate for at least five years and be capable of being renewed, without significant wear-out. And it must be relatively inexpensive.

The television campaign must also be capable of translation into various print components, which can be applied to specific community projects. While the look may change to take advantage of the medium, the tonality should remain constant.

Our idea for a freshly defined and sustaining advertising campaign for Dialogue involves the dynamics of *action*. The program, to date, has created awareness of drinking problems, at least of the importance of bringing them out into the open, of talk being the beginning of understanding and remedy.

Now we feel we *need action*.

We need to translate the positive thoughts of moderation grown over the past years into action. We want people to think they can actually do something to control *overdrinking*.

A simple theme which will fit nicely with the existing Dialogue theme apparatus is: TAKE ACTION ON OVERDRINKING. The word "overdrinking" tacitly states that moderate drinking is okay. It places the problem and the danger together in one word. It has connotations with overeating, etc., and it effectively removes us from the WCTU and tee-totaller image.

"Overdrinking" is a useful word when selling moderation.

It defines a state of excess without resorting to a tangle of ounces or glasses or bottles per kilo of body weight.

It is easily understood by everyone, as is overeating, overworking, overtraining. It is something of which you have done too much.

It lets us stay away from numbers while getting our point across.

REFERENCES

Altheide, D., and R. Snow. *Media Logic*. Beverly Hills: Sage Publications, 1979.

Barthes, Roland. *Elements of Semiology*. A. Lavers and C. Smith, trans. New York: Hill and Wang, 1968.

Barthes, Roland. *S/Z*. Paris: Seuil, 1970.

Bennett, Tony. "Media, 'Reality,' Signification," in Gurevitch *et al.*, eds., *Culture, Society and the Media*. Toronto: Methuen, 1982.

Berelson, Bernard. *Content Analysis in Communication Research*. New York: Hafner, 1972.

Eco, Umberto. *The Name of the Rose*. New York: Warner Books, 1984.

Eco, Umberto. *Travels in Hyperreality*. Orlando, Fla.: Harcourt Brace Jovanovich, 1986.

Frye, N. *The Critical Path: An Essay on the Social Context of Literary Criticism*. Bloomington: Indiana University Press, 1971.

Gans, Herbert. *Deciding What's News: A Study of CBS Evening News, NBC Nightly News, Newsweek, and Time*. New York: Pantheon Books, 1979.

Grady, Wayne. "The Budweiser Gamble," *Saturday Night* (February, 1983), pp. 28-30.

Hackett, R.A. "KAL: the media exploited story," *Gateway*, Edmonton, October 25, 1983, p. 5. Reprinted as "Massacres and the media: the KAL story," *Canadian Dimension* (December, 1983), pp. 17–19.

Hackett, R.A. "Decline of a paradigm bias and objectivity in news media studies," *Critical Studies in Mass Communication*, 1, 3 (1984), pp. 229-59.

Hall, S., *et al. Policing the Crisis: Mugging, the State and Law and Order*. London: Macmillan, 1978.

Heydon, Elizabeth. "The Land of the Soaps," unpublished paper, Simon Fraser University, 1984.

Laba, M., and R. Lorimer, prods. *Video, Vinyl and Culture* (30 min. video), Part 3 of Mass Communication in Canada. Burnaby: Simon Fraser University, 1986. Distributor: Magic Lantern, Oakville, Ontario.

Lorimer, R. "Canada in an expanding, industrialized communications environment," in R. Lorimer and D.C. Wilson, eds., *Communications Canada.* Forthcoming, 1988.

Olive, D. "Ads vs. editorials: have new lines been drawn," *Quill and Quire* (September, 1984), pp. 71-73.

Orwell, G. *Homage to Catalonia.* Harmondsworth: Penguin, 1974.

Pollack, D. "Mister Flashdance," *Saturday Night* (October, 1984).

Tuchman, Gaye. *Making News: a Study in the Construction of Reality.* New York: Free Press, 1987.

Woollacott, J. "Messages and Meanings," in Gurevitch *et al.,* eds., *Culture, Society and the Media.*

STUDY QUESTIONS

1. Semiotics is a basic technique of research and a basic point of view that every student of communications should understand. Provide examples of sign, signifier, and signified in the print medium, in painting, and in the movies. Specify the dyadic relations for each example.

2. Content analysis is another basic technique. Perform a content analysis of an individual article, then of an entire magazine. In the case of the magazine you might leave it at setting up the analytic categories. If you carry the example through, you may be surprised at the results.

3. The power of an ad, a newspaper story, a rock video, a television drama, or even a newsmagazine derives partly from the uniqueness of each and partly from characteristics in common. Discuss, using examples.

4. In the CBC documentary *The Press and the Prime Minister,* gossip columnist Nigel Dempster refers to the storybook nature of newspaper content. One might say that the news content overlaps with that of soap operas. What advantages and disadvantages are there to that overlap?

5. Emphasis on design of information over content is extreme in ads. Discuss the image and the reality of CP Air's Royal Canadian Class (to the Orient) or Labatt's ad campaign for Budweiser.

6. One would think that a mass market would encourage a great variety of products. But in the example of beer, at least, all brands are fairly much the same in taste. Comment.

CHAPTER

5

The Media and the Audience

INTRODUCTION: THE LIMITATIONS OF EFFECTS ANALYSIS

IN MANY textbooks the topics discussed in this chapter are categorized as "effects." For example, the question of the effects of rock videos may be considered. Or, for example, what effect does the format of television news have on our views of the world, our political choices at the ballot box, or even our views of journalists? Similarly, are television soap operas a form of escape for people who are bored, and do they change the attitudes of their viewers, perhaps giving them unrealistic expectations that may lead to marriage problems, family problems, and, ultimately, social instability? All of the above are "effects" questions and, of course, many more could be asked.

This manner of conceiving the interaction between the audience and the media derives from early research into the media conducted primarily by American social psychologists, e.g., Katz and Lazarsfeld (1955) and Klapper (1960). The primary question that interested these psychologists was the *influence of the media*. They were working to dispel the formulations of a set of European social theorists known as the Frankfurt School. The claim of the Frankfurt School was that the media were destroying culture, in the sense of culture as that which knits a nation or people together, including the common assumptions, behaviour patterns, attitudes toward the world, and so on. These Europeans claimed also that the media were destroying folk culture, those traditions that were distinctive to the peasant and working classes of a nation or country (see, for example, Adorno and Horkheimer, 1972). The ideological assumption of the American psychologists who set out to counteract these notions was that the media were a marvellous democratic institution that brought all people into the mainstream of the culture. They set out to document the "effects" of exposure to the information and entertainment the media were able to bring into the homes and neighbourhoods of all Americans.

Conceiving of the link between the media and people as "effects" tends to narrow the scope of the kind of questions one might ask about media-audience interactions; also, it is difficult to point to the exact connections clearly and unambiguously. Formulations can be clear and unambiguous only in cases that are simple and not of great social import. Thus, while experiments certainly can be designed to test the memories of members of an audience for some particular statement made as part of a television presentation, unless that statement is trivial or very specific in its detail, similar or related messages would have been encountered elsewhere in the social environment. Because of the impossibility of controlling the prior exposure of audience members to the message in question, let alone what they have made of that exposure, it is therefore impossible to isolate the "effects" of the media

contribution to a wide selection of people's opinions or behaviour. Consequently, discussion of the "effects" of media on society becomes problematic.

MEDIA AND SOCIETY: AN INTERACTION OF MEANING-GENERATING SYSTEMS

Once we reconceive media-society interaction as a question of media content and audience behaviour, we move away from a limited, causal equation to a more open consideration of people and media messages and forms. In such a discussion we do not need to assume that the media program messages into people in the same manner that a computer is programmed. Nor do we need to try to make the case that, subject to the receptivity of individuals, the media can pour or program in certain messages. The point is to discuss and compare media content to audience behaviour without assuming a direct path that connects the two and makes the latter dependent on the former.

Determination versus Interaction

As meaning- and image-generating entities, both individuals and the media affect one another, but they do not determine one another. They do so because both generate meaning and each is an active part of the environment of the other. If one is not an active element in the environment of the other, then the relation does not hold. Once we accept such a relation we can discuss the interaction between audience behaviour and the information presented by the media. They can be compared with one another and analysed for their relation to broader forms of social behaviour and conceptions in society as a whole.

In general, both individuals and the media select elements from each other, re-stylize those elements, and display them for possible reappropriation by others. The dynamics of this system are the basis for Eco's posed dilemma over the alligator on the polo shirt at the end of Chapter 1. Stated differently, *lived reality and media reality interact with one another through a constant process of mutual selection, re-stylization (or appropriation), and re-display.* Built into this system as its motive force is human frailty, the felt necessity to construct and present an acceptable self to the world (Goffman, 1959). Or, as Berger (1972) puts it in emphasizing the media side of the equation, ads are designed to make us envy the models. Simultaneously, they provide a means whereby we can apparently achieve an equivalent status – by purchasing the product displayed.

John Lekich (1982) provides an illustration (but not an explanation like Berger's) of media-audience interaction. Basically, in an amusing and vivid manner, he illustrates by example the role television played in his childhood. He talks of his mother's attention to the set as a valued piece of furniture. He talks of his early wonder about how so many people came to be inside the set. He recreates the child's wonder and naive embrace of mother figures like June Allyson, the literal interpretation of Camay ads, and his persistent if not desperate attempt to touch the people behind the television screen.

Perhaps what makes his piece so interesting is the detail of his memory. These details evoke memories and the images come rolling back to anyone who grew up in the same era. The memories include not only the content of the programs but the entire family dynamic that the television programs created: what restrictions there were on viewing, how late one was allowed to stay up, parental differences in viewing habits and involvement in programs,

and so forth. In short, he gives us access to his memory of the world created for him by his television set. Whether his model was June Allyson, Van Johnson, Jimmy Stewart, Robert Young, or Donna Reed, they and the situations in which they were placed, including intervening commercials, provided the fabric of his dreams. As he says, based on the television world:

> My wife would be ideal. She would have no cavities, an embroidered hanky for each day of the week, and a hairdo with crash helmet durability. She would never do the upsetting things that mothers did, like making you eat creamed corn or sticking name tags on the inside of your underwear. At night we would walk up a long staircase to our separate beds, and read books across to each other. Just like Donna Reed.

The power of the article is that it makes the futility of calculating the percentage influence of television versus social interaction versus movies versus books quite apparent. It forces upon us a recognition of the extent to which the material presented on television can become fodder for a child's imagination. Lekich and the various producers of the television shows he watched can be seen as semi-autonomous, meaning-generating systems each in interaction with the other. Lekich was in interaction with the programming through viewing. It was in interaction with him through his willingness, along with millions of others, to tune in each week to these various shows and through the sponsors' interest in having access to him and his fellow audience members. The nature of this interaction is that neither is free from the influence of the other, yet neither is determined by the other.

However, there is certainly not a lack of interaction. The dynamics of the interaction from the media side are not entirely invisible. They are the ratings game and all that transpires in the creation and presentation of programs. It is a game played constantly by the networks as they assess the audience shares of each of their programs.

In "How *Quest*'s crew charted a suicide course," former managing editor Lynn Cunningham documents some aspects of audience-media interaction from the media side. As much as being killed by the owners, the staff led the magazine down a suicide road. *Quest* offered writers, photographers, layout artists, editors, and other creative people a chance to do their best work. The result was that the magazine appealed editorially as interesting, exciting, and unpredictable, but from the point of view of media buyers, the people who locate vehicles for advertisers to reach known audiences in a known frame of mind, it was denounced. As Cunningham says: "good journalism ... as media buyers are fond of pointing out, has little to do with good numbers."

THE INVASION OF THE IMAGINATION OF AN INDIVIDUAL

For the audience, their interaction with the media has a longer-term aspect to it and probably more profound implications. What does it mean to have an imagination filled with the characters, events, and settings of the media? Because Lekich has given us such an engaging self-report, let us continue with the example provided in his article. First we will propose some elements of the identity of a viewer such as John Lekich. In doing this we do not pretend to be exhaustive in defining all the characteristics that make up the identity of a person. We will stick to a social identity and ignore the psychological, economic, and partisan political identities. Also, it should be pointed out that, as with readings of media

materials, there can be as many readings of the identity of a person as there are people to do the readings.

For our purposes, let us propose three elements of a social identity for our fictitious viewer: he is young and male, Canadian, and of non-British stock. How might these elements interact with the content of the programs he watched as a child?

If what Lekich says might be considered to be typical, our viewer could easily have used the women he saw on television as the basis for idealized versions of two female roles, mother and partner. Rather humorously, Lekich points out how he made invidious comparisons between the television ideals and his own family. While this presentation of women the programs put forward was available to all viewers of both sexes, it has a particular significance to a growing boy. It provides a basis for a restricted view of women as home-based partners in a child-rearing enterprise or as ever-solicitous caretakers of one's every want and need. By implication (and at times explicitly) it puts forward a role model for the males as persons who can expect such solicitous behaviour from women.

A second element of our viewer's social identity is his nationality. In our discussion of soaps we noted how many of the shots were of interiors. We claimed that these interiors served the function of making the material "generic," as capable of happening everywhere but happening nowhere in particular. Generic material is not peculiar to soap operas. It is to be found in all mass-market materials from ads to school textbooks. But, rather than actually erasing all specifics, it tends to erase only up-front cultural particularities, the kinds of elements that communicate that the story is set in the U.S. or Canada, Montreal or Vancouver, the Prairies or the Maritimes. But generic material does not erase cultural assumptions. Nor does it erase the background cultural particularities that require that the story could only have happened in one particular culture or country.

Television's Pantheon of the 1950s

In the programs mentioned in Lekich's "Horizontal Hold," a great many cultural assumptions are intrinsic to the material:

* the authority of the father, father as breadwinner, mother as homemaker, all in *Father Knows Best*;
* woman as pretty if not beautiful seductress-servant in *I Dream of Jeannie*;
* the dream of being a millionaire in *The Millionaire*;
* the theatre of wrestling;
* the role of the lawyer for the defendant as opposed to the lawyer for the state in *Perry Mason*;
* the association of physical handicap with limited intellectual ability and the sexual and community politics of lawmen and madam in *Gunsmoke*.

The list could continue.

Hidden Culture

All these cultural assumptions are very much American assumptions. Some of them we share with the Americans as well as other nationals around the world. But some, such as being a millionaire as opposed to being well off in general, have a particular American flavour in the way they are presented. In *Gunsmoke* the background assumptions of relative lawlessness and in *Perry Mason* the presentation of the power of oratory in the courts (which links back to Daniel Webster) are both quite American in their manifestation. These background cultural particularities are not erased at all but are actually infused into the programs. Canadian frontier towns did not have sheriffs as lawmen, nor was lawlessness a character of the Canadian West. Madams and houses of prostitution were tolerated but there were few saloons filled with gun-toting patrons. Similarly, while oratory is not unknown to Canadian courts, there is no strong oratorical tradition with known historical figures. Nor is there a strong preference for the sanctity of the individual over the state or the community as *Perry Mason* would lead a viewer to sense.

In other words, while apparently generic, these mass media materials have built into them a host of cultural particularities of the producing culture. To an American audience they would appear to be culturally non-specific or generic. To any other audience they would appear as extrapolations or generalizations of the American world view onto events with no exact time, place, or culture. The further distant the viewer is from American culture, the more apparent will be the cultural roots or ethnocentrism of the material.

The third aspect of our viewer's social identity is his descent from non-British stock, as might be indicated by his last name. Consider the names of the actors and actresses and of the characters they play: Donna Reed, June Allyson, Jimmy Stewart, Loretta Young, Robert Young, Jane Wyatt, John Beresford Tipton, Mr. Anthony, the Andersons, the Nelsons, Perry Mason, Hamilton Berger, the Cartwrights, Mr. Dillon, Miss Kitty (not Pussy Galore), etc. All are British-derived, reflective of a melting-pot society whose only official language is English. Clearly, to be an acceptable member of society one must come from the right English stock.

Even a character meant to represent the fool, i.e., Chester, has a British name, which suggests a certain marginality. Similarly with Hamilton Berger, his Christian name, while casting back to the Declaration of Independence of the U.S., also connotes an excessive formality or a certain clumsiness that a monosyllabic or even disyllabic name lacks. The exceptions to this general rule are names with an element of the estoric built into them, such as Shelley Fabares, Van Johnson, or, for that matter, Paladin. In contrast, with characters such as Ethel Mertz we have a symbol of a dowdy, raspy-voiced woman whose name tells us that, amusing as she is, she can never fully participate in the American Dream. All of these can be seen as variations on an acceptable English theme.

The Extent of the Invasion

Does the above analysis mean that our viewer would see women only as wives or mothers, that as a Canadian he would feel cast out of the American Dream, and, as a person with a non-British last name, forever marginalized? The straight answer is no. Were he a meaning-generating individual working solely from the elements of his identity we have put forward, and if he saw only those aspects of the programs we have emphasized in this analysis, then one might expect our analysis to be the basis for the meaning-generation we have outlined. However, media programs and individuals are very complex entities rich in subtlety and attuned to a far greater range of meaning than any one book could ever identify. Our analysis cannot predict what our viewer would make out of his television childhood. But were we to know his opinions on all the matters we have discussed we could understand how these programs complemented or contradicted those opinions. Moreover, were someone to report on the overall attitudes of his generation to these matters we would again have some idea of how television programming might have strengthened or weakened such attitudes.

THE INVASION OF THE IMAGINATION OF A CULTURE

The prospect of a generation or indeed a nation being tuned into the same set of programs is not terribly unrealistic. While these days we have a greater variety of programs and channels to choose from than Lekich did in his childhood, Canadians are still inundated with American programs, perhaps even to a greater extent than before. Moreover, with financial and ideological pressure on the CBC, it would seem that every time a series of cutbacks is announced the likelihood of a significant level of Canadian program production in drama, the stuff of the imagination, becomes more distant.

What does it mean to have a whole nation tuned into the imagination of another? The general answer is parallel to what we described of the interaction between an individual and media programming.

Cultures as Meaning-Generating Systems

Cultures, like individuals and like media programs, are **meaning-generating systems**. They derive their identity from their history, their laws, various institutions that mediate interaction, governing structures, opportunities afforded by their cultural and physical geography, and so forth. They generate meaning through interacting on the basis of this identity in a particular style with the events of the day. How Canada responds to famine in other countries is derived from our wealth, our history, and our present-day attitudes. It creates meaning at a cultural level by exemplifying principles of action for both Canadians and others to see.

In the context of media and culture there are

at least two levels of interaction. On the one hand is the extent to which Canadians import cultural material. Related to this is the effort our public bodies spend to discourage other nations from pouring their cultural overflow into our country. For example:

- What ratio of foreign versus domestic information do we allow, through our regulatory body, the CRTC, to circulate freely?
- From another perspective, how much effort and money do both public and commercial media spend making opportunities available for the creation of Canadian cultural products?
- At a second level, how much and what kinds of foreign and domestic programming do individual Canadians choose to watch?
- When Canadians are given a choice do they watch Canadian programming?
- When Canadian performers are given access to the airwaves do Canadian audiences respond by buying their records?
- When political parties suggest making cuts to the CBC how do Canadians respond?

These are questions we cannot answer directly or in the space of a few paragraphs. In a sense they are addressed throughout this book, in describing the dynamics of Canada's communication system and environment, and in the nature of the analysis we provide of the various issues we bring forward. What the above understanding of media and culture does allow us to consider are some of the *mechanisms through which media and culture interact*. And as we saw in Chapter 1, the interaction is at least eight-dimensional.

Three case studies that examine the interaction of media and culture are to be found in Lorimer and Wilson (1988). In that volume Laba examines both sound recording and broadcasting in the context of continental market organization, centralized national production, and local and

regional cultures. McLarty's analysis contrasts to Laba's in her discussion of national televisual expression within the context of U.S. dominance in the industry. Valaskakis considers the influence of television on cultural integration in native communities in the Canadian North. She argues that while television's impact has been dramatic, native communities and individuals are now turning it to their own community and individual priorities and needs.

THE INTERPENETRATION OF MEDIA AND CULTURE: ENTERTAINMENT AND ADVERTISING

In the last chapter, in a discussion of beer commercials, we argued that the audience was sold an image of itself. Further, we claimed that the advertiser added the element of the presence of its product with high-status members of the target population and noted that at least one advertiser was sponsoring events in which members of the public were able to re-enact a commercial. In that series of ads and events is found an obvious interpenetration of media and culture. Advertisers identify valued behaviour of the target audience. They then portray it and adapt it to their needs to serve as a promotional vehicle for their products. They may even go so far as to establish audience behaviour (the slalom contest) that associates the product with recreational enjoyment.

The media interact with everyday life in a variety of other ways. Catchy tunes played countless times or repeatable phrases that float through one's head at the oddest times are not infrequent, nor are they intended to be. And they are not confined to ads. The media teach us how to kiss, how to smoke cigarettes (Humphrey Bogart had a style that was immortalized in his movies and even reappeared in a popular song in the phrase, "Don't Bogart that joint, my friend"), how to rob banks, how to dance. The list is endless. But the interaction is not a one-way process. The media take their content out of the lives of real individuals and groups. Everything, from the surfing movies to portrayals of the life and times of F. Scott Fitzgerald, emerges not from a vacuum but from real life.

The Case of *Annie Hall*

Perhaps the most vivid example of this sort of thing can be found in the relation between clothing fashions and movies. In 1977 a Woody Allen movie, *Annie Hall*, was released. In this movie the title character wore various versions of thrift-store derivative loose-fitting clothes (see photograph). These clothes were not the simple invention of the costume designer for the movie but rather expressed a growing trend for clothing like that worn by the hippies in the late sixties. * Following *Annie Hall* a great many women and clothing designers, who had heretofore spurned such clothing as unstylish, adopted clothing derived from the movie and its roots. For a while such clothing was even dubbed the *Annie Hall* look.

What makes *Annie Hall* such a good example is that the fashion of 1987 was still building on variations of what was introduced to the broad public in that movie. The point to take from this is not that *Annie Hall* transformed the designs of North American clothing, but rather that the fashion was brought out of a limited sector in society through *Annie Hall*. The

movie confirmed the fashion and placed it firmly in the mass market. In other words, the fashion of a subgroup of society penetrated the movie, which in turn transformed and propelled it into mass fashion.

Elvis Presley and Béla Bartók

The same phenomenon is observable in popular music. In the best-known case, Elvis Presley took southern black music and transformed it into something white teenagers would consume, largely by simply being white because mainstream white radio stations did not play recordings by blacks in this genre. That is not the sum total of what Presley did, but it was the basis of his fame. Lesser-known examples of the same thing come from any popular singer taking musical material from its folk origins, stylizing it, and offering it up for mass consumption, for example, Carl Perkins, Jerry Lee Lewis, and even Bob Dylan. The phenomenon is known equally in popular music and in classical music. Béla Bartók was a pioneer user of sound recordings to collect folk music, which he then used as the basis for his classical compositions. Anton Dvorak's *New World Symphony* transformed southern black music, as did Gershwin, into contemporary orchestral form. In Canada, James R. Wilson has used New Brunswick folk tunes for his classical pieces.

One point should be emphasized about this process of interpenetration. In picking up material from other sources the mass media transform it, whether it is clothes, music, or, as we will see in the next section, information. At a first level they stylize it for mass audiences, smoothing its edges and in general making it something distinctive – but not too much so, or else it would not have mass market appeal. They also transform it to suit the particular characteristics of the medium.

---

*The "costume designer" in this case was Ralph Lauren, a man who has shaped a whole career around making high-quality versions of classic designs from romantic periods of American history, first in clothing and later in furniture, soaps, towels, rugs, wallpaper, sheets, comforters, dishes, and so on.

Ralph Lauren's *Annie Hall* look in the Woody Allen film. *Canapress Photo Service.*

The movies, for example, require visual overstatement of a fashion style for that style to be noticed. In being picked back up in the world of mass fashions, that overstatement does not disappear. This process thus tends to encourage extremes. Consequently, when movie costumes emphasize aggressiveness (through military-inspired styles) or sexual characteristics (through the portrayal of high-class prostitutes), styles also follow that overstatement. Because fashions are purchased most often by the young and those with disposable income, class and generational differences are increased. However, the other side of this issue is that so extensive is the feed of styles derived from entertainment into the production of other consumer products that few sectors of the population are left out. Children's clothing frequently is emblazoned with media personalities. Media-derived styles, many now coming from rock videos, are as easily found in Sears as in Holt Renfrew, al-

Echoes of *Annie Hall* in 1987.
Courtesy Jeanette Maternities.

though their expression is somewhat different in these two markets. The photograph on the following page illustrates the derivation from top-rated *Miami Vice* of boys' clothing.

INFORMATION AND INFORMATION PROGRAMMING: MEDIA AND AGENDAS

The interpenetration of culture and the media is not confined to the domain of en-

tertainment. Real political, economic, and social events are reported in and affect the operations of the media. On the other hand, the media also have a considerable influence on the shape of events and certainly of ideas, as mentioned in Chapter 2 and as will be considered more fully in Chapter 7.

A tragic personal example of how the media shape events took place in 1983 in Alabama. According to *The Globe and Mail* (1984), on March 4, 1983, Cecil Andrews, an unem-

Miami Vice makes it to Sears. *Photo © Sears Canada Inc.*

ployed roofer, phoned the local television station in Anniston, Alabama, and announced that he would burn himself in a Jacksonville square to protest against the high rate of unemployment. The television news crew dutifully got itself together and travelled to where the man was going to enact his scene. As he doused himself with lighter fluid for his television crew audience (no one else was present) the cameras rolled. After setting himself on fire the news crew extinguished the blaze, but not before the man suffered con-

siderable burns to his body. The man subsequently sued the television station and news crew for being negligent in not having tried to prevent him.

A fuller account of the incident is contained in an article in the *Journal of Communication* (Bennett, Gressett, and Haltom, 1985), which we will introduce in our discussion in Chapter 7. However, in the context of our discussion here, bizarre as that example is, it brings up two issues. The first is the idea that the man was performing for television. Had the crew not shown up, it is questionable whether he would have burned himself. But the second issue is the responsibility of the crew in such a circumstance. Whatever the American courts decide, the issue will remain an open one. Should the media intervene actively in ongoing events? We know that they interact with them and cannot help but be a factor in them as they go about their job collecting and organizing information, but do they also have a responsibility to intervene?

Even more unsettling is the case of Pennsylvania's state treasurer, the late R. Budd Dwyer, who, facing a number of criminal charges, called a press conference, read a half-hour statement, admonished camera crews who began to dismantle their equipment, and then killed himself with a shot to the head while the cameras rolled – a media induced event? – who is to say? (*Globe and Mail*, 1987)

The Press and Prime Minister Trudeau

Less bizarre and more broadly significant examples of the interaction of the media and culture are numerous. The political life of Pierre Elliott Trudeau is surrounded with media-culture issues worthy of some attention. Richard Gwyn reports in *The Northern Magus* an event that occurred early in Trudeau's career as

Prime Minister. The incident arose from a reporter's question on Canadian policy regarding Biafra and its many starving people. Trudeau's reply was "Where's Biafra?"

Gwyn notes that most of the media interpreted Trudeau's remark as arising from a mixture of ignorance, inhumanity, and arrogance. How could any Canadian Prime Minister not bother himself to know where thousands of people were starving to death? Gwyn claims that Trudeau posed the question as a means of asking a larger question: what should Canadian policy be toward a region of which most Canadians know little? And faced with incomplete knowledge of the fate of millions around the world, should Canadian policy leap at the chance to prove itself humane just because the press happens to have broken a story of famine?

In the heat of the pursuit of stories journalists tend to believe that they are on top of all the major stories of the day. However, after cool reflection only the rare journalist will not admit to a woeful inability to cover even major world stories. For one thing, they may simply be unable to obtain visas to enter a region where millions are dying of starvation.

Trudeau's point can be seen as derived from the presence of information-gathering services governments have in their external affairs departments. Biafra may very well have been only one of many regions that External Affairs, if not Trudeau, knew was experiencing food shortages at the time.

A second example is better known to Canadians. In shooting some news footage at the time of the October crisis of 1970, during which a British trade commissioner and a Quebec cabinet minister were kidnapped, Trudeau took up the issue of the role of the media in ongoing events. He pointed out to the reporters that their interviewing him about the presence of Armed Forces troops in Ottawa was playing into the interests of the FLQ (Front de Libération du Québec). By publicizing the situation the media were giving publicity if not legitimacy to the concerns of the FLQ. The media were aiding the FLQ in terrorizing the population by reporting the feared possibility of more kidnappings and other forms of violence. This footage has been used many times, including in the CBC documentary, *The Press and the Prime Minister*.

Subsequent information and analysis of the events of October, 1970, suggest that the government itself, by invoking the War Measures Act and calling out the troops, contributed to the view that the FLQ was a broadly based terrorist organization. On reflection it also appeared that a remark of Trudeau's was the most significant aspect of that interview. The remark, made in reply to a reporter's question on how far Trudeau was prepared to go in infringing on the civil liberties of Canadians, was "Just watch me." Rather a bald statement of autocratic power.

Nearly two decades later the Canadian media and all media are still discussing how they ought to respond to terrorism. On April 2, 1985, *The Journal* broadcast a panel discussion on the subject in the wake of a threat by some Armenian extremists to bomb the Toronto transit system. The conclusion of the panel appeared to be that the media should not heighten the tension, for example, by putting through phone calls to the terrorists. Nor should they play into the theatre of terror the terrorists attempt to create. But given Western news values, it appears that the media will continue to respond to terrorist activities by using them to bring forward a broader discussion of the issues behind what the terrorists are fighting about, while at the same time condemning the means and co-operating with the police in bringing them to the courts. It was recognized that, to an extent, this plays into the hands of terrorists, but the majority of the panel could not see a way around this problem without the creation of a new set of problems just as serious as those created by reporting terrorism.

The effects of all this are dependent, of course, both on what is presented and on the active meaning-structuring process of the audience. As the CBC documentary, *The Press and the Prime Minister*, notes in narration – over a picture of the Parliament Buildings as seen distortedly through the reflective glass of a neighbouring building – the media are not the only ones who have an informed view of their relations to society. Politicians do, too, but theirs is no more disinterested or valid than that of the media. The viewer must decide, often in the absence of much other reliable information, whose story makes the most sense (see Gans, 1979).

The view Canadians had of Pierre Trudeau seems to have been derived from many of these interactions between the press and the Prime Minister that accumulated over the years. To what extent that view influenced their voting patterns or their attitudes to government or even their fellow countrymen and women is indeterminate. In terms of our earlier discussion, while the effects are not clear, very significant interaction obviously took place between the press, the PM, and the populace.

The Grenada Adventure

A final example illustrates the undoubted but precisely indeterminable involvement of the media in world affairs. In November of 1983 the U.S. invaded Grenada. The American government claimed it did so because of the presence of U.S. citizens in the country who might have been in danger as a result of an uprising in which the Prime Minister had been killed. It also claimed that Grenada was on the verge of becoming a military base for Cuba and the Soviet Union because an airstrip was being built there. According to various publications, including the normally regime-supportive *Time* magazine, the U.S. invaded Grenada because it had been suffering considerably from a number of blows to its prestige. These included Vietnam, the Bay of Pigs invasion of Cuba, the occupation of the U.S. embassy in Iran, and, most recently, the deaths of a number of soldiers in Beirut, caused by a major explosion. According to *Time* as well as other sources, the U.S. had been looking for some time for an opportunity to take decisive military action and receive local, domestic, and world praise for it. Grenada seemed, and proved to be, almost the perfect opportunity.

Now the role of the media in these matters, especially with such events as Beirut, Iran, and Vietnam, is that they have been so close to the actual events that the shoddy, tragic, embarrassing, inept aspects of each were perfectly visible to U.S. citizens and the world at large. The world had very little information about Grenada, for very little was available. In fact, it was not entirely clear what the situation was at the time of the invasion.

The U.S. attempted to use this lack of information to its advantage. In face of a lack of information U.S. President Ronald Reagan announced to the world: "Grenada ... was a Soviet-Cuban colony being readied as a major bastion to export terror and undermine democracy. We got there just in time" (*Time*, November 7, 1983, p. 44). None of the media, on the basis of background evidence, could contradict Reagan. Nor could they on the basis of on-the-scene reporting. The U.S. took no chances that this image-enhancing exercise

President Reagan and the U.S. Marines grill a hapless Grenadian in this Plantu cartoon that originally appeared in *Le Monde. Courtesy Plantu.*

would be marred by on-the-spot reporting: the American government barred the press from access to Grenada until most of the dirty work was complete. The U.S. military issued its own information, complete with pictures, some of which proved to be quite misleading (see Taylor, 1983). One photograph was identified as being of a dead American soldier. It turned out to be a dead Grenadian.

The question can again be asked, did the media cause the invasion of Grenada as a result of seeing too much, thereby dealing a series of blows to the international prestige of the U.S.? The question is exactly parallel to asking whether, by covering terrorists, the media encourages terrorism. Most people would answer no, giving as a reason that the image any country maintains is not totally dependent on the media but is part of the world of international politics and diplomacy. But neither would they deny that the media play a significant role in international politics and diplomacy, especially when the press has access to events and circumstances that would otherwise be unknown to other countries.

The Nicaraguan Information War

Events subsequent to the U.S. invasion of Grenada have shown yet another aspect of the interaction between international politics and the media. A cartoon in *Le Monde* captures the position of the hapless Grenadians rather well. How could they have known that their actions would have been assessed in terms of the past two decades of struggle the U.S. has had in enforcing its will around the world? While the Grenadians might not have anticipated such a situation, another country, Nicaragua, is doing everything it can to keep the U.S. from performing on the world stage at its expense. It has learned from the Grenada affair.

Nicaragua has mounted a campaign of action and information that has kept the Americans at bay. At one level of symbolism it has asked numbers of Soviet advisers, whom the Americans could see as military and political advisers, to leave. It could then claim that it was not a Soviet base for operations in Latin America. Nicaragua has also refrained from importing advanced levels of weaponry, which would provide the Americans with an excuse to interfere directly in the war.

These actions in themselves are significant. But in taking them and announcing them to the world, Nicaragua has mounted an information war against the U.S. at another level of symbolism. The Sandinista government is playing out in public its attempt to rule the country by a set of unspecified rules that are sufficient to make it a greater embarrassment for the U.S. to invade than it would be a victory to oust the leftist regime of President Daniel Ortega.

In these circumstances it is clear that the media are right in the middle of this intrigue. What role they are playing and what control they have over that role are not easily defined.

THE FREEDOM OF THE MEDIA TO CREATE MEANING

The examples given in the previous section concern the role or interference of the media as they go about their task of collecting and disseminating information. However, these examples do not address the limitations that exist on the media to define issues, or, to

couch it in a theoretical framework, to *create a discourse* within which issues are defined (see Mitchell, 1988).

Enoch Powell and the Consensus on Race

In Birmingham, England, in 1968, a Conservative politician, Enoch Powell, made a speech designed to sweep away an artificial consensus on race that had been constructed by the media in alliance with the politicians and the civil service of Britain. That consensus was really to ignore any racially oriented protestations. In the words of Jeremy Issacs, a television producer:

> Television current affairs deliberately underplayed the strength of racist feelings for years, out of the misguided but honourable feelings that inflammatory utterances could only do damage. But the way feelings erupted after Enoch Powell's speech this year was evidence to me that the feeling had been underrepresented on television, and other media. (Quoted in Braham, 1982, p. 280.)

It would appear that Issacs was right. Powell received 110,000 letters containing 180,000 signatures in the days following the speech. Only 2,000 did not express approval for what he had said. The majority of the letters of support contained reports of real and imagined sufferings that white Britons had experienced as a result of the immigration of "black" workers from Africa, India, Pakistan, and the Caribbean, among other countries and regions. They were allowed to immigrate by virtue of being citizens of the Commonwealth, in other words, citizens of former British colonies.

Enoch Powell opened the floodgates to an outpouring of feeling that had had no means for representation in the media. The principle the situation illustrated is the potential peril the media court in defining issues purely on their own terms, or on terms developed with those other than their readership.

Carving Out and Serving Up a Monopoly

The Enoch Powell incident is quite unusual. Certainly in North America it is extremely rare for the media to suspend "news values" for "the greater good of the country." More often we are presented with an array of styles that do exactly the opposite. They play to the known attitudes of various sectors of the population. McCormack (1983) argues that the newspapers of large urban markets seek out separate population subgroups for whom they are in a monopoly position as sources of information. This may occur through a realignment of a newspaper, as happened with *The Province* in Vancouver. It became a morning tabloid (while not totally giving in to sensationalism) where previously it had been a morning broadsheet. Or it may happen more dramatically through the closure and subsequent opening of a new paper with new owners. For example, not long after the demise of the middle-of-the-road *Toronto Telegram* the sensationalist morning tabloid *Toronto Sun* arose. Similarly, soon after the middle market, evening broadsheet *Winnipeg Tribune* closed, the tabloid *Winnipeg Sun* opened for business.

In a draft paper Sullivan (1982) supports McCormack's thesis with an examination of the content of two Toronto papers. *The Globe and Mail*, he notes, defined news as events that are unusual and significant to a readership composed of persons who are in positions of responsibility in society. Teenage gang conflicts are not the stuff of news in *The Globe* unless they begin to threaten the peace of the broader community. *The Globe* explains why an event

occurred and what measures are being taken by what persons in what positions to ensure against its recurrence.

The advertising in *The Globe* further reinforces the target reader's comfort with the publication. A typical ad is an understated corporate advocacy ad, one that puts the name of the company forward and lets the reader know it is a member of the club of high-class businesses that advertise in *The Globe*. Any ads intended to sell items directly are promoting prestige items of considerable cost.

Sullivan raises one other interesting point. In past times of perceived substantial threat to its "community of readers," as happened during the FLQ crisis, the normally ordered and ordering front page of *The Globe* has taken on more of the characteristics of a tabloid.

The *Toronto Sun*, on the other hand, is a typical tabloid intended for readers who have very little power in society. The *Toronto Sun* bombards the reader with an unordered melange of events that are at once trivialized and at the same time symbols of a profound disorder. For example, on January 21, 1982, the *Sun's* headline read, "235,000 JOBS VANISH." Inside, the expansion of this statement in another headline was "THE BUDGET'S A BUST" just above the picture of the Sunshine Girl complete with emphasized bust.

Sullivan argues that the juxtapositioning of completely unrelated stories in conjunction with a treatment that emphasizes the dramatic, the unexplainable, the bizarre, the futility of trying to make sense, in general the lack of patterns and the randomness of events, trivializes all subject matter from the Sunshine Girl to the federal budget. Such treatment, he argues, produces a low-grade paranoia because, just as one never knows when one might win a lottery, one never knows when the lottery that dishes out disasters might deal a wild card. In keeping with this presentation of news, Sullivan argues that the *Sun* attracts ads that encourage its readers to exert the only power they have, the power of spending money. They are encouraged to comfort themselves through the purchase of the trinkets of the marketplace. A typical ad is a two-page spread on a stereo equipment sale lasting only the weekend and filled with items from top to bottom.

The *Sun* presents to its readers a fragmentation of consciousness. Nothing is related to anything else. There is no pattern that connects, only a series of random, threatening events. One's date with fate can never be anticipated. One might best wait it out buffered by technological playthings. In contrast, *The Globe and Mail* presents an integration of consciousness. Each event is placed in a context of understanding. It is made clear how the occurrence will be managed and who will manage it. In due course all will be right with the world and those who should rule will continue ruling.

A final example of the manner in which the media create meaning and of the limitations on their ability to do so deals with television news. Television news, merely by its format, gives the impression that everything one really needs to know is included. The familiar pattern – a dramatic beginning, followed by more significant but less dramatic middle stories, followed by a lighter ending – has the comfort of a bedtime story, squalid as it may be. For example, one-line summaries or other summarizing devices are rarely used. The viewer is treated as someone who has no real interest in knowing about the multiplicity of events that might be going on in the world. Rather, she or he is treated as a person who wants to be entertained by what the television station can do in packaging the events of the day into an entertaining and somewhat informative program. It is more important that the producers get cheers for the production than that the audience come away as informed as possible.

Similar to entertainment programs, information programming takes events of the real world and transforms them into "programs." As with entertainment, it, too, stylizes content while seeking to inform. Information programming is involved in a trialogue with its audience and with world events upon which it comments and of which it is a part. It assigns meaning to events, but not arbitrarily, or at least not forever arbitrarily, as Enoch Powell proved. Information programs tend to read events back to their audience in the categories that suit the audience. At the same time, they maintain the dominant order. They court disaster only in the long term, if their categories of analysis contradict life's experience.

MEDIA AND REALITY

Here we consider the interaction between signification or representation and the events themselves. Let us start the discussion with literature to provide some background for consideration of the basic issues.

Literary Devices and Real Life

When a novelist kills off someone in a novel he or she is using a convenient literary device to advance the plot or shape the plot in ways that otherwise would be impossible or at least difficult. The death of a person provides opportunity for all manner of human action and drama. However, the meaning of this device for the reader may be quite different. It is not unusual for the average reader to be distraught or indeed to cry at the death of a character.

The reader has suspended disbelief and in so doing may identify with some or all of the characters and, as a result, become emotionally involved. Indeed, to some extent this is exactly what the novelist is trying to accomplish in writing a tale for the reader. While few people in this era would identify so strongly with the characters and interaction of a novel that they would confuse the world of the novel with their day-to-day world, in past times such an intermingling has not been unknown.

Intermingling of the Media and the "Real" World

In our times such intermingling is more likely to happen in other media. Soap opera characters, for example, regularly receive letters advising them of the intent of other characters or giving them gifts for their upcoming television marriages. Some observers have suggested that this means that viewers do not distinguish between real life and the soaps. It may be more the case that they want to test the system. If they send gifts, will their gifts be included in what the couple received? Or if they warn the character of the intent of another, will a warning be built into the plot somehow?

When we move out of literature and into other media, whether radio, television, or movies, the distance between reality and signification shrinks. To take another example, in 1939 Orson Welles produced a radio play called *The War of the Worlds* in which he presented, in pseudo-documentary style, an invasion of the earth by Martians. Great numbers of listeners phoned in, some as the program was being aired, reporting sightings of the landings of other Martians. Some listeners seemed genuinely in fear of their lives.

Chernobyl and *Challenger*

Two recent events, which stand the *War of the Worlds* phenomenon on its head, appear to demonstrate a considerable intermingling of the real world with media fictions in everyone's mind. In 1986, the U.S. space shuttle, *Challenger*, blew up shortly after takeoff. Later the same year a nuclear plant at Chernobyl, in the U.S.S.R., underwent a partial core meltdown sending radiation throughout the Northern Hemisphere. In both cases, the pattern of coverage was considerably different from that for a normal news story. In the case of *Challenger*, for example, for the following hour or so, almost nothing else could be seen or heard except pictures or commentary on the tragedy on every North American channel. And for the following days, it was the lead story on the newscasts and in the newspapers. Approximately the same pattern of coverage emerged subsequent to Chernobyl.

The point to be drawn from these events and their coverage is that when the unanticipated but not to be unexpected happens, when "our worst fears materialize," the media recognize the special identity of the event with saturation coverage and thereby signal to us that this is no fictitious event. In other words, they make a special effort to signal to us that the event is real. Without such signals of verification, the event is not assumed to be necessarily fictitious but rather, like a rumour, is in a limbo somewhere between truth and reality.

"Freeze, buddy, or you're dead!"

In the early eighties a group of teenagers broke into a house in Sackville, Nova Scotia. One boy was shot and killed in darkness as he apparently turned to run back down the stairs when the man of the house said something like "Freeze, buddy, or you're dead!" In his judgement in the case the judge, while finding the man not guilty of murder, severely chastised him. He pointed out that the manner in which he had held the gun, the position he took before firing, and the language he used in talking to the boy were derived directly from the gun culture the man lived within as a result of, among other things, subscribing to gun magazines.

The dominant mode of the presentation of information in our electronic society is dramatic. Ads are mini-dramas; entertainment is rarely anything but drama; news and information programming is increasingly presented in a dramatic style. Investigative television programming is more a detective story that happens to be non-fiction than a presentation of the results and the consequences of an investigation. The investigation is presented in dramatic form complete with a star, the intrepid reporter, like *60 Minutes'* Mike Wallace, who runs into various adventures as he or she seeks out the villain and demands to know the truth. The scene is reminiscent of the confrontational but crude CBC program *This Hour Has Seven Days* as opposed to the more exploratory *the fifth estate.* Superimposed on this dramatic form, whether fiction or nonfiction, is often graphic realism. Breakthroughs in the realistic portrayal of sex and violence are regarded as great achievements.

The difficulty with graphic realism combined with a dramatic form is that it succeeds too well. It simulates events so well that they are almost indistinguishable from real life and art. At a second level is the frequency with which members of the audience encounter these dramatic devices. There are two views of what appear to be the results of this over-encounter with dramatic realism. The research of George Gerbner presents one view, research on children points to another.

Research Findings

Gerbner has concentrated his research over the years on the portrayal of violence on television (see, for example, Gerbner, 1977). He has argued that the frequent use of violence results from its being a cheap way to portray power. But his central concern has been the effects this constant use of violence has had on television viewers. In his studies Gerbner has pointed out how people who watch a great deal of television overestimate the amount of violence in society. They tend also to have a "bunker mentality," to protect themselves from what they perceive to be a violent world.

In a variety of studies of children's play, Bandura (1976) has shown that those children who watch a great deal of television tend to engage in more aggressive play than those who watch less or see none at all. Also, following a television session in which aggression has been shown, there is an increase in the amount of aggressiveness in the interactions between children.

In both of these studies, obviously, only a certain amount of control over the exposure of the subjects to the media can be achieved, and only a certain level of confidence in the results is appropriate because of other such uncontrolled variables as socio-economic status. However, there is little doubt that Bandura's work points to effects that make sense if one takes a more analytic perspective, as we have done in postulating persons, cultures, and the media to be meaning-generating systems in interaction with one another. Let us return to that perspective and return once again to signification or media presentation on the one hand as opposed to real life on the other.

Pornography and Erotica

In discussions of pornography a distinction is often drawn between pornography and erotica. The former is put forward as unacceptable, the latter as permissible. The argument usually goes something like this: there is nothing wrong with having literature that is designed to stimulate the sexuality of males and females; there is, however, something wrong with portraying the exploitation of females or children, or, in fact, anyone, when, if such actions were real, the person could be charged with a criminal offence.

While such a distinction can be made, another position questions the acceptability but certainly does not argue for the criminalization of erotica. This position is useful for viewing all activities of the media. Erotic magazines for men do two things. They idealize the female body. Only attractive women are photographed and, in addition, the photographs are touched up to remove what are regarded as imperfections. Second, they give men easy access to (pictures of) naked women in poses intended to encourage fantasies and masturbation. We must take into account a third point as well. Much of the erotic magazine market is accounted for by young men who have not yet formed a permanent attachment to a woman.

By virtue of providing erotica for the young, unattached male market, its producers have the potential to encourage exactly the same type of comparison between the real and the media ideal as John Lekich reported in "Horizontal Hold." Whether or not such comparisons lead to unrealistic expectations on the part of young men depends on a great many unknowns. When this idealized form is combined with an unimpeded visual access, what we have is a rather dramatic rift between community norms and the norms of the medium. To put it another way, the presence of such erotica is a continual challenge to the norms of the community. If one were to assume a direct effect of these materials, one would assume that rather large numbers of young men walk around in a state of unconscious wonder as to why they can have easy visual access to beautiful women in magazines whereas they have no such thing in real life. To carry the matter one step further, it might be similarly argued that rather large numbers of young women compare themselves to the idealized form presented in these magazine and ask themselves whether they should be willing to grant numbers of men access to their bodies.

In the same manner in which sexual portrayals challenge community standards, so do other portrayals, whether they are violent, idealizations of family, or dramatic or even humorous portrayals of the life of anyone the media care to portray. The positive side of such portrayals is that they provide the viewer with another view of life besides the one he or she lives. Such a view may encourage the striving for excellence, or the movement from the farm to the city, or vice versa, in order to take advantage of what is offered in a milieu other than the one in which one has grown up. On the negative side, they may discourage an allegiance to community values in favour of the values of a world of signification.

SUMMARY

There are inherent limitations in seeing the interaction between the audience and the media as "effects." Audience-media relations are better seen as the interaction between meaning-generating systems in that both interact with and affect the other. Since neither system can be fully defined or understood *a priori*, audience-media interaction can be well understood but only predicted within broad categories.

The imaginations of many individuals may be filled with the pantheon of characters and situations television provides. Further, a television-dominated imagination can lead to unrealistic expectations or to feelings of marginalization. However, for that to be the case depends on the identity of the individual and his or her relations with lived culture.

Whole cultures, too, may be bombarded by the imaginative output of other cultures. Specifically, Canada's pattern of importation of programming as opposed to its domestic production makes our culture vulnerable to living inside the media-based collective imagination of the United States. Its actual effects, however, depend on the programs we are willing to put in place to build our own culture.

The mass media select images and symbols out of lived culture, transform them, and display them in a restylized form to mass culture. In doing so they contribute both to the fashion and to the political agenda. However, again here, their influence can be circumscribed by the redefinition of the significance of events by key personages such as, in the political realm, prime ministers.

The freedom of the media to create meaning, or, in other words, to define the elements of a discourse, for example, on race, is fundamentally limited by the lived experience of their audiences and the attitudes, social processes, cultural institutions, etc. that are created by such a life.

What the media say about the world and what the world is are two quite different things. Pornography is becoming less acceptable because it portrays the violation of the legal rights of certain people. Erotica is accepted by greater numbers of society; however, it challenges the world of normal social relations. It is important to find a conceptual framework to provide a basis for consideration of the role of the media in society.

REFERENCES

Adorno, T., and M. Horkheimer. *Dialectic of Enlightment.* New York: Herder and Herder, 1972.

Bandura, Albert. *Analysis of Delinquency and Aggression.* Hillsdale, New Jersey: L. Erlbaum Associates, 1976.

Bennett, W.L., L.A. Gressett, and W. Haltom. "Repairing the news: a case study of the news paradigm," *Journal of Communication,* 35, 2 (Spring, 1985), pp. 50-68.

Berger, John. *Ways of Seeing.* London: British Broadcasting Corporation and Penguin Books, 1972.

Braham, Peter. "How the Media Report Race," in Gurevitch *et al.,* eds., *Culture, Society and the Media.* Toronto: Methuen, 1982.

Canadian Broadcasting Corporation. *The Press and the Prime Minister,* directed and produced by George Robertson. Toronto: CBC, 1977.

Cunningham, L. "How *Quest's* crew charted a suicide course," *Quill and Quire* (January, 1985), pp. 18-19.

Gans, H.J. *Deciding What's News: A Study of CBS Evening News, NBC Nightly News, Newsweek, and Time.* New York: Pantheon, 1979.

Gerbner, George. *Trends in Network Drama and Viewer Conceptions of Social Reality, 1967-76.* Philadelphia: Annenburg School of Communications, University of Pennsylvania, 1977.

Globe and Mail. "Burned man sues station over filming," January 31, 1984, p. 5.

Globe and Mail. "Pennsylvania official shoots himself dead at news conference," January 23, 1987, p. 49.

Goffman, Erving. *Presentation of Self in Everyday Life.* Garden City, New York: Doubleday, 1959.

Gwyn, Richard. *The Northern Magus.* Toronto: McClelland and Stewart, 1980.

Katz, E., and P. Lazarsfeld. *Personal Influence: the Part Played by People in the Flow of Mass Communications.* New York: Free Press, 1965.

Klapper, Joseph. *The Effects of Mass Communications.* New York: Free Press, 1960.

Laba, M. "Popular culture as local culture: regions, limits and Canadianism," in R. Lorimer and D.C. Wilson, eds., *Communications Canada.* Forthcoming, 1988.

Lekich, J. "Horizontal Hold," *Vancouver* (April, 1982), pp. 48-53.

McCormack, Thelma. "The Political Culture and the Press in Canada," *Canadian Journal of Political Science,* XVI, 3 (September, 1983).

McLarty, L. "Seeing Things: Canadian popular culture and the experience of marginality," in R. Lorimer and D.C. Wilson, eds., *Communications Canada.* Forthcoming, 1988.

Mitchell, D. "Culture as political discourse in Canada," in R. Lorimer and D.C. Wilson, eds., *Communications Canada.* Forthcoming, 1988.

Sullivan, Edmund. "Mass Media and Political Integration: Thematizing Three Major Dailies in a Canadian City," unpublished, 1982.

Taylor, S. "Sifting U.S. statements for the facts," *Globe and Mail,* November 7, 1983, p. 10.

Time magazine, November 7, 1983, p. 44.

Valaskakis, G. "Television and cultural integration: native communities and the Canadian North," in R. Lorimer and D.C. Wilson, eds., *Communications Canada.* Forthcoming, 1988.

STUDY QUESTIONS

1. How do the media capture the imagination of the individual and whole cultures?

2. Describe a meaning-generating system and how such systems impinge on the interaction between media and audiences.

3. "The media create their own realities." Discuss.

Cartoon by Jean-Marc Phaneuf, Beloeil, Quebec. *From Royal Commission on Newspapers, 1981. Reproduced with permission of the Minister of Supply and Services Canada.*

CHAPTER

6

The Structure and Role of Ownership

INTRODUCTION: PEOPLE AND PROPERTY

M ANY OF us in capitalistic societies grow up in blissful ignorance of the power of ownership. For example, we think of our houses and apartments as our homes. The texture of their very walls figures prominently in our imaginations. Their interiors are our private domain, a domain over which we control access. Their exteriors are the face we show to the world both as an invitation and a barrier. In the same way a farmer's field becomes his in a personal and private way as a result of the years of toil he spends in it and his ability to know its behaviour under all kinds of circumstances.

Capitalism has no respect for such relations between people and property. No economic system does. In capitalist countries, at certain times, such as the Great Depression, vast numbers are expelled from their homes and denied the right of access to what is more humanly theirs than anyone else's. If the rent is not paid, if the mortgage is not kept up, the landlord or lender evicts. At other times in history fewer feel the brunt of the owner's exercise of his or her property rights. But at all times, numbers of people live out their days with the conscious or subconscious realization that they carry out their private daily routine in surroundings that are granted to them at the pleasure of an owner. It is something that we tend to hide from our children.

The other side of capitalism is that each citizen has the right to own property if he or she can find the money to buy it. Essentially, that right or privilege allows people to build houses, set up businesses, and own land for a variety of purposes; to live in, make money from, or rent to others; to respond to opportunities in the marketplace. Such an arrangement means that we do not have to depend on the state to discover needs, plan ways of meeting those needs, and begin programs to address such needs as reinterpreted by government study. And there is a magic to the marketplace. Capitalist societies, especially rich capitalist societies, do manage to manufacture and distribute goods and services fairly well.

However, while capitalism creates a certain amount of individual freedom in that way and a certain level of distribution of goods and services, it also pits individual against individual for scarce resources. The price of a house is set, in theory, by market conditions. Market conditions are the variables that determine the price people in general are willing to pay for a house. Thus, while person A may need a house and house A may be empty and for sale, unless person A is prepared to pay market value, then he has no right to live in the house. For a lesser short-term amount he may rent the house, but he may not even be able to afford that alternative.

Individuals are pitted against one another in the sense that they must compete in the marketplace. So person B may purchase house A and rent to person A essentially because person B has the money or capital to buy the house, although B may not need it to live in. Moreover, purchasing and renting it may just make B that much richer than person A.

In the case of larger properties, such as business institutions rather than houses, the little guy who cannot even afford his own home has no chance of participating in ownership. There is, of course, a group of reasonably well-off people who can participate, but not equally with a third and richer group, those who own and control large business enterprises. Substantial numbers of Canadians can and do participate in ownership through the purchase of small blocks of shares in public companies. But as we will see in this chapter, they have very little say in what goes on in such corporations.

This third group of owners, who exert effective control, is made up of men (rarely women) with copious amounts of surplus resources they use to invest to make more money to reinvest further. This group, which holds controlling ownership of a significant percentage of the larger business institutions of our country, consists of very few people.

Culture and Capitalism

Ownership of land and property is not quite the same as ownership of media institutions. There is a size difference but there is a kind of social equivalence. Communication, as we pointed out in Chapter 1, is infused into every aspect of personal, societal, and cultural life. It is a necessity of modern civilization. Just as a person's home or a farmer's field is the private domain and the public face of an individual, so a nation's communication system is essential to and an expression of the culture of which it is a part.

Yet communication in modern society is increasingly dependent on privately owned media institutions whose primary aim is to make money. Communication, therefore, takes place within the structures of an economic regime. Were it not for the CBC, the very fabric of our culture, what we have to say to one another, what insights our artists and writers have to share, our distinctive national imagination, our domestic reality, might depend for its dissemination on the pleasure, which is to say the profit, of a small group of owners of media institutions. Even the CBC lives within an increasingly parsimonious regime where it must weigh the value of the message against the number of viewers or listeners a particular program might attract.

Private Enterprise and the Public Purpose in Media

These two opposing forces, public good and private interest, are enshrined in The Broadcasting Act (1968) (see Chapter 2). A more recent discussion of them can be found in the *Report of the Task Force on Broadcasting Policy* (1986). Hardin (1988) has provided a useful commentary on that report from the perspective of public broadcasting. As the Act itself makes clear, while accepting the participation of the private sector as a complement to public enterprise, the primary purpose of broadcasting is cultural and is stated explicitly in Section 3(h):

> where any conflict arises between the objectives of the national broadcasting service and the interests of the private element of the Canadian broadcasting system, it shall be resolved in the public interest but paramount consideration shall be given to the national broadcasting service ....

The Act empowers the CRTC to oversee these opposing forces, giving it the job of persuading capitalists to spend their profits on items of cultural value, at times, at the expense of economic gain.

In media other than broadcasting, for example in the print media, the profession (i.e., journalists, as distinct from the owners) usually takes up the cultural issue. Owners represent business concerns. This is especially true in newspapers and, to some extent, in magazines. However, with small magazines and with many Canadian-owned book publishers, the owners are as concerned with cultural content as the writers who contribute to their pages.

In this chapter we will review the structure and role of ownership, predominantly private ownership, as it exists in media institutions in Canada.

HISTORICAL BACKGROUND: FUNCTION AND OWNERSHIP

The roots of media institutions are found in social, cultural, and political opportunities. Gutenberg's press was an invention that responded to growing literacy, to a need to make the Bible and other tracts available to a wider audience. The establishment of the press in Canada, in the sense of an institution rather than a machine, was a response, at first, to the needs of government to print official information as official records and to make such information widely available. It soon evolved into an institution capable of responding to other social and political pressures for the distribution of information and ideas.

With such roots, the intensive involvement of government, that is, the public sector, is not difficult to understand. In the case of the British press at least, which provided a model for Britain's colonies, while ownership was not exclusive to the public domain, numbers of laws and taxes were used to control press output so that it would reflect the interests of those who allowed its operation. However, as printers as a group became less and less dependent on government largesse, and with the general economic and political rise of the bourgeoisie, intense, insistent pressure grew for the freedom of printers to pursue their economic interest.

Free Press, Free Market

As we saw in Chapter 3, the fight for the establishment of the economic interests of private press owners was not fought on economic grounds. Rather, the press put itself forward as an estate representative of a distinct set of interests, not those of church, business, or landowners but of "the people." However, the press won recognition because the basis of its pursuit of its economic interests was in accordance with the generally accepted theory and practice of the day. That theory, which still holds sway in capitalist countries today, posits that the pursuit by individuals of their own economic self-interest will maximize the economic interests of the whole. The mechanism that leads to this happy confluence of interests is Adam Smith's "invisible hand," named after the theorist who proposed it. The invisible hand guides individuals to pursue a social need through each responding to a self-interested, economic opportunity.

The press asked for nothing more than any other business. But in dealing with information, which, even during the Industrial Revolution, was recognized as somehow different from other commodities, the press found it prudent to fight and win the battle on non-economic grounds.

The Public Role in Broadcasting

We can probably attribute public involvement in broadcasting to the capitalistic instincts of Giuglielmo Marconi. Marconi was the first person to be able to transmit intelligence electronically from one point to another without the use of connecting wires. As a result of this, and with other extensive experiments and achievements and considerable business acumen, Marconi was able to create for himself a virtual international monopoly of the airwaves through the patenting of his inventions. Faced with that monopoly and the differences of interests between nations, which one monopolist would be hard-pressed to serve without rancour, the nations of the world were only able to break his monopoly by declaring the airwaves to be a public resource. They were then able, and to some extent forced, to regulate the airwaves.

Once in the business of regulation, governments found that the obvious immediate issue was the principle of regulation. In virtually every country, regulation of the public airwaves for the public good was accepted. The early stages of broadcasting saw a high degree of public involvement. But the inevitable pressures of capital, especially in the United States, made it questionable whether this public resource could be licensed for exploitation by private investors and still reflect the public good. As in the case of the press, market theory, i.e., Adam Smith's invisible hand, came to play an underlying role in the acceptance of exploitation of the airwaves by private, licensed owners. (Of the major Western countries, only the U.S. rejected the involvement of public institutions in the early years of broadcasting.)

In both major areas of communication, broadcasting and newspapers, there was an early involvement of public institutions. At the same time in the Western world, pressure for private exploitation has never been distant from communications institutions.

Media Ownership in Canada

The nature of ownership has been especially significant in Canada. As we noted earlier, communications serve an important role in binding the nation together. They bring isolated communities and individuals into the nation and are intended to reflect our regional differences, our two official languages and cultures, and our multiethnicity.

The mesh of these public goals with private economic interests is not smooth. The Broadcasting Act recognizes that collision of interests in assigning special responsibilities to the public sector. These special responsibilities include:

- attention to balance in types of programming;
- programming for all population groups;
- extension to all parts of Canada as funds permit;
- contribution to national unity and a Canadian identity;
- the primacy of the national system;
- provision for educational broadcasting;
- attention to technical advance.

The difficulty of meshing public goals and private interests has been recognized in other ways in Canadian communications. Foreign private interests have been especially problematic. In contrast to other industries, every encouragement has been given to Canadian entrepreneurs and corporations to keep newspapers Canadian. In book publishing, governments, beginning with Ontario and followed by the federal government and other provincial governments, have reviewed ownership and granted direct subsidies to ensure Canadian participation in the Canadian publishing industry. For Canadian magazines, Bill C-58 was intended to bolster the advertising base in comparison with those from foreign countries. Tax breaks and direct subsidies have also been put in place to encourage the development of a Canadian-owned film industry.

In education, the production of educational programming has been a public-sector activity involving educational authorities and the National Film Board. Such activities have been a major basis of resistance of the energetic export initiatives of the U.S.

In broadcasting, through licensing, while private ownership has long been a *de facto* element of the overall system, only in 1968 did the Broadcasting Act give formal recognition to the private sector as part of Canada's overall broadcasting system. Prior to 1968 it was still an open question whether the entire system should be in public hands.

These media traditions and initiatives were designed to allow Canadians to keep control of their communication system through public ownership, which was seen as the best means of allowing Canadians to use communications to pursue public, cultural desiderata. However, private ownership of media, with its unavoidable pursuit of profits and audiences with whatever products work, has come to play a large role, and, in fact, has come to predominate communications in Canada.

FORMS OF OWNERSHIP

A variety of enterprises operate in the marketplace. We will differentiate between two major types and discuss the second in some detail.

The Single Enterprise

The **single enterprise** is a business form in which control rests with a group of shareholders who do not represent other companies. Examples of this form of ownership were plentiful in small Canadian towns until press barons began buying them all up. Roy Thomson, for example, created a chain of small-town papers from which he was able to launch his newspaper and now conglomerate empire.

The Chain: Horizontal Integration

The second major type of firm is the **linked company**. In this case, the nature of the links is significant. On the one hand a company may be part of a chain of similar companies. The group of cable companies owned by Rogers Cablesystems Inc. and of newspapers owned by Quebecor and Southam are examples of groups of companies that constitute chains. Each chain can also be described as horizontally integrated; the links do not buy or sell to or from one another but are a number of enterprises, usually in different locations, doing the same business.

Vertical Integration

Another form of linkage is through **vertical integration**. In this circumstance companies under the same owner are suppliers and consumers of the products of each other. Thus, when the telephone companies purchase from equipment companies owned (or controlled) by the same group of investors, or when a major newspaper owns a newsprint supplier, such companies could be said to be vertically integrated. One example here is Selkirk Communications, which owns radio station CKKS-FM, CKWX, and Quality Records. Another is Western Broadcasting, which owns CKNW and the Vancouver Canucks and broadcasts Canuck games. Pierre Peladeau's Quebecor, as of late 1986, published 37 weeklies and three dailies, thus being horizontally integrated, but it is also vertically integrated through its distribution companies. Eaton's ownership of CFTO, Toronto, the main CTV station, and of

Glen Warren productions, the main CTV production studio, is yet another example.

Cross-Ownership

A further type of linkage more closely associated with horizontal than vertical integration is **cross-ownership**. Cross-ownership of media companies refers to companies that own more than one type of media company, e.g., a television station, a radio station, a newspaper, a magazine publisher, a book publisher, a cable company, a telephone company, etc. Maclean Hunter is an example of cross-ownership. It owns *The Financial Post*, *Maclean's*, and the *Toronto, Calgary, and Edmonton Sun* newpapers, as well as several radio, TV, and cable companies.

The Conglomerate

The last type of linked ownership is the **conglomerate**, which combines a variety of linkages, usually inclusive of horizontally and vertically integrated companies. The conglomerate operates in more than one field, for example the media and travel, or oil exploration and retailing. It is a conglomeration of all sorts of different companies. Power Corporation, which owns, among other companies, Montreal Trust, Investor's Syndicate, *La Presse*, and radio interests is an example of a rather powerful Canadian conglomerate.

FORCES TOWARD INCREASED CONCENTRATION OF OWNERSHIP

Corporate Concentration, a Definition

When ownership within an industry shifts increasingly to the hands of the few rather than the many, the emergent business structure is said to have an increasing degree of corporate or ownership concentration. Corporate concentration in any single industry, such as the media, arises through a combination of chain ownership and cross-ownership, two different forms of horizontal integration. The resulting situation is that a small number of chains take on a national presence as information and entertainment providers and in some markets all media are owned by one of those few. Most markets are affected in some way or other by these dominant few. Industry in a country is said to be concentrated when chains and cross-ownership are combined with vertical integration. The economy is thus dominated by relatively few, large corporations.

One of Canada's media giants, Télémédia, exemplifies a corporate size and cross-ownership typical of the industry. It is a private company and is second only to the CBC in combined audiences. With *TV Guide* and *Canadian Living* it produces more copies of consumer magazines than any other Canadian company. However, Télémédia is no higher than 17th among Canada's largest media companies. It has no television, cable, or newspaper holdings, but it does own 22 radio stations in Quebec and Ontario, publishes eight magazines, maintains controlling interest in a Toronto-based promotion and marketing company, and holds equity investments in Canadian Satellite Communications Inc. and in Cantel Inc., a national radio service.

It is usually assumed that corporate expansion is stimulated by the expectation of greater efficiency. The first type of efficiency is derived from a greater number of companies doing the same thing under one overall owner (i.e., horizontal integration). The second derives from cutting suppliers and those whom one supplies out of the market by becoming supplier and end-product producer oneself. If an owner can buy from another company he already owns and sell to a third he owns as well, then nobody but the one owner makes a profit. Vertical integration is another level of efficiency. The average person might consider efficiency to be the major reason for growing concentration, but a number of other reasons are no less significant.

Growth for Its Own Sake

While efficiencies are often important, there is a prior reason for expansion, especially with extremely large corporations. Simply, they are in a position to expand. Maclean Hunter, for example, has increased its revenue not so much by increased sales but from expanded activities (Table 6.1). According to company president Ronald Osborne, "Maclean Hunter could comfortably handle a cable-television acquisition of $300 million to $400 million and a publishing venture of $100 million to $200 million" (Enchin, 1985). Note here that the company does not have that much spare cash, nor does Maclean Hunter necessarily think it could manage things better than existent companies (at the time of the announcement apparently it didn't even know who it would try to buy out). Simply, it has the borrowing power to take on such an expansion.

Borrowing Power

Access to financial resources often results in corporate expansion. A small company may not be able to borrow enough money to upgrade its physical plant to remain competitive, but frequently a larger company will buy out the smaller company, even paying a premium to the owner, and then will be successful in borrowing the money for upgrading. The necessity of borrowing for technological

TABLE 6.1

Maclean Hunter's Growing Empire
($millions)

	1986 (9 mos.)	1985	1984	1983
Revenue	822.5	973.0	902.6	634.1
Newspapers	242.2	323.0	317.6	131.5
Periodicals and printing	283.0	289.9	261.3	224.3
Cable TV	131.8	162.1	137.1	115.1
Business forms	106.4	111.6	103.7	83.0
Broadcasting	37.2	51.1	52.1	51.5
Info. Services	21.9	35.2	30.9	28.7
Profit	44.0	64.6	49.2	47.7

SOURCE: Maclean Hunter *Annual Reports*.

upgrading can lead to corporate concentration. It is often easier and, for a number of reasons, cheaper for a company to buy an existing company than to build one up from the ground. And sometimes, just when an individual entrepreneur has brought an enterprise to the verge of real financial success, a conglomerate with the needed financial resources to provide the final expansion or marketing will buy out the entrepreneur and subsequently reap the profits.

Replacement of the Rich

People die, and shareholders are people. When shareholders die their shares often come on the market. When these holdings are large, often only large corporations have the resources to take up the shares. Ownership thus becomes further concentrated. An interest-

ing case of this type, which also represented a major cross-ownership issue, emerged in the fall of 1985 when Paul Desmarais's Power Corp. agreed to purchase controlling interest of Télé-Métropole through the purchase of 1.4 million class A and 6.2 million class B nonvoting shares from the estate and foundation of J. Alexander DeSève and Ciné-Monde Inc. for $97.8 million. Obviously, few would be in a position to match the Desmarais offer (Phillips, 1985). As it turned out, the CRTC refused permission for this Power Corp. purchase. The eventual purchaser was Télécable Vidéotron, the largest cable TV company in Quebec.

A Small Canadian Club

In some media, restrictions against foreign ownership lead to increased concentration of ownership. In broadcasting companies no more than 20 per cent of shares can be foreign owned. In newspapers both tradition and the strength of near monopoly, not to mention journalistic ire, scare off foreign investors. In other media Investment Canada, in spite of its general encouragement to foreign investors, operates within an overall concern for maintaining cultural sovereignty. The result is that foreign owners are effectively prevented from entering the marketplace.

Large blocks of holdings, however, are quite characteristic in the industry, and only the rich few and large businesses have the necessary borrowing power to acquire available blocks of holdings when they come on the market. The point is not that Canadians do not have the money, but that financial clout is organized by these financial brokers. Thereby they gain enormously while we gain the crumbs, that is, the interest the banks are prepared to give us to pave the way for these people to use our money.

Large companies may also wish to buy into emerging industries because they represent potential competitors or outlets for products they are already producing. For example, the Famous Players movie theatre chain was an early investor in cable television, which represented a new and potentially dominant outlet for movies that might have ruined Famous Players. Similarly, in the U.S., Warner Brothers investment in cable television represented a potential outlet for its products.

Media Ownership as Status

Media companies can also be status symbols for companies in more mundane industries, such as farm equipment. It is difficult to know what Conrad and Montegu Black want in their financial dealings other than power and money, but it is certainly apparent that Conrad has some sort of affair with the media. His purchase of various media properties (including the prestigious *Sunday Telegraph* in London) does not appear to be explainable purely from a financial point of view. Coupled with his literary efforts and his letters to editors defending against attacks on the position, ideology, and individuals in the international elite, he appears to associate some element of status with the media. In England, Roy Thomson acquired *The Times* and the *Sunday Times* for that reason and his son was able to sell them to Rupert Murdoch for the very same reason.

Sunset-to-Sunrise Industries

Traditional industries may also buy up certain media properties as a means of diversifying for survival. The newspapers were lured into investing in Telidon for this reason, and Famous Players, in its original investments, undoubtedly saw cable in the same light. The cable TV companies and the movie producers are both trying to set themselves up strategically so that whatever emerges as the dominant form of movie distribution, they will not be in a losing position.

The big do get bigger. For example, as of 1985 there were far too many players in the video rental business. When some order returns to the marketplace and a way of predicting and buying success becomes apparent, the big boys will step in to make it impossible for the little guys to have anything but a marginal place in the market. Recent statistics on the recording industry demonstrate how difficult it is for the small companies to get a piece of the action once the big companies have moved in, even in an expanding market. Ten foreign-owned firms in Canada earned 82 per cent of the domestic profit in 1983. The remaining 18 per cent was divided among 84 Canadian companies (Off, 1985).

The CRTC Contribution

A final factor leading to increased concentration in cable TV as a regulated industry has to do with the manner in which the CRTC operates. While the CRTC regulates cable subscriber rates, it does not generally pass judgement on the price a company might pay to take over another company. Thus, one of the biggies – Southam-Selkirk, Rogers, or Maclean Hunter – might decide to buy out a small company at a high price and do it all with borrowed money. It can then go to the CRTC with a request for an increase in rates because it paid an exorbitant amount for the shares and must now keep up the interest payments on the borrowed money. It is not asking to make undue profit, just a reasonable return on its (unwise) investment. In other words, the subscribers are the ones who pay for the takeover. Because the company is protected by virtue of being a monopoly, it has only consumer resistance to worry about, certainly not competition.

The CRTC is content to allow another monopolistic subterfuge by not requiring full disclosure of the finances of the parent and sister companies of the regulated company. Given this shortsightedness, arrangements can be worked out whereby profit is centred in unregulated companies while regulated companies become burdened with debt.

Policy on Ownership

Warnings regarding ownership concentration are not new. As far back as 1929 the Aird Commission registered concern about the ownership of media industries. Various committees and royal commissions have also sounded the alarm. Federal Combines Investigation officials have taken on a variety of cases (which they have consistently lost). The CRTC itself has expressed alarm at growing concentration but seemingly has lacked the will to take decisive action. The Kent Royal Commission's strongest point was that there was far too high a level of corporate concentration in the newspapers. In response, Trudeau's federal Liberal cabinet passed a now-rescinded order-in-council discouraging a greater degree of cross-ownership between newspapers and broadcasting. No other action has been taken by any government to enforce Kent's recommendations.

At the same time as these alarms have been raised, government policy has been to proceed without delay on the development of high-technology communications. But who benefits from such high technology? While it could be argued that Canadians do, the greater beneficiaries lie elsewhere. First, large enterprises get the information systems they need for world-scale operations. Firms able to pursue the manufacturing and marketing of these technologies in the world market also benefit. All the while these same firms are going into partnership with the federal government for development of such technologies. The very firms that dominate the market are being placed in an even more advantageous position by the commitment of the Department of Communications to high technology. It would appear that Canadians both want and don't want these firms in their position of dominance.

IMPLICATIONS OF OWNERSHIP FORM

Public Enterprise

Public ownership has a long and distinguished tradition in Canada. As Herschel Hardin (1974) points out, we Canadians have made extensive use of public enterprise throughout our history. We have used public enterprise – its most common form is the Crown corporation – in instances when we saw that the market was incapable of adequately serving the needs of the country. At times, as in the case of the CPR, we have combined public enterprise with private ownership to produce the same end, public service.

The prime example of public ownership in the media is hard to ignore. The CBC, originally a radio operation, was set up essentially in fear of inundation by programming from the U.S. In television, in the face of the small costs of purchasing U.S. programming, it was not apparent how Canadian production and display could be a money-making venture. To bring information reflective of the variety that makes up Canada to the greatest number of Canadians in order that we might all see ourselves as members of a single nation did not look like a private-enterprise project. As a consequence the CBC extended its activities into television.

The Ethic of Public Enterprise

Public corporations such as the CBC do not, like some public enterprises, go off on their own and act like private corporations, assiduously pursuing profit. To do so would be, in a sense, counter-productive. In the case of the CBC, this is not within its mandate.

For the public corporation, economics is only one factor to be considered in an overall equation. The amount of money exchanged must be considered within the broader reality of being able to provide a service to Canadians. In a democratic society, to provide national benefits to as many citizens as possible, in as attractive a way as possible, is extremely important. It is, to some extent, part of the fabric of a nation.

To bring radio and television services to every Canadian community of 500, whether those 500 people can consume enough to make them a market sufficiently attractive to advertisers to pay for the service, is surely a national achievement. Not to provide such services would threaten the maintenance of national sovereignty: if we find ourselves unable to provide services another nation, most likely the U.S., will find it in its interest to provide them.

The central ethic of the public corporation is **public service**, to both the users of the service provided and to the population as a whole. Under such an ethic charges are levied for services rendered, determined by what other Canadians must pay, not how much the service actually costs. Government corporations engage in scientific and technological research that is then licensed out to Canadian companies, largely to the benefit of the latter. Such an ethic, for example, justifies the creation of umbrella export corporations to aid private companies in developing foreign markets. The variety of such "transfers of technology" continues.

Public versus Private

The point in laying out the general *modus operandi* of the public corporation is that at times we assume that private corporations operate in the same way. Canadians tend to assume that public corporations also are means of providing sinecures for aging and out-of-office politicians and that they are notoriously inefficient. While Crown corporations are vulnerable to such problems there is no systematic evidence to suggest they are more vulnerable to mismanagement than private corporations. The point to emphasize is that they are generally in business for a different reason. They aim at public service rather than profit.

While the private media outlets can talk about how they must scramble to attract audiences and sponsors, the CBC must weigh its special responsibilities, such as training top-level journalists, against audience size and type. The CBC can consider, on the merit of the case itself, whether it will or will not, for instance, carry children's programs without ads, develop socially oriented programs for the poor, underwrite programs for the aged, and so forth. The private station must consider such issues within the context of the long-term economic equation. It is responsible to its shareholders to do just that. But through regulatory insistence private enterprise can turn aside economic concerns for whatever ends the CRTC feels are warranted.

Private Enterprise: The Private, Independent Media Corporation

The private corporation exists in a different world from that of the public corporation. Private corporations exist to make a profit. They perform a service in order to remain in business so that they can generate wealth for their owners. There are two major perceived social benefits of private enterprise. The first is that by virtue of Adam Smith's invisible hand, needed, desired, and affordable services are stimulated by economic opportunity. Second, because communication services are advertiser-supported, they are "free" to the consumer.

The prospect of a single independent media corporation operating a newspaper or a television or radio station, or publishing magazines or books, is not at all an unpleasant one. Certainly there is no hint of hidden power and behind-the-scenes manipulations. In all likelihood the scale of operations is such that the owner lives in the community, is anxious for the development of the community, and attempts to provide a service to the community while seeking to make a healthy profit.

As with any independent operator, one expects a certain personal bias, a kind of bias toned down but nonetheless present as a result of the outlook of any managing editor, for example. One would also expect to find personal quirks of the owner reflected in the paper's or station's output. One might further expect that no stories denigrating the owner or the owner's close associates would be found in the company's products.

About the only unknown, given the present state of media industries and ignoring the spectre of possible takeover for the moment, is the degree to which the owner might feel it necessary to purchase professional advice, for example, material and formats from outside. That is, as the CBC's *Inside TV News* points out, various consultancy firms exist to advise on nearly every aspect of the design of information services. The degree to which such services and their resulting formats interfere with a media company's responsiveness to the community in which it exists is considerable.

To put the matter bluntly, the community to which the company refers if it hires such consultants, or even highly specialized editors, managers, and the like, is the state-of-the-art media manipulators rather than the audience it has been licensed to serve. The responsibility for decisions passes out of the hands of the owners themselves and into the hands of those whose sole purpose it is to develop formats that maximize audiences everywhere, especially in the larger media markets.

The Multi-enterprise Media Corporation: Horizontal and Vertical Integration

Once we leave the environment of the independent media corporation and enter the world of companies related in ownership to other media and non-media companies, the whole scene, save the pursuit of profit, changes. Essentially, these dramatic changes are brought about because, as much research and commentary argue, the emergent identity of the multi-enterprise corporation comes to be represented in the output of its media arm. That emergent identity is affected by two types of internal integration, the first called horizontal, the second, vertical.

A simple horizontal combination of one media company with a non-media company can serve as a first example. With such a combination normal horizontal relations suggest that taboo subjects are extended from the personal affairs of the owner to the business affairs of his (or her) other company. Court proceedings, labour practices, any news that might reflect on the owner become, if not taboo subjects, then subjects that are treated very carefully by the employees. It is rare for a multi-enterprise company or conglomerate not to make its overall holdings known to its employees so that the employees cannot plead ignorance of these matters.

The media company will ease the business atmosphere for the non-media company to the extent that it can without being charged with undue bias. The relation is parallel to any intra-company dealings. Related companies, while concentrating on their primary responsibilities, do what they can along the way to ease things for their sister companies. The apparent difference when one is a media company is that, in dealing with information, the media company is in a fairly powerful position to make matters easier.

For example, when the Australian Broadcasting Tribunal issued a gag order to Australian newspapers early in 1982 not to print the contents of a submission by a Murdoch-owned television station to the Tribunal, it neglected to send the order to Murdoch-owned newspapers, *The Daily Telegraph* (Sydney) and *The Australian*. Apparently it assumed, quite rightly as it turned out, that the Murdoch-owned papers would not print material of detriment to a sister company (*Sydney Morning Herald*, November 2, 1982, p. 2).

Vertical relations also come into play in a simple media–non-media association. To explain, most companies use advertising. While the placement and pricing of ads is standardized by rating cards, such cards are only the beginning of negotiations.

As the mistaken submission by Murdoch's Channel Ten 10 to the Australian Broadcasting Tribunal demonstrated, item by item (see Table 6.2) the amount paid by companies for advertising varies a great deal with the identity of the company concerned. Presumably, variations are normally based on the amount of advertising taken out by the company itself, the firm the ad is about, and so forth. But advertising by a related company can be discounted or overpriced depending on the wishes of the owner. Advertising or related companies can also be given space references unavailable to others. As an illustration, figures from one hour of one day of Channel Ten 10 are included here. The station's logs also show the general level of advertising on a daily basis – rarely less than $200,000, most garnered at prime time, and little on such programs as children's shows.

The newspaper holdings of International Thomson and the advertising of the various retail (The Bay, Zeller's, and Simpson Sears)

TABLE 6.2

An Hour in the Life of Ten 10
(7 to 8 p.m., November 11, 1981)

Time	Client	Length (seconds)	Cost $
1901	Chesebrough Ponds	30	1417
1901	Dairy Prom CNL (M)*	30	1319
1914	Aust Motoro Ind.	30	1251
1914	Cadbury	30	1026
1925	Angus and Coote (M)*	60	1806
1940	United Permanent	30	1159
1940	Malvern Star	30	1352
1941	Waltons (M)*	60	1990
1942	Cadbury	30	1026
1947	Sportsplan P/L*	60	1557
1948	Pulsar	30	1382
1948	McDonalds	30	1275
1949	Rose Music P/L*	60	2151
1954	Unilever	30	1275
1954	Norman Ross	60	1450
1955	Beecham (M)*	30	1275
1956	Meyers Taylor P/L*	30	1224
2001	Mars Incorp (M)*	30	1275

*The meaning of these terms was not specified in the source used.
SOURCE: *Financial Review*, 1982, p. 12.

and travel companies Thomson also owns are a good case in point. It appears that no one has attempted to analyse the actual financial dealings between these media and non-media holdings. These would be internal company records. But International Thomson must be careful not to be seen to exploit its advantage, because the potential for non-arm's length relations are certainly undeniable. To exploit those advantages would earn the disfavour of those concerned with media and other business monopolies. It would also raise objections from Thomson's various competitors at each level of its operations.

Conglomerate Relations

When the simple association of media and non-media companies is extended into a reasonably sized conglomerate, the potential extension of self-censorship and insider financial relations also extends in lock step. What employee journalists find themselves able to talk about, what potential favouritism exists in advertising rates and placement, what potential abuse there is for tailoring soft news items to the travel and business interests of the conglomerate – all become major items of concern not only for employees but for the public and, in the case of broadcasting, for the regulator.

Said thus, it might appear, for instance, that a newspaper that is part of a conglomerate will be nothing but a propaganda tool for its sister companies. Thankfully, such is not the case. The primary role of the newspaper is to capture and maintain a market of readers to sell to advertisers of all types. Were a newspaper to be seen solely as a propaganda tool of a larger group of companies, it would begin to lose this readership and jeopardize its primary function as a company dealing in the capture and sale of audiences. That primary function significantly curtails narrow-minded, self-serving journalism done in the context of a narrow set of economic interests.

However, just as bigotry attracts its own audience, so the personal prejudices of media magnates can be found in various media. Rupert Murdoch is a prime example. When his papers have not reflected his point of view he has been known to write editorials himself. But were the opinions of owners to be found with such a frequency and in such a form that they jeopardized the journalistic identity of the outlet, they would also destroy the market position of the paper.

Matters such as these are both interesting and subtle. The human face or personality of a media outlet can go a long way to making outright bias and prejudice acceptable. The various writings in *Canadian Newspapers: The Inside Story*, which are documented in the following chapter, make that apparent (Stewart, 1980). But when such biases extend beyond those common in the community, as we saw in the Enoch Powell story, the journalistic integrity of the outlet is indeed jeopardized.

A Subtle Transformation in Content: Chain Journalism

The environment of the conglomerates has created and is creating nothing less than a transformation of journalism. In the atmosphere of an increasing number of media-related and non-media-related conglomerates, there is good reason to discourage in-depth investigative reporting. In its place comes soft news that is vaguely boosteristic of this or that community cause and that complements advertising or expected advertising. Advertorials and photographic editorials create a complementary visual environment for other commercial products.

These developments are not a crude representation of a set of narrow prejudices. They represent nothing less than a change in function and approach of the newspaper or other media company. What is most surprising is that, according to the Kent Commission, the journalists who work on the forefront of such a weakening of the ideals of journalism (e.g., the tabloids) are often more satisfied with their jobs than those who work on more traditional papers.

The problems of conglomeration increase when the likely form of the conglomerate is examined in more detail. It is rare to find a conglomerate with only one media company among a group of non-media enterprises. The more usual situation is a group or chain of media companies that are either unconnected to non-media companies or exist within a set of larger corporate holdings.

Economies of Scale

A chain, whether of media companies or otherwise, allows for so-called **economies of scale**. For example, a chain such as Southam can employ a columnist and use him or her throughout the chain. Beneath the surface, managerial techniques successful in one location can be adopted all along the chain, as can promotional strategies, special features, and the like. The Thomson chain is said to have a set of managerial techniques and other corporate guidelines that appear to define, among other things, the ratio of advertising to editorial content. These guidelines apply to all its papers except *The Globe and Mail* (Stewart, 1980). In another case, one radio station of the CHUM group, CFUN in Vancouver, switched its market from teenagers to yuppies. Once the formula proved workable, other stations followed suit.

In television, because of the network status of CTV, not strictly speaking a chain, negotiations can be carried out for the national market by CTV on behalf of all its affiliates. The bargaining position of the network is that much stronger than if the stations came to the negotiations singly. Programs can be acquired and production undertaken for the use of all affiliates. Such factors minimize costs. Similarly, consultants can be hired by a chain for all its stations rather than separately, treating each station as a unique instance.

Managers as well as managerial techniques can be transferred from paper to paper or station to station. With a chain there are opportunities for advancement within the company, a situation that encourages company loyalty in managerial echelons. If a loyal editor cannot get along in one location but appears to have talent, she or he can always be transferred to another location to have a fresh start.

Service to the Consumer

While all of these points have to do with production efficiency, they may have little to do with the enhancement of the service the paper is able to provide as a result of being a member of a chain. Media companies would argue that any economies of scale that can be achieved mean a higher level of service to the consumer. No single paper, for example, could afford to hire the number of columnists any member of a chain offers readers. In television, negotiations for city and province-wide rights rather than national rights would introduce a great deal of uncertainty in the importation of foreign television programs. Similarly, were stations to be limited to an initial local audience, media companies would argue that little which is now produced would appear.

On the surface, these economies are not to be denied, but McCormack (1983) has argued that the pursuit of such economies distances newspapers from their traditional readership. In achieving such economies the newspapers are neglecting content that would expand their readership. While her argument bears attention, the case is by no means proved.

In book publishing it is particularly interesting to compare independent with chain-owned bookstores. The two tend to operate quite differently. The former are usually in the traditional mould of providing a wide range of books from the classics to the contemporary for their clients. The chains stock only fast-selling items that are given limited shelf life, depending on their computer-monitored sales. The cultural values of the two types of stores are vastly different. The possibility of a vibrant national literary community being maintained through the marketing practices of the chains is zero.

Cross-Ownership

Complementary to the media chain is cross-ownership of different kinds of media companies. The chain is constituted of a series of geographically distant companies, each operating in a separate market, but any one company is confined to a geographical boundary as a result of its distribution system. The physical delivery of newspapers and the strength of the local signal for broadcasting are the operative variables; today, however, both variables are being much changed by the introduction of satellite transmission.

With cross-ownership, a newspaper and a radio station, for example, might operate in the same market and be owned or controlled by the same person or group of persons. The best-known example of cross-ownership in the media is the holdings of the Irving family in New Brunswick. The Irvings own all five English-language daily newspapers in the province plus a certain number of television and radio stations. Another example of extensive cross-ownership exists in London, Ontario, where the Blackburn family controls the *London Free Press* newspaper, AM and FM radio stations, and a TV station. The interesting aspect of this latter example is that in recent CRTC licence renewal hearings the company received rave reviews from the community for the services it provides. In other words, the potential for monopoly exploitation need not be taken up, especially with family holdings.

Monopoly Control

The central issue of cross-ownership is **monopoly control**. The two types of monopoly are a natural monopoly and effective monopoly. A **natural monopoly** is created when, by virtue of limited technology, competition cannot exist over the long run except by duplication of facilities. A licensing and regulatory structure is put in place to substitute for competition. The monopoly ensures that by avoiding duplication the greatest number of households can be "wired" for the lowest cost. In Canada, the telephone and hydroelectric companies are principal examples of natural monopolies. These also avoid any competitive friction that might work to the detriment of the consumer.

An **effective monopoly**, rather than being granted to a company by government, is gained by a company buying up or establishing companies that have control over the market in which they operate. In media, the combination of radio, television, and newspapers can provide a company with an effective monopoly over the local media.

When natural monopolies are granted they are regulated in an attempt to ensure that the interests of the consumer and the public are looked after. When effective monopolies are gained no such mechanism exists. The resulting situation can be seen as follows. The various media companies of a community are major information resources for the community. The ownership structure of each leads to particular biases, but with a multiplicity of owners at least some range of content can be expected. (This is the liberal-pluralist argument.) However, if all of the media are controlled by the same owners, then a potential for outright manipulation certainly exists. It is not that somehow these media outlets will work to try to turn our minds to jelly, but rather that they are quite free to work in their own economic self-interest.

So problematic is the potential for monopoly exploitation in the normal course of events that legislation has been put in place (The Restrictive Trade Practices Act) to prevent such market monopolies from emerging. Faced with lack of success in the prosecution of the Irvings and subsequently Southam and Thomson in their simultaneous closure of the *Ottawa Journal* and the *Winnipeg Tribune* respectively, the Liberal cabinet of Pierre Trudeau passed an order-in-council designed to discourage further cross-media acquisitions. However, during the time it was in effect (it was withdrawn by the Mulroney government), though it may have discouraged some new cross-media acquisitions, the CRTC was not single-minded in disallowing cross-ownership from continuing. Southam was allowed to keep 20 per cent of its holdings in Selkirk Broadcasting (reduced from 30 per cent) through the formation of a "voting trust" in which Selkirk voted Southam's shares (*Marketing*, 1982, p. 2).

Maclean Hunter was seen to be in contravention of the directive because it held 49.7 per cent of the Toronto Sun Publishing Co., publisher of *Sun* papers in Toronto, Edmonton, and Calgary. Its other holdings included CFCN Communications Ltd., holder of one television and two radio licences in Calgary. However, at the hearings Maclean Hunter argued that it did not control the *Sun* papers because of a standstill agreement, part of which was that Maclean Hunter could only elect two of the twelve members of the board of directors. The CRTC renewed the broadcasting licences in question.

In a third and last case, involving the renewal application of CHSJ-TV, the CRTC ruled that the cabinet directive held because the licence holder, New Brunswick Broadcasting Ltd., was owned and controlled by the Irving group, publishers of two daily newspapers in the area. However, the CRTC saw fit, in spite of complaints that the station was not living up to its promise of performance, to renew the licence for 2.5 years (rather than five years) be-

cause there was no CBC station in the area and little likelihood of there being one within the next two to three years (Skinner, 1984).

Manipulation and thoroughness in coverage of the news are not the only problems created by media monopolies. Media monopolies have full control over advertising rates and can abuse that control. Media monopolies also have a considerable advantage in wage negotiations with labour. They know full well that what revenue they lose in one company will be picked up to a great extent by one of their other holdings.

CORPORATE CONCENTRATION: THE SOCIAL ISSUE

In an article in *The Financial Post Magazine*, Henry Knowles, former chairman of the Ontario Securities Commission, is cited for his comments on corporate concentration in Canada and its problems. His basic concern is that if the corporate barons become too powerful, Canadians may lose control of their economic destiny. If control is lost to an elite group of super-rich businessmen, who are not responsible to the public or who are too powerful for anyone to force them to live up to their public responsibilities, such a concentration of control may lead to social and cultural instability (Hatter, 1985).

Participatory Capitalism

Hatter delves into other aspects of corporate concentration in Canada. He notes that as things now stand, some observers feel that Canadian stock prices are already too high because of the level of control exercised by major players in Canadian industry. The small shareholder stands only to gain by shifts in the price of the stock and by declared revenues.

The controlling shareholder stands to gain beyond the small shareholder in any way he can use the company, its assets, and its production capacity to lever gains where he has holdings elsewhere. Many stocks are therefore worth more to the controlling shareholder than to the non-controlling shareholder.

Hatter notes also that the degree of concentration in Canadian industry can be conservatively estimated by knowing that only 78 of the 300 stocks on the Toronto Stock Exchange (TSE) index (a wide cross-section of Canada's major publicly traded companies) can be said to be widely held in that no more than 20 per cent of the shares are in the hands of any one individual, equity, or group. Further, 112 companies on the TSE index have single shareholders with 50 per cent of the stock or more, thereby giving that shareholder legal as well as effective control. Comparative American (1983) figures show that 85.2 per cent of companies listed in Standard and Poor's 500 index are widely held, that is, no shareholder controls more than 20 per cent.

Hatter reveals also that eight major power brokers – two branches of the Bronfman family, Paul Desmarais, Ken Thomson, the Blacks, Galen Weston, Hal Jackman, and the Reichmanns – control 15 per cent of the TSE index. This figure does not include any of their private (i.e., not publicly traded) companies because such companies are not listed on the TSE index. Hatter's figures do not account for nonparticipation by the average Canadian by virtue of wholly owned foreign subsidiaries operating in Canada. Given the percentage of such corporations operating throughout the economy, it would be surprising if Canadians were not more greatly disenfranchised by them than by the Canadian super rich.

Participatory Capitalism in the Media

In comparison to industry in general, the Canadian privately owned media are even more highly concentrated in ownership. Robert Babe reports that in 1980 two chains, Thomson and Southam, controlled 59 per cent of the English-language daily newspaper circulation. In broadcasting, as of 1975, the four largest television broadcasters, Baton Broadcasting, Télé-Métropole, Southam-Selkirk, and Western Broadcasting, accounted for 40 per cent of private-sector advertising revenues. Further, again as of 1975, the 10 largest radio chains controlled 75 stations accounting for 44 per cent of private-sector revenues. The largest, CHUM, owns 21 radio stations across the country, five television stations, and the cable video-music channel, Muchmusic. Finally, as of 1980, the top three cable television companies – Rogers Cablesystems, Télécable Vidéotron, and Maclean Hunter – accounted for about 50 per cent of cable subscribers. The tables in Chapter 2 plus the ones that follow here (Tables 6.3 to 6.9) provide a sense of the overall degree of concentration of media ownership in Canada.

The Effects of Concentrated Ownership in the Media

The general ramifications of corporate concentration are usually not emphasized in discussions of corporate concentration in the media. This is not because they are unimportant but because they take second place to direct, observable effects on content. For example, when a group of newspapers or radio stations forms a chain, elements of the content can be used throughout the whole chain. An Ottawa commentator for a chain must therefore comment differently from a commentator

TABLE 6.3

Selected Financial Data: Major Newspaper Groups
($000's)

	1969	1974	1979
Southam Inc.			
Revenue from operations	104,765	221,920	484,235
Pre-tax operating income	12,261	28,484	55,507
Pre-tax return on equity	34.1%	48.6%	34.8%
Thomson Newspapers Ltd.*			
Total revenue	92,860	170,113	319,650
Pre-tax income	28,673	63,179	125,511
Pre-tax return on equity	47.9%	37.1%	39.3%
Torstar Corporation			
Total Revenue	52,275	114,836	371,100
Pre-tax income	5,826	16,735	51,996
Pre-tax return on equity	28.9%	43.6%	49.3%

*For Thomson Newspapers, the first column of figures is for 1968 rather than 1969. Data for 1969 were not available.
SOURCE: Audley, *Canada's Cultural Industries*, which used annual reports for each company.

whose material will be used only in Vancouver, Montreal, or Halifax. Programs can be developed in a central location and shipped out to the hinterlands.

Formats and management techniques can also be developed in one place and made known or adapted for sister companies. Most significantly, if equipment needs upgrading, an operation that is part of a chain can go to the bank with the chain's assets and borrowing power behind it.

Monopoly Power

In markets with monopolies, now the common situation for newspapers, the monopoly completely controls what news is covered, how it is covered, the ratio of ads to news, and the slant taken on the news, i.e., analytic and informative or sensational. The only threats to such a monopoly are the possible alienation of its audience and the remote possibility of some other company taking a run on its market. The monopolist is also constrained to some degree by the other media in the same market, provided that it does not own those media outlets.

Alienation is a very real threat, for that readership or audience is what the company sells to advertisers. However, it would be a mistake to assume that media outlets are continually seeking ways to enhance the informative value of their product and thus please their audiences. More often they attempt to capture

TABLE 6.4

Share of Gross Advertising Revenue for Five Major Consumer Magazine Publishers, English- and French-Language, 1978 and 1979

	1978		1979	
	$000's	% of Total	$000's	% of Total
English-language				
Maclean Hunter	25,512	34.4	31,553	36.1
Comac Communications*	14,376	12.3	15,656	17.9
Reader's Digest	9,090	12.3	10,631	12.2
TV Guide Ltd.	8,582	11.6	9,949	11.4
Time Canada Ltd.	6,884	9.3	8,764	10.0
Total	64,444	87.0	76,553	87.6
French-language				
Maclean Hunter	5,557	40.1	6,807	44.3
TV Guide Ltd.	3,874	27.9	4,316	28.1
Reader's Digest	2,182	15.7	2,593	16.9
Comac Communications	1,622	11.7	1,639	10.7
Nous Magazine Ltd.**	633	4.6	Not available	
Total	13,235	100.0	15,355	100.0

*Comac, a subsidiary of Torstar, is involved exclusively in the publishing of controlled-circulation magazines.
**Includes *Nous* only.

SOURCE: Audley, *Canada's Cultural Industries*, which used: *Interim Profile of the Periodical Industry in Canada*, vol. 1.

the audience with anything that works and is not too costly to produce, such as game shows. The advertorial is also a good case in point. It fills the "news space" in that it is not advertising. Because it is not advertising it costs the advertiser nothing. And because it is not written by the journalist it costs the paper nothing for the generation of the content. Everyone gains, except journalists and readers (if readers expect reasonably independent commentary).

A second concern, that of an emergent competitor, is minimal because the chain-linked company has the financial resources to withstand any kind of circulation or ratings war by virtue of its membership in a larger company. Another constraint on emergent competition is

TABLE 6.5

Revenue of Recording Industry by Source and Country of Controlling Interest, 1977–80
($000's/% of total)

	Sale of Discs/Tapes		Revenue from Lease of Master Tapes		Revenue from Related Activity		Total Revenue from Recording Industry Activity	
Canadian-controlled								
1977	30,092	16.5%	1,818	48.4%	14,548	13.4%	46,458	15.8%
1978	48,859	21.8	2,471	43.6	15,146	10.7	66,476	17.9
1979	29,079	12.2	1,682	27.8	18,471	16.3	49,232	13.7
1980	36,731	15.6	1,221	24.7	12,243	12.2	50,195	14.8
Foreign-controlled								
1977	151,938	83.5	1,936	51.6	94,111	86.6	247,985	84.2
1978	175,256	78.2	3,194	56.4	126,588	89.3	305,039	82.1
1979	209,749	87.8	4,375	72.2	94,942	83.7	309,066	86.3
1980	198,332	84.4	3,720	75.3	87,753	87.8	289,807	85.2
Total								
1977	182,030		3,754		108,659		294,443	
1978	224,114		5,665		141,734		371,515	
1979	238,829		6,057		113,413		358,299	
1980	235,063		4,942		99,996		340,001	

SOURCE: Audley, *Canada's Cultural Industries*, which used: Statistics Canada, *Recording Industry, 1978* and *1979*, and unpublished 1980 data.

that for any company in the media business to undertake such a run would mean counterpressures on some of its other holdings in other markets. For a new player to emerge with sufficient financial resources to make a go of it is unlikely because of the interlocking interests of the Canadian business elite. This leaves open the possibility of a foreign company. In broadcast-ing, foreign ownership beyond 20 per cent is not possible because of an order-in-council dating back to the 1960s. With newspapers, the traditional strength first derived from the local nature of the newspaper, which was then transformed into the strength of a chain, together with weak combines legislation, has managed to keep foreign owners at bay.

TABLE 6.6

Major Companies' Share of U.S.–Canadian Market Receipts for Films Earning Rentals Over $1 Million 1970–78 (percentages)

Companies	1970	1971	1972	1973	1974	1975	1976	1977	1978
Columbia	14.1	10.2	9.1	7.0	7.0	13.1	8.3	11.5	11.6
Metro-Goldwyn-Mayer*	3.4	9.3	6.0	4.6	—	—	—	—	—
Paramount	11.8	17.0	21.6	8.6	10.0	11.3	9.6	10.0	23.8
Twentieth Century Fox	19.4	11.5	9.1	18.8	10.9	14.0	13.4	19.5	13.4
United Artists	8.7	7.4	15.0	10.7	8.5	10.7	16.2	17.8	10.3
Universal	13.1	5.2	5.0	10.0	18.6	25.1	13.0	11.5	16.8
Warner Bros.	5.3	9.3	17.6	16.4	23.2	9.1	18.0	13.7	13.2
Total: 7 largest, 1978	75.8	69.9	83.4	76.1	78.2	83.3	78.5	84.0	89.1
Buena Vista	9.1	8.0	5.0	6.5	7.0	6.0	6.7	5.6	4.8
Amer. International	—	—	—	—	3.8	3.4	3.8	3.4	1.4
Total: 9 largest, 1978	84.9	77.9	88.4	82.6	89.0	92.7	89.0	93.0	95.3

*Distributed by United Artists since 1974.

SOURCE: Benjamin M. Compaine, ed., *Who Owns the Media?* (Knowledge Industry Publications, 1979), p. 223 (based on information from *Variety*).

The emergence of the tabloids in markets already served by broadsheets is a special case. It appears that they were allowed to enter essentially because they targeted their publications at a different market of readers. The broadsheet publishers did not want to abandon their traditional readership. Once established, however, the tabloids became direct competitors for advertising dollars and for the sub-population of readers who are equally happy with either a tabloid or a broadsheet.

All of these dynamics are being played out in Vancouver in the boardroom of the *Vancouver Sun* and *The Province*. Having recognized the emergent competition just described and owning both Vancouver dailies, Southam decided to convert *The Province* to a morning tabloid and create a style that would attract the untapped sensationalist tabloid market but not lose its traditional readership. Five or so years after the conversion, *The Province* is still losing money. However, its existence prevents the emergence of a tabloid that would compete for advertising dollars with the *Sun*.

As for the third constraint, there is some real effect of the presence of other media (and media targeted at slightly different markets, as we just explained), as there is with the general level of rates across the country for similar sized markets. No media outlet is in a very good position to gouge its advertisers and maintain good business relations.

TABLE 6.7

Numbers of Private Radio Stations Owned by the 13 Most Important Groups, 1985

Groups	Atlantic	Quebec	Ontario	Prairies	British Columbia	Canada	Stations Share %
CHUM	8	2	8	5	1	24	5.4
Telemedia	—	10	10	—	—	20	4.9
Selkirk	—	—	1	7	4	12	2.7
Maclean Hunter*	2	—	6	3	—	11	2.7
CUC Group	—	—	11	—	—	11	2.7
Moffat	—	—	1	6	2	9	2.0
WIC	—	—	4	3	2	9	2.0
AGRA Industries	1	1	3	2	1	8	1.8
Claude Pratte and Paul Desmarais Group	—	2	6	—	—	8	1.8
Eastern Broadcasting	7	—	—	—	—	7	1.6
Radiomutuel	—	7	—	—	—	7	1.6
Gordon Rawlinson Group	—	—	—	7	—	7	1.6
Standard Broadcasting	—	2	5	—	—	7	1.6
Number of Stations Owned by the 13 Groups	11	24	55	33	10	133	31.4
Total Number of Originating Stations in Operation	58	85	135	91	74	446	100.0
Relative Share of Total of the 13 Groups in Each Region (%)	19.0	28.2	40.7	36.3	13.5	29.8	

*Excluding shortwave stations.

SOURCE: *Report of the Task Force on Broadcasting Policy,* which used: CRTC, Financial Statistics and Analysis Division, Financial and Corporate Analysis.

TABLE 6.8

Number of Private Television Stations Owned by the 21 Most Important Groups, 1985*

Groups	Atlantic	Quebec	Ontario	Prairie	British Columbia	Canada	Share of all Canadian stations (%)
CUC Ltd.	—	—	7	—	—	7	8.6
CHUM Ltd.	4	—	2	—	—	6	7.4
Skinner Holdings	—	—	—	6	—	6	7.4
Pathonic Inc.	—	5	—	—	—	5	6.2
Selkirk Communications Ltd.	—	—	1	2	1	4	4.9
Moffat Communications Ltd.**	—	—	—	3	—	3	3.7
Newfoundland Broadcasting Co.	3	—	—	—	—	3	3.7
Radio Nord	—	3	—	—	—	3	3.7
Claude Pratte and Paul Desmarais Group	—	1	2	—	—	3	3.7
Number of stations controlled by nine largest groups	7	9	12	11	1	40	49.4
Baton Broadcasting	—	—	1	1	—	2	2.5
Canwest Communications	—	—	1	1	—	2	2.5
Cogeco	—	2	—	—	—	2	2.5
Harvard Developments	—	—	—	2	—	2	2.5
Huron Broadcasting	—	—	2	—	—	2	2.5
London Free Press Holdings	—	—	2	—	—	2	2.5
Monarch Broadcasting	—	—	—	2	—	2	2.5
Shortell Ltd.	—	—	—	2	—	2	2.5
"Marc and Luc Simard" Group	—	2	—	—	—	2	2.5
Télé-Métropole	—	2	—	—	—	2	2.5
Thunder Bay Electronics	—	—	2	—	—	2	2.5
WIC	—	—	—	—	2	2	2.5
Number of stations controlled by the 21 television industry groups	7	15	20	19	3	64	79.0
Total number of private stations in operation	8	17	24	24	8	81	100.0
Regional holdings by 21 groups (%)	87.5	88.2	83.3	79.2	37.5	79.0	

*Some of these stations may be termed rebroadcaster stations with a small amount of local programming and/or advertising sold locally; they file revenue reports with the CRTC and in this way are considered separate entities.
**Two of Moffat's three TV stations are 50 per cent owned through Relay Communications Ltd.
SOURCE: *Report of the Task Force on Broadcasting Policy*, which used: CRTC, Industry Statistics and Analysis Division, Financial and Corporate Analysis.

TABLE 6.9

Cable Ownership Patterns (1973, 1980, 1985)

1973

Holding/Cable Company	Province	Subscribers	% of Canadian Total	Cumulative %
1. Premier Cablevision	Ont., B.C.	300,200	14.2	14.2
2. Canadian Cablesystems	Ont., B.C.	291,700	13.4	27.6
3. Cablevision Nationale	Que.	189,000	8.9	36.5
4. Maclean Hunter	Ont.	187,000	8.8	45.3
5. Selkirk Holdings	Ont., Man., Alta.	100,800	4.8	50.1
6. Cablecasting Ltd.	Ont., Man., Alta.	91,500	4.3	54.4
7. Bushnell Communications	Ont.	67,700	3.2	57.6
Total Canadian Subscribers:		2,116,000		

1980

Holding/Cable Company	Province	Subscribers	% of Canadian Total	Cumulative %
1. Rogers Cablesystems	Ont., Alta., B.C.	1,270,300	29.6	29.6
2. Vidéotron Ltée	Que.	500,100	11.7	41.3
3. Maclean Hunter	Ont.	339,600	7.9	49.2
4. Cablecasting Ltd.	Ont., Man., Alta.	156,800	3.7	52.9
5. Moffat Communications	Man.	133,300	3.1	56.0
6. Agra Industries	Ont., Sask., Alta., B.C.	131,300	3.0	59.0
7. Cable TV (CFCF)	Que.	130,000	3.0	62.0
8. Selkirk Communications	Ont., Man.	127,100	2.9	64.9
9. Cable West	Alta., B.C.	105,600	2.5	67.4
10. Bushnell Communications	Ont., Que.	104,800	2.4	69.8
11. Capital Cable	Alta., B.C.	96,200	2.2	72.0
Total Canadian Subscribers:		4,293,000		

1985

Holding/Cable Company	Province	Subscribers	% of Canadian Total	Cumulative %
1. Rogers Cablesystems	Ont., Alta., B.C.	1,280,400	23.5	23.5
2. Vidéotron Ltée*	Que.	621,700	11.4	34.9
3. Maclean Hunter	Ont.	370,100	6.8	41.7
4. Shaw Cablesystems	Alta., B.C., N.S., Nfld.	319,300	5.9	47.6
5. CUC Holdings	Ont.	290,800	5.4	53.0
6. Cablecasting (excluding Greater Winnipeg)	Ont., Alta.	210,400	3.9	56.9
7. Selkirk Communications	Ont., Man.	177,100	3.3	60.2
8. CFCF	Que.	167,300	3.1	63.3
9. Cablenet (AGRA)	Ont., Alta., B.C.	161,600	3.0	66.3
10. Moffat Communications	Man.	142,900	2.7	69.0
11. Bushnell Communications (Standard)	Que., Ont.	141,500	2.0	71.0
12. QCTV Limited*	Alta.	110,700	2.0	73.0
Total Canadian Subscribers:		5,438,000		

*QCTV has been acquired by Vidéotron, CRTC approval pending.
SOURCE: *Report of the Task Force on Broadcasting Policy.*

A highly concentrated media industry also leads to a *narrowing of perspective*. This is not because journalists become narrow-minded but because the sources of news become fewer. As things stand, news is generated internationally by the global agencies. Within Canada, Canadian Press and its derivative, Broadcast News, generate national news for the vast majority of papers and for radio and television stations that do not have reporters in locations other than their home base. Local papers normally generate most of their own local news, which they then feed to other companies within their chain. These sources are supplemented indirectly and at all levels by the continuing investigative reporting of the CBC.

It is difficult to believe that sources can get much narrower, but it would work as follows. At the international level, as concentration increased, costs could be cut by subscribing just to the global agencies and having no other sources whatsoever, that is, no foreign correspondents and no subscriptions to secondary news agencies such as Tanjug. At the national level, as concentration increased, the owners of Canadian Press could decide that there was no longer any need for duplication of reporters between Canadian Press and its subscribing papers. Canadian Press could dispense with all of its reporters and adapt what local reporters write for their local papers. At the local level, the number of beats would be decreased. For example, after the *Winnipeg Tribune* closed, the *Winnipeg Free Press* dispensed with regular coverage of education.

Superconcentration: Beyond Monopoly Power

As mentioned previously, if the Kent Commission accomplished anything, it put the Thomson organization on notice that further expansion in the media field would not, if tolerated at all, be approved without a great deal of public debate. The matter was not so much quality of journalism, although Thomson newspapers compare unfavourably with those of the Southam chain, and not that there were not areas of the country that Thomson does not dominate, but rather that the Thomson organization was growing too large for Canada.

A more recent example of this same phenomenon occurred when Paul Desmarais's Power Corporation attempted to obtain regulatory approval for its takeover of the TVA flagship station, Télé-Métropole. Power Corp. is an extremely large Quebec-based conglomerate with extensive interests in a variety of areas of the economy. As Peter S. Anderson notes in the *Canadian Encyclopedia* (1985), it is

> a large diversified company engaged in newspapers, financial services, pulp, paper and packaging. Through its subsidiary, Gesca Ltée, Power publishes 4 daily newspapers, including *La Presse*. In addition, Gesca has 2 separate book-publishing operations. Its financial services include controlling interest in Great-West Life Assurance Co, Montreal Trustco Inc and the Investors Group. The company's pulp, paper and packaging interests are held in Consolidated-Bathurst Inc, a major Canadian pulp and paper firm. Total assets of all operations associated with Power Corporation exceeded $12.7 billion in 1983, with revenues exceeding $4 billion.

When Power came before the CRTC, as happened with Thomson and the Kent Commission, numerous individuals and organizations came forward to oppose the takeover. *Le Devoir* devoted a series of articles and editorials to the matter. On February 21, *Le Devoir*'s editor-in-chief, Paul-André Comeau, noted that the CRTC had the responsibility to protect a pluralism in information sources in the name of the public interest. This approach was turned into an argument against the takeover (*Le Devoir*, March 18, 19, 1986). With newspaper and radio holdings in both Montreal and Quebec City, the Power takeover would diminish the diversity of voices in Quebec. Citing the referendum crisis of 1980, *Le Devoir* on March 18 questioned whether a Power-dominated media would have allowed for the expression of separatist sentiments in a matter so clearly against the interests of Power. A third argument coming from this March 18 article was that since Power had suggested no improvements to the news programming, none would take place, and thus there was no public benefit to the takeover.

The judgement of the CRTC against the takeover emphasized some of the same arguments. But if one reads between the lines of all these various statements, it would appear that Power is simply too large to be allowed to expand further into more media holdings. As *Le Devoir* put it in a March 18 headline, "Télé-metropolé: une super-concentration injustifiée."

It would appear that a political will exists to resist monopoly power not at the level of one industry but at a level in which the power of private capital threatens political power. Thus, when no political action can be taken in a region or in a political sphere (such as agriculture) that does not impinge on the interests of a single company, Canadian governments and their regulatory bodies apparently are prepared to take a stand.

Trends in Ownership

In this chapter we have stressed the negative side of corporate concentration over the positive benefits. The positive benefits accrue primarily to the owners. But it is true that an independent city newspaper, based, say, in Vancouver and not hooked into the global agencies and Canadian Press, would not be much more than a local paper. For all the curses world-wide news services bring, they do provide important information for an industrialized society. Without this information our economy would disintegrate.

However, if corporate concentration brings certain advantages, an optimal level of concentration doubtless brings that advantage. A greater level brings into play the disadvantages we have discussed. Most observers see that the level of corporate concentration in the media in Canada is beyond the level necessary to obtain that advantage.

Faced with this situation, we perhaps could predict that trends in ownership patterns would be toward a lessening of corporate concentration, either by policy or in anticipation of the advantage of moving in front of policy. But no such trend is visible.

SUMMARY

Capitalism or private ownership deals with relations between people and property in a manner that is at odds with the role of communication in society. Yet private enterprise has come to own and control much of this cultural domain in Western society and specifically in Canada. The nature of that control derives directly from the dynamics of the dominant business form in the mass media, the multi-enterprise conglomerate. Three major elements of those dynamics are horizontal and vertical integration and cross-ownership.

Increased concentration of ownership has been viewed with some alarm over the years almost universally by Canadian observers.

Moreover, forces leading to increased concentration are clearly identifiable. They include growth for its own sake, acquired borrowing power, the greater ease of buying a company over starting one from scratch, providing capital to financially strapped entrepreneurs, taking over large share blocks from the estates of the rich, the limited number of wealthy people in Canada, buying up the competition, diversification, and a nurturant legal, tax, and regulatory framework. However, little has been done to combat continuing trends toward increased concentration.

The implications of ownership form, whether public or private, are many. The goals and operations of public enterprise are directed differently from those of the private corporation. They are, essentially, to serve the public interest. Private media enterprises cannot help but transform journalism, whether electronic or print, by their increased size and scope of activities. This does not mean that journalists will become the lackeys of big business. It is more that the style of journalism practised within large media companies will come increasingly to resemble the production of any other commodity by mass manufacturing for the mass market, a trend that does not appear to be of any great concern to our legislators. However, when the power of such corporations begins to rival the total power of the state, then there are indications that counteraction may be taken.

Two forms of ownership are not discussed in any detail in this chapter. The first is co-operative ownership, a form common enough in Quebec-based community radio stations but much less common in English Canada. It is a type of public ownership. A co-operative is open to any person who wishes to become a member. In that way it is public. Co-operative or community radio stations in Canada tend to be oriented to their local community and involved in cultural animation.

A second form of ownership, now evolving on the Canadian scene, is characterized by the identity and purpose of the owners. Whereas private stations are usually in business to make money, there are now groups, such as churches, interested in owning their own radio and television stations so that they will have greater access to audiences. It appears that the CRTC is prepared to allow such groups ownership, given the emerging capacity brought by cable and satellites, if various members of such groups, for example, a variety of churches, are prepared to submit an application for joint ownership and management (see Salter, 1988).

REFERENCES

Anderson, Peter S. "Power Corporation of Canada," *The Canadian Encyclopedia* (Edmonton: Hurtig, 1985), p. 1464.

Babe, R. "Media Ownership," *The Canadian Encyclopedia* (Edmonton: Hurtig, 1985), pp. 1014-15.

Canada. *Report of the Task Force on Broadcasting Policy.* Ottawa: Ministry of Supply and Services, 1986.

Canada. *Royal Commission on Newspapers.* Ottawa: Canadian Government Publishing Centre, 1981.

Canadian Broadcasting Corporation. *The Press and the Prime Minister,* directed and produced by George Robertson. Toronto, 1977.

Canadian Broadcasting Corporation. *Inside TV News,* directed by F. Steele, produced by H. Gendron and F. Steele. Montreal, 1982.

Enchin, H. "Southam faced total 'destruction' if taken over by Maclean Hunter," *Globe and Mail,* October 11, 1985, p. B1.

Hardin, H. "Pushing public broadcasting forward: advances and evasions," in R. Lorimer and D.C. Wilson, eds., *Communications Canada.* Forthcoming, 1988.

Hardin, H. *A Nation Unaware*. Vancouver: Douglas and McIntyre, 1974.

Hatter, D. "Corporate concentration: Charmed circle still firmly in control," *Financial Post 500* (Summer, 1985), pp. 58-61.

Marketing, May 23, 1982, p. 2.

McCormack, T. "The political culture and the press in Canada," *Canadian Journal of Political Science* (September, 1983).

Off, C. "Statscan report casts doubt on culture's economic clout," *Financial Post*, October 12, 1985, p. 11.

Phillips, F. "Rough reception for Power Corp. TV deal," *Financial Post*, September 28, 1985, p. 2.

Financial Review, February 17, 1982, p. 12.

Salter, L. "Reconceiving the public in public broadcasting," in R. Lorimer and D.C. Wilson, eds., *Communications Canada*. Forthcoming, 1988.

Skinner, Dave. Unpublished student paper, Department of Communication, Simon Fraser University, 1984.

Stewart, W. *Canadian Newspapers: The Inside Story*. Edmonton: Hurtig, 1980.

Sydney Morning Herald, November 28, 1982, p. 1.

STUDY QUESTIONS

1. The first Lord Thomson of Fleet said: "It is the business of newspapers to make money." What are the arguments for and against this viewpoint?

2. The mass media systems in Canada have specific organizational and ownership characteristics. What are they and how do they affect the content received by Canadians? Use examples from newspapers, radio, or TV (or all these media).

3. "Freedom of the press is for those who own one." Discuss.

4. Wallace Clement, in *The Canadian Corporate Elite* (Toronto: McClelland and Stewart, 1975), p. 235, has written: "The conclusion must be that together the economic and media elite are simply two sides of the same upper class; between them they hold two of the key sources of power – economic and ideological – in Canadian society and form the corporate elite." Do you agree or disagree with his statement?

CHAPTER

7

The Functions of
Media Professionals

INTRODUCTION

THE MEDIA of the Western world bring together in their production activities two groups of individuals, capitalist (or sometimes state or co-operative) owners and professionals of various types, including journalists, announcers, typesetters, camera operators, and so on. The focus of the present chapter will be on these *professionals*, specifically *journalists*. Throughout this chapter we will sometimes talk about print journalism, sometimes about electronic journalism. Unless stated otherwise, comments apply to both. The chapter is divided into three sections.

1. We begin by looking at the ideals of journalism, some of the issues of dispute within the profession, accounts of the day-to-day realities of working for newspapers, career patterns, and finally the relations between journalists and newsmakers.

2. In a second section, management processes (the editorial side of journalism) are outlined and consideration is given to how infor-

...there are, however, certain indications from head office that ours is a troubled paper...

PUBLISHER MOOSE CHIP TIMES

Cartoon by Phil Mallette, Winnipeg. *From Royal Commission on Newspapers. Reproduced with permission of the Minister of Supply and Services Canada.*

mation is programmed both at the gathering stage and in its dissemination.

3. Finally, some of the various influences on media professionals, in their jobs as information coordinators and disseminators, are discussed.

THE IDEALS OF JOURNALISM

The journalistic profession, just like the teaching, legal, and medical professions, has a set of ideals to which it makes primary reference. Contemporary journalism finds the basis of those ideals in the notion of **social responsibility**. Freed from the yoke of government through the achievement of a libertarian ideal (see Chapter 3) only to be constrained by large capitalist employer-owners (see Chapter 6), the profession has asserted this ideal as a way of establishing its right to seek information and to maintain a measure of independence

from its employers. In the view of the profession, its quest for information is based on a commitment to treat "events and persons with fairness and impartiality, but also ... [to consider] the welfare of the community and of humanity in general in a spirit devoid of cynicism" (*Royal Commission on Newspapers*, 1981, p. 24). Journalists see, and most declarations of human rights enshrine, this ideal of freedom of the press as an extension of the basic right given to all individuals, **freedom of expression**.

The 1960 Canadian Bill of Rights, brought in by John Diefenbaker's government, speaks to freedom of expression and freedom of the press in two different sections, Sections 1(d) and 1(f). The Canadian Charter of Rights and Freedoms addresses both freedom of expression and freedom of the press in Section 2 under the heading "Fundamental Freedoms":

2. Everyone has the following fundamental freedoms:
(a) freedom of conscience and religion;
(b) freedom of thought, belief, opinion and expression, including freedom of the press and other media of communication;
(c) freedom of peaceful assembly; and
(d) freedom of association.

Journalists do not take the ideals of their profession lightly, nor do they consider those ideals and their profession as peripheral to the workings of Western democratic society. As Royal Commissioner Tom Kent points out, most journalists believe that press freedoms are the very reason we have responsible democracy, rather than vice versa. They see press freedoms as the prime mover.

The classic self-image of journalists is that of inveterate seekers after truth, devoted to the facts and to the reader. If they err in excess, it is in their view of the ideal reader who may bear a closer resemblance to an ideal self or ideal rational citizen than to the average citizen. At another extreme is the journalist who believes in attending to the public's wants and needs. Usually these wants and needs are prescribed by the market and therefore the corporate values of the newspaper for whom the journalist works. But the wants-and-needs approach may also be found in those oriented to left-wing politics. There the journalist may see his job to be to combat a false consciousness, to persuade the public how to view various issues and events.

Two recent cases in British Columbia illustrate the normal split on what is considered to be appropriate professional behaviour. In one case five people, who at the time of their arrest were in the possession of a quantity of arms and ammunition, were charged with a variety of offences, including blowing up a hydro substation. Almost immediately they were named the "Squamish 5" and local television news had a field day exploiting the situation and depicting them in the image of terrorists after the style of European groups. Other journalists were quick to sense this exploitation and monitored it. One CBC television program prepared an extensive item questioning the role of the media. To place this "field day" in a slightly fuller context, the trial judge later placed a ban on the use of the term "Squamish 5" for the duration of the trials of all of the accused, apparently because he felt it was prejudicing the right of the accused to a fair trial by casting them as terrorists. On the other side, the news journalists who hyped the story saw their brethren as self-appointed media watchdogs.

In terms of the two general perspectives we spoke of above, those who were anxious to hype the five into modern-day political terrorists could be said to have been fulfilling the wants if not needs of the public for intrigue and high drama. Those who were more circumspect could be said to have been playing out the role of rational, disinterested citizens, committed to the principles of justice for all.

A second case involved a man who was accused of killing members of two families in northern British Columbia and burning their car and camper. Once again representatives of the media differed as to the appropriate course of action. Some explored every lead surrounding the accused once the man was arrested. Others questioned the wisdom of such story creation prior to the trial of the accused.

The two positions in both these cases express two differing views of the role of the journalist. One group espouses what could be called a traditional role: to seek after information surrounding any case and bring all the information that can be uncovered to the public eye. The second group sees the responsibilities of journalists as including a consciousness of the consequences of their own action. Inflammatory presentation of the accused as terrorists or amateur psychologizing on what might have caused an accused to do a terrible deed potentionally jeopardizes a fair trial and certainly creates a problem for an innocent person after his name has been cleared.

This point seems to have motivated a specific comment by a presiding judge. In an incest case reported in the *Vancouver Sun*, County Court Judge Peter van der Hoop found it necessary to say, "This is not just an acquittal based on reasonable doubt. This is a declaration of the innocence of the accused" (June 21, 1985, p. A3). As the accused in this case noted to an inquiring reporter, seemingly more in reference to the media than to the legal treatment, "I have no comment. This whole thing has already caused me too much grief."

One other point is implicit in the reasoning of the "self-aware" group of journalists, and especially applicable to the case of the Squamish 5. In a society where institutions are able to orchestrate the rule of law to favour their own ends, some individuals may find that their only available tactic is illegality and/or violence. Immediate branding of such groups as terrorists may prevent them from obtaining a fair hearing for their grievances.

The same division of opinion was apparent on a *Journal* program aired early in 1985 following a threat by a political group to place bombs in the Toronto transit system. A number of journalists from the print and electronic media, along with some representatives of the "oppressed" community to which the bombing was intended to draw attention, were interviewed as a group. Most of the Canadian journalists felt that while coverage plays into the hands of terrorists by giving them publicity, that coverage must continue in order that the

public be informed. They believed that the responsibility of the media was to refrain from heating up the issue through its coverage, for example by opening a "hotline" to those doing the threatening. The extreme position on this side of the argument was that the media are responsible to pursue the collection of information to the extent that the law allows. That opinion was put forward by an American journalist and former White House adviser. Several non-journalists argued for no coverage at all.

A more recent example of media-terrorist interaction emerged in the summer of 1985. In this instance, involving the hijacking of a TWA jet out of Athens, there seemed to be little leeway for the two perspectives on the role of the media, so powerless did they become as they were swept up in the events. Journalist Glenda Korporaal, writing in the *Australian Financial Review* (July 3, 1985, p. 1) under the title "How the U.S. media hijacked foreign policy," saw the event as a turning point in the role of the media in global politics. Very quickly the hijackers realized what power the U.S. media had in producing movement in the Reagan administration. The hijackers stated: "The Central Press Bureau of the Amal declares that all the film taken of the hostages can be used freely by all press agencies and television networks."

Thus they milked the media for all the publicity they could get. But perhaps the hostages and their families had more at stake in the media treatment of the event. As Korporaal put it, the event established a precedent: television is both an essential part of an effective hijacking and an important tool for the families of the hostages to keep the pressure up for the release of the captives.

In summary, while journalists accept the notion of "social responsibility" as a guiding principle, they are certainly not united in applying its meaning. They do agree, however, that no matter how social responsibility is applied, it is an extension of freedom of expression and is fundamental both to democracy and to press freedoms.

A further level of agreement among journalists is indicated by the Kent Commission. Journalists account for a fall in the prestige of the press by citing its lack of depth. If they were allowed to:

> get to the bottom of facts and events, go beyond the tip of the iceberg, grapple with difficult, complex, but important subjects, and expose them, explain them clearly to the public, bring out the deeper significance of events, in short, assume the responsibility of finding and publishing what the public should know rather than seeking to satisfy the lowest common denominator of public demand as determined by market studies and advertising surveys then the former prestige of the press would be regained. (*Royal Commission on Newspapers*, p. 31)

University professors sometimes feel that they, too, would be more respected if they had the freedom to pursue truth to its very base and make it known to all.

Canadian Newspapers: The Inside Story

If the Kent Commission lays out the ideals of the journalistic profession, its realities are to be discovered in a book edited by Walter Stewart, *Canadian Newspapers: The Inside Story*. In this book some fifteen journalists provide their perspectives on working for Canada's newspapers. Several important general points emerge.

The strongest point made by these journalists is the extremely *influential role of the owner*

on journalism as practised in a variety of Canada's newspapers. There seem almost to be as many styles of owner influence as there are owners. The ideal is the rare case in which the owner has a fundamental respect for the profession of journalism and sees his role to be that of standing behind the decisions of the editor. This ideal passes on to the reporters through the editor in the form of respect for their judgements, and the reporters, in turn, must accept the responsibility of this freedom.

At the other extreme is the type of owner, personified by Beland H. Honderich of *The Toronto Star*, whose tastes and predispositions guide the entire operation of the paper. Stewart, writing about *The Star*, claims that the paper, although it has a readership of 640,000, is edited with one reader in mind at all times – the owner. He tells how series were dropped because it was anticipated that Honderich wouldn't like them. In another instance a *Star* book editor was removed from his post for no other reason than that Honderich did not want him in the post. *The Star* engages in Metro (Toronto) boosterism because that is what Honderich wants. Pictures of people in profile rarely appear because the boss has laid down a rule forbidding such pictures. A comparable owner is Rupert Murdoch: his intrusions into his papers and TV stations are discussed in the hearings of the Australian Broadcasting Tribunal of 1981-82, as well as in many other places.

Other owners are no less idiosyncratic. Halifax papers go in for highway safety and support of the monarchy on account of the predispositions of the owner. And intrusion on major issues is certainly not the exception. Back in 1955 Charles Woodsworth, son of J.S. Woodsworth, the founder of the CCF, predecessor to the NDP, was fired as editor of the *Ottawa Citizen* by R.W. Southam mainly because of his last name and to a lesser extent because his editorial policies were seen to be "socialist." Throughout the reign of the CCF in Saskatchewan, by reason of the views of the owner, the *Saskatoon Star-Phoenix* continually did battle with the government and only made peace with the government when Ross Thatcher's Liberals were elected.

Our point here is not the behaviour of owners but the behaviour of journalists in response to the realities of ownership. It is important to emphasize that the presence of the owner is, seemingly, the most strongly felt influence in the day-to-day lives of practising journalists. Wedding those influences with the ideals of journalism – truth-seeking, social responsibility, etc. – causes continual tension and intrigue in the profession.

As to the ideals themselves, in Stewart's book and in other accounts of journalistic practices, it is extremely rare to find accusations of being handed orders to write on an issue from a particular perspective contrary to the facts or to one's conscience. The kind of selection that takes place is more subtle. If an editor wants a certain perspective taken, he or she will choose the reporter who will give that perspective and will often inform the reporter about that perspective. In many other cases the reporter is left with the "responsibility" to do something that fits in with the perspective of the paper. The reporter knows that perspective simply by having worked for the paper for some time, by having read it previous to employment, and by its general reputation in the profession. If a reporter turns up something that is not pleasing to the editor or publisher but cannot be faulted factually, the piece is either killed because of "space limitations" or indirect pressure is applied to the reporter to produce something that balances the reporter's perspective with that of the editor or owner.

One example of the journalist as "hired gun" is an article called "The Corporation Haters" (*Fortune*, June 16, 1980), which argued that the Nestlé baby formula boycott had been engineered by corporation-hating radicals, not by those concerned about infant deaths in Third World countries. The author, Herman Nickel, received a $5,000 fee from a Washington, D.C., conservative think tank (MacLean, 1979) and ended up, not long after, as U.S. ambassador to South Africa, a handy man for the Reagan government to have in such a position. Nestlé, by the way, ultimately accepted some responsibility for the infant deaths by pulling back on its marketing efforts in underdeveloped countries.

Should reporter and editor or owner continually disagree, the reporter finds opportunities narrowing sufficiently to encourage him or her to move to another paper. Journalists who are uncompromising tend to become freelancers whose articles and programs are purchased as single items. The same kind of relationship, one level up, may develop between the publisher of a newspaper and the owner. While the journalist may find the opportunities of his assignments narrowing, a publisher may find the resources with which he has to work unduly diminished as the owner allocates fewer and fewer resources to create a good paper. (See Murdock, 1982, on allocation control.)

First-rate reporters such as John Sawatsky operate as freelancers, it would appear, by choice. They sell individual articles to newspapers as they are developing their research for a book, which is then published and excerpted. The quality of work Sawatsky and other freelancers produce would suggest that this is a good way around the limitations that journalists most often complain about, namely, the lack of the time or resources to do investigative reporting in any depth. The paper may not be interested for fear of uncovering things embarrassing to its advertisers or setting a tone with which advertisers are uncomfortable. Or the paper may be interested enough but unprepared, purely for reason of profit, to devote enough resources to the task.

Television Journalism

It is rare for a television station owner to exert the kind of pressure common to newspaper owners over the shape if not the content of the news. The person who plays that role is the news director, whose opinions about what should be covered and how it should be covered or followed up shape television news. The documentary footage in the CBC's *Inside TV News* tells us as much about the role of journalists as does anything.

As that program points out, on the basis of agency feeds, morning newspapers, and other credible sources, a news program begins to take shape early in the day. The task for the central office is to get reporters and crews to the right places and to obtain the right information to construct visually compelling "on-the-spot" stories about what they already know is news. The task for the journalists is to obtain access to people and places in order to collect information in a manner in which it can be used to build the story.

In *Memoirs*, René Lévesque tells of his involvement in 1956 with the beginnings of the current affairs genre in Canadian television.

> According to the experts in program planning, it was hard to imagine anything more stillborn than my idea to introduce real stories from far-off lands into the family living room after the local soap opera.... Everyone was crazy about our little family dramas perpetuated on TV from one series to the next. As distant as they

might be from Saint-Denis and Saint-Catherine streets, couldn't the crises of world events be made just as captivating, given that the cast was made up of highly dramatic characters and the plot was fuller of jolts and surprises than anything Grignon or Lemelin could invent? ...

Lévesque and his producer proceeded to construct a story on the Suez crisis in soap opera terms. Their basic notion was that Suez was "the joint tragedy of colonial empires and their humiliated subjects, of the unconscious arrogance of their rulers and, finally after years of resignation, the angry revolt of the subjugated." Lévesque continues:

> That night, signing off, I risked saying to the TV audience that from the look of things we'd soon be speaking of Suez again. The next day or the day after war was declared.... and our friend Pearson was awarded the Nobel Peace Prize.... on a more modest level I was considered to be something of a sorcerer. Or better still, a prophet in my own country, however minor. (pp. 143-45)

Similar stories unfolded with other CBC reporters as a tradition of foreign and domestic reporting and storytelling was built up. Luck and informed judgement sometimes put the right people in the right spot at the right time. More often, and increasingly frequently because of budget constraints, the CBC's foreign correspondents, in contrast to the large American networks, are either confined to news hot spots or they are covering several countries or entire continents. However, the CBC backs itself up with the feeds of the major U.S. networks. The U.S. networks make it a point of pride to operate on their own resources, to be in the right place at the right time, and to be sufficiently informed that they are used by the U.S. government as a source of information. The U.S. networks also use feeds, but to a more limited degree.

Where Canadian radio and television shine, in part because they do not have the resources to be on top of every event, is in follow-up journalism. In the case of radio, because the telephone may be used for "phone out" interviews, programs such as *Sunday Morning* and *As It Happens* can be much more immediate in their reaction to events. The fancy technology of *The Journal* also allows a certain amount of up-to-date coverage. But planned, in-depth documentary pieces that combine both issues and events by anticipating occasions of contemporary significance are particularly good opportunities for Canadian television journalists and producers to show their mettle. Such was the case, for example, with Lévesque's current affairs program, *Point de Mire*, in the 1950s.

Career Patterns in Journalism

One might not expect the career patterns of journalists to be relevant to an analysis of the broader significance of their role. Usually a profession has a slightly skewed distribution toward younger members, enough to give it new blood but not enough to set norms for the profession as a whole. The situation in journalism has been summarized with respect to the parliamentary press gallery by Roy MacGregor. He writes:

> If we could distill one composite reporter from the two hundred thirty or so that make up the present Parliamentary Press Gallery we would come up with one male, close to thirty years of age, middle-class background (perhaps slightly higher), university educated (rarely in journalism) earning in excess of $25,000 a year, somewhat concerned about his weak backhand in tennis, and frightfully testy about his lack of knowledge of political history. He would be fairly conservative in his soul, Liberal in print and NDP in the bar. (Stewart, 1980, p. 196)

Is the parliamentary press gallery a place where the relatively young congregate? Are older journalists found elsewhere? Not at all. Journalists tend to advance relatively quickly out of their basic role as reporters to become editors and columnists or, just as often, to leave journalism to work on the other side of the fence, for government or private enterprise as information officers. For example, Prime Minister Mulroney's former press secretary, Bill Fox, was lured away from his position as Washington correspondent for *The Toronto Star* when he was 36 years old (MacDonald, 1984, p. 230).

When journalists move on to private enterprise and to government, they often find positions that offer more money and less immediate, day-to-day pressure. Such jobs involve designing and orchestrating information to be fed to the media. Knowing from their journalistic background what makes reporters pay attention, they design press releases so that certain information is bound to be emphasized in the papers. Or they cook up photo opportunities for television crews. Or they advise ministers on how to leak and whom to leak to in order to float trial balloons or achieve other secretive purposes.

As a consequence, the public is left with the relatively young and the idealists to pursue journalism on their behalf. On the other hand, for every orchestrating information officer working to create press releases there is an equally and perhaps more competent editor assigning his reporters to uncover other aspects of the story that may not be immediately apparent. (A fuller account of the functioning of the parliamentary press gallery, following Fletcher, 1981, was provided in Chapter 3.)

One final point on the journalist-information officer interaction. It is quite interesting that journalists find themselves able to move back and forth between government, private corporations, and the media with relative ease. Such ease of movement illustrates the degree to which such institutions share the same basic viewpoint. It also illustrates a basic pluralism to which they all adhere with relative comfort.

Relations between Journalists and Newsmakers

Journalists need information. Formally speaking, information can be acquired by interview and by virtue of the Access to Information Act. The journalist can also search through records that private companies, for example, are required to make public. Equally important to a journalist are informal channels of information.

One example of a journalist who makes extremely good use of a combination of officially available and informal information, acquired through other sources, is John Sawatsky. His books on the RCMP and on spies could never have been written without his ability to solicit information off the record from various unnamed individuals. The more usual example is referred to in the CBC documentary *The Press and The Prime Minister*. As columnist Allan Fotheringham points out, in Ottawa at least, there is a kind of incest between politicians and journalists. Journalists need politicians to give them good stories. Politicians need journalists to get things into the press. They extend favours to one another in exchange for return considerations. It is an intricate game played according to certain rules that could not be described as the pure pursuit of truth. The journalist must develop a host of relationships with a wide variety of newsmakers in order to get the occasional scoop and quickly check the veracity of, or get another opinion on, the many stories he or she must write.

THE MANAGEMENT OF INFORMATION

Journalists are not hired as autonomous information seekers and given the freedom to pursue and reveal what truth they personally deem worthy of their efforts. Their activities are constrained by their bosses, owners and/or editors, news directors, or anonymous bureaucrats who lay down policy and allocate the necessary resources to do the job. Their bosses, if they are not owners, are usually former journalists who have advanced to the editorial stage in the collection and organization of information. The responsibility of these editors is to deploy strategically the troops to whichever fronts appear to be potentially active and then to sort through what information is gathered for the "best stories."

In carrying out this function, the editor-managers must provide a credible information product that attracts listeners, viewers, or readership to a great enough extent to stave off the competition. In other words, their jobs are to maintain a penetration rate that does not leave room for a competitor to enter. They must assemble a large enough audience to sell to advertisers at a sufficient price to pay for expenditures made producing information and to provide the requisite percentage profit that the owner demands.

The division of responsibilities between reporter and editor or between the reporter and the person acting in the name of the publisher is recognized in law in Section 267 (1) of the Criminal Libel Act. In a 1981 libel case involving the CBC and reporter Chris Bird versus the deputy attorney-general of B.C., Richard Vogel, in which Bird, through the facilities of the CBC, accused Vogel of misusing his office, the presiding judge drew distinctions between the responsibilities of the journalist involved and his editors who represent the institution. The judge wrote:

> Mr. Bird's conduct was in the course of his employment as a reporter. Had his employer exercised a reasonable degree of editorial judgment and control, that conduct would have caused no harm to anyone. The damage came, not from the investigation, but from the publication. The responsibility for deciding whether to publish rested with those above Mr. Bird. The most seriously reprehensible conduct was their abdication of that responsibility. That was an abdication not by individuals, but by an organization possessing a unique degree of power and influence.
>
> The circumstances of the case call for the award of an additional amount against the CBC as exemplary damages.
>
> That amount should not depart from the traditional moderate awards but should be sufficient to mark the court's disapproval of the conduct of the CBC and provide some element of deterrence from similar conduct....
>
> The defendants CBC and Bird will be liable jointly for damages in the amount of $100,000. The defendant CBC will be liable for the further amount of $25,000.

Editors as Gatekeepers

The manner in which this judgement has been written leads us directly into what is perhaps the dominant way of seeing the functions of editors in the media, that is, as gatekeepers.

The notion of **gatekeeper** was originally conceived and coined by social psychologist Kurt Lewin in 1947 in reference to the consumption of food. The question he posed was, why do people eat what they eat? To answer his question he developed a "channel theory" – food comes to the table through various channels, for example, buying in the store, picking from the garden, etc. Food moves step by step through a channel, for example, from gatherer

to processor, to wholesaler, to retailer, to family, to freezer, fridge, or cupboard, to table, to eater. He then questioned who controls the flow of food along those channels. In general, the answer is gatekeepers. He noted also that gate sections were either governed by impartial rules or by the decision-making of the gatekeepers (Cartwright, 1951, p. 186).

Obviously this model can be applied to just about any social phenomenon that involves gathering objects or materials and transforming them into consumable products. As Hester (in Wells, 1974, p. 210) points out in a diagram in his article on international news agencies, the reporter selects from a universe of events:

- which are then selected for transmittal by a national agency,
- which are then selected for transmittal by the global agency,
- which are then selected for transmittal by the media users,
- which are then selected for reading or watching by the individual consumer.

What is of particular interest in this process is that the notion of gatekeeping is usually applied in academic literature only to some stages of selection, that is, specifically not to the reporter's gathering and the consumer's choice. More broadly speaking, the cognitive selection process, in which both reporter and audience engage, is not considered to be "gatekeeping." Moreover, there are limitations of the gatekeeping model for describing the process by which newspapers and television programs are created. The gatekeeper metaphor causes us to focus our attention on the refusal or negative-selecting function of editors and owners. By implication, truth and value are in the hands of the reporters or writers, and editors allow only acceptable truths through the gates.

A major element neglected in the gatekeeping analysis is the construction function that the

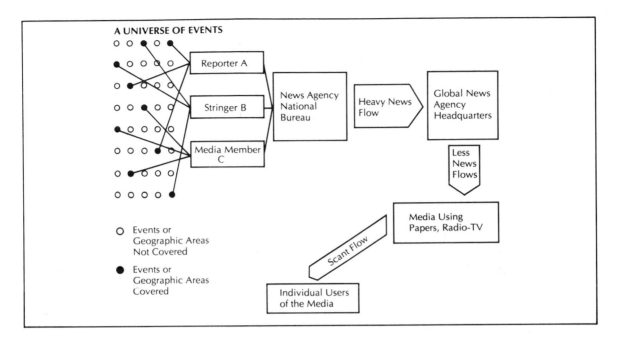

FIGURE 7.1. *International news flow via a news service.* Of the many potential news events, only some are covered by reporters, "stringers," or members relaying stories to the bureau of the global news agency. Editors there forward important news items to the world headquarters of the agency. Editors at world headquarters select what they think newsworthy. Finally, the individual reader, listener, or viewer decides what international news he will be attentive to. What began as hundreds of events and items has gradually dwindled to only a handful. SOURCE: Al Hester, "International News Agencies," in Alan Wells, ed., *Mass Communications, A World View* (Palo Alto: Mayfield Publishing, 1974). Reproduced with permission of the author.

editor, news director, or program producer serves. From this perspective it might be argued that the significance of the editor or producer, or for that matter any others involved, is to help transform or construct something from the raw material, which reporters gather or writers produce, to form the greater whole of the program, magazine, newspaper, and so on. Only then does the material become fully contextualized and take on its full significance. What a racy tabloid makes of a political assassination is usually quite different from what a national broadsheet makes of it. More generally stated, the whole is greater than the sum of its parts.

Incidentally, owners, too, serve a construction function in providing the institution within which journalists operate and by allocating the necessary resources to the news-gathering and editorial processes. The challenge of the editor/producer role is to negotiate a place for material that is culturally valuable. It is to the construction function that we now turn.

The Editorial Construction Function

The *Royal Commission on Newspapers* provides a description of the workings of management in the newsroom. That description provides a sense of the mechanics of the construction of various elements of a newspaper and of the newspaper as a whole.

The *head of the editorial department* or *editor-in-chief*, who reports directly to the publisher, is responsible for the editorial content of the newspaper. He or she usually creates the character of the paper both in its day-to-day operations and in the context of its broader relations with readers, politicians, and other opinion leaders.

The *executive editor* or *editorial page editor* works under the editor-in-chief, as does the *managing editor*, the person who manages the newsroom, hires and fires, and negotiates editorial space with the advertising department.

The *news editor*, as might be expected, looks after the news desk, sorting items for placement in the paper and on the front page, asking for rewrites, obtaining headlines, etc. Again here, this sorting process is influential in determining the character of a paper.

The role of the news editor comes closest to the simple notion of gatekeeper. But the news editor builds and creates an emergent reality as much as he excludes pieces. And even in his exclusion it is not so much that he censors or refuses to let events interfere with his and the paper's world view, but rather that he requires of the reported events an interpretive context consistent with his sense of what his paper is all about.

Apparently the strongest negative editorial influence, which is potentially censoring, is related to the type of ownership of a newspaper. As the Kent Commission (p. 114) reported from the testimony of Professor Henry Mintzberg:

> [Chain ownership] tends to insulate management from local pressures, local situations. The loyalty is to the corporation, the loyalty is to the bottom line, and there is a certain mobility built into the fact that, if you don't

make it in Montreal, then you can move to Toronto or Winnipeg or what have you, within the corporation. I think that creates certain tendencies to be less sensitive to local needs, and perhaps sometimes to be less in touch with them.

Beyond the Mechanics of Construction

Journalists and the entertainment industry have celebrated the construction function for some time. The "good editor/good newspaper" tradition and the reverence held for John Grierson of the National Film Board are elements of that celebration. So, in the entertainment field, are such awards as the Oscars, Genies, Emmies, Rockies, Junos, etc. The construction function is also discussed in "Their Finest Hour," an article by Martin Knelman (1983) in *Saturday Night*.

Knelman points to a fine Canadian tradition in documentaries, beginning with John Grierson. But his focus of attention is on *The Journal*, its executive producer, Mark Starowicz, and the other central figures involved in the creation of *The Journal*. An extensive effort went into the creation of *The Journal* months before it ever went to air. More than a year was spent in conceiving and developing the format and personnel for the show before any content was ever introduced. All this attention, some $10 million worth by Knelman's guess, can be seen as attention to format, to the processing of information as opposed to content, to the editorial rather than the information-gathering side.

While few shows are able to spend $10 million setting themselves up, it could be argued that the capital costs of setting up a newspaper are equivalent. However the costs are reckoned, a great deal of attention is paid to the matter of how one will present information, how one will construct and package information to appeal to one audience or another.

Neither is this activity confined to the preproduction phase. Once in operation all media maintain a constant surveillance of their audiences.

The editorial/management function is not confined to the broad design of the program as a whole. The gatekeeping view would have us assume that on a day-to-day basis editors are rather like St. Peter manning the gates to heaven. In fact, more often, at least in the Canadian media, the editor works with the journalist/writer to shape an initial draft into something suitable for the editor's particular program or series. The process involves much give and take.

This process is not confined to news and information programming. While much emphasis has been paid to the gatekeeping function, constructive interaction is frequent. Writers, whether for television, periodicals, or book publishers, seek out the programs, magazines, or publishing houses respectively for which they anticipate they can write. They feel that they understand the approach and the style of the production. On that basis they develop scripts, pieces, or book outlines they believe fit their target program or publication. After the material is submitted, if it is seen to have possibilities, the editor then sits down with the writer to try and maximize possibilities inherent in the script. Together they reconstruct the piece with regard to both the creativity of the writer and the contingencies of production or publication in the particular outlet.

The differences emerge between, say, book publishers and program producers in the degrees of freedom within which each feels it must operate. Clearly a publisher known for encouraging new and innovative writing has a much broader range of possibilities than do the producers and editors of *Seeing Things* or *The Beachcombers*.

A More Academic View

Extensive research has been conducted into the function of editors, but from a more abstract perspective than the one we have been discussing so far. Some of it derives from a gatekeeping model but manages to move to varying extents into a discussion of the editorial construction function.

Take, for example, the claim introduced in Chapter 2 and extended in Chapter 5 that the media are an ideological control apparatus. That notion derives, to a considerable extent, from a view of the media as gatekeepers. According to this model news is a constructed entity which, by numerous journalistic means such as story format, use of beats, pursuit of accepted angles, use of authorities as primary definers of events, etc., reproduces the dominant ideology. Such a viewpoint de-emphasizes the creative act of making the world comprehensible – the work of consolidating or articulating culture – in favour of seeing such activities as an ideological reproduction process aimed at extending powerful and dominant interests. The gatekeepers, so the model goes, let in stories that conform or can be made to conform to standard acceptable themes played out in the daily news. When stories appear to but do not conform to the implicit definition of news that results from these procedures, as Bennett, Gressett, and Haltom (1985) put it, they must be repaired and made to fit.

Thus, in the example of the Alabama man setting himself on fire, the U.S. national media felt compelled to transform that story from the story Andrews wanted told about unemployment, but for which he had no media-understandable credibility as teller, to a story of journalistic ethics. Similarly with other examples we have cited, such as Trudeau's "Just watch me!" and "Where's Biafra?" senior journalists such as Richard Gwyn feel the need to repair the story to make it conform with our image of authority as knowledgeable and "the closest perspective we have to objectivity."

Much of the academic work in this area tends to be slanted toward a basic gatekeeping model, e.g., Epstein (1973), Gans (1979), Gitlin (1980), Tuchman (1978). Such writings are not devoid of insight, nor is the reader steered away from any sense of the creative construction function that is basic to media functioning. Indeed, Gaye Tuchman's *Making News: A Study in the Construction of Reality* emphasizes the construction function in its title. Some British work (see Gurevitch *et al.*, 1982) has also been done on how the assigned work patterns of journalists, which are customarily defined by management, affect the information collected. This research also gets at the construction function. However, this construction is conceived from within a larger system of maintenance of ideological dominance.

Tuchman, for example, points out that both editors and reporters are continually searching for frames of reference within which to present news. By identifying a frame or a perspective on an occurrence, as Tuchman says,

> an occurrence is transformed into an event, and an event is transformed into a news story. The news frame organizes everyday reality and the news frame is part and parcel of everyday reality, for, as we have seen, the public character of news is an essential feature of news.

In other words, news frames tap accepted social and ideological categories of lived culture for the frames of reference of their productions and news consumers select, use, and transform those productions in the context of everyday life. Both the media and the audience construct meaning in interaction with one another.

In the British literature on the work patterns of journalists (see, for example, the Glasgow Media Group's *Bad News* and its sequels) much attention is paid to the daily beats of the reporters. The very existence of a crime beat – a daily visit or check with the central or local police – ensures there will be stories centred on police matters. Moreover, in such a beat the common factor is the police. Hence, their behaviour will not be worthy of note but the behaviours they collect as a result of their law enforcement action will be seen as newsworthy. Other beats work exactly in the same way. A business beat without a labour beat ensures labour will be treated continually as a disruptive force. Long-term labour concerns and initiatives are almost certain to be ignored. Conversely, a labour beat without a business beat would probably turn into a running grievance column.

The structure of beats comes together with the relations journalists have with newsmakers, that cast of characters who are vehicles or agents through which the news is brought to the attention of the journalist or editor. The personal and professional adventures of these people – prominent citizens in political office, business, labour, law, etc. – become the background against which news is defined. But they also play off against one another to catapult social behaviour of other groups into the limelight. In an imaginative book called *Folk Devils and Moral Panics*, Cohen traces the attribution of meaning and escalation in significance by those "in authority" of some relatively contained concrete action. They also point out the role of the media in helping certain groups extend their definitions of the behaviour of others to name and control the lives of those named.

An example of this same phenomenon, which goes beyond content and delves into ownership and long-term marketing dynamics, is to be found in a study on the presentation of welfare in the British press over the past 50 or so years. In *Images of Welfare: Press and Public Attitudes to Poverty*, Golding and Middleton identify four factors contributing to a definition of public attitudes toward problems of poverty:

1. four centuries of cultural history in which poverty was seen as a mixture of unavoidable misfortune and morally culpable behaviour;
2. the disappearance of an alternative, labour-oriented press in the 1960s;
3. the economic crisis of 1973 in Britain, which sent welfare costs soaring for both the unemployed and elderly;
4. how news-gathering organizations picked up the dominant, culturally based explanation of poverty in their regular beats with welfare bureaucracies, the courts, the police, and ultra-conservative British MPs.

There is also an extensive literature on balance and fairness (e.g., Cook, 1984). This literature exists because there are formal (in the case of the electronic media) and informal (in the case of the print media) expectations of "objectivity" in news reporting. As a result, interest groups, regulators, and the media themselves often monitor the treatment of issues from these perspectives. The irony of such monitoring, as many academic researchers have come to realize, is that it is a very limited perspective on what one might call the constraints on discourse.

The work of Tuchman, the Glasgow Media Group, and many other researchers demonstrates the limitation of the notion of balance as an analytical category. What is deemed to be the other side of the balance defines the issue in a particular way, as the semiologists point out (see Chapter 4). Put somewhat differently, the choice of a **primary definer** of an issue is an interpretative act in itself and, inherently, is ideologically oriented. The *values of journalists* also play a role in how information is managed. The degree to which the journalistic community is exorcised by a simple statement that, overall, they have a left-wing bias (e.g., Cooper, Miljan, and Vigilante, 1986) reveals both the probability of the truth of the statement and the degree to which they strive to avoid an explicit expression of it.

Perhaps the greatest lack in the literature is a sense of the media's contribution to the articulation and consolidation of culture. As both Chapters 3 and 8 demonstrate, debates dealing with the establishment and support of media industries and those focused on licence renewals of both the CBC and private stations are an indication that Canadians see the media, especially the CBC, as major, albeit imperfect, contributors to the articulation and consolidation of national culture. Such testimony as is to be found in Gzowski's *Morningside Papers* (1985) exposes a major inadequacy in dominant conceptions of the media.

OTHER STRUCTURAL INFLUENCES

Media editor/managers are torn between the ideals of their profession, the realities of the market, the politics of the market, and the structural constraints imposed by the owner or ownership form. In the previous section we discussed how such individuals negotiated a constructive and creative course amidst such constraints. In this section we will consider some specific examples of other structural influences that are part of the environment of the media.

Libel

As we have noted, the presence of libel laws is at all times a constraint on media content. The federal law of criminal libel (criminal defamation), not to be confused with provincially administered civil libel, defines (in Section 262 [1]) an offence as:

> matter published, without lawful justification or excuse, that is likely to injure the reputation of any person by exposing him to hatred, contempt or ridicule, or that is designed to insult the person of or concerning whom it is published.

Conviction for publishing such libel is punishable by imprisonment for two years. Conviction for publishing such libel with the knowledge of its falsity is punishable by up to five years in prison.

Cases of criminal libel are extremely rare in Canadian law. More common are cases of civil defamation. The law varies between provinces and, as a result of many judgements, is fairly complex. As noted in Chapter 3, the complexity of the law can be accounted for by the necessity of balancing two basic rights, freedom of expression and the individual's right to his reputation.

The journalist's job is to collect information and to ensure its authenticity. However, it is also the responsibility of the publisher to account for the presence of any piece of information in his publication. Reporter, editor, and publisher thus share the responsibility of ensuring that what they publish is not libelous.

The easiest way of avoiding libel, of course, is to publish non-controversial material. Indeed, soft news, positive news, and boosterism get around libel in this very way. But there is a vibrant tradition in journalism of engaging in the critical and controversial. The profession appears to believe that this approach attracts audiences. Journalists deem it to be the cutting edge of the duty of the media to inform, to pursue truth. While the law may seem like a censoring device it can be claimed that libel law does not censor but rather contributes positively to the reporting of what would be agreed upon by a community of fair-minded people as true.

The Media and Business

In two major studies of business and Canadian society (Porter, 1965; Clement, 1975) the argument is advanced that the Canadian media are closely interwoven with the Canadian and North American business elite. One manifestation of that interweave is that members of boards of directors of banks and other corporations are found regularly on the boards of directors of media corporations. In Chapter 3 we discussed the general influence of business on the press; here our interest is centred on the influence this has on media professionals and the significance of this influence for the media consumers, the audience.

The media see themselves generally as the fourth estate or as watchdogs, yet they watch government in an entirely different way from how they examine business. When particular policies are being developed or a controversial law is passed by Parliament, the media consider it a source of pride to hound it out of existence. The members of the Canadian media saw it as their duty to bring down the government of John Diefenbaker. The role they play is that of an articulate, informed citizen with independent ideas.

By contrast, the watchdog role toward business, in general, appears to be confined to identifying the transgressors of the law or what is considered to be proper conduct. They do not voice, on a day-to-day basis, criticisms of the behaviour of business with respect to the public interest. Indeed, the business section and additional special regional or national development sections are customarily directed at informing the public of new developments. These sections are complemented by advertisements placed by the very companies that are crucial to those developments.

The newspapers, television, and magazines serve to some extent as the ideological arm of the business community. They provide the background within which the contribution of business to society is made to seem primary. Even in television sitcoms, the job identity of the person is often placed up front. The adventures presented are derived from his or her function as a working person.

This orientation toward business creates an environment within which advertising is well received. An ad puts forward the accomplishments of an individual corporation just a little less critically, with just a little more specificity and a little more hoopla, than does the journalism that surrounds it. If this advertising/journalism relationship is true of the "news" media, it is even truer of the media that do not see themselves as engaged in the pursuit of truth in the name of public interest. As fashion photographer Howard Fry points out in the video program, *The Fashionable Image*, in doing a photographic editorial piece his job is to enhance the environment within which the advertisers' ads appear. A journalist writing for the same magazine might say the same. Their job is to make the package within which the ads appear sufficiently attractive to bring to the ads an audience of a particular type.

In television, attracting and delivering a suitably prepared audience to advertisers has quite an immediate, temporal connotation. In the same way that a front page is designed to take the reader further into a paper, an evening of programs is designed initially to attract an audience and then deliver that audience in a frame of mind suited to the acceptance of the advertisers' messages from program to program throughout the night. Usually that is accomplished through the use of known quantities, i.e., programs that are part of familiar series and non-threatening but adventurous enough to capture the attention of the viewer.

In one class project at Simon Fraser University, about fifty students viewed a documentary dealing with the trials of a young teenage girl whose parents had recently separated. In mid-program an ad for a charter flight to Las Vegas was shown. The self-indulgence implied in the ad hit a raw nerve with nearly all of the viewers. It was certainly the wrong ad for the program content. The example highlights the general situation rather well. Advertisers are not interested in having audiences delivered to them whose frame of mind is not open to a fairly non-critical acceptance of their message. As a result, there is a real constraint on programming not to involve the viewer too deeply in the subject of the program so that he or she resents the intrusion of the ad. Also, the subjects chosen must not show the ads in a bad light. This restriction in advertiser-supported communications argues most strongly against the privatization of the public media.

The CBC and Its Affiliates

In Canada we have a particularly interesting, living example of the contrasting pulls within private and public enterprise. In the world of privately owned television production, just as in magazines and many newspapers, a station and network stay alive by delivering audiences to advertisers. This life-sustaining act is more obvious in television, radio, and controlled-circulation magazines (magazines delivered free in certain city areas, or to certain professionals or income groups) because there is no purchase price for access.

The CBC lives partly in this reality and partly in the reality of its annual parliamentary appropriation. However, it has a number of privately owned affiliates that do not get parliamentary appropriations and thus are continually pressing for the CBC to provide them with programming that will net the largest audiences possible. They object to Canadian cultural programming, which may develop "unity and identity" but which garners relatively fewer viewers than would American dramas.

So successful have they been in their complaints that they are subsidized by the CBC to carry its programming, to compensate them for the perceived loss of audience. (They are tied to CBC programming by the conditions of their licence.) This situation is rather like the tail continually threatening to wag the dog. The CBC has neither completely capitulated to its affiliates nor felt free to ignore their protestations.

Community Politics and Standards

In a narrow sense of the term "community standards," the programmer or editor must at all times be aware of how content will be received by the target audience. For example, while Playboy programming may have seemed like a big mistake when First Choice announced the signing of an agreement to air the programs on its pay TV channel, its decision not to withdraw from the agreement suggests that it understood its own audience and the manner in which their standards and values differed from those of the general public.

The media play to or with community stan-dards and with the politics of acceptability. A survey done in 1984 reported that violence was more frequently portrayed on CTV than on any other network, more than on the CBC, ABC, NBC, or CBS. Presumably this was because CTV buys programming on the basis of its ratings and pays less attention to program balance and production cost because it does not produce the programs. But bringing the matter to the attention of the network would not necessarily lead to change. One of the many interesting revelations of Channel Ten 10's submission to the Australian Broadcasting Tribunal was an item-by-item description of how much each advertiser paid for each ad during the course of one week (see Chapter 6). The submission revealed that the station, owned by Rupert Murdoch, made very little money on advertising on children's programming. This led to increased pressure from parent groups to ban advertising from children's programming altogether. Murdoch would have none of it; the advertising stayed.

CONTINUING STRUCTURAL ISSUES IN MANAGEMENT: THE PROBLEM OF POLITICAL BIAS

In Chapter 1 we discussed Innis's idea that communications media structure the society in which they exist. In Chapter 10 we discuss a study of political bias in the media. At this point these two ideas can be brought together to anticipate some of that discussion and to illustrate Innis's point.

Journalists and the viewing and reading public sometimes assume that bias in the media is put there consciously by journalists who perceive it to be their duty to write biased articles or who are biased by their own ideological convictions. In the case of a CRTC study of political bias in the media, there seemed to be an assumption by those commissioning the study and those doing the study that the roots of bias are in the minds and activities of journalists. The response of Pierre Juneau indicates otherwise, or indicates, at least, that this is not the whole story.

When Juneau took over as CBC president one of his first major acts was to realign the basic structure of the radio and television service. Prior to his intervention the corporation was divided into the French-language service and the English-language service. Within each of these services were radio and television divisions. Much to the consternation of some near the top of the organization, Juneau made the simple but elegant move of switching the fundamental divisions from a linguistic to a media base. Now radio is separated from television but the languages are not separated from each other.

One interpretation of this move is that it could never have been attempted prior to the prime ministership of Trudeau. His regime was so successful in bringing French Canadians into all walks of public life that Juneau felt able to amalgamate the languages without the fear that the French would be drowned by the English or that they would be separated off into Quebec affairs. To put the matter rather simply, this realignment means that any journalist striving to advance in the CBC will be under pressure to be bilingual. Not only will bilingual individuals have increased opportunities but the closer an individual comes to the top of the organization the more likely it will be that the responsibilities of the position will require familiarity with services in both languages. In one bureaucratic move Juneau gave the CBC's responsibility to nurture Canadian unity and our bilingual identity an unshakeable structural foundation, one that will affect continually the management of the corporation.

A negative perspective on the reality of such optimism can be found in the Broadcasting Task Force Report (1986). The view expressed there is that the two services cannot reflect the cultural distinctiveness of the anglophone and francophone communities if the services are integrated as Juneau has done. Unfortunately, as of early 1987, Juneau's plan does not appear to be working. Amid cutbacks and the CBC's disfavour with the Mulroney government, interchange between the French and English networks is low on nearly everyone's agenda.

SUMMARY: PROFESSIONAL EXCELLENCE VERSUS IDEALS OF EQUAL ACCESS

The major point of this chapter is that *in every medium a rather thick layer of organization affects the content we receive as consumers.* Whether such a layer represents the ideals of a journalist/editor tempered by years of experience, the marketing orientation of a glossy magazine editor, or the attempt by a programmer to tailor a program idea to the image a particular client wishes to project, there is no doubt that it exists. The relative failure of community programming on community cable channels speaks to the necessity of that layer to produce "acceptable" programming.

In the same way that a symphony orchestra represents an extremely elegant, hierarchically organized use of the potentialities of the many musicians and instruments of an orchestra, so the production of a newspaper, a program or series, a magazine, is also a sophisticated integration of the talents and potentialities of the many crafts and interests of the production team. However, just as an orchestra excludes the untrained musician who might wish either to join in or to have a musical composition played, so media production excludes the single individual who may wish to communicate a simple idea. For that communication the individual must rely on the co-ordination of the talents of a group of professionals who all have different but crucial roles to play in getting his or her message across in an effective manner.

The musical analogy is relevant in other ways. Both music and communication are social processes. Through these processes a community can express and enhance itself. If the mode of expression is layered with complexities, however, the ideas of a community have a rather limited possibility of being expressed in a manner that is true to their nature. They are professionalized along the way and, as this happens, some of the ideas become so transformed that they are extinguished. In the end, and to a significant degree, the very social nature of communication is lost to a class and a profession. In that loss there may be some damage to the community's ability to express and renew itself in order to adapt to its changing environment. The media may become alienated; they may no longer mediate but, instead, become semi-autonomous image-generating processes.

REFERENCES

Bennett, W.L., L.A. Gressett, and W. Haltom. "Repairing the News: A Case Study of News Paradigm," *Journal of Communications*, 35, 2 (Spring, 1985), pp. 50–68.

Canada. *Royal Commission on Newspapers.* Hull, Quebec: Canadian Government Publishing Centre, 1981.

Canadian Broadcasting Corporation. *Inside TV News*, executive producer, M. Blandford, directed by F. Steele, produced by H. Gendron and F. Steele. Montreal, 1982.

Cartwright, E., ed. *Field Theory in Social Science: Selected Theoretical Papers, Kurt Levin.* New York: Harper & Row, 1951.

Clement, Wallace. *The Canadian Corporate Elite.* Toronto: McClelland and Stewart, 1975.

Cohen, S. *Folk Devils and Moral Panics: The Creation of the Mods and Rockers.* London: MacGibbon and Kee, 1972.

Cook, Peter. "The Concept of Balance in the Supervision and Regulation of Canadian Broadcasting," M.A. thesis, Simon Fraser University, 1982.

Cooper, B., L. Miljan, and M. Vigilante. "Bias on the CBC? A study of network AM radio," paper presented at the Learned Societies meetings, Winnipeg, May-June, 1981.

Epstein, E.J. *News From Nowhere: Television and the News.* New York: Vintage, 1973.

Fletcher, F. *The Newspapers and Public Affairs.* Vol. 7, Research Publications, Canada, *Royal Commission on Newspapers.* Ottawa: Ministry of Supply and Services, 1981.

Gans, H.J. *Deciding What's News: A Study of CBS Evening News, NBC Nightly News, Newsweek, and Time.* New York: Vintage, 1979.

Gitlin, T. *The Whole World is Watching.* Berkeley: University of California Press, 1980.

Glasgow Media Group. *Really Bad News.* London: Writers and Readers Publishing Cooperative, 1982.

Golding, Peter, and Sue Middleton. *Images of Welfare: Press and Public Attitudes to Poverty.* Oxford: Martin Robertson & Company, 1982.

Gurevitch, M., et al., eds. *Culture, Society and the Media.* Toronto: Methuen, 1982.

Gzowski, P. *The Morningside Papers.* Toronto: McClelland and Stewart, 1985.

Hester, Al. "International News Agencies," in Alan Wells, ed., *Mass Communications: a World View.* Palo Alto: Mayfield, 1974.

Korporaal, G. "How the U.S. media hijacked foreign policy," *Australian Financial Review,* July 3, 1985, p. 1.

Knelman, Martin. "Their Finest Hour," *Saturday Night* (March, 1983).

Lévesque, René. *Memoirs.* Toronto: McClelland and Stewart, 1986.

MacDonald, L. Ian. *Mulroney: The Making of the Prime Minister*. Toronto: McClelland and Stewart, 1984.

MacLean, E. *Between the Lines*. Montreal: Black Rose, 1979.

Murdock, G. "Large corporations and the control of the communications industries," in Gurevitch *et al.*, eds., *Culture, Society and the Media*.

Porter, John. *The Vertical Mosaic*. Toronto: University of Toronto Press, 1965.

Simon Fraser University. *The Fashionable Image*. Videotape, Communications Department, 1985. Distributor: Magic Lantern, Oakville, Ontario.

Stewart, Walter, ed. *Canadian Newspapers: The Inside Story*. Edmonton: Hurtig, 1980.

Tuchman, Gaye. *Making News: A Study in the Construction of Reality*. New York: Free Press, 1978.

Vancouver Sun, June 21, 1985, p. A3.

Vogel vs. CBC/Bird. #C802500 Vancouver Registry, in the Supreme Court of Canada, 1981.

STUDY QUESTIONS

1. The label "gatekeeper" hides much of the creative side of the work of editors, news directors, and program supervisors. Discuss the role of the information manager in the context of the aims of information seekers.

2. Dan Phelan, senior program editor for the CBC radio program *World Reports*, has said: "I was a reporter a long time so I know basically what I want. It's like a parade, and each story is a float and you have to put it together so that there's a beginning and an ending." How do you think Phelan defines the news and what does his role as journalist appear to be? Comment on the pros and cons of this type of journalistic approach to news.

3. "The ideals of journalism play an important role in structuring our media environment." Discuss.

CHAPTER

8

Communications Policy in Canada

INTRODUCTION

THERE ARE basically two different ways to study a nation's communications policies. One consists of looking at explicit policy: the official statements about goals and means that are embodied in laws, regulations, reports, ministers' speeches, statements, and so on. The other consists of observing implicit policy: the results of policy decisions and practices. From this latter observation, it is possible to infer the social, economic, and political policies that have given rise to the practices. Not surprisingly, this second kind of analysis often shows major discrepancies and contradictions between the policy goals officially endorsed and the policy decisions actually made.

This chapter concentrates on the explicit and implicit policies on telecommunications and broadcasting in Canada. At the end of the chapter, we take a brief look at policy relevant to the so-called "cultural industries" such as film, music recording, and book publishing.

In studying the *implicit* policies underlying the development of communications services and practices in Canada, the heritage of British influences is encountered side by side with the powerful and sometimes contradictory influences from the United States. Adding spice to the pot are the dynamics of ethnicity, language, and geography. For instance, while Canada is a parliamentary democracy modeled on that of Britain, Canada has existed as a federal state only since 1867. It was built upon older traditions in English Canada and Quebec, both of which had evolved patterns of social structure quite unlike those in the American version of a democratic society.

In addition, a significant part of the present-day Canadian population is not of British or French descent. The western provinces in particular were settled by large numbers of immigrants from Europe. More recently, large urban communities of European, Latin American, Asian, and Commonwealth peoples have arisen in all of Canada's major cities.

At the same time, the attitudes of many Canadians have been, and continue to be, shaped by American society and its communications media. While Canadians as a whole have never adopted the American distaste for government involvement in communications media, private interests in Canadian media can count on a certain amount of sympathy when they invoke American ideals such as "First Amendment" rights of free speech and the "free marketplace of ideas" in their protests against specific Canadian regulations.

THE POLICY ENVIRONMENT

B oth explicit and implicit policy are developed and exist within what might be called a policy environment. *We can define the environment of the communications policy field in Canada as those factors outside the policy field itself that influence the structures,* *processes, and ideas at the core of policy but which are more appropriately seen as part of the society as a whole.* First of all, an important determining element in the policy environment is the Canadian constitution. The *constitutional allocation of political powers* between the federal and provincial governments has been an active cause for debate periodically since 1867 but perhaps especially since the late 1960s in such areas as natural resources and communications. Quebec has been particularly determined in demanding autonomy over communications matters as one means of protecting the cultural distinctiveness of its society. This tension between the provincial and federal governments has been a continuing and significant factor in the development of Canadian communications policy since the late 1960s (Woodrow *et al.*, 1980).

Two other factors that contribute to the complexity of policy formulation in Canada are ones that we identified in Chapter 1 as influential over the whole society. First is the *size and distribution of its population*, which was over 25 million at the time of the 1986 census. This makes the Canadian population about 10 per cent of that of the U.S., a proportion that has remained steady for about forty years and an obvious factor in the balance of power between the two countries. The distribution of people across Canada is heavily concentrated in southern Ontario and Quebec. Between them, these two provinces have about two-thirds of the country's total population. The remainder is spread thinly over four western provinces, four eastern provinces, and two northern territories. Such a population distribution has led to the particular mixture of regional differentiation, dual language use, and multicultural communities unique to Canadian society.

Proximity to the United States (Canada's only

contiguous neighbour), together with a large land mass and a relatively small, scattered population, is another major factor in the evolution of Canadian communications systems and policy, as can be seen in the early history of radio broadcasting. By 1928, virtually all of the radio broadcasting frequencies then available for the North American continent had been claimed by American broadcasters. Nearly everywhere along the Canadian border (where most of the population has always lived and most of the cities are located) it was possible to receive American radio programs. Almost nowhere outside of Toronto and Montreal was it possible to receive Canadian radio programming until explicit government policy and government action led to the creation of a Canada-wide service receivable by most Canadians.

The combination of American proximity and the high cost of providing Canadian-based communications services has given rise to the unique Canadian mixture of public and private ownership in communications institutions. Canada's British and French heritages predisposed it to accept the commitment to public communications systems similar to those in Western Europe (for broadcasting, specifically, the model of the BBC). Furthermore, Canadian policy-makers were faced with the practical realization that providing communications services to a majority of the scattered population could probably not be accomplished through private enterprise anyway and this would require some form of public support. Nevertheless, there had to be room for private entrepreneurs to develop communications systems and services where this could easily be done. The development of broadcasting, telephone systems, the transcontinental microwave networks, and the domestic satel-

lite system all provide examples of this curious marriage of private enterprise and public ownership.

A fourth factor in the policy environment in Canada has been the *relative openness of the policy process* and discussion about which directions to take regarding communications media. Perhaps because of the complex mixture of people living in Canada, and consequently the lack of a strong consensus on many issues related to communications, it has been the practice of the federal government – and more recently of some provincial governments – to encourage public discussion and comment about current issues requiring policy action. Under the procedures of the Canadian Radio-television and Telecommunications Commission (CRTC), matters concerning (for example) policy questions, licence renewals, conditions of service, and rate structures for federally regulated common carriers and broadcasters are all considered at public hearings. In addition, the federal Minister of Communications may encourage public discussion and reaction through the issue of Green Papers on proposed policy.

Further to the openness of the policy process, on a number of occasions since the mid-1960s, task forces, commissions of inquiry, and special committees have been set up to examine particular problems and their reports have been made available to the general public. Indeed, since 1928, it has been the practice of the federal government to employ the inquiry processes of royal commissions and parliamentary committees on many occasions to examine particular aspects of broadcasting development and to obtain public comments. This public involvement, as well as the more usual consultations with industry associations and between the government agencies and departments themselves, provides the federal government with considerable information upon which to draw in establishing policies. Of course, the number of the members of the general public who participate is often quite small but the opportunity is there, unlike the situation in most other countries.

A fifth and crucial factor in the environment of the communications policy field is often referred to as *technology*. This element is most frequently misunderstood and needs the closer attention we provide here.

The Influence of Technology on Policy

If the influence of technology on the communications systems is frequently alluded to, this does not mean it is an easy phenomenon to define or describe. As Langdon Winner has observed, it is useful to distinguish between three different levels of meaning in common usage (Winner, 1977). First, there are pieces of apparatus (tools, instruments, machines, appliances, gadgets) that are the "physical devices of technical performance." Second is the type of techniques needed to operate the apparatus and accomplish tasks (skills, methods, procedures, routines). Third is the type of social organization that can encompass various technical activities (networks, factories, bureaucracies). In the following discussion, our definition of technology encompasses all three levels of meaning distinguished by Winner.

It has been suggested by some writers that to view technology as the starting point of one's inquiry is to treat it largely as a given rather than as a social phenomenon. Thus, this view accepts that technological innovation is occurring and will continue to occur, without questioning from where the innovative pressure comes. Scholars such as Herbert Schiller and Vincent Mosco have argued that communications technologies and pressures for further innovations in communications in the U.S. come mainly from major, multinational corporations and from interests in the armed forces and government favouring increased expenditures on military R&D and hardware production (Schiller, 1984; Mosco, 1982).

Technological change appears to be proceeding at an ever-increasing rate in recent decades and this trend is attributed mostly to the creation of computer technology. Its widespread diffusion throughout manufacturing, processing, and service industries, as well as in communications networks and in the introduction of new computer-communications systems and processes, has made the computer the key technology of this time. The short term often given to this period of rapid change is the "computer revolution" or the "information revolution."

Canada today is said to be one of the technologically most advanced nations in communications, spending more per capita on communications equipment than any other country. Covering the country with networks of radio stations and later of television stations, as well as encouraging the growth of a national grid of telephone (later telecommunications) networks, has been the primary preoccupation of Canadian communications planners and policy-makers. While these developments have encouraged equal access to services, critics have argued frequently that the emphasis on hardware and distribution capability has been at the expense of production and programming capability – that is, the content these expensive systems carry. The question of what is the "right" balance between spending on hardware and software is probably the most vexing one in Canadian policy-making on communications.

Political Responses to Technology

In Canada, political responses to the perceived communications revolution in technology have been going on in various ways since the late 1960s, with the establishment of the Department of Communications and the launching of the Telecommission studies and other task forces. Recent versions of this type of study are the Clyne Committee Report (Clyne, 1979) and the Broadcasting Task Force Report (Caplan-Sauvageau, 1986). Provincial governments have also produced studies and reports. The general tone of these documents is that the "revolution" is going ahead, with or without Canada's active contributions to it, and Canada must take account of (if not accommodate itself to) the changes that will occur internationally and, therefore, domestically. These changes are expected to occur in Canadian communications systems as well as in the economic system as a whole.

The federal government's conclusion, in response to these reports and studies, is that Canada cannot afford to be left behind in the technological race. The provincial governments appear to agree with this. The argument is that, if we are left behind, then the Canadian economy is fated to become increasingly dependent on foreign technology. This prospect does not make an appealing picture for a society that sees itself to be advanced.

Despite these concerns about the costs of not participating in the communications revolution and a general enthusiasm for technology, there is an ambivalence in Canadian policy attitudes toward communications technology. While the technologies can offer – and, it is usually argued, *should* offer – the opportunity to enhance political cohesion, economic growth, and cultural development, these systems are being used most often as additional carriers of non-Canadian information. It is frequently claimed by federal policy-makers that the increased diffusion of foreign information in Canada could decrease national unity and prevent economic and cultural development. So, communications technology is seen as both potential national saviour and potential trojan horse.

New Technologies

New communications technologies that have been introduced in recent years have had and continue to have effects on the economics and politics of Canadian communications sytems. Those with the most noticeable effects are: communications satellites, pay TV and specialty TV systems, videocassette recorders (VCRs), computers, computer network services, videotex services, and optical fibre networks. Individually and collectively, they are changing communications services by enabling production and distribution techniques to be transformed through digitalized processes and microelectronic devices. The main change, however, is through the actual or potential creation of competing electronic distribution networks (such as cable, satellite, optical fibre, microwave, and so on) for broadcast-type material and of other content formats such as data.

These new distribution methods and formats create more competition for customers, thus putting the traditional broadcasters and telecommunications carriers on the defensive. Some, by enhancing the services available, also affect the market for cable TV services. The increased competition for market share, which must inevitably result from the new possibilities, probably means lower profits for private communications system-operators and higher net costs for the publicly owned systems. Increasingly, policy questions arise about the economic survival of the whole broadcasting system in Canada and how the telecommunications networks can adapt to increased competition.

Today, broadcasting is more often seen by governments as part of the wider communications infrastructure, not as a separate and exclusive category. The media of electronic communications (which now include broadcasting, coaxial cable, telephony, telegraphy, data communications, and satellite systems) are becoming increasingly interchangeable and interconnected. As the systems converge in their usage of digital transmission and their interconnections, thereby creating a new environment for the development of policy, it becomes increasingly difficult to regard any of them as technically separable from the others. However, the policy field has been slow to recognize this.

POLICY AND THE POLICY FIELD

As we have seen, a strong theme in the environment affecting the current phase of communications policy in Canada is the pressure for rapid technological change in the communications distribution systems. The speed by which policy can be adapted to new circumstances is affected by (among other things) the degree to which certain ideas are entrenched within the institutions and processes through which policy decisions are taken and implemented. Rapid adaptabilility is not necessarily a desirable characteristic in any policy field because those who are affected need to have policy consistency in order to plan their future activities. On the other side, the inability to adapt policy and the policy field to major and long-term changes in the policy en-

vironment means the field becomes increasingly out of touch with its society.

The policy assumptions about technology, as well as the particular character of Canadian society, are built into the numerous communications policy structures that have accumulated over time. These structures are represented by statutes (laws), regulations, corporations, commissions, boards, departments, and other government institutions at the federal and provincial levels of government (with a little still at the municipal level). Several institutions play a leading role in the policy field. Two are outlined here by way of illustration. Others are introduced in the following discussion of telecommunications, broadcasting, and cultural industries.

The Federal Department of Communications

The federal Department of Communications and its minister have been playing an increasingly important role in the policy field since the early 1970s. The establishing statute is extremely short and gives the duties of the Minister as follows:

> The duties, powers and functions of the Minister of Communications extend to and include all matters over which the Parliament of Canada has jurisdiction, not by law assigned to any other department, branch or agency of the Government of Canada, relating to
> (a) telecommunications;
> (b) the development and utilization generally of communication undertakings, facilities, systems and services for Canada. (Department of Communications Act, RSC 1970, s.4.)

Under the authority of the Radio Act the Minister exercises regulatory authority over all technical licences for the use of the radio spectrum, including its use for broadcasting purposes. Related to his responsibility within Canada for spectrum management, the Minister is also empowered to negotiate international agreements to protect "the rights of Canada in communication matters."

However, the ministerial portfolio is not solely technical, and this has become more clearly the case since 1980. Basically, the Communications portfolio contains two elements, one technical and the other social or cultural. The former, which still needs most of the department's resources, is concerned with the technical matters of the radio spectrum and its usage, and advanced research and design of communications technologies. The latter is concerned with the development of communications (including broadcasting) policy and cultural policy.

In 1980, various duties and responsibilities were transferred from the Secretary of State to the Minister of Communications. Specifically, the Minister became responsible for the CBC and for a group of nine other agencies. In addition, a major portion of the Arts and Culture Branch of the Secretary of State was transferred to the Department of Communications.

It has been suggested that the Minister of Communications is "really six ministers in one" and the job is "an almost impossible one" (Fortin and Winn, 1983). Indeed, the Minister has a widely diverse portfolio, as can be seen in the range of the statutes for which he or she has some responsibility:

Department of Communications Act
Telegraphs Act
Canadian Radio-television and Telecommunications Commission Act
Teleglobe Canada Act
National Transportation Act
Telesat Canada Act
Radio Act

Railway Act
Broadcasting Act
Canada Council Act
Canadian Film Development Corporation Act
Cultural Property Export & Import Act
Social Science and Humanities Research Council Act
National Arts Centre Act
National Film Act
National Library Act
National Museums of Canada Act
Public Archives of Canada Act

The degree of control the Minister can exercise over the agencies in the portfolio depends on the scope of the statutes concerned and on the kind of control the Minister would like to exercise. For example, the Minister can determine the amount of money made available to the Canada Council but cannot influence directly who receives that money for book publishing. However, a publishing support fund managed by the Department of Communications would be much more subject to ministerial supervision. All of the agencies operate at some sort of arm's length from the Minister and from department officials, but, as some have observed, the arm may not be very long at times.

From its inception in 1969, the department focused its attention on telecommunications, computer-communications, and the observed convergence of communications technologies that was leading toward the promised information revolution. The nucleus of the department's staff came from the Department of Transport and the Defence Research Board. The establishment of a task force (called the Telecommission), made up of public servants from various government departments, to collect and publish information about the imminent communications explosion helped to alert federal and provincial policy-makers about the importance of these developments for Canada.

In 1971, the Telecommission published a series of over forty studies and a summary report called *Instant World*. It was anticipated that the materials gathered and responses to the studies would allow the Minister to table in Parliament a White Paper on communications policy.* Sixteen years later – and after the introduction of many different, discrete programs and policies – this still has not been achieved. The reasons for the inaction are complex, but one factor that stands out is the federal-provincial disagreement over jurisdiction, a second structural factor that has a continuing influence over communications policy development.

The Federal-Provincial Dispute

Attempts made in the early 1970s by the federal government to develop macro-policies on communications for Canada ran afoul of provincial jurisdiction over certain elements of the telecommunications infrastructure, particularly the telephone systems in the Prairie provinces and in the Atlantic region. By March, 1973, the government was able to produce only a Green Paper for discussion (Minister of Communications, 1973). The Minister at that time, Gérard Pelletier, held the view there was a need, due to the technological revolution, for a national policy to co-ordinate federal and provincial regulations of telecommunications and to integrate that policy with the federal field of broadcasting. Somewhat to the surprise of the federal minister and his officials, the provincial governments strongly objected to the federal view, seeing it as an attempt to

*In parliamentary language, a White Paper is a statement of *actual* government policy while a Green Paper is a statement of *possible* policy that is issued in order to elicit public response and suggestions for improvement.

encroach on provincial jurisdiction and to override provincial priorities. A second Green Paper in 1975 was not well-received either; consequently, no formalized "national" policy exists.

What we have is a piecemeal collection of policies, federal and provincial; it may be we are none the worse for having it that way. Developing a national policy means one must produce a set of objectives and rules that are equally suitable for all regions of the country. This is difficult to achieve in a society as widely scattered and diverse as Canada's. Since 1975, behind-the-scenes work by federal and provincial politicians and officials to co-operate in developing nation-wide policies on telecommunications services and equipment has been slow, but some progress has been made through consensus.

Particularly prominent in the public disagreements between Ottawa and the provinces in the early 1970s were Quebec and the Prairie provinces. Quebec's objections were based on the argument that the provinces needed to control broadcasting developments in order to meet the cultural objectives of the francophone majority in the province. While the whole field of communications (understood to cover both telecommunications and broadcasting) was and still is of interest to Quebec, it concentrated for some years on the need for provincial jurisdiction over broadcasting, particularly cable TV. In 1973, the Quebec government tried to regulate some aspects of cable TV systems through the introduction of a licensing procedure administered by a regulatory board (Régie des services publics). This action forced the Quebec cable TV operators to deal with a dual licensing system and created acute problems for a few licensees. A series of court actions followed, which took until 1977 to be resolved by the

Supreme Court of Canada when it confirmed that the federal government had exclusive jurisdiction over cable television (but not over closed-circuit cable TV systems that do not carry broadcasting signals).

The Prairie provinces were also concerned in the early 1970s about what they saw as the extension of exclusive federal jurisdiction from over-air broadcasting to cable television and the proposed intrusion of federal authority into what had been a provincially controlled area of telephone company regulation and ownership. As far as the Prairie provinces could see at that time, cable TV systems (not much was developed in Saskatchewan or Manitoba then) could become competitors of the telephone companies in the provision of some services such as pay TV or information services. To prevent this, the Prairie provinces sought to exert control over the physical installation of cable TV technology.

While it would be incorrect to say that the Prairie provinces were not interested in the cultural arguments advanced by Quebec, they placed a higher value on arguments concerning their historic rights to own and control telecommunications carriers and systems in their territory. Any technological developments that threatened the provincial telephone systems and their economic viability concerned those provincial governments for social as well as economic reasons. As they saw it, changes in the availability of telecommunications services, especially in the rural areas, would affect the survival of small towns and farming communities throughout the region.

TELECOMMUNICATIONS POLICY

Telecommunication is defined this way in federal legislation: "Telecommunication means any transmission, emission or reception of signs, signals, writing, images or sounds or intelligence of any nature by wire, radio, visual or other electromagnetic system" (Radio Act, RSC 1970, s.2). In strictly technical terms, then, broadcasting is a type of telecommunication. However, in policy terms, broadcasting is treated separately. In less technical terms, the telecommunications sector refers mainly to the telephone industry and the services it provides. It refers, as well, to those telecommunications companies and services outside the telephone industry (for example, CNCP Telecommunications), and to the satellite communications industry, the most significant part of which is Telesat Canada.

The Common Carriers

All of the companies in these industries are referred to as "common carriers." The basic characteristic of a common carrier is its obligation to carry whatever messages (i.e., content) any customer wants to have sent and to charge equitable rates for that carriage service. A carrier may not tamper with the message, nor is it involved in creating any of the messages carried for customers (although this requirement may be modified through changing technological opportunities). The creation of the "content" is what makes broadcasters different from common carriers; broadcasters are involved in content creation and are legally responsible for all the content they transmit even if some programming is purchased from other sources.

There are two nation-wide telecommunications systems and one international system, which provides telecommunications links overseas. The two domestic systems are Telecom Canada and CNCP Telecommunications; the international system is Teleglobe Canada. A brief description of each is useful here.

Telecom Canada (which was known as the TransCanada Telephone System until 1983) is an unincorporated association of the nine largest telephone companies as well as Telesat Canada, the domestic satellite company. The Telecom phone companies are:

British Columbia Telephone Co.
Alberta Government Telephones
Saskatchewan Telecommunications
Manitoba Telephone System
Bell Canada
New Brunswick Telephone Co. Ltd.
Maritime Telegraph and Telephone Co.
Island Telephone Co. Ltd.
Newfoundland Telephone Co. Ltd.

CNCP Telecommunications is a partnership formed from what used to be the telegraph subsidiaries operated by the two major railway companies, Canadian National Railways and Canadian Pacific. CNCP competes against Telecom Canada for the domestic market in telecommunications services although some services are provided by each of them on a monopoly basis. The competition is not exactly on an equal footing, however, because Telecom companies hold about 88 per cent of the domestic telecommunications market compared to the 4 per cent share held by CNCP.* The competition between them is keenest in the area of data communications.

Teleglobe Canada was established as a federal Crown corporation whose role is to provide telecommunications between Canada and other countries across the Atlantic and Pacific oceans (links to the United States and other American countries are provided through

---

*The remaining 8 per cent is shared between many small telephone companies, Teleglobe Canada, and radio common carriers (Department of Communications, 1983).

the domestic telecommunications carriers, mostly the telephone companies). Teleglobe is not competing against any of the domestic carriers. Its monopoly may be reduced with the further international development of satellite communications. In 1987, Teleglobe was sold to private owners as part of a shift away from public ownership and a government wish to deregulate as many markets as possible. At present, Teleglobe represents Canada in the operation of several international communications organizations; one example is IN-TELSAT, the satellite consortium owned by over 100 countries that provides international satellite services to most of the world outside the Soviet bloc.

Basically, telecommunications services can be categorized into five types: voice telephony; public message (telegram); switched teleprinter and other text services (Telex and TWX); data communications; and program transmission (audio and video signals, especially for broadcasting). Telecom Canada and CNCP compete in the provision of the last three service categories. In the first category, CNCP can compete only in the provision of leased circuits (private lines) and not in the public switched systems that we are most familiar with as a telephone company service. The second category of public message is the monopoly of CNCP.

The National Telephone System

There are over 160 telephone companies in Canada but only a handful are nationally significant. There are also over 200 radio common carriers that provide mobile radio and radio-paging services in competition with the telephone companies. Recently, cellular radio service, provided by Cantel in competition with telephone companies, has been added.

Even so, for most Canadians, telecommunications services are still provided by one of sixteen telephone companies. Some of these companies are privately owned while others are government-owned at the federal, provincial, or municipal level.

The two largest entities in the telephone industry, Bell Canada (serving most of Ontario and Quebec) and British Columbia Telephone (serving most of B.C.), are shareholder-owned. The three largest public companies operate in the Prairie provinces, a region where distances between subscribers are often great and initial costs of building distribution networks are high. There are still some municipally owned telephone systems although most of them were taken over years ago by the bigger telephone companies. Examples of municipal telephone systems are 'edmonton telephones,' Thunder Bay Telephone System, and Prince Rupert Telephone System.

System interconnection to ensure compatible equipment and revenue-sharing agreements has been resolved partly by non-governmental means such as Telecom Canada. First, through arrangements with the many smaller companies, Telecom Canada can provide telecommunications links from coast to coast and from the southern border to the North. For example, Telesat Canada (the Canadian satellite communications corporation, discussed below) and the major telephone companies also provide much of the cross-country distribution networks for the broadcasting networks. System compatibility is also ensured by technical standards set by the federal Department of Communications and by provincial bodies responsible for regulating telephone services in their territories. The request by one carrier for the right to link its system with another is the subject of regulatory decisions at the federal and provincial levels.

Regulation of Telecommunications

Since its beginning in the 1840s, the telegraph industry in Canada has been under federal regulation; in turn, telephone companies were regulated when they began in the 1880s, but not necessarily at the federal level. Regulation of telephone and telegraph rates and service was deemed necessary for protection of the public interest because of the companies' operation as natural monopolies – that is, in the longer term, it was believed that only one company could provide efficient service in any one area. (It is a moot point whether such monopolies could ever have been described as "natural" since they were authorized by statute and regulation.) In any case, due to the proliferating technologies of communications transmission, it is no longer taken for granted that one large company should have exclusive rights to provide any telecommunications service in a specific territory.

The regulation can occur provincially or federally, depending on historical and jurisdictional circumstances (English, 1973). For example, the major prairie telephone systems are owned and regulated by the province concerned. The two largest privately owned systems of Bell and B.C. Tel are both regulated federally. To carry on the pattern of public-private mix noted earlier, transnational telegraph and data communications services provided by CNCP are the joint efforts of a Crown corporation (Canadian National Railway) and a private corporation (Canadian Pacific); CNCP is regulated federally. So also are Telesat Canada (about which more later) and two small telephone companies operating in the Northwest Territories and Newfoundland. Altogether, the federal government regulates only six telecommunications companies. This does not seem to be much until one discovers that the six provide services to about 70 per cent of the entire Canadian telecommunications market. Bell Canada alone supplies 52 per cent of the market (Department of Communications, 1983).

The basis for government control over a telephone or telecommunications company in Canada is regulation as a public utility with a view to ensuring that "just and reasonable" rates are charged to customers. The CRTC is responsible for regulating the rates of the federally regulated carriers, including Telesat Canada (as well as regulating all broadcasting licensees). However, having broadcasting and common-carrier regulation within one body does not mean the CRTC administers an overall communications policy. Further legislative changes are still needed, in the form of a telecommunications act, to provide a unified policy and regulatory framework at the federal level.

At the provincial level, each province has organized its regulatory function somewhat differently but most have a regulatory board responsible for the telephone companies that come within their jurisdiction. All provinces now have a minister responsible for communications policy, although only the Quebec government has a minister with a department solely concerned with communications. Several provinces have a department of transport and communications while others simply name any minister to be the government spokesman on communications matters and to attend federal-provincial ministers' meetings as the provincial representative.

Satellite Communications

Canada has been a pioneer of non-military satellite applications since the early 1960s; the possibility of improving trans-Canada communications links through the use of communications satellites has appealed to federal policy-makers since at least 1965. A White Paper on satellite policy was issued in 1968, in which the following statement was made: "A domestic satellite system should be a national undertaking stretching across Canada from coast to coast, north to Ellesmere Island and operating under the jurisdiction of the Government of Canada" (Minister of Industry, 1968).

In 1969, the Telesat Canada Act established the corporation given the responsibility to own and operate the Canadian satellite communications system and to provide communications services to Canadian locations on a commmercial basis. Despite the fact that Telesat was established by statute and given a monopoly position, it is not a Crown corporation – as its officials have pointed out on many occasions. They often describe the corporation as "the carriers' carrier," a reference to the fact that most of the signals carried on satellite are being transmitted on behalf of another carrier, such as a telephone or telecommunications company. The ownership of Telesat is shared between the federal government (with 50 per cent) and a number of telecommunications carriers, principally the members of Telecom Canada.

Telesat's first satellite was launched in 1972 and shortly thereafter the company initiated the first domestic satellite communications service in the world. (In 1964, Canada had joined IN-TELSAT, the international consortium that operated the first-ever commercial satellite service, but Intelsat's mandate was to provide only international communications linkages.) By 1986, the corporation had launched several series of satellites and had four in operation with two more launched but not yet in service.

The Telesat satellite system was designed

originally to have two different transmission capacities: (1) a "heavy route" linkage between Toronto and Vancouver via major earth stations at Allan Park and Cowichan Bay, respectively; (2) a "thin route" network that could provide at least telephone service via small earth stations in isolated communities in northern Canada. Technical integration of the ground facilities of the satellite system with the ground-based networks of the telephone system was arranged efficiently so that, from the start in 1972, the satellite system was interconnected with the major telecommunications carriers' networks.

Historically, the primary use for the satellites has been for telecommunications (mostly voice telephone and data communications) traffic. However, by 1987, it was apparent that broadcasting services were becoming at least as important to Telesat. The Canadian common carriers have been the major users of the satellites, and the large telephone companies have been the beneficiaries of Telesat policies that require customers to contract for point-to-point services through their local telecommunications carrier. Thus, it should not have been surprising when, in 1976, Telesat announced that it planned to become a member of the TransCanada Telephone System (since renamed Telecom Canada); by joining TCTS, Telesat hoped to be assured that TCTS members would continue to use the satellite facilities and, thus, ensure that Telesat remained financially viable. Telesat's membership in TCTS was reviewed by the CRTC, which refused to permit such a move. The CRTC declared that the Telesat-TCTS arrangement would not be in the public interest mainly because it would make regulation of Telesat's service rates more difficult and also because Telesat's ability to serve *all* common carriers might be impaired. The CRTC's decision was overturned by the

federal cabinet and Telesat has been a member of the telephone industry group since 1977.

Three types of network have been developed to provide or improve broadcasting service coverage in northern Canada, to take advantage of the existence of the Canadian satellite system and despite the high cost of leasing a full satellite channel (around $1 million per year). Since 1973, the CBC, with special funding from Parliament, has leased several full channels; part of this capacity is used to distribute a Northern Television service to communities in the territories. Since 1981, a broadcasting consortium known as Cancom (Canadian Satellite Communications Inc.) has leased satellite channels to distribute its package of Canadian TV and radio signals to remote and under-served communities across the country. In 1983, Cancom received CRTC permission to redistribute several American signals as well. Most recently, Cancom was given CRTC permission to provide service in more urban, southern communities. A third kind of system has been the Inukshuk TV network set up by the Inuit Broadcasting Corporation for a number of native communities in the eastern Arctic. However, this part-time network depends on federal funds and access to CBC-leased satellite channels for its operation. While commercial radio or television networks in southern Canada make use of the satellite system, none has opted to abandon terrestrial links to use satellites only.

Although the effects of satellite development on communications policy may not have been fully anticipated, some possible impact on the broadcasting system and on telecommunications carriers should have been expected. The 1968 White Paper noted that a domestic satellite system could have significant benefits for the distribution of television service in Canada. However, the benefits and costs of the changes were not completely assessed at that time – nor could they be. Unanticipated changes (such as in the low cost and high accessibility of small earth stations, new rules established by the FCC in the United States, the launching of numerous U.S. satellites and satellite TV services) have made the 1968 prognostications seriously inaccurate. The predictions were most seriously wrong in the degree to which rural and northern Canadians would seek and obtain access to many satellite TV services, especially American ones.

BROADCASTING POLICY

Since the establishment of the first royal commission into broadcasting in 1928, the federal government has regularly returned to the establishment of commissions or special parliamentary committees as a chief instrument of policy formulation in the broadcasting area. The 1932 Radio Reference case, heard by the Judicial Committee of the British Privy Council (then the final court of appeal for Canadian law), decided that the federal government had *exclusive* jurisdiction over radio communication in Canada. This was taken to include broadcasting, and no court case since has seriously challenged this interpretation.

The only role remaining to the provinces in broadcasting policy is in the area of educational broadcasting although this was rather unclear for many years. In the early 1970s, it was finally agreed that provinces could set up educational broadcasting organizations as long as they were at arm's length from the provincial government itself. Thus, we have seen the setting up of Radio Québec, ACCESS Alberta, TVOntario, and the Knowledge Network of the West (KNOW) in British Columbia.

The legal definitions relevant to broadcasting are provided by the current Broadcasting Act, Section 2:

> "broadcasting" means any radiocommunication in which the transmissions are intended for direct reception by the general public;
>
> "broadcasting licence" or . . . "licence" means a licence to carry on a broadcasting undertaking issued under the Act;
>
> "broadcasting undertaking" includes a broadcasting transmitting undertaking, a broadcasting receiving undertaking and a network operation, located in whole or in part within Canada or on a ship or aircraft registered in Canada.

Cable television systems are deemed to be "broadcasting receiving undertakings" and, therefore, are required to be licensed under the Act. Altogether, cable television, pay television, and satellite carriage of TV and radio signals have made the technical concept of "broadcasting" much broader than was originally imagined when radio broadcasts began in Canada in 1919. These technological changes have prompted efforts to change the legislative definition to ensure effective political control over licensing of the whole broadcasting system.

Based on the 1932 judicial decision, Parliament has passed a series of statutes related directly or indirectly to broadcasting:

1932   Canadian Radio Broadcasting Commission Act
1936   Canadian Broadcasting Act
1958   Broadcasting Act
1968   Broadcasting Act
1969   Department of Communications Act
1970   Telesat Canada Act
1976   Canadian Radio-television and Telecommunications Act

Under these statutes, various federal institutions have been set up:

1932-36 Canadian Radio Broadcasting Commission (CRBC)
1936- Canadian Broadcasting Corporation (CBC)
1958-68 Board of Broadcast Governors (BBG)
1968-76 Canadian Radio Television Commission (CRTC)
1969- Department of Communications (DOC)
1970- Telesat Canada
1976- Canadian Radio-television and Telecommunications Commission (CRTC), an expanded version of the one set up in 1968.

Regulation and the CRTC

Regulation of broadcasting has taken various forms, mostly aimed at encouraging the production of Canadian programming content or at extension of service coverage to less urban areas. One type of regulation that has affected international control of the broadcasting system is the restriction on levels of foreign ownership. As long as the CBC was the predominant broadcaster, less concern was expressed about the existence of foreign companies owning broadcasting stations. However, by the 1960s when the private sector had grown and cable TV was expanding quite rapidly (often with the help of foreign capital), political concern about foreign control of broadcasting became greater. Direct and effective action was finally taken in 1969 when the CRTC was directed by the cabinet not to issue licences to corporations with less than 80 per cent Canadian ownership or where the corporation board was not made up wholly of Canadian citizens (CRTC, 1974).

Because of the strong federal authority over broadcasting, much attention is given to the body that holds this power on a day-to-day basis. The CRTC has a central role in the policy processes regarding broadcasting in Canada.

Historically, the CRTC is the successor of a long line of state regulation of Canadian broadcasting going back to 1932. In the first twenty years after 1936, the CBC exerted some regulatory control over private broadcasters through its organization of national networks to which the private stations belonged. Not until 1958 was a separate regulatory authority set up for non-technical regulation; this was the Board of Broadcast Governors (BBG).

From the earliest years of radio broadcasting (the years immediately after the First World War), technical licences were issued by the Minister of Marine and Fisheries; later the Minister of Transport had the job, which was eventually moved to the Minister of Communications in 1969. In the technical licensing process, considerations of signal coverage, signal quality, and potential interference with other users of the radio spectrum are the main criteria for issuance or non-issuance of a licence although the CBC, as the national broadcaster, has the opportunity to reserve specific frequencies for its own immediate or future needs in serving the country as a whole. Once having received a technical licence, a private broadcaster until the late 1950s had to meet some minimal standards and categories of programming content in his broadcast airtime; these standards were set by the CBC but apparently not strictly enforced.

In 1958, non-technical regulation was changed by the establishment of an independent regulatory body, the BBG. However, the new statute under which this was done did not specify clearly what should be the relationship of authority between the CBC and the BBG. As a consequence, the CBC tried to continue its operations as it had in the past while the Board was left to exert whatever control it could over private broadcasters. This confusing situation was resolved by the next statute, in 1968, which set up the CRTC as the Board's successor and gave the Commission full regulatory powers over all licensees, including the CBC networks and stations.

The purpose of the Commission is to regulate and supervise the Canadian broadcasting system and to do this with the intent of achieving the social and cultural objectives of the broadcasting policy stated in Section 3 of the current Broadcasting Act. The basis for the CRTC's authority stems from this section, called the "Broadcasting Policy for Canada." Typical CRTC policy actions can be setting general regulations applying to broad classes of licensees (for example, AM radio, FM radio, TV, cable TV) or directed toward certain kinds of programming content (for example, political broadcasts, commercials, foreign-language programs, programs intended for children). The CRTC also engages in policy action through the attachment of specific conditions of licence on individual licensees. In addition to having the responsibility to implement the stated broadcasting policy, the CRTC is also obliged to act in response to direction from the Governor-in-Council (i.e., the federal cabinet) on certain matters specified in the statute.

Much of the CRTC's work revolves around public hearings and the issuance of broadcasting licences. The hearings are held virtually year round and across the country in the larger cities. Each year, the Commission has to decide on thousands of licence applications: new applications, amendments, renewals, securities-related matters (affecting the ultimate control of a licensee or changes in assets), and network licences. In 1985-86, the CTRC made decisions on 3,309 applications, of which 2,131 were on cable TV, 223 on TV, 326 on securities, 269 on FM radio, 175 on AM radio, 76 on Cancom retransmitters, and 56 on networks (CRTC Annual Report, 1985-86).

To say that the CRTC is merely regulating the broadcasting system to achieve policy objectives set by Parliament understates the extent to which the CRTC has been obliged to interpret the policy before it could draw up regulations. It also understates the extent to which the CRTC has established sub-policies of its own in areas such as cable television, for which no explicit government policy existed prior to 1968 and about which the policy section of the statute remains too vague to be useful to the Commission. An implicit obligation placed on the CRTC in 1968 was the need to establish policies and regulations regarding cable TV systems and their operation with regard to over-air broadcasting.

While cable TV is the outstanding example of an area where policy-making by the CRTC has involved much more than simply implementing a statutory policy section, there have been other areas as well, some of which may turn out to be equally significant in terms of substantive broadcasting policy. One such area is concentration of private ownership in broadcasting licensee companies. Another is the introduction of pay television and other new broadcast-related specialty TV services. A third is the use of satellites for the distribution of broadcasting signals.

None of these is directly mentioned in the 1968 statute. Since the middle of the 1970s, there has been considerable discussion in the policy field about the degree to which the CRTC can and should initiate or resist policy action. There has also been discussion about the extent to which the federal government or Parliament should maintain policy control over the CRTC. The desirable balance between the autonomous authority of the regulatory commission and the cabinet's need to retain overall policy authority is difficult to determine and depends a good deal on where one is standing.

For example, views differ between those in government and those outside, between lawyers and economists, between industry associations and consumers representatives, and so on.

The Canadian Broadcasting Corporation

The CRTC is not the only important federal institution in broadcasting policy and the broadcasting system; aside from the technical regulation administered by the Department of Communications, the Canadian Broadcasting Corporation must be considered. The CBC is now fifty years old and, for many of those years, it has provided the major portion of Canadian radio and television programming. To do justice to the CBC's complex history and organization would require a substantial book – indeed, several books have been written largely about it (see, for example, Peers, 1969; Peers, 1979; Weir, 1965).

The mandate of the CBC comes mainly from Section 3 of the 1968 Broadcasting Act; it is cited in Chapter 2 and repeated here:

(f) there should be provided, through a corporation established by Parliament for the purpose, a national broadcasting service that is predominantly Canadian in content and character;

(g) the national broadcasting service should

(i)　be a balanced service of information, enlightenment and entertainment for people of different ages, interests and tastes covering the whole range of programming in fair proportion,

(ii)　be extended to all parts of Canada, as public funds become available,

(iii)　be in English and French, serving the special needs of geographic regions, and actively contributing to the flow and exchanges of cultural and regional information and entertainment, and

(iv)　contribute to the development of national unity and provide for a continuing expression of Canadian identity;

(h) where any conflict arises between the objectives of the national broadcasting service and the interests of the private element of the broadcasting system, it shall be resolved in the public interest but paramount consideration shall be given to the objectives of the national broadcasting service.

Since 1968, the CBC has tried to carry out its mandate "as public funds become available." The Corporation has six national networks, three in each official language; of each three, one is television, one AM radio, and one FM stereo radio. The English-language networks extend across the country although not fully in Quebec; the French-language networks are fully developed in Quebec but only partly available elsewhere. "Extension of service," as it is usually called by CRTC, is a special obligation of the CBC (much more so than for private broadcasters). While only a small percentage (less than one per cent) of Canadians remain unserved by Canadian broadcasting, the CBC is obliged to extend its signals to reach these people whenever possible.

Aside from the six major networks, the CBC also maintains other services:

- northern radio and television services including native-language program production in seven dialects for radio (over 7,400 hours in 1984-85) and six dialects for television (about 60 hours); the CBC also carries "access" programming by community organizations on both media;
- two national satellite-to-cable House of Commons networks, one for each official language;
- a TV captioning service for the hearing-disabled;

- an international short-wave radio programming service in eleven languages to countries around the world; and
- host broadcasting services for foreign broadcasters when international events occur in Canada.

Public ownership of broadcasting is usually considered to have started in 1932 with the establishment of the CBC's predecessor, the Canadian Radio Broadcasting Commission. During those years, the government's declared intention was for the public broadcaster to acquire all existing private stations and to set up new stations where those were needed. However, the elimination of private ownership may not have been as firmly intended as is sometimes claimed. Frank Peers has argued that it was never intended that all private stations be taken over by the CBC but rather that the Corporation should provide and control a national system of broadcasting – a minor part of which could be small, local stations owned by private companies (Peers, 1969). In any case, the CBC found it impossible to buy all private stations because sufficient funds were never made available by Parliament.

Despite this limitation, it can be argued that the public broadcaster still dominated the broadcasting system until the early 1960s. In 1961, the first licensed private network of broadcasting stations (the CTV network) began operating. Until then, the CBC was the only broadcaster allowed to form permanent networks. The first private radio network (the CKO chain) was approved by the CRTC in 1976.

Although the numbers of stations (radio or TV) owned by the CBC are considerably overwhelmed now by the numbers of private stations, the CBC still remains a significantly large corporate entity compared to any one of the private companies involved in broadcasting. In 1984-85, the CBC had over 11,000 employees and paid out more than $120 million in freelance payments to creative artists (CBC Annual Report, 1984-85). In hours of production, the CBC far outweighs any single private broadcaster; totals for 1982-83 of original production were over 115,000 hours for radio and over 36,000 hours for television.

Statistics for comparison between the public and private sectors of broadcasting are difficult to get, partly because of their different purposes and corporate structures. Statistics Canada data on public and private broadcasters exclude non-commercial stations such as educational, community, and religious broadcasters so that the CBC alone is compared with the private, commercial broadcasters. Generally speaking, the CBC represents about half of the expenditures on programming and about three-quarters of technical costs (production facilities and distribution facilities) in the broadcasting system.

The policy significance of the CBC relates to several factors: its corporate size and history; the dependence on public funds for most of its revenue; the provision of radio and TV services to almost all Canadians in one or both official languages; and the large expenditures on program productions and creative artists' fees. The more than $800 million a year now received by the CBC from Parliament makes the Corporation the largest recipient by far of public funds assigned to cultural purposes.

Canadian Content

Canadian content regulations stem from the CRTC's obligation under the Broadcasting Act to ensure that the programming provided by each licensee uses "predominantly Canadian creative and other resources." The CBC is under the extra obligation that its national broadcasting service should be "predominantly Canadian in content and character."

The idea of requiring a minimum percentage of broadcast time to be used for transmitting Canadian productions did not originate with the CRTC but had been in place since 1959 under the Board of Broadcast Governors regulations. The Canadian content quota was never well received by the private broadcasters, who protested each rule and rule change vigorously and sought to minimize their carriage of Canadian material as far as possible (Babe, 1979). This is the case for both radio and television; cable TV, being almost entirely a carrier of other licensees' content, is not subject to the same sort of rules. The CRTC requires television licensees to have at least 60 per cent of all programming hours be given to Canadian productions (50 per cent in prime time for private broadcasters). Licensees for AM radio stations must have Canadian productions as at least 30 per cent of music selections; there is no standard quota for FM stations.

Canadian content quotas on radio are generally not a big issue either with the broadcasters or with the general public (although there was much complaining when the regulations were first introduced). It is generally agreed that the Canadian record production industry has benefited enormously from the quota, which has given the companies and their artists some assurance of access to the Canadian audience. However, it is on television that the major problems have always existed. During the 1970s, a good deal of evidence was produced to show that, while the majority of programs aired by Canadian TV broadcasters were "Canadian" in the regulatory definition, the Canadian audience showed a strong preference for American entertainment series and movies.

There was clearly a strong demand for TV drama yet very little of this was being produced in Canada. Independent producers said they would like to produce this type of program but were unable to persuade Canadian broadcasters to pay them adequately for their productions. The CRTC re-examined the Canadian content rules to see whether they could be changed to encourage the production of more and higher-quality entertainment for television. There was some hope expressed that the introduction of pay TV in Canada would open up a big new market for Canadian popular entertainment production. As is discussed in Chapter 11, this hope proved to be ill-founded when the pay TV services launched in Canada did not attract enough subscribers to support the large expenditures needed.

Towards a New National Broadcasting Policy

In 1982, the federal Minister of Communications announced he was developing a comprehensive broadcasting strategy. The strategy was revealed in March, 1983, in a paper entitled *Towards a New National Broadcasting Policy*. The paper was subtitled: "New policies and initiatives to provide Canadians with greater program choice and make the Canadian broadcasting industry more competitive: A response to new technologies and a changing environment." The "Broadcasting Strategy for Canada" was given these fundamental goals:

1. To maintain the Canadian broadcasting system as an effective vehicle of social and cultural policy in light of a renewed commitment to the spirit of the broadcasting objectives set out in the 1968 Broadcasting Act.
2. To make available to all Canadians a solid core of attractive Canadian programming in all program categories, through the

development of strong Canadian broadcast and program production industries.

3. To provide a significantly increased choice of programming of all kinds in both official languages in all parts of Canada.

One key action taken by the federal government was the creation of the Canadian Broadcast Program Development Fund to be administered by Telefilm Canada. This fund was intended to provide greater resources to Canadian producers so that they could produce "attractive high-quality Canadian programming in both official languages and of international calibre – Canadian programming that people will choose to watch." The Fund was to be $35 million in its first year of operation and would rise to $60 million in its fifth year.

To receive funds, producers had to show their program would be exhibited by a Canadian broadcaster and initially they had to raise two-thirds of the money needed from other sources. (This rule has since been modified to allow Telefilm to contribute a larger share.) Further, the funds were earmarked for three program categories: drama, children's programming, and variety. Since its beginning in 1983, the Fund has been well-received by independent producers and has also been acceptable to the CBC and to some of the private stations. Given the lengthy lead-time needed to create high-quality television productions, although positive signs are on the horizon it is still rather early to say if the productions assisted by the Fund will be as popular with the Canadian public as the policy-makers and the producers have hoped.

The Broadcasting Task Force

In May,1985, then Minister of Communications Marcel Masse appointed a task force to make recommendations on "an industrial and cul-

tural strategy to govern the future evolution of the Canadian broadcasting system through the remainder of this century, recognizing the importance of broadcasting to Canadian life."* The task force was co-chaired by Gerald Caplan and Florian Sauvageau and had five other members selected from across the country and with different perspectives. The task force report, originally due in January, 1986, was not issued to the public until the following September. The 700-page report proved to be very complex, and a set of linked recommendations were made to the Minister of Communications. By this time, a new Minister of Communications, Flora MacDonald, had been appointed. Even if the new minister decides to support the recommendations fully, the political will to change the broadcasting system requires the active support of the cabinet and the co-operation of all parties in the House of Commons. Many of the task force's recommendations need legislative action and this is usually slow to occur in the Canadian Parliament.

CULTURAL INDUSTRIES POLICY

So far in this chapter we have discussed communications policy largely in the context of telecommunications and broadcasting. In recent years, however, broadcasting has been combined with the film, publishing, and recording industries to form what are called "cultural industries." The term derives from the

---

*For those interested in how the task force interpreted its mandate, the secretary to the task force, Paul Audley, has written an article on just that subject: "The Agenda of Broadcasting Policy: Reflections on the Caplan-Sauvageau Task Force," in R. Lorimer and D.C. Wilson, eds., *Communications Canada* (forthcoming, 1988).

fact that each of these industries is involved in manufacturing, distributing, and retailing cultural materials for mass markets. In this section we will look at those cultural industries other than broadcasting.

As Audley (1983, p. 320) suggests in *Canada's Cultural Industries*, the major challenge for policy in cultural industries "is not that properly financed Canadian cultural materials are being offered to the Canadian public and rejected, but that as a general rule, they are in limited supply, have limited financing available, and receive inadequate distribution or exhibition." Why do these barriers to production, financing, and distribution exist? Audley identifies two reasons. First, cheap foreign content is available at run-on prices. Second, Canadian companies must unfairly compete with foreign-owned branch plants who supply such materials to the market.

Given such barriers to Canadian participation and the nature of cultural materials themselves, cultural industries policy has been founded on two arguments. The first is an economic one: because there are structural barriers to the participation of Canadian businesses, an "infant industries" argument has guided a certain amount of government intervention in the marketplace. The purpose of such intervention is to allow Canadian businesses to gain a foothold under protective or supporting legislation, then, eventually, to re-open the doors to international competition.

A contrary reading of the economic context places a different interpretation on the significance of competition and industry structures. This reading has two elements. First, Canada has weak copyright laws that do not insist on the separation of Canadian rights from either North American or British rights.

Second, as a result of this, foreign-owned branch plants can have exclusive and prior rights to the output of their parent companies. The consequence is that, for the most part, Canadian companies are unable to compete for the right to manufacture and distribute cultural products in Canada produced by foreigners. Support programs help to counteract this restricted competition.

The second and perhaps more fundamental argument used to establish cultural industries policy is a cultural one. This argument has been cited by all the public bodies that have examined cultural industries and cultural policy – even those with a preference for minimizing state intervention. A recent example of this could be seen in the Nielsen Task Force on Program Review, whose task was to find where government spending could be cut. The study team charged with examining communications and culture programs stated:

> The analyses of this paper suggest that while the economic impact of cultural activity is positive, economic reasons alone are probably not sufficient to justify the allocations of public resources to culture. The study team suggests that the main rationale for public support has to reside in the political and social value of cultural activities and their ability to contribute to the definition of the Canadian character. (Nielsen, 1986, p. 45)

As reviews of policy have pointed out, it is important that both economic (sometimes called industrial) and cultural considerations be built into policy. The predominance of economic considerations can lead to culturally undistinguished products. However, if cultural considerations dominate, this can perpetuate the international dominance of foreign cultural industries.

Film and Video

There is no comprehensive policy for film and video at the federal or provincial levels. This is an area in which the provinces could play an active role if they so chose. In May, 1984, the federal Minister of Communications issued a National Film and Video Policy, but this was more a statement of intent than a program that has been actively pursued. The key goals of the policy statement were given as: (a) the development of the private-sector Canadian film and video industry; (b) a more focused and smaller production role for the National Film Board (NFB). This latter objective has not been followed up yet although some decisions may be made within the next few years. At present, the NFB absorbs about 40 per cent of federal government expenditures in the film sector so it is clearly an important part of public policy. Among policy-makers, there has been dissatisfaction with the NFB for some years, as well as increasing uncertainty within the NFB itself about what its proper role is, now that the private film and video production industry is growing.

With regard to the private-sector initiatives, the most important federal policies have been Telefilm Canada's Broadcast Program Development Fund (already mentioned in the broadcasting section of this chapter) and the development of the Capital Cost Allowance (CCA).* Other policies relate to the funding of the NFB to produce and distribute films, the

___
*The CCA is part of the Income Tax Act and allows investors in certified Canadian film and video productions to deduct capital costs from their taxable income over a two-year period. This type of policy action is called a tax expenditure; that is, the government forgoes collection of taxes in exchange for some other type of benefit.

support of film (and video to a lesser extent) as art by the Canada Council, and establishment of Cité du Cinema, which is a jointly funded federal and Quebec production facility in Montreal.

Most of the policies focus on production support of one kind or another but the major problem is the lack of screen time for Canadian production on Canadian cinema screens. About 2 per cent of screen time in Canada goes to Canadian films. This obviously makes the film production industry very weak in terms of its own "natural" market. The reason for lack of market access is the historic, structural relationship between the major American studios and the Canadian exhibitor chains (who own the vast majority of first-run, urban cinemas). There are now only two major chains of Canadian movie theatres today, Famous Players and Cineplex Odeon. They have established contractual arrangements with the seven Hollywood majors, who are both producers and distributors of film products. From a business point of view, these agreements are beneficial to the financial security of all the parties involved. The problem is that the independent Canadian producers and distributors are largely excluded from the arrangements.

There is a problem also in using political power to free up the exhibition of films. First, the federal government cannot act directly in this area because cinemas are a matter of provincial jurisdiction, and provinces have been most reluctant to intrude on the business decisions of cinema-owners. Furthermore, such government action is often perceived as dictatorial interference with the open market – even though it can easily be demonstrated that there is no free market in this sector. On the other hand, efforts to get the exhibitors to agree voluntarily to give access to more Canadian films have not worked well at all. The access to the Canadian cinema audience for Canadian films is crucial to later access to the television and pay TV markets. So, even though the cinema audience is now much smaller than the TV audience, the initial cinema market remains important for structural reasons. No policies yet have been established to deal effectively with this bottleneck.

Publishing

Publishing, a term that normally includes book and magazine publishing but not newspapers because they are usually not seen as a cultural industry, has its own collection of policies attempting to deal with specific aspects of the sector. There is no comprehensive policy and this is another industry in which provincial governments can and do play a policy role.

Book publishing is generally regarded as having four kinds of markets: educational, trade, mass paperback, and scholarly. All of these kinds of publishing show structural weaknesses that harm their effectiveness both as transmitters of culture and as industrial sectors in Canada. Essentially, there are two separate linguistic markets for published materials (as well as many minuscule markets for other languages). This divides the country into a small French-language publishing industry based in Quebec, largely restricted to that province, and a somewhat larger English-language publishing industry, largely based in Ontario but also spread across a wide, relatively underpopulated country.

Foreign presences loom over both of these industries. In the case of the English-language industry it is the giant U.S. book industry, together with the British, with their lower per unit costs for published material and heavy promotions of best-selling authors. In the case

of the French-language industry it is French publishing, with slightly higher than American per unit costs but still an ability to supply the Canadian market with books at run-on prices. In addition, because of foreign-owned branch plants and weak copyright laws, there are problems of poor access for Canadian-owned publishers to the Canadian rights of foreign works (such rights are usually already held by foreign publishers and their Canadian subsidiaries act as exclusive agents for distribution in Canada). Because of weaknesses in other cultural industries, such as film and broadcasting (already mentioned), the Canadian book publishers do not benefit much from the sale of subsidiary rights for their published works for movies or TV programs. This reduces their profit potential.

Altogether, Canadian-owned publishing companies operate under severe structural handicaps and both the federal and provincial levels of government have support programs that try to develop a vibrant (and eventually self-sufficient) book publishing industry. The latest program of support for book publishing entrenches the cultural support the Canada Council is able to provide for "culturally valuable" books. The Department of Communications policy is oriented to increasing the participation of Canadian companies in the more profitable areas of publishing: educational books and, to a lesser extent, mass paperbacks.

Periodicals publishing also shows a division between different kinds of publications. In this case, the differentiation is between general interest, special interest, literary, and academic periodicals. Each type is supported by government programs designed to deal with the problems of that particular market segment. Periodicals publishers have all the same structural weaknesses associated with the lack of an adequate advertising base. One policy that gives significant aid to periodicals published in Canada is the establishment of postal subsidies.

Government policies are usually intended to help only Canadian-owned publishers, but it is extremely difficult to design support programs that exclude foreign-owned publishers from benefiting as well. This is very much the case with postal subsidies, which are also used extensively by foreign publishers. Since this was never the intention of the policy-makers, a re-examination of the program seems in order. The Nielsen Task Force recommended the gradual abolition of the subsidy and, if this is done, another way to aid Canadian periodicals publishers would likely have to be developed.

CONTINUING ISSUES IN COMMUNICATIONS POLICY

The perennial issues in communications can be summarized in this way:

Area	Issues
For telecommunications:	access, competition
For broadcasting:	content, choice, participation
For cultural industries:	ownership, content

The details of the issues can vary over time but the basic questions do not change.

Telecommunications Issues

For telecommunications, the fundamental issue is always that of **fair access**. This revolves around the principle that individuals (households or businesses) are entitled to receive adequate service at equitable and non-discriminatory rates. While no one seriously expects that a person living in an isolated area will receive exactly the same range and price of services as someone living in downtown Vancouver or Montreal, there must be no deliberate deprivation of service and the rates charged must be shown to be "just and reasonable." These principles govern all telecommunications regulation on this continent.

Related to them is the principle that all customers in similar circumstances must be treated equally and the charges for services must be publicly known. This requires all telecommunications carriers to post their rates and to specify clearly who pays what for which level of service. Specific issues that arise in telecommunications are related to disputes about the equity of established rates, whether one type of customer service is being cross-subsidized at the expense of another (e.g., households by businesses, rural residents by urban residents, and so on), and whether the costs of service are being properly calculated by the carrier.

Another major issue in telecommunications that has become much more important in recent years is **competition**. As outlined above, telephone companies in the past were regarded as providing a "natural monopoly" type of service. This is no longer agreed upon because new distribution technologies allow for different ways of delivering essentially the same service within any one area. The question here is the extent to which competition between telephone companies and others should be encouraged. In theory, full competition is better than monopoly but there are costs involved, especially for customers in less profitable regions. Competitors for market shares in large cities, for example, are eager to step forward but there is not a rush to compete in serving small towns and rural areas.

Here is a situation where the benefits accruing to urban, business-oriented customers have to be balanced against the costs accruing to rural and other less profitable customers. In Canada, a high priority has always been placed on the widest possible availability of telecommunications services to all Canadians so there is no presumption that competition is invariably beneficial. Arguments swirl around the question of who is going to win and who will lose in an increasingly competitive environment for telecommunications services. New technologies allow for new arrangements in providing service, but Canadian policy-makers are not necessarily in favour of deregulation without careful consideration of the likely consequences. These consequences can be effects on the telecommunications carriers themselves as well as effects on consumers and on new companies that would like to enter the telecommunications marketplace.

A whole series of issues that have been discussed and to some extent dealt with in recent years include the following: The question of system interconnection – can CNCP be allowed to interconnect its system with those of major Telecom Canada members even though they compete with each other? Can customers buy their own communications terminals and attach them to the telecommunications system without the approval or knowledge of the carrier? If so, under what conditions? Can the carriers be compelled to buy equipment from manufacturing companies not linked to themselves or their parent company? Can satellite systems or other new distribution systems be allowed or required to compete with telephone companies in providing data communications or voice telephony services? Can the satellite company be required to allow anyone to own an earth station and, if so, under what conditions so as to prevent unauthorized reception or transmission of signals? How can the monopoly services of the carrier be separated for accounting and regulating purposes from the competitive services they offer? Can large telephone companies such as Bell Canada

evade regulation of some of their telecommunications activities simply by reorganizing their corporate structure?

Broadcasting Issues

The key issue in broadcasting is **content**. As with telecommunications, though, this issue is not isolated from others (in this case, choice and participation). **Choice** refers to consumer choice and is akin to the telecommunications issue of access. In recent years, because of an increasing number of technological systems that can deliver broadcasting-type (especially video) signals to households – over-air, cable television, satellites, VCRs – there is a growing demand from consumers for greater choice between delivery systems. This is *assumed* to provide consumers with greater choice of content, although that is not assured. The Canadian broadcasting system has economic difficulty in delivering greater choice and even in delivering popular Canadian entertainment content.

Some will argue that, if Canadians do not want Canadian content, there is no way it should be pushed on them. First of all, it is not clear that Canadians don't want to watch or listen to Canadian programming. There is not enough good quality programming available to most Canadians for anyone to answer this question. Second, it must be stressed that without Canadian content as an essential component there is really no justification for having a Canadian-owned broadcasting system at all. We have ownership rules to keep foreigners out and we have a clearly demonstrated and undisputed popular demand for Canadian news, current affairs, and sports on radio and television. What we don't have is a strongly based popular entertainment industry to feed content into the Canadian broadcasting stations and networks. Hollywood and New York provide an overwhelming presence in this field and Canada has trouble creating a place for its own industry.

Questions abound here. Should we bother about a Canadian production capacity if the American entertainment industry does the job so well and its product is popular with Canadians? If we should bother, then how much protection do we give our own industry and for how long? If we do protect it, what types of protection are appropriate and effective – guaranteed air-time (in a way the Canadian content rules provide this)? Subsidies for production? Subsidies to aid distribution? Subsidies for exporting to other countries? Should we rely entirely on public broadcasters such as the CBC and forget about the majority of private broadcasters who don't want to do this anyway? Should we change the nature of the Canadian content quota? If so, how? Reduce it? Drop it altogether? Develop incentives for particular types of content? Should we encourage independent producers more? If so, which ones and who will choose them?

The issues surrounding Canadian content are linked, of course, to questions about content in general. Canadian content increases the range of choice that Canadian consumers have. So does foreign content other than the American content, of which we have an abundance. Content diversity within Canadian content can also be useful; Canadian content need not mean only Toronto for English Canadians and Montreal for French Canadians. How much are Canadians (as consumers or as taxpayers) prepared to pay to encourage production outside of these two dominant cities?

In choosing content in terms of source, diversity, and so on, we are also choosing between methods of payment. Of course, all broadcasting must be paid for. If it is a com-mercial service, we pay indirectly through the reception of advertisements and the purchase of advertised products or we pay directly as in pay TV. If it is a public or educational service, we pay through taxes. If it is non-commercial, then the community pays through local taxes or voluntary contributions of various kinds.

There are really two kinds of payment, direct and indirect. Increasing attention is being given lately to direct forms of payment in systems such as pay TV, specialty TV, and VCR cassette rentals. These are not necessarily better or worse than the older payment systems; they are different and we have to consider the different effects of their development on content and on consumer choice. Indirect payment methods tend to have a redistributive effect in that wealthier people pay more through taxes than those less well-off although they all can receive the same service. Direct forms of payment tend to discriminate against those with the least amount of disposable income. The policy choice between payment systems is a social one and cannot be made solely on technical grounds if the broadcasting services provided are regarded as an important and basic requirement of nationhood.

Participation is a third and usually much less publicized issue in Canadian broadcasting policy. It refers to the access permitted to people outside the professional broadcasting companies to the production decisions on content. Ironically perhaps, access in the North for native people to the facilities of the CBC is actually a good deal better than is access for most southern Canadians to any broadcast facilities. Participation issues can be about the difficulties of using the local cable TV system's community channel for a discussion of local politics, about the problems of selling independent productions to any broadcaster (CBC or otherwise), or about the difficulties of regional producers in the CBC getting the opportunity to produce a nationally aired program series, not just a local news hour or current affairs show.

There are a few community radio stations in Canada, mostly in Quebec where the provincial government has encouraged their establishment and provided basic funding for their operation. There is the access policy in the CBC's Northern Service. There are, as well, an "ethnic broadcasting" policy and some third-language programming. Also, the picture is improving for independent producers to sell their products to TV broadcasters. But there is still a long way to go before most Canadians have a chance to use the broadcasting system to say anything to their fellow citizens.

Cultural Industries Issues

With regard to all the cultural industries, the issues are largely the same as for broadcasting, with the addition of the key issue of **ownership**. Unlike in broadcasting, foreign ownership of other cultural industries cannot be limited by laws equivalent to the Broadcasting Act. Federal and provincial governments both have jurisdiction over various aspects of the film and publishing industries. These governments do not usually act in unison to implement a coherent policy. Many underlying problems of the industrial process of production, distribution, and retailing in the Canadian cultural industries relate to the small size of the domestic market and the strong intrusion of foreign-owned companies into that market.

The dominance of foreign companies in cultural industries (other than newspaper publishing) has significance not only because it weakens the cultural sovereignty of Canadian society but also because it clearly affects the **content** of the cultural products that are made available to Canadians. The industrial aspect of cultural products for the mass market shows that the flow of Canadian products from production through distribution to retailing is not a smooth process but is restricted by business practices that often favour large (usually foreign) corporations based outside Canada.

In terms of the international trade in cultural products, Canada is a very small player indeed and Canadian companies operate from a weak domestic base. In industrial terms, decisions about what kinds of content to develop and promote are affected by the market potential. The cultural industries face a tough choice of trying to sell Canadian materials to a very small domestic market or aiming to produce "international" products that appeal to a world-wide audience accustomed to American mass culture products. Neither choice is particularly appealing in industrial or cultural terms, yet the choice has to be made.

SUMMARY

Electronic communications media are usually divided into two categories: telecommunications and broadcasting. It is becoming increasingly difficult to treat them separately in technical terms because their systems are converging in terms of usage. In policy terms, however, these systems are still dealt with separately even though newer technologies like satellite communications clearly affect the usage of both types of systems. While the specific issues of concern in broadcasting policy are somewhat different from those in telecommunications, there are increasing overlaps. In other cultural industries, film is increasingly pulled into broadcasting policy actions while book publishing remains largely dominated by foreign companies.

The primary problem is how to develop an overall communications policy in the sense of encompassing all electronic media nationwide. There are many difficulties in coordinating Canadian policies toward communications, not least of which is the federal-provincial tension. Different perceptions exist between federal and provincial governments about what kinds of policy direction are needed; the provinces also do not agree among themselves. Another difficulty in harmonizing policies is in the historic growth of statutes, corporations, and regulatory bodies each designed to focus on one aspect of communications. It is difficult to amend legislation or change institutions to meet changing circumstances. Also, policymakers' attitudes toward the communications revolution, and the wider phenomenon of rapid technological change, are confused and need to be clarified so that communications policies are more consistent.

REFERENCES

Audley, Paul. *Canada's Cultural Industries: Broadcasting, Publishing, Records and Film*. Toronto: James Lorimer, 1983.

Babe, Robert E. *Canadian Broadcasting Structure, Performance and Regulation*. Ottawa: Economic Council of Canada, 1979.

Canada, Task Force on Program Review (Nielsen Task Force). *Culture and Communications*. Ottawa: Minister of Supply and Services, 1986.

Canadian Broadcasting Corporation. Annual Reports.

Canadian Radio Television Commission. *Canadian Ownership in Broadcasting: A Report on the Foreign Divestiture Process*. Ottawa: Information Canada, 1974.

Department of Communications. *Canadian Telecommunications: An Overview of the Canadian Telecommunications Carriage Industry*. Ottawa: Minister of Supply and Services, 1983.

English, H. Edward, ed. *Telecommunications for Canada: An Interface of Business and Government*. Toronto: Methuen, 1973.

Fortin, Luc, and Conrad Winn. "Communications and Culture: Evaluating an Impossible Portfolio," in G. Bruce Doern, ed., *How Ottawa Spends: The Liberals, the Opposition and Federal Priorities 1983*. Toronto: James Lorimer, 1983.

Globerman, Steven. *Cultural Regulation in Canada*. Montreal: Institute for Research on Public Policy, 1983.

Minister of Communications. *Proposals for a Communications Policy for Canada: A Position Paper of the Government of Canada*. Ottawa: Information Canada, 1973.

Minister of Communications. *The National Film and Video Policy*. Ottawa: Minister of Supply and Services, 1984.

Minister of Communications, Consultative Committee on the Implications of Telecommunications for Canadian Sovereignty (Clyne Committee). *Telecommunications and Canada*. Ottawa: Minister of Supply and Services Canada, 1979.

Minister of Communications, Federal Cultural Policy Review Committee (Applebaum-Hébert Committee). *Report*. Ottawa: Minister of Supply and Services, 1982.

Minister of Industry. *White Paper on a Domestic Satellite Communication System for Canada*. Ottawa: Queen's Printer, 1968.

Mosco, Vincent. *Pushbutton Fantasies: Critical Perspectives on Videotex and Information Technology*. Norwood, N.J.: Ablex Publishing, 1982.

Peers, Frank W. *The Politics of Canadian Broadcasting: 1920-1951*. Toronto: University of Toronto Press, 1969.

Peers, Frank W. *The Public Eye: Television and the Politics of Canadian Broadcasting, 1952-1968*. Toronto: University of Toronto Press, 1979.

Schiller, Herbert I. *Information and the Crisis Economy*. Norwood, N.J.: Ablex Publishing, 1984.

Weir, E. Austin. *The Struggle for National Broadcasting in Canada*. Toronto: McClelland and Stewart, 1965.

Winner, Langdon. *Autonomous Technology: Tech-*

nics-out-of-Control as a Theme in Political Thought. Cambridge: MIT Press, 1977.

Woodrow, R. Brian, *et al. Conflict over Communications Policy: A Study of Federal-Provincial Relations and Public Policy.* Montreal: C.D. Howe Institute, 1980.

STUDY QUESTIONS

1. Canada does not have a clear and unified national policy on communications. Discuss the pros and cons of developing such a policy framework.

2. It has been suggested in this chapter that assumptions about the power of technology have influenced Canadian policy-making on communications. Give two examples of how this influence has been exerted recently.

3. The most crucial issue in telecommunications policy today is the proper balance between competition and monopoly service provision. Why is this a policy issue at all and how do you think it will be resolved?

4. The Fowler Committee Report in 1965 began with this statement, "The only thing that really matters in broadcasting is program content; all the rest is housekeeping." Do you agree? Explain your reasons.

5. "Cultural sovereignty" is an important term used in policy discussions about the cultural industries. What does this term mean? How does it translate into policy actions regarding the film industry?

CHAPTER

9

The Global Geopolitics Of Information

INTRODUCTION: JOURNALISM IN HISTORICAL PERSPECTIVE

IN THE OPENING chapter of *The Geopolitics of Information*, Anthony Smith quotes a speech given to the Manchester Chamber of Commerce by the famous explorer-journalist, H.M. Stanley, the man who found Livingstone in "deepest Africa."

> There are 50 millions of people beyond the gateway to the Congo, and the cotton spinners of Manchester are waiting to clothe them. Birmingham foundries are glowing with the red metal that will presently be made into ironwork for them and the trinkets that shall adorn those dusky bosoms, and the ministers of Christ are zealous to bring them, the poor benighted heathen, into the Christian fold. (Smith, 1980, p. 25)

Smith notes that, far from being a servant of some set of business interests, Stanley was first and foremost a newsman. Moreover,

> His professional integrity was unassailable. But his information was collected under the

inspiration of a socially accepted doctrine of colonialism, in which the pursuit of loot, markets and the Christian faith were subsumed into a single quest, which was undoubtedly emotionally uplifting for his audience in imperial England. (p. 25)

Smith's example is not atypical of the attitude to the gathering of information and its transformation into news at the height of the British Empire. Nor is it atypical of all of the information-gathering services the British had at their disposal. A review of nineteenth-century studies of "exotic" societies reveals a rendering of whole cultures through the eyes of colonialists. Indeed, Smith makes the claim that the Stanley example is simply a reading of the world view of the dominant culture.

Contemporary Equivalents

The penetration of the interests of the information-gathering culture into the information-gathering process has not abated in modern times. While those interests may be expressed less blatantly, they are nevertheless as present now as they were in Stanley's days. Consider the example of U.S. involvement in Grenada. The United States insisted that the airport runway being built in Grenada was being built for strategic purposes, to allow the landing of Soviet military supplies and personnel. Once in control, the Americans resumed building the runway to allow the landing of Boeing 747s with jumbo loads of tourists, a different form of strategic control. The Americans claimed that the runway would allow the development of the tourist trade. This was exactly the reason for building the runway the Grenadians had been giving prior to the U.S. invasion.

Such an obvious bias is not confined to special events. Third World nations have claimed

for some time that the manner in which the developed world collects information continually puts the developing nations at risk by portraying them according to Western, developed-world news values instead of evaluating them in their own context. Thus, in the eyes of those affected by the news, things have not changed. World views are still very much the foundation of the structuring of information in the news.

Neither have things changed much in social science. Intelligence tests developed in the United States are routinely administered the world over and results talked about as if people of other countries really were of lower intelligence than Americans. Parallel comparisons have been made between population groups in developed nations. The working class repeatedly scores lower than the middle class, a testing result that has led to theories of differentials in intelligence between races (Jensen, 1980). Even studies using relatively sophisticated theories, such as Piaget's or Bruner's (Bruner *et al.*, 1966), make comparisons (which are inevitably invidious) between people in the U.S. and people of the Third World.

Knowledge Serves the Interests of Those Who Collect It

The news is neither disinterested nor objective; nor is social science; nor, in fact, is science. *Knowledge serves the interests of those who collect it.* Knowledge and news reporters conceive of what information is to be sought, what elements of it are important, and how it should be discussed. For those who are written about and who have no access to telling their own story, the consequences are rather drastic. As Smith (p. 27) says: "To be imprisoned inside the misinterpretation and misunderstanding of others can be a withering form of incarceration. It is a fate which can afflict whole nations and cultures as painfully as individuals."

To understand the problems inherent in the dissemination of information we must know who the collectors and distributors are in the global scene. Also, we must know how their interests are reflected in the structure and content of global information.

The Free Press in an Open Society

As we have outlined in previous chapters, the doctrine of a free press and a free and open information system is entrenched in Western societies and is crucial to their continued existence as free and open societies.

As it is understood in Western countries, democratic rule requires that political parties be able to put their opinions before the electorate in order to gain the opportunity to govern a nation or region. Once one party has gained power other parties still need to put their views forward, either as criticism or as alternative policies. In other words, in keeping with democratic principles, the ruling party is required to act in a way that is apparently not in its own interest but is in the interest of a democratic society.

Another important element of the notion of free and open information, as we have come to know it, is the freedom of access to information, the right to know. A free press requires open access to information governments collect and create so that informed comment can be made on their policies. It is not difficult to understand why access to information and the freedom to publish are fragile freedoms when so much is at stake for those who have the power to restrict information access and flows.

The principle of a free press gives competing elites the right of access and allows comment on anything they might so choose, especially government policy. It provides the general public with a range of alternatives that can provide the basis for electing a government, taking broader political action, or, more generally, considering options and understanding society.

The freedom to inquire and to know and freedom of expression, however, are only part of the story. A further freedom has come to be associated with a free press – the freedom to make information and ideas known as widely as possible, that is, the freedom to distribute information. Essentially this is a freedom to pursue markets for information unencumbered by restrictive regulations. For a free press in the hands of private owners to operate in a capitalistic society those gathering the information must be free to exploit their markets. They must be free to sell the fruit of their labours in information-gathering and interpreting to whomever might want it. This extension of the principles of a free press is known as **free flow of information**. It means that the press believes that it must be free not only to gather information from anywhere but also to circulate it to anywhere a potential consumer of the information might be found.

The whole sector of information industries is founded on the principles of access to information, freedom to publish, and freedom to exploit markets. The press and media empires of the Western world depend for their existence on these principles and are certainly not interested in any reformation for dealing with information that would undermine their operations. They are most vociferous in protecting these freedoms with respect to information-gathering and distribution. The principle of free flow also very conveniently protects their entertainment arms. While protecting information against restrictive policies, they can rather easily extend the principle to any cultural or information product, i.e., movies, books, television programming, etc.

As Smith points out, this leads us, increasingly quickly, into a conundrum. International agreements that create consistent policies world-wide for the seeking after and exploitation of information provide the foundation for the emergence of immense information corporations. While these corporations serve the needs of equally immense countries, their size and power dwarf that of many small countries. The bargaining power of such countries to have their information needs attended to or even respected is slight.

THE GLOBAL NEWS AGENCIES AS EMBODIMENTS OF A FREE PRESS

On any single day there is a high degree of similarity in the media in the coverage and treatment of stories. This is especially true with the international stories. The reason is that most papers and other news media subscribe to common sources for their foreign material, any of several global news agencies.

A Portrait of the Globals

Approximately 1,200 news agencies operate in the world; the four large Western agencies are Reuters, Agence France Presse (AFP), Associated Press (AP), and United Press International (UPI). Together these four agencies put out 34 million words per day and claim to provide nine-tenths of the entire foreign news output of the world's newspapers and radio and television stations (Smith, 1980, p. 72). Other international agencies worth noting are DPA of West Germany, ADN of East Germany, Tanjug of Yugoslavia, EFE of Spain, and Kyodo of Japan. There are also several regional or ideologically alternative agencies for the non-

developed, non-capitalist world, such as ASIN, a Latin American and Caribbean news exchange pool, and NANAP, the Non-Aligned News Agency Pool (Boyd-Barrett, 1980). Table 9.1 provides information on the operations of these agencies as well as others of some influence, including TASS, the news agency of the Soviet Union.

Dominance by the Large and Non-Profitable

The Western agencies maintain dominance over the market by being large and in some cases non-profitable. While the Western press considers it anathema to operate with direct government subsidies, AFP operates with a set of indirect subsidies involving the purchase of the service by officers within the French government. An agency must have a great many subscribers to support its operation, yet if there is little profit in the venture, except when the scale of operation is vast and its market predictable and secure (as with AP and Reuters), other entrepreneurs are effectively blocked from setting up rival services. In other words, the agencies provide news so cheaply that no one else can compete. UPI itself seems continually on the verge of bankruptcy. Consequently, for its global coverage much of the Western world has come to rely on one French, one British, and two American organizations to collect and write up the international news. A review of the dynamics and history of the news agencies and their relations to national governments points out why the identity of the agencies is so important.

The Colonial Roots of the Globals

Anthony Smith maintains that it is impossible to examine the global news agencies without considering their relation to capitalism. He maintains that capitalism is as much an information system as a system of finance and production, as we are beginning to see more clearly as we enter the "information age." The imperial nations of the nineteenth century accomplished the integration of the world's resources into the markets of Europe. Such an accomplishment depended as much on an information network as it did on physical resources and transportation. In fighting for privileged trading positions over a period of several hundred years, the various European nations became masters at seeing economic potential in the appetites of their compatriots and in the resources, human or physical, of newly "discovered" nations. So keen was their appetite that they were able to cast aside fraternal connections with human beings of different races, question whether they had souls, and, as if to decide the matter in advance, create slaves of them.

These same nations and nationals acquired a position as purveyors of information, whether of the mundane sort to the newspapers of the land or of the more esoteric variety, as, for example, Darwin's several works inspired by his travels on the ship *Beagle*.

These systems of transportation and information were the foundation of contact between Europe and other world civilizations. However, they were structured in such a way to benefit Europe. Europe defined itself not as a civilization that had created untenable living conditions for its population, thus forcing emigration on the underprivileged, but as the colonizer, the spreader of the one true civilization and religion to a heathen and more or less empty world. For a time the communication of information depended on its physical carriage along with goods and people from Europe to the colonies and back. Eventually, submarine cables, laid along sea routes, and cables across land outpaced the speed of physical carriage. The British especially were eager to put the latest and best communications technology in place to span their empire.

The news agencies built their routes on the backs of the colonial information system and transformed the whole scope of news dissemination. Founded by a Frenchman, Charles Havas, in 1835, the first news agency grew out of a translation agency that then sold its translations to newspapers. With the coming of the telegraph, the number of newspapers the agency could sell to increased enormously. With the primacy of national interests in the nineteenth century and the division of the world into various European "empires," other nationally based agencies soon emerged. The first two were begun by two of Havas's employees, Bernard Wolff (Germany) and Paul Julius Reuter (England).

Havas, Reuter, and Wolff were all expansionist entrepreneurs working at the edges and propelled by the energy of three European empires. The world was split three ways among them with Havas gaining monopoly control of Latin America, which he held from 1870 to 1920 when his monopoly was broken by the U.S.-based United Press Association. From his base in Britain, Reuter took over the Low Countries and moved into Austria, Greece, and the area surrounding the Black Sea. Thwarted by the refusal of *The Times* to use his service, he provided information for other, mostly provincial, British newspapers. His service was so creditable that he was allowed to use British government telegrams as a source of news from India. Reuters was seen as an independent news service operating at arm's length from the British government; however, during the First World War the managing director of Reuters doubled as director of propaganda.

TABLE 9.1

Some Internationally Active Agencies

Press Agency	Number of countries served	Number of subscribers	Number of countries covered by correspondents and stringers	Number of words issued daily	Number of regular staff	Number of correspondents in foreign countries
AP (U.S.A.)	108	1,320 newspapers 3,400 broadcasters in U.S. 1,000 private subscribers	62 foreign bureaus	17 million		559
UPI (U.S.A.)	92	7,079 newspapers 2,246 clients outside U.S.A. +36 national news agencies	81 foreign bureaus	11 million 200 news pictures	1,823	578
AFP (France)	152	12,000 newspapers 69 national agencies	167 countries 108 foreign bureaus	3,350,000 +50 news pictures	1,990 incl.	171 full-time corres. 1,200 stringers
Reuters (U.K.)	147	6,500 newspapers 400 radio and TV stations	153 countries	1,500,000	2,000 incl.	350 full-time corres. 800 stringers
TASS (U.S.S.R.)	80	13,000 subscribers 200 subscribers to TASS photo 325 foreign subscribers	110 countries 40 bureaus		professional staff 560	61 corres.
DPA (FRG)	78	144 foreign subscribers 55 film services	80 countries 37 film services	115,000	800 incl.	105 full-time corres.
ANSA (Italy)	69	1,600 (approx.)	69 bureaus	300,000	568 incl.	47 full-time corres. 295 stringers

EFE (Spain)	32	1,734	52	500,000	545	123
Kyodo (Japan)	37	33 national agencies 40 foreign news agencies 64 Japanese newspapers 59 commercial radio and TV stations 14 non-members newspapers	37 bureaus	220,000 letters in Japanese 35,000 words in English	1,900	
Tanjug (Yugoslavia)	103		46	75,000 to 120,000 +40-50 news pictures	896 incl.	46 full-time corres.
IPS Inter Press Service (Latin America)	36	19 national agencies 400 newspapers, weeklies, and institutions	50	100,000	390	44
MENA (Middle East)	25	13 national agencies for exchange of news 21 national agencies for exchange of photos	35	185,000 200 documentary films 200 news pictures	500 incl. corres.	35 full-time

SOURCE: The World of News Agencies Working Paper No. 11 of the UNESCO Commission for the Study of Communication Problems, 1978.

The Entry of the Americans

The First World War brought the United States and the American news agencies onto the world stage. The obvious connections between the European agencies and their national governments and the virtual news blockade of Latin America provided the Americans with the opportunity to move out of their domestic confines. So successful have the Americans been in their operations that Smith claims that the whole of Latin America operates on the same news values as the U.S. The territorial monopolies have disappeared and been replaced with a scale of operations that ensures market dominance. As we noted earlier, the big four claim 90 per cent of the world's foreign news.

Since the entry of the American agencies during and following World War I, a variety of other agencies have attempted to gain a foothold in the international market. Some, such as the Chinese agency, Hsin Hua, have been national efforts, while others, representing numbers of developing countries, have been aided by UNESCO. Many of these later agencies have exchange or service relations with parallel organizations in other regions and also with the larger agencies to give them access to world news in exchange for what they provide on the local scene.

Inevitable problems arise in the use that other countries and regions make of the material the regional agencies create. Smith cites the coverage of Surinam independence: not a single Latin American paper carried the story on its front page on Surinam's first day of independence, November 26, 1975 (Smith, 1980, p. 71), despite Surinam being in South America. Apparently the absence of coverage was simply the result of the U.S. agencies not feeding the story. At times there are also problems of access to news sources for Third World agencies, which do not exist for the larger agencies. Such access problems are typical. When Canada's first astronaut was being interviewed shortly before he was launched into space, individual interviews were scheduled for Voice of America, AP, and UPI. Twenty minutes were set aside for all Canadian journalists (*Saturday Night*, March, 1985, p. 27).

The Performance of the News Agencies: The Bias of News Values

The most publicized shortcoming associated with the global agencies is the type of coverage given to Third World countries. The general view has been that there is an overemphasis on tragedy and disaster. Table 9.2 summarizes the actual pattern of coverage. A separate study carried out for UNESCO by Phil Harris of Leicester University found that the weakest aspect of the agency-created news story was the presentation of the Third World in a rather sketchy and ethnocentric form (Smith, 1980, p. 91). According to Western news values, only the unusual or exceptional is newsworthy. Such a definition is politically biased against those whose access to power is not usual. It favours the status quo and entrenched interests and provides a basis whereby society can continually restate its dominant ideology to the perpetual disadvantage of disenfranchised groups.

GLOBAL NEWS FLOWS

Hester (1974) identifies another major contributing factor to the distortion of the news from the Third World. While the definition of news causes journalists to select a certain minority of events out of the possible universe of events, several filtering or gatekeeping processes further select the material

TABLE 9.2

Subjects of AP Latin American News

Subject Categories	From Latin American Bureaus %	On U.S. AP Trunk Wire %
Accidents	5.01	2.34
Agriculture	0.86	1.36
Art, culture, and entertainment	1.16	0.00
Crime and criminal violence	13.81	47.66
Disasters	3.61	11.72
Domestic government and politics	15.65	14.06
Economics and business	7.58	2.34*
Education	1.04	0.00
Foreign relations	19.19	6.25
Human interest features	2.81	5.47
Labour	2.20	0.00
Military and defence	1.16	0.00
Miscellaneous	1.04	0.78
Prominent people	1.47	3.91
Religion	0.79	1.56
Science and medicine	1.34	2.34
Sports	23.23	0.00*
Totals (per cent)†	101.95	99.79
Number of items	1,636	128

*A few sports items were retransmitted on AP sports wires in the United States. A few business items were used on the AP-Dow Economic Wire.

†Totals do not equal 100 per cent because of rounding.

SOURCE: Al Hester, "International News Flows," in Alan Wells, ed., *Mass Communications: A World View* (Palo Alto: Mayfield Publishing, 1974). Reproduced with permission of the author.

that ends up in the newspaper. What we see in our papers is the result of news values being applied several times over. They are applied by the global agencies, but are also applied by the reporters for the national bureaus, the national bureaus themselves, the media who subscribe to the agency services, and the individual users of the media. As they are successively applied by people who have a very limited knowledge of the country being discussed, it is easy to understand why certain subjects of AP Latin American News – such events as coups, floods,

and debt defaults – are overrepresented. Hester points out the amplification of distortions at one site, between what arrives from the Latin American bureaus and what Associated Press puts on its trunk wire (Table 9.2).

Attempts To Compensate

Whoever shoulders the heaviest burden of guilt, the problem is recognized but the solution has yet to present itself. Few newspeople would deny the existence of a systematic distortion of what we in the developed world receive as news about the developing world. That distortion does indeed appear to come about through the definition of news. But the majority of newspeople would claim that it is precisely that definition of news which sells papers and captures audiences for television. Soft news on development, for example, is not read. It is not even picked up by countries and regions in the Third World when it is provided. The relative lack of success the Soviets have in their short-wave radio services compared to the BBC points to the crux of the problem in assessing how far one can go in using the media for the direct presentation of ideologically based issues. Smith discusses this problem in some depth and points out the efforts made by Tanjug, the Yugoslavian agency, to ensure a world-wide circulation of Third World news. (See also Robinson, 1981.)

There are two central issues with regard to the agencies. The first is the dominance the French, British, and Americans have over foreign news. The second is the perspective presented along with "the facts of the matter." If the U.S. government relies on ABC television news for information on foreign events, as a spokesperson for ABC claims in the television documentary *Inside TV News*, might we not assume that an American viewpoint pervades the operation? And if the BBC can be berated in the British House of Commons for failing to provide a sufficiently British perspective on the Falklands War, can we not assume that there is a certain pressure on all journalists to maintain a national perspective?

Smith uses the example of the overthrow of the shah of Iran to clinch the argument that the news agencies provide an ethnocentric perspective on foreign news. He points out that prior to the collapse of the Pahlavi dynasty there was no inkling in the Western press that the

"reforms" brought in by the shah were progressively unacceptable to the people of the country. The Ayatollah Khomeini was portrayed, if at all, as a religious zealot and not given any credibility as a spokesperson of a firmly entrenched set of values. The British press reported on the jobs lost to British and American firms, ignoring the plight of the Iranians themselves. The land reforms that consolidated the shah's power did less than nothing for putting land in the hands of a greater number of people, and these reforms obliged the country to import 50 per cent of its food, where previously it had been self-supporting. In the American press, they were presented as positive modernizations. After thousands had been killed in riots during the shah's regime, it was still presented as having a broad base of popular support.

In general, a viewpoint emphasizing modernization versus reactionary religious zealotry was put forward. As AP put it late in 1978, "modernization has collided with ancient social and religious traditions, whose proponents have refused to budge" (Smith, 1980, p. 99). Suppose a Canadian newspaper had reported at the end of the Trudeau era and after John Turner's failure to be elected Prime Minister that "liberalization and social development have collided with the traditional vested interests of business whose proponents have yet to come to grips with the 1980s." While no doubt some Canadians are of that opinion, it certainly distorts, as does the AP statement on Iran, the vibrancy of and popular support for the ideologies now voiced by the governments both in Canada and in Iran.

THE PRODUCERS AND CONSUMERS OF WORLD CULTURAL PRODUCTS

In the same way that world news is dominated by a few very large players, so are the

FIGURE 9.1
Domestic and Imported Television Programs

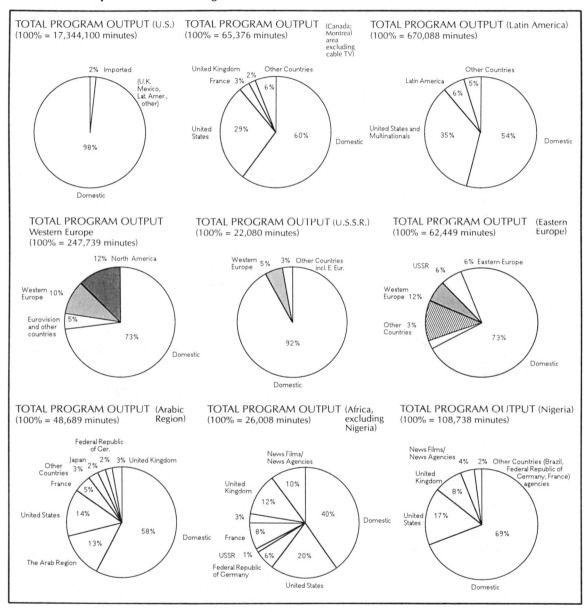

SOURCE: UNESCO, Reports and Papers on Mass Communication:
Tapio Varis, No. 100 International Flow of Television Programs. UNESCO, 1985.

entertainment industries, especially television and movie production. The difference is that the Americans play an even larger role than they do in the news agency business.

In Chapter 1 we presented some tables showing that Canada imports a vast number of "cultural products" from the U.S. and, to a limited degree, from other countries as well. Canada is not alone in being an avid importer of the imagination industries of the U.S. and other countries. Many nations and virtually all of the Third World find themselves in exactly the same position. Figure 9.1 shows comparative imports of television programs in a number of different countries and regions.

Consuming Exported Cultural Products

As with news, the issue is not just one of the amount that is generated elsewhere and imported. We must also understand the nature of the content. In work done over the past few years, a number of students and Lorimer have pointed out the kind of content that finds its way into school learning materials not imported directly but adapted for use in Canada or created from "scratch" by branch plants of multinational companies.

- In certain elementary readers a preponderance of American authors tell American stories about American events in American settings.
- In others, only the non-fiction was written by Canadians. The fiction was written by Americans and a few Britons. Table 9.3 illustrates the limited amount of Canadian authorship found in some major reading programs.
- In social studies an emphasis on the process of inquiry pushed out a systematic treatment of concrete information that would be necessarily Canadian.
- In a dictionary, American words such as the

names of all the states of the U.S. were deleted in favour of an odd collection of substitutes such as "deke" and "micmac," the latter being described as a canoe rather than the indigenous people of the Atlantic region of Canada (Lorimer, 1984). Subsequent work showed that science books put forward a view of scientific investigation that eclipses the relevance of the subject matter to the student's life in favour of understanding the position of the scientific investigator (Carscallen, 1984).

More recent inquiry on the basis for the appalling absence of Canadian content has focused beyond the identities of educational publishers and beyond the American-oriented traditions of Canadian education. We are now looking at the proposition that the inadequacy of market demand mechanisms accounts for the lack of a cultural character in school texts. Another researcher is inquiring more deeply into the thought of the American educational philosopher, John Dewey, in an attempt to explain why Canadian education is so profoundly anti-cultural in orientation (Keeney, 1985).

How To Read Donald Duck

Other investigators have examined entertainment products for their ideological content. One of the better-known studies of the introduction of ideology, in this case into comic books, is Dorfman and Mattelart's *How To Read Donald Duck, Imperialist Ideology in the Disney Comic*. The authors make a strong case for a high level of ideological intrusion into material assumed by most to be free of "political" content.

On the basis of an extensive review of some 200 Disney comics available in Latin America, Dorfman and Mattelart claim that the Disney world denies the political realm, yet simul-

TABLE 9.3

Canadian Authorship in Canadian Publishers' Reading Series

Programs	% of Pages by Canadians
1. Copp Clark Voyager Program (grades 4–6)	19
Dent Developing Comprehension in Reading	
2. (grades 2–3)	95
3. (grades 4–6)	43
4. Gage Expressways	80
5 Gage Strategies for Language Arts (grades 4–6)	37
6. Ginn Starting Points in Language Arts (grades K–3)	73
7. Ginn Starting Points in Reading (grades 4–6)	14
8. Holt Language Patterns Program (K–3)	55
9a. Nelson Language Developmental Reading Program (K–3): "Hickory Hollow ABC" to "Heads & Tails"	100
9b. "Make-Believe Time" to "Treasure Chest"	89
10. Nelson Language Developmental Reading Program (4–6)	84
11. Science Research Associates	71
Individualized Reading Skills Program	

SOURCE: R. Lorimer, *The Nation in the Schools*, which used: Office of the Director of Education, Toronto Board of Education Study, Canadian Authorship of Reading Programs, 22 Jan. 1980.)

taneously it has a clear politics. That politics is profoundly personal, centring on personality characteristics and family interactions. Donald Duck lives a life of the idle rich, yet he has the consciousness of the dominated. He blames his constant unemployment on his personality just as he sees the rich as "lucky" in that they seem to "attract wealth." Moreover, the rich are made morally legitimate by being unhappy victims of their own wealth. These politics are profoundly personal and highly adventuristic, but they lack the crucial nurturant elements of childhood, especially the guidance of child-parent relations. For Huey, Louie, and Dewey, it is not unlike a prettified Dickensian orphanage.

Other countries are presented in caricatures based on the very symbols those countries use to attract tourists. Such names as "Unsteady-stan" (Vietnam), "Aztecland" (Mexico), "Inca

Blinka" (Peru), and "Sphinxia" (Egypt) even mock Third World countries. More significantly, they provide a basis for a distorted self-knowledge, a device that divides Third World people among themselves in negative stereotypical understandings of one another. People who object to oppression are dismissed as eccentrics and egomaniacs with charisma, and are trivialized (e.g., Soy Bhien and Char Ming). Protest movements are portrayed as completely lacking in seriousness. The people can be totally diverted from their causes by a lemonade stand.

The exploitation of the Third World is legitimized from within a comparative context. The ducks, working with the unknowing participation of the natives, are contrasted to the up-front criminality of the Beagle Boys. The ducks, implicit citizens of the U.S., are put forward as representatives of "civilization, wealth and industrialization." As such, they lay claim to the treasures and resources of Third World backwaters that would merely be corrupted if they knew the value of their own wealth.

The politics of exploitation and, at times, of outright robbery and injustice is cleansed in the waters of innocence we normally attribute to the imaginative world of the child. It is justified implicitly as a process of civilizing and modernizing.

The World Information Order: A Free Press in a Global Context

In our examination of information generation and international information flows, several points have been made. The first is that information is gathered, organized, and distributed within a doctrine that applauds free access to information, freedom of expression, and the free flow or the freedom to distribute information. These notions are rooted in the liberal democracies of the industrialized world.

The major characteristic of these democracies is a sufficient political consensus to allow for the coexistence of a number of sets of confluent or overlapping interests. This coexistence is enshrined in information policy by the respect paid to these press freedoms, a respect that allows for private ownership of the press and free inquiry, expression, and distribution. It is a stable society indeed that can hand over to the marketplace the generation and responsibility for distribution of ideas.

These freedoms have contributed to the political, social, and economic health of the developed world. However, their entrenchment has led to a lack of thorough understanding of the value and dynamics of other systems at both the practical and theoretical levels. The *potential* of a "free" press is often compared to the *realities* of a state press.

The global news agencies illustrate the actual operations of a major element in the international operations of a "free" press. The agencies were built to serve the colonizing activities and the industrial development of Europe. Just as the New World was divided for its resources among the European powers, so it was similarly divided among the early European news agencies. World War I heralded an end to these territorial monopolies and the arrival of major American players.

The present overwhelming dominance of AP, UPI, Reuters, and AFP over the world's foreign news continues that colonization and has had unfortunate consequences for the developing world. Third World countries are represented to the developed world within news values that emphasize the exception over the rule, and they know of each other through the unusual, or exception-oriented, information-gathering and editing processes of the developed world.

Stories about them are written and edited by people who have sketchy and simplified notions of their countries and peoples. Myths are held to be true, as in the case of Iran, despite obviously contradictory social phenomena. Yet, to counteract such distortions and maintain readership is not a simple matter.

A similar problem exists in regard to education and entertainment. A massive, highly capitalized industrial production of movies and television programs based in the U.S. distorts our knowledge of other cultures and swamps attempts at national expression and distribution for all but a few countries in the developed world, let alone the developing world.

The press traditions that have protected and are protecting the liberal democracies of the developed world are ill-suited to serve the developing world. While developed nations gain the information they need for the exploitation of the developing world, the developing world receives little it can use to begin to redress the gross inequalities between North and South. In more political terms, having gained political independence and having expected to gain from that formal move overall sovereignty, the nations of the Third World are discovering to what degree they are dependent for their often very low standard of living on the information institutions and markets of the developed world. Trade and information routes still run to the old imperial centres rather than between points of the periphery. Moreover, participation in international markets demands the acceptance of certain business practices and ultimately the evolution of a certain class of people whose manner of thinking and overall ideology must be consonant with those of the business world in which they live.

The pattern of global information creation and flow, who owns and controls it, along with its characteristic content, we can term the **world information order**. The systematic jeopardy it introduces to some nations, especially those of the Third World, and the systematic advantage it creates for others, especially the U.S. as well as other developed countries, are the reasons why there has emerged a call for a **new world information order**.

THE NEW WORLD INFORMATION ORDER

Conceptually, the call for a new world information order arises out of an attempt to redress the imbalance in how the various nations of the world are served by the evolved international system of communication. Politically, it arises from a shift in the balance of power in the United Nations and specifically within UNESCO. With the achievement of formal political independence, Third World nations, the vast majority of which were former colonies of Europe, have obtained an independent voice in the United Nations.

The Exploitation of Dominance

The international debate focuses on three points. (1) Historically, communications services together with evolved information technologies have allowed dominant states to exploit their dominance. They have assumed a presence in the cultures and ideologies of less dominant states, i.e., other nations throughout the world. Whether that presence comes through being the only source of foreign news or from beaming satellite signals into another country, such a presence is strongly felt by nations of the Third World. In this equation Canada plays both sides of the fence. On the one hand we complain about the invasion of American programs and put in place Canadian content regulations on television and radio. On the other hand we have a foreign short-wave service called Radio Canada International and we endeavour to sell Canadian programs through CBC Enterprises and through private production companies to other nations, including Third World nations.

Economies of Scale and Dominance

(2) The second central point of the international debate is that economies of scale in information flows threaten to give increased dominance to those already dominant. However, any attempt to counteract a worsening situation must avoid feeding into the hands of repressive governments that would curtail freedom of expression and information circulation.

Who Controls the Technology

(3) The mobilization of technology has been accomplished by a few transnationals as a vehicle for the exploitation of markets rather than to serve the cultural, social, and political needs of nations. In other words, the large corporations have seized the opportunity to use communications technologies, but the use they have made of these technologies emphasizes the exploitation of audiences as opposed to providing information, education, and entertainment to these audiences for their benefit or for the benefit of the larger cultural whole.

The MacBride Report

International debate over the design of a world information order is based on the MacBride Report, a 312-page report by a UNESCO commission that studied communication problems on a global scale. The theoretical underpinnings of this report are found in two principles that were accepted by two intergovernmental

conferences, the first held in San Jose de Costa Rica in 1976 and the second in Kuala Lumpur in 1979. They are:

1. Communication policies should be conceived in the context of national realities, free expression of thought, and respect for individual and social rights. (UNESCO, 1980, p. 40)
2. Communication, considered both as a means of affirming a nation's collective identity and as an instrument of social integration, has a decisive role to play in the democratization of social relations in so far as it permits a multidirectional flow of ... messages, both from the media to their public and from this public to the media. (UNESCO, 1980, p. 41)

To conceive of communication policies as national realities rather than as the right of any individual to communicate with any other individual in any place in the world is a fundamental delimitation of free flows of information. Because corporations are conceived legally to be persons with some accompanying rights, large multinational or transnational corporations have been able to translate the right of the individual to communicate freely into a right for them to broadcast their programs or sell their papers in any market in the world.

When communications are seen as national realities, then, the individualistic claims of corporations are defused without being directly attacked. This approach puts in its place a respect for a collectivity, the nation. It also recognizes the contribution that information can make to that collectivity. It is easy to understand how respect for national realities could cause a nation to be wary of importing the standard fare of American or Canadian television with its sumptuous surroundings and, especially in game shows, easy access to wealth.

Respect for collectivities, however, can be abused and become unnecessarily restrictive of individual freedoms. Hence, communications policies must also be conceived in the context of free expression of thought, which curtails the ability of the state to infringe on individual freedom and insists on an acceptance of plurality. In other words, ideas should be freely considered in order that the collectivity can enrich itself.

A third element in this first accepted principle further limits the freedom of the national collectivity: communication policies should be conceived in the context of individual and social rights. While such a phrase may appear open to interpretation, and indeed there is a wide difference among nations as to how it is and might be interpreted, the concept is not totally lacking in anchorage. Individual and social rights are dealt with in the Universal Declaration of Human Rights to which all nations are signatories. In addition, there are various "accords," including the Helsinki accords that address individual and social rights. These documents provide a foundation for the interpretation of this phrase by speaking of the rights of individuals and social groups to think and act in a manner they see as best within the necessary confines of a social order; the rights of individuals and groups are not to be subordinated to narrow state-defined interests. Western nations, especially, are concerned for individual and sub-national group rights, which are indeed abused in both the developed and developing world.

The second principle, accepted by the intergovernmental meeting in Kuala Lumpur, manages to restate the first principle in terms likely to be slightly more satisfactory to those concerned with bringing about a new world information order. It puts forward the integrity of a culture or nation, "its collective identity and social integration," while maintaining that communication has a key role to play in enhancing that identity through its power to democratize information flows. It might be claimed that such a statement respects core freedoms of individuals and groups and that such a respect is the necessary foundation for any collectivity to thrive. Note that while it is difficult to object to such a principle, it is a potential threat to the vast economic interests of the producers of information and cultural products in the developed world. Not only is it threatening to the standard content of entertainment programs, but also it challenges technologies that only serve to increase the flow of information from the top down, or from the centre to the periphery.

THE CONTINUING DEBATE ON THE NEW WORLD INFORMATION ORDER

The call for a new world information order and principles such as the ones passed in San Jose de Costa Rica and Kuala Lumpur have not been universally heralded as a foundation for a new, just world society. Objection has been especially strong in the Western world and specifically within the Western press. It is not difficult to see why they might object. From the point of view of the owners, the possibility of collapse of foreign markets is alarming. From the point of view of journalists, while the report comes up short of recommending the licensing of journalists (indeed, it states that "we share the anxiety aroused by the prospect of licensing and consider that it contains dangers to freedom of information" [p. 236]), many journalists see the report as chipping away at the freedom they need to do their job properly. Whether they are misinformed about the report or whether there is a solid basis for a real fear remains to be seen.

CBC Foreign Correspondents at Ryerson

The typical responses of Western journalists were audible in an annual symposium held in 1983 by the School of Journalism at Ryerson Polytechnical Institute in Toronto. Each year the CBC brings its foreign correspondents home for a short debriefing session to discuss the past year and make decisions for the following year. At this time they make themselves available to an audience composed primarily of journalism students at Ryerson. In the 1983 session a question was asked about the new world information order.

Jan Lazowski: You're talking about something that is going on at UNESCO and that is being sponsored by the Soviet Union, the Eastern Bloc and a lot of the Third World countries. The Western countries are absolutely opposed to it because, among other things, it makes provisions for the licensing of journalists.

Knowlton Nash: The idea is that the licensing is supposed to be a safeguard for journalists but it seems to most of us, or many of us certainly, and certainly I think it seems to the spokesmen for the government of Canada, and certainly the United States, that it's a first step toward the controlling of journalists and controlling what they report and how they report it. I think the essential motivation for those who want the New World Information Order in UNESCO is really to make the media an instrument of the state so that it reflects what the government of the day happens to think is the best thing for the people of that state. And that's a concept of journalism, or a concept of the media that Western nations ...

David Halton: If I could just come in here I think there is a danger in seeing this issue in too starkly black and white terms. Understandably we've all been upset by the idea of licensing foreign correspondents and

an attack on press liberties and so on. At the same time, the notion that the Western media are doing a good job of reporting on Third World problems is, I think, at best, a debatable one. I think there is a tendency for Western coverage of Third World countries to be crisis-oriented, to concentrate on wars, on coups, – this gentleman's question, when are we going to have ongoing coverage of Grenada now that the troops are coming out, certainly is a legitimate one. I think a perfectly understandable complaint of some Third World countries is that the Western media, the wire services in particular, do not focus on the kinds of developmental problems that are absolutely essential for many of these countries, when your first priority is to feed your people and so on. This is the kind of reportage we're not getting in the Western wire services.

Knowlton Nash: Yes, there is a journalistic problem there, of course, but how you resolve it, whether you resolve it by making, in effect, the news media an instrument of government is really the question.

Don Murray: I'd like to take a little issue with you here because at UNESCO, this whole issue has just been debated in ... Paris .... As Jan was saying there were resolutions put forward by the Soviet Union which would tend toward the licensing of journalists and the U.S. stood up and said very clearly, "Anybody votes for that and we pull out." The resolution was dumped. UNESCO pulled back considerably knowing full well that the U.S. was very angry. The U.S. still pulled out or announced that it was going to pull out and, in my opinion, having looked at the conference and watched it, I suspect that the Reagan administration really wasn't too concerned ... [speaker trails off] ... Last week when it made this decision to pull out of UNESCO it simply used the New World Information Order, which has become extremely diluted in the hands of UNESCO authorities. The U.S. was looking for a cheap foreign policy victory and they decided to give a shock to UNESCO which doesn't have a lot of backers in the United States but I think on pretty flimsy grounds.

Joe Schlesinger: What is journalism for? Is it to put out stuff that pleases the people that you write about, the countries that you write about? Or is it to put out information that others may be interested in, and that's put in a way that interests other people? It's all right to say that you should have more news about development in the Third World countries [but people] aren't going to read it – we find it hard, for instance, to put even Canadian news into American papers.

David Halton: … there's really a certain hypocrisy in this debate. We, in Canada, have been debating and passing legislation on Canadian content on the Canadian airwaves for years …. Here we are, a lot of people in Canada, a lot of editorialists saying "Why should the Third World be concerned about their intake? Let them take the American movies and the Dallases along with Nestlé's milk and so on." Surely there's an element of hypocrisy there when in Canada we're concerned about our identity and protecting it to some degree from things like American programming and we say the Third World countries shouldn't bother about this.

Two Other Perspectives

Two other commentaries on the new world information order are worth noting. The first is Tom McPhail's *Electronic Colonialism*. McPhail takes much the same stance as David Halton, claiming, in essence, that developed nations practise a kind of journalism designed to augment their own national interests. He takes Canada as an example. A "free press," he argues, is a "development" press supportive of capitalism. The purpose of the Western press is to "confer a rightness on the social order."

Canada has developed a series of cultural and regulatory agencies such as the National Film Board, Telefilm Canada, the CRTC, even the CBC, which are designed to interfere with the "free flow of information." Further, we have a number of national media-enhancing acts, such as Bill C-58, which makes advertising tax deductible only when Canadian media are the vehicle for the advertising. Finally, he argues, we show every sign of continuing in the same vein with the advent of new technologies. (Note, however, that we do not have parallel regulatory measures for newspapers.)

The thrust of McPhail's argument is that developing nations should be allowed to do the same not only for the electronic media but also for the press. They should be allowed to develop print and electronic communication systems that foster their national development and integrity as separate and distinct cultures. It would follow that our responsibility would be to aid as much as we can in that process.

Anthony Smith takes quite a different perspective in *The Geopolitics of Information*, maintaining that there is little doubt that the developing nations have a legitimate complaint. However, it appears to him that the Western media cannot accept the articulation of the solutions such as were emerging, at the time he was writing, in the activities of UNESCO and the MacBride Commission.

What bothered Smith most was that the statements of the strongest proponents of the new world information order did not capture how humankind might be improved through a different use of information, communications, knowledge, and entertainment. Rather, Smith saw in these writings the very limited imagination of a bureaucrat whose aim it was to control information generation and distribution so well that the result would be more equitable for all. Smith's view seemed to be that the approach to the task was not up to the task it had set itself.

If Smith's perspective can be summarized in a sentence, it would be that although the cause is just and changes need to be made, we have yet to find a manner of thinking about the issue that will cause us all to seize the matter and work toward a resolution.

SUMMARY

Here we have perhaps the most fundamental issue facing global communication today. Within Canada and Britain there is already a considerable range of opinion. Media owners and some journalists dismiss the whole matter as something that fundamentally interferes with the process of gathering and distributing news. Other journalists (and one commentator) are sympathetic but do not see anything that has emerged as a resolution to an admitted problem. And another commentator would have us extend aid to empower others to do more than follow the Canadian example. He would have them extend the principles Canada has evidenced in its electronic communications to all forms of communications systems of the Third World.

What we have not represented here is the diehard capitalist position, which is undoubtedly working to prevent any such considerations as are being brought forward under the rubric of a new world information order from gaining any ground whatsoever. It would not be unreasonable to assume that these are at least part of the motive behind the withdrawal of the United States from UNESCO and the threat of Great Britain to do the same.

REFERENCES

Boyd-Barrett, J.O. "Cultural Dependency and the Mass Media," in Gurevitch et al., eds., Culture, Society and the Media. Toronto: Methuen, 1982.

Bruner, J., R.R. Olver, and P.M. Greenfield. Studies in Cognitive Growth. New York: Wiley, 1966.

Carscallen, Anne. Untitled Master's thesis draft, Simon Fraser University, 1984.

Dorfman, A., and A. Mattelart. How To Read Donald Duck: Imperialist Ideology in the Disney Comic. New York: International General Editions, 1975.

Hester, Al. "International News Agencies," in Alan Wells, ed., Mass Communications: A World View. Palo Alto: Mayfield Publishing, 1974.

Jensen, Arthur R. Bias in Mental Testing. New York: Free Press, 1980.

Keeney, Patrick. "Deweyan Pedagogy and the Multinational Text," unpublished manuscript, Simon Fraser University, 1984.

Lorimer, Rowland. The Nation in the Schools. Toronto: OISE Press, 1984.

McPhail, Thomas. Electronic Colonialism: The Future of International Broadcasting and Communication. Beverly Hills: Sage Publications, 1981.

Robinson, G.J. News Agencies and World News: in Canada, the United States and Yugoslavia. Fribourg, Switzerland: University of Fribourg Press, 1981.

Ryerson, School of Journalism. Round Table discussion of CBC journalists, 1983.

Siebert, F., T. Peterson, and W. Schramm. Four Theories of the Press. Urbana: University of Illinois Press, 1956.

Saturday Night (March, 1985), p. 27.

Smith, Anthony. The Geopolitics of Information: How Western Culture Dominates the World. London: Faber and Faber, 1980.

UNESCO, Commission for the Study of Communication Problems (MacBride Commission). The World of News Agencies, Working Paper #11, 1978.

UNESCO. Many Voices, One World: Communication and Society, Today and Tomorrow (MacBride Report). Paris: Unipub, 1980.

Wells, Alan, ed. *Mass Communications: A World View*. Palo Alto: Mayfield Publishing, 1974.

STUDY QUESTIONS

1. Media managers sort out important news from the trivial. As a result we get a good selection of all the important news of the world. Is this a simplistic statement? Using examples, argue your case.

2. Walt Disney was once nominated for the Nobel Peace Prize. Did he deserve it?

3. Define the new world information order and discuss the reasons why a call for such an order exists.

4. Complex communications technologies have been developed (and are continually being developed) in the leading industrialized countries; these technologies have come to be used also in the Third World. What are the challenges facing various people in Third World countries (e.g., government officials, politicians, businessmen, teachers, consumers) in their use and adaptation of the technologies for their own needs?

CHAPTER

10

The Domestic Geopolitics of Information

INTRODUCTION

A S WE HAVE seen in the previous chapter, certain patterns have emerged in considering how information is generated and distributed throughout the world. These patterns are connected to history, the relative power of nations, and political ideology. The global wire services serve the long-established, powerful, capitalist, industrialized nations. In serving such nations the global information systems do not merely fail to serve business, government, and cultural interests of less powerful, less industrialized, and politically different nations, but, more significantly, they clearly interfere with the industrial development and the ability to develop and sustain distinct national cultures in such nations.

THE POLITICS OF INFORMATION

T he disparities in opportunity that are introduced by the way information is organized do not result from a planned malevolence on the part of powerful capitalist nations. Rather, the pursuit of their own self-interest conflicts with the independently articulated and pursued self-interest of the less developed nations. Only when the less developed co-ordinate their interests exactly with the developed nations can both exist in "beneficial" coexistence.

Metropolis-Hinterland Theory

The view that an inevitable conflict of interest exists between developed and developing nations is not merely a political perspective. It can also be derived from a well-accepted theory most often used by geographers but that has also been applied in economics, sociology, and communication. That theory is variously called metropolis-hinterland, centre-periphery, centre-margin, empire-colony, and several other combinations of the above. Its major proponent was the Canadian economic historian, Harold Innis. The centre-periphery theory can be applied equally to global and to national or, for that matter, regional or local affairs.

The Writings of Harold Innis

The writings of Innis on the fur trade, the cod fishery, the bias of communication, and relations of empire and communication contain various statements of his metropolis-hinterland theory. The theory can be summarized in the following manner. A metropolis or centre or empire is to be regarded as a seat of power. The most fundamental aspect of that power is its organizing dimension. Thus, North America was "explored" by various European powers for what it could contribute to European economies. The European economies were the centres or metropolises reaching out into the hinterlands to gather materials to enhance themselves as powers. What we learn of the history of the period was how well those colonies functioned as hinterlands, that is, how well the fisheries or the fur trade served the Europeans. These were the significant aspects of North America as opposed to, for example, what Indian confederations had to offer for enlightened government in Europe. It was not a relationship between equals.

Centre-Hinterland Dynamics in Canadian History

The power of the metropolis was not only expressed in what became historically significant. The activities or dominant patterns of life of the hinterland directly flowed from their relation to the centre. For example, for a great number of years the British attempted to enforce a ban on settlement in Newfoundland because this would give an unfair advantage to those who wintered-over to bring their goods to market in the spring. No self-respecting member of the bourgeoisie would want to winter-over, so all were forbidden to do so. Similarly, after the conquest of New France, the British survey system was introduced into Quebec and effectively disrupted the French system of long and narrow river lots with a "common" up behind those lots. It also diminished the ability of the French Canadians to continue to form tightly knit village communities (Rioux, 1978). The same survey system played a major role in the Red River Rebellion of 1869 and was imposed upon the region after the rebellion was quashed in 1870.

More fundamentally, the activities of explorers, traders, and settlers were governed by the centre. If the centre needed fish, fish were caught, not so much to eat in the colonies but to make money to fish more or better or to bring the fisherman's life closer to the style of living at the centre. If the centre needed fur for fashionable beaver hats, then fur was gathered. If the taste for furs radically declined with changes in fashion, as indeed it did, then the whole of the economic and therefore social and political activity of the periphery was altered. Not only did various traders become bankrupt but the primary producer, or at least gatherer, the Indian, often starved. The Indian had been brought into an economy that depended on the whims of European fashion and had come to depend on the money and goods supplied by the trader.

Things are no different today. Thanks to the efforts of certain interest groups in the urban centres of North America and Europe, the hunt for seal pups off the coast of Newfoundland has been brought virtually to a halt. Numerous Newfoundland families have lost not only their income but their sense of self-worth as a result of the instability of these markets.

Other manifestations of centre-periphery relations could be seen in the political arrangements of the day. When the British conquered the French at the Plains of Abraham, the consequence was the replacement of one bourgeoisie, the French, with another, the English. In those days there was no question of each business having equal right to do business. Licences were granted only to those the governor saw fit to license.

Similarly, the Family Compact was the group in Upper Canada given political and effective business control over the affairs of the colony. As Canadian history shows, even William Lyon Mackenzie's popular uprising was not enough to dislodge them from the empire-anointed position of power. Likewise, until well into the twentieth century the Canadian Prairies were touted as the "breadbasket of the empire." And more than

one British farmer, inspired or not by Kipling, saw himself as manning the "outpost of empire" on the Canadian frontier. If he faltered in his vision he could rely on his children who were encouraged in their schoolbooks to see themselves accordingly.

Social and cultural relations also derived from the relation of the hinterland to the metropolis. The defeat of the North West Company at the hands of the Hudson's Bay Company is a story that cannot be told without due attention to the privileges granted to the latter by the (British) court of the empire. Similarly, one can only understand ethnic relations and the defeat of the Métis led by Louis Riel and Gabriel Dumont by reference to anglophone Ontario, the Orangemen, and ultimately the power of the English over the French in Canada. (Beale, 1988, provides a particularly interesting discussion on the organization of Canadian geography into a social space. Her paper develops the ideas outlined here.)

Hinterland Relations

The relations of the hinterland, not just to the centre but also to other points on the periphery, are centre-dominated. Two neighbouring farmers, like two towns, are more liable to be producing goods in competition for the market of the centre than to be producing goods that complement each other. Also, it may be easier to travel to another town twenty miles down the track than to one three miles distant because the former is on the route to the centre whereas the latter is on no "route" at all. The history of land speculation and personal wealth in Canada is tied closely to the choices made by the railroad builders. Whole towns as well as people were destined to oblivion because they bet on the wrong route for the iron horse.

Transportation routes became communication routes with the development of wire services. Just as the patterns of trade and settlement were derived from the needs of the centre, so information of significance to the centre was both gathered from and distributed to the hinterlands. The running of telegraph lines along the routes of the railroad is the most obvious physical manifestation of the parallel relation of communications to transportation, trade, and settlement. Letters and newspapers also travelled the same routes. Just as important to Sir John A. Macdonald's dream of binding the nation together with a railroad was a notion that encompassed the transmission of information as well as the transportation of people and goods.

The emplacement of the telegraph, quickly followed by radio, the telephone, and television, and the emphasis on the availability of Canadian radio and television signals to all Canadians (which Parliament has insisted be a major part of the mandate of the CBC) demonstrate how important to our politicians is the job of organizing the nation around the eastern centres of Montreal and Toronto. As spokespersons for western Canadian resource-based economies are so fond of pointing out, trade relations are governed by the interests of the manufacturing centres, not the interests of the hinterland resource provinces. Were Alberta, Saskatchewan, and British Columbia allowed to sell their resources without interference from Ottawa in terms of export limits and prices, there is little doubt that these provinces would be better off financially, at least in the short term. However, perhaps a more fundamental question is, would there have been and would there be a Canada had the various settlements in British North America not been integrated with the eastern manufacturing centres?

COMMUNICATIONS IN A CULTURAL, CENTRE-HINTERLAND PERSPECTIVE

While communications can be studied as a separate entity with its own separate dynamics, communications are a part of a social system. Structurally, they both complement and reinforce the way society is organized. In this section we will examine one perspective on the role of communications in northern Canada.

The Berger Report and the Position of Northern Native People

In a landmark report resulting from an inquiry into the advisability of building a gigantic oil and gas pipeline down the MacKenzie River Valley, Mr. Justice Thomas Berger outlined the issues he saw as background to the interaction between southern Canadians and the Inuit and Dene in the North. The perspective we summarize here is taken from "Cultural Impact," a chapter in Volume I of the Berger Report, *Northern Frontier: Northern Homeland.*

Two elements predominated in white-native interactions in the early days of contact, now over two centuries ago. They were trade (in furs) and religion. Both were powerful devices of transformation of native life. Religion represented a broad challenge to traditional patterns of life. To Europeans, the hunting and gathering of food and material goods as a way of providing the necessities of life seemed not only lazy but somehow also extravagant and irreligious. The Christian practice of the cultivation and maximal exploitation of resources was seen, by Europeans, as a necessary condition for the emergence and development of civilization.

The land needed to be put to use by the native people under the guidance of whites in order that the native people themselves could be integrated into Christian civilization. In the context of the North that meant a systematic gathering of furs for European markets in exchange for the "products of civilization." Such a trade represented a systematic exploitation of the only retrievable resource (for the time) in an otherwise "barren" land. In the context of the North, Christian ideology stopped short of forcing land into a system of private ownership, as had been the case in the Canadian Prairies. Essentially, this was because whites were unable to see a benefit in their ownership of the land.

This fur-based interaction, if we ignore for a moment the ethnocentric bias inherent in it and the power relations emanating from that bias, provided mutual benefit for native and white. The native people participated in the fur trade with comparatively little disruption in their patterns of living. They continued as semi-nomads, living in small groups off the land, and merely modified their yearly cycle to include visits to the Hudson's Bay Company outpost to trade furs for food, guns, and, in the neighbouring church, prayer. So satisfactorily did this interaction work out that when northern natives talk of a traditional life, what they are referring to is not pre-white, pre-fur trade days but rather the days of the fur trade.

Stable and beneficial as this situation was, it did not change the reality of the growing dependence of the native people on the markets, the technology, and the food and other staples of the south. The instability of the markets would eventually reveal that dependency in a rather cruel manner and envelop native people in the web of Western civilization.

Communications and the Spiral of Dependency

After World War II the northern fur economy collapsed. Its collapse brought the welfare state into Canada's northern communities. The elements of the welfare state included family allowances, old age pensions, welfare payments, government housing, nursing stations, schools, and wage labour. While each aspect of the welfare state was benign in intent and was intended to meet a particular set of needs, it was nevertheless designed on the assumption that the traditional way of life was no longer tenable. And it was to transform every aspect of northern native life.

The welfare measures set up a spiral of growing dependency that has undermined northern native culture. Let us run through that spiral of dependency in the general case to illustrate some of the dynamics. We will start at the point where a hunter finds that he does not have enough money to pay off the debts he has incurred from the previous season, essentially because the bottom has dropped out of the fur market.

Faced with this situation he can either turn to wage labour or to welfare. If he engages in wage labour he must stay near the settlement to be near his job. This prevents him from hunting so that he becomes almost fully dependent on wages. If he goes hunting and misses any more than a few days on the job, he is fired. If he goes on welfare, the welfare officer becomes interested in the whole family, especially the children and their education. The welfare officer points out that his application for assistance will be given more favourable consideration if he shows that he is "responsible" by sending his children to school.

Then, once he is on welfare, looking for

wage labour becomes a desirable thing in the eyes of the welfare agency; hunting is seen to be neglect of his responsibility to earn a living. Similarly, if chances present themselves to return to the traditional way of life, in abandoning the settlement the man and his family are seen as irresponsible, or at best as romantics who do not have the discipline to live in a civilized setting.

If ever the man is forced to return for assistance such interpretations of his behaviour are presented to him. Behaviour not patterned after the white way of doing things is denigrated, while things that are white, even though they may be less self-sustaining, are praised. If the man complains further, when confronted with these interpretations, for example by complaining that the school teaches little that his son can use to learn to fish, trap, and hunt, he is seen to be simple, refusing to accept the inevitable decline of the old ways.

Each move he makes in accepting further assistance from white civilization draws him further away from his ability to sustain himself and his family independently. Not only do work and welfare encourage him to stay near the settlement, which usually is distant from any hunting grounds, but other forms of assistance have the same effect. If he has taken up housing in the settlement, his subsequent departure with family can be seen as abandonment. Certainly it is a queer idea to continue to pay for a house while he and his family are absent. Likewise, if his children enter school, taking them out of school is a sign of lack of value for education. Medical services also require, at the very best, remaining near the settlement. Often, they require extended care in southern cities such as Edmonton, Toronto, or Montreal.

As the children reach high school age, if they have not been in a residential school already, they usually must leave their family to attend school in one of the larger settlements. The longer the children attend school the more their abilities are limited and focused on survival only in the wage economy. They do not learn how to hunt, trap, and fish and find their way through the frozen and apparently featureless snow and ice. Instead, they learn how to operate heavy equipment so that they can be employed as wage earners for southern development companies. Should they fall prey to the shock of this transformation of their lives, of course, they can always seek solace in the church, whose values are fundamental to southern, white civilization.

Well-meaning as each of these support programs may be, each further envelops the family in a dependency relation to southern white culture. Each program is intended to provide a more satisfactory level of service, schooling, welfare, health, job training, etc. Each program, in its turn, cannot help but exacerbate dependency problems.

Magic in the Sky

Communications is essentially an add-on component intended to enhance the level of "service" in information to northern communities but which directly envelops northern native peoples in the culture of the south. The NFB's *Magic in the Sky* explores some of the dynamics of how that envelopment takes place. Some of the history of Canadian developments in communications provides a fuller background.

Canada began experimenting with communications in the North because of the irregularity in radio signals. The problem was that the same electrical disturbances that produced the northern lights also interfered with radio signals. At times radio was perfectly adequate; at other times it was impossible. The quality of the signals was improved, but various experiments showed that the interaction of radio signals and this electrical activity in the atmosphere was inevitable and that there were firm limitations on the use of radio signals as a means of communication in the North. Reliable communications in the North could not depend on the airwaves. Since land lines were impossible the answer was satellites.

Early satellites were designed to enable individuals and communities to communicate with each other. Because the satellites were fairly low powered, fairly powerful ground stations were required to send and receive signals. Once this was discovered to be a satisfactory means of communicating, development moved quickly. Satellite power was increased, as was their capability to transmit numbers of signals until, with a four-foot stationary receiving dish, it was possible to receive good-quality signals of any kind, including television.

Suddenly, communication between individuals and communities was replaced with the possibility of receiving as many or more channels as any southern Canadian could. By means of satellites and dishes people in isolated northern communities had beamed through history almost from the days of Fessenden's rudimentary experiments with voice transmission to the present day.

The significance of these developments for Inuit and other northern native communities, as *Magic in the Sky* points out, was considerable. In place of traditional values of sharing, young people were introduced to individualism and greed. Social status was linked not to an ability to provide for more than one's own family but to the ability to collect and hold material goods for oneself. The personal politics we have discussed as endemic to popular culture items, where status is conferred upon those of particular body types, with particular ethnic backgrounds, and with particular personality traits, suddenly became the way the outside world worked. Most of all, consumerism, the necessity to have all manner of consumer products, as well as the necessity of a culture to produce all manner of consumer products, became a guiding force. All these things were made doubly attractive by the sumptuousness of the settings in which both advertised products and entertainment programs were presented.

Imagine having lived in an environment where a crackling radio brought sporadic items of world news on an erratic basis. The qualities of the technology itself suggest distance. Contrast that with sitting down one day and seeing the crowded, bustling streets of Toronto or New York, the luxurious shoreline of Howe Sound where *The Beachcombers* is shot, and so forth. Suddenly it is all there in full living colour, right in the living room, 400 miles from the North Pole and $1,000 plane fare from Montreal. In the same way that a whining and crackling radio would lead a listener to perceive world events as distant, the daily fare of murders, assassinations, coups, wars, plane crashes, social unrest, and the like has also crept into the daily life of northern native people much in the same way that DDT has found its way into the egg shells of the gyrfalcon. A fine welcome to the modern world.

In spite of the news, satellite communications have served to draw northern communities further into the ideology of the industrialized world. They are given values and viewpoints that make them aliens in their own culture. Thereby, their culture is made vulnerable to eclipse by the industrialized south. This especially affects the children. Communications is the latest of the services southern Canadians have provided to northern native communities, which, while offering them relief from immediate discomforts, lock them into a dependency relationship to our culture.

The preceding description is intended to be an overview of the process of acculturation. Numerous studies have explored this process in detail. One particularly useful compilation is, a publication by the Department of Communication Studies of Concordia University: *Communication and the Canadian North* (1983). An even more recent discussion can be found in Valaskakis (1988).

Reinforcement of the Prevailing Order

As Chapter 9 has shown and as this section of this chapter also demonstrates, communications services are part of the social order. One Marxist commentator calls them an ideological state apparatus (Althusser, 1971). Just like economic arrangements (the fur trade), education, health, and welfare, in their structure these services re-express the power relations of the state. In drawing people into them, as producers or consumers, they force such people to participate in relationships consistent with the dominant relations and ideology of the state (McNulty, 1987). As we have argued here, communications forms one more level of social activity that further reinforces the relation of particular groups to the prevailing order.

CANADA AS A CULTURAL HINTERLAND

One of the strengths of Innis's concepts of centre and hinterland is that there is no one centre, nor does a country or region have solely a hinterland relationship to a variety of other industrialized countries, such as West Germany and Japan.

In various ways Canada can be seen as a cultural hinterland of the United States. What effect does this have on Canadian cultural expression? How might the metropolis-hinterland perspective allow us to understand our cultural relations with the U.S. and plan policy accordingly? We will concentrate here on two areas of cultural expression, the writing contained in school learning materials and television broadcasting.

The Domestic Politics of Learning Materials: Textbooks and the Structure of Knowledge

In the previous chapter several examples were introduced illustrating the kind of content to be found in learning materials in Canadian schools. We noted that the content was not Canadian when it might have been and that some of the Canadian content inserted into materials adapted from foreign sources was either trivial or wrong. To add two other examples in that vein from one reading series published by Ginn (Clymer, 1972), in the American edition 60 milk trucks deliver 50,000 quarts of milk whereas in the Canadian edition 60 milk trucks deliver 2,000 quarts of milk. In another place in the series, in the American edition 2,500 postal workers sort 5 million letters while in Canada hundreds of workers sort thousands of letters and packages.

The importance of these and other examples is multilayered. In the first place Canadian school children are deprived of a body of basic information about themselves and their country, which should be a key aspect of school learning. As the oft-repeated phrase goes, Canadian school children seem to know more about the U.S. than they do about Canada. Second, the structure of the subject matter as it is developed in the centre actually persuades educators of the hinterlands that information about the hinterlands is relatively unimportant compared to information oriented to the centre. In the previous chapter we used the example of science: by emphasizing scientific inquiry over scientific knowledge about the environment in which one lives, examples become secondary and therefore less appropriate to the lives of the students.

Science is just like nearly every other subject in as much as the structure of inquiry has been developed to play down knowledge of direct relevance to students in their immediate cultural and physical milieu. In the study of language arts and literature, the structure of language is first stressed, followed by examples of "quality" prose. This allows learning materials to be developed that entirely neglect to introduce students to the literature of their own country. In a third subject area, social studies, a similar structural change has held sway for some time but now seems to be on the wane. This perspective emphasizes inquiry (just as in science) and decision-making over the study of the social fabric itself. One publisher, McGraw-Hill Ryerson, has designed a series for grades 1 to 6 called *Social and Environmental Studies* that devotes one grade to the study of Canada and all other grades to the abstract study of neighbourhood, community, region, nation, and so on. This approach, which emphasizes universals over particulars, is to be found in many other subjects. The study of "great" artists over contemporary art of the nation and region similarly neglects that which is familiar to the child. The study of "world renowned" musicians also isolates students from serious consideration of music produced in Canada.

The point of these examples is that the structure of knowledge is defined at the centre. It serves the centre not so much by infiltrating the materials with information about the centre but by putting forward a perspective that emphasizes the development of knowledge that will be of greatest use to the centre. For example, the acquisition of scientific knowledge is of primary benefit to industries based at the centre. It allows them to expand their power to produce products for any environment. It may benefit the regions. It may allow them to control some local conditions. Similarly, the acquisition of social scientific information enables us to understand the dynamics of new, evolving social situations that heretofore we have not experienced. It is rare for those new social relations to emerge in the more stable environment of the periphery.

If we delve further into metropolis-hinterland relations we can see how this redefinition of knowledge to the detriment of the hinterlands comes about. *The Nation in the Schools* (Lorimer, 1984) examines two areas that shed light on this process. The first is the education of teachers; the second, the business of educational publishing.

The Politics of Teacher Education

The major findings of the work on teacher training indicated the presence of an extremely strong centre-margin process. In the first place, many of the professors appointed to teach teachers in Canadian universities are foreign born and trained. In recent years this problem has decreased somewhat as a result of Department of Immigration rulings favouring the hiring of Canadians. But throughout the 1970s only 60 to 70 per cent of professors hired to teach all subjects in the university were Canadian, 55 to 60 per cent of whom received first degrees in Canada (von Zur Muehlen, 1981). (Data were not reported in the above study on final degrees.) Other studies have reported that up to 90 per cent of books sold in university bookstores are foreign authored and produced. These statistics are not introduced to be anti-foreign. Canada has benefited greatly both from foreign-born academics and from foreign-produced information. The point is that in training Canadian university students in general, and Canadian education students in particular, we rely on *imported* personnel and *imported* materials. As a result we cannot avoid an imported perspective.

Nor can it be claimed that once these foreign academics come to Canada they are immersed in a Canadian environment and leave behind that of the country in which they were trained. A survey (Lorimer, 1984) found that nearly 50 per cent of conference attendance and academic publishing involved American conferences and publishers. The other 50 per cent was accounted for by both local and national Canadian conferences and journals.

Centre-margin processes could be seen further in the hiring practices of school boards. Only approximately 15 per cent indicated definitely that they gave preference to teachers with a knowledge of Canadian phenomena over non-Canadian phenomena, for example, Canadian history over world, European, or American history. Even when the job involved Canadian geography or history, preference was rarely given to Canadians. Nor were teachers, once hired, encouraged by very many school boards to upgrade themselves with Canadian subject matter.

As we got closer to the actual courses teachers take in their training, we found no better a picture. Not a single university in Canada requires more than one course introducing the Canadian educational system in its social, legal, cultural, or historical context. Many do not require even one course. Further, in educational foundations in general, there are approximately double the number of psychologically oriented courses as social, cultural, historical, and legal courses combined.

The Politics of Educational Publishing

Educational publishing presents essentially parallel phenomena. The Canadian elementary-high school market is dominated by large multinational publishers, some of which are Canadian-owned although most are not. Data collected in the seventies indicate that two-thirds of the market was accounted for by eight multinational firms. Eighty-six per cent of the market was controlled by these plus a further ten firms, only three of which could be said to be nationally oriented, Canadian-owned companies. When we combined these statistics with our prior knowledge of the content and design of textbooks and the structure of knowledge they advance, we argued that these companies are oriented essentially to the mass market. They attempt to produce materials that are easily transferable between markets by dealing in generalities and emphasizing knowledge of benefit to the centre, to which every province and state is a hinterland.

Beyond content that favours mass market-oriented materials, a number of other practices were identified. Multinational publishers, sometimes in concert with educators, seek to ensure their continued, centre-oriented dominance of the market by using expensive "cosmetics," such as four-colour printing that can only be afforded in a very large market. Also, massive pre-publishing investments soften the market to receive the learning materials. This softening consists of a continual presence of sales reps in the school system for at least one year prior to a major adoption, plus contracting with numbers of opinion-leading educators as consultants in a variety of regions. Their consultancies naturally lead them to promote the product as well as to pilot test the materials. Most importantly, this massive investment softens the market by means of publication of the materials prior to a decision being taken by the province to purchase: nothing less than a very high stakes poker game.

We found also that the publishers were not actively engaged in trying to promote interprovincial co-operation in the acquisition of materials. Their reluctance to push this rationalization very hard appears to originate in the fear that it would give more power to the province-consumers once they pooled their purchasing power. In a situation where the materials are not developed under contract, the publishers have sufficient bargaining power to publish materials that are potentially saleable in a wide variety of markets.

The Nation in the Schools also discusses the long-term interactions between publishers and the education profession. As both Keeney (1985) and Lorimer (1984) argue, educational philosophy has become married to the interests of centre or mass market producers.

The conclusion to be drawn is that while the content of learning materials itself reflects metropolis-hinterland relations, the processes involved in the production of both learning materials and teachers indicates a profound infusion of metropolis-hinterland dynamics in the education system as a whole. The implication from this conclusion is that the Canadian educational system is not serving Canada or Canadians particularly well and is likely to prolong our hinterland status.

The Domestic Politics of Canadian Television Services

The structure and content of educational materials are not as often debated as are television services. But the dynamics, although played out differently, are much the same. Television began in Canada with the importation of signals from the U.S. Before any Canadian station was on the air, Canadians had purchased television sets and were receiving U.S. signals.

Television production itself began in Canada as a public enterprise. In the face of a vigorous American entertainment industry spilling over into the new medium of television this initial conception was intended to help hinterland Canada survive the onslaught of the entertainment centres in New York and Los Angeles. As Judy LaMarsh reiterated in a 1967 White Paper, broadcasting is "a means of preserving and strengthening the cultural, social and political fabric of Canada ...." In the early days of television a great number of productions were mounted, and many live broadcasts of plays and programs were produced in television studios in Toronto. At the same time, a certain amount of material was also purchased for rebroadcast.

The CBC and Its Complement

Not long after the first public television broadcasts, private entrepreneurs were allowed to inaugurate services to "complement" the offerings of public television. However, because the motivations of private television were so different from the public service the nature of the "complement" was different from what many expected. Whereas the public service was conceived from a cultural perspective, private stations were conceived by their owners as vehicles for making money. That is, they saw themselves as capable of delivering sufficiently large audiences to advertisers to attract their advertising. They reasoned that they would be able to ask enough for the access to these audiences that they would have sufficient funds not only for the acquisition of programs but also for a healthy profit besides. The basis of this belief was the assumption that there were all sorts of American-produced materials that could be acquired for a fraction of the cost of production. As the first Lord Thomson said, "a television broadcasting licence is a licence to print money." To the private broadcaster, content is only important for its ability to attract audiences. It is obvious how a great emphasis on gratuitous sex and violence can emerge from such an orientation.

The Pursuit of Profit

The notion the private broadcasters had of "complement" was any programming the public broadcaster was not providing. More importantly, this notion included a fundamentally different, profit-seeking operation. The private broadcasters thus were happy enough to let the CBC go its own cultural way. While the CBC pursued the good of the nation, they would pursue the maximization of audiences for sale to advertisers. Only when the CBC stumbled on something that garnered large audiences, such as *Hockey Night in Canada*, were the private stations concerned about competition with the public broadcaster. As competition heated up between the two services in the bidding for foreign programming, complaints about subsidized competition could be heard.

The Dance of the Entrepreneurs

In addition to the private contingent came another set of players, the border stations. American businesspeople soon realized that from a position just inside the American bor-

der, television signals could assemble audiences and sell them to advertisers in competition with the Canadian stations. Since Canadians had built the majority of their major cities within broadcast distance of the border, why not make a profit in providing them with American television?

The Canadians were not far behind. If Americans were going to provide technically mediocre television signals that required a jungle of roof aerials in every Canadian city near the U.S. border, and if these signals were unlicensed in Canada, why not put up one first-class aerial and run wires from that aerial to everyone in the neighbourhood. Thus was born yet another set of television entrepreneurs, the cable companies.

There was a brief lull after the cable companies were licensed to bring in a maximum of four U.S. signals in exchange for providing access to members of the community to create programming. But recently yet another set of entrepreneurs has entered the field, the pay television companies. They were allowed to enter the market for two reasons. The first was technological development. One of the original reasons for regulating the air waves was the finite amount of space available for stations, but technology that vastly increases the number of signals that can be fitted on to various parts of the radio spectrum is now in place. The second reason was that pay TV companies promised to divert a certain amount of their profits to the development of Canadian production. This promise has so far proved to be as much a dream as the large profits that were to be the basis of funding.

Profits and Hinterland Dynamics

The centre-hinterland relations that this account of television services illustrates arise both from the expansionist activities of the American entertainment centres and their outpost messengers just south of the border and from the assimilative activities of our private sector to import entertainment products from the U.S.

Living as we do in the shadow of the American empire, we are continually aware, partly because of centre-hinterland processes, of the production of the United States. As the Americans capitalize on each new technology, we spend a certain amount of time worrying over the consequences for us of their exploitation and exportation of that technology and its products. But before long it becomes apparent to the private sector that there is money to be made in importing those products. In combination with the profits to be made by the Americans exporting, Canadian importers have good reason to want to bring in such products, as they have proved to be popular with Canadians. The incentive structure, i.e., the ease and reliability of profit-making, favours the importer. Thus, rather than set up in competition with the Americans, we merely transport to our country (and their hinterland) their products.

While this activity creates profits for the private sector that allow it to grow and provides services for us to attain a certain "quality of life," it diminishes our ability to create cultural products for ourselves. It creates growth but not development. With minimal production on the periphery, creative artists must make the pilgrimage to the centre. Once arrived, no matter how great their talent, they must produce within the dominant genres. At the same time, as they move and begin to participate in the industry, they confirm the possibilities of export back to Canada (and elsewhere) by their ability to understand how the genres must be adapted to that end. A CBC

documentary, *Solid Gold*, reviews the various Canadian groups that have been internationally successful in popular music over the years. One of the surprising aspects of this presentation is the number of Canadian groups, from the Crewcuts and the Diamonds to the Band. It is doubtful that many Canadians realize how extensive our participation has been. Certainly, no claim was advanced that the music produced by Canadians was distinguishable from that produced by the Americans.

The matter is not confined to production dynamics. It is not hard to understand how the force of four U.S. channels, together with CTV, Global (an Ontario network), the other private stations, and the CBC's own importing activity, has developed in Canadians a taste for American entertainment programs. When Canadians produce something distinctive it must run counter to centre-hinterland forces and fight an uphill battle to attract a Canadian audience away from its accustomed diet. The power and expansiveness of the American centre is evident in the tiers of both American and Canadian entrepreneurs that it supports, from the border stations to the private networks and stations, to the cable companies and pay TV operators.

One bright cultural light that runs counter to the forces of American centre dominance over the Canadian hinterland is our news and information programming. Figures 10.1-10.4, from the Annual Report of the CBC (1985), present viewing statistics for various categories of programming. These figures illustrate that Canadians have almost opposite viewing habits for information programs than for drama and movies. This is especially true of CBC English viewers. Comparing CBC English (Figure 10.2) with all English viewing (Figure 10.1) and comparing both those sets of data with the data presented on French viewing in Figures 10.3

FIGURE 10.1

**Proportion of Viewing Time in Canada Devoted to Various
Types of Canadian and Foreign Programs on all English TV**

**Monday to Sunday, 6:00 a.m.–2:00 a.m.
(January–December, 1984)**

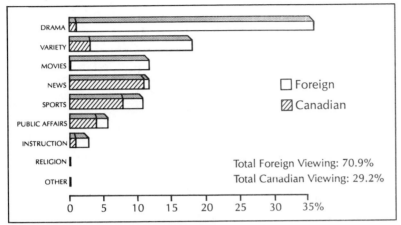

SOURCE: *TV and Radio: Figures That Count.* CBC, 1985.

FIGURE 10.2

**Proportion of Viewing Time in Canada Devoted to Various
Types of Canadian and Foreign Programs on CBC English TV**

**Monday to Sunday, 6:00 a.m.–2:00 a.m.
(January–December, 1984)**

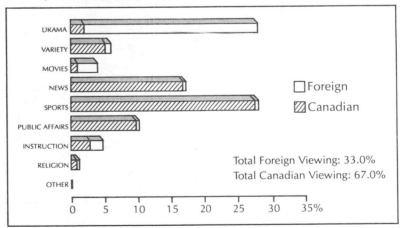

N.B. Excluding CBC affiliates in own time.
SOURCE: *TV and Radio: Figures That Count.* CBC, 1985.

FIGURE 10.3

Proportion of Viewing Time in Canada Devoted to Various Types of Canadian and Foreign Programs on all French TV

Monday to Sunday, 6:00 a.m.–2:00 a.m.
(January–December, 1984)

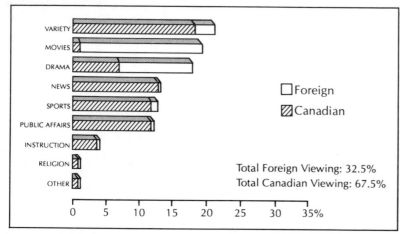

SOURCE: *TV and Radio: Figures That Count.* CBC, 1985.

FIGURE 10.4

Proportion of Viewing Time in Canada Devoted to Various Types of Canadian and Foreign Programs on CBC French TV

Monday to Sunday, 6:00 a.m.–2:00 a.m.
(January–December, 1984)

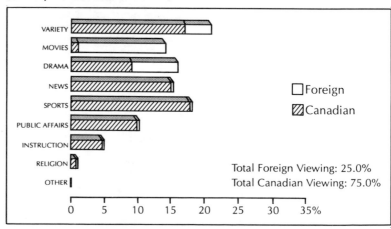

N.B. Excluding CBC affiliates in own time.
SOURCE: *TV and Radio: Figures That Count.* CBC, 1985.

and 10.4, the hypothesis presents itself that Canadians view Canadian programs to the degree that they are available in the general mix of programming. While insufficient research has been conducted on this question, it certainly runs counter to the general thesis that we are a nation absolutely lost in a colonial consciousness.

THE CANADIAN NEWS AND CENTRE-HINTERLAND RELATIONS

A basic question for our purposes in studying centre-hinterland dynamics is whether news programming contributes to these dynamics or works to counteract them. Two studies, one of CBC English radio news (Lorimer, 1984), the other of English- and French-language television news (Siegel, 1983), will help to answer this important question.

CBC National Radio News (in English)*

The first thing to note about CBC radio news is that it is Canadian in focus. As Tables 10.1 and 10.2 show, more than half the stories are Canadian. The frequency then drops to 14.1 per cent. These are stories about the U.S., our closest neighbour and a "newsworthy" nation. Then follow European countries and the Middle East. The Middle East was a particular hot spot in 1982, the year these data were collected.

The second noteworthy point is the dominant categories of content covered in the news stories. As Table 10.3 shows, political stories stood out as the most frequent (43.9 per cent). (Table 10.4 breaks down the political stories into sub-categories.) Following politics

---

*Kate Cockerill, Laine Lynde, and Bill Richards helped to collect and analyse the data for this study, which was directed by Rowland Lorimer.

TABLE 10.1

Distribution of Stories by Region

Region	Percentage
North America	68.3
Europe	13.2
Middle East	5.8
Eastern Bloc	4.3
South America	2.9
Asia	2.7
Africa	2.2
International	.6

TABLE 10.2

Distribution of Stories by Country

Country	Percentage
Canada	54.2
United States	14.1
Britain	4.7
Russia	2.9
Israel	2.5
France	2.0
Others (each)	<2.0

TABLE 10.3

Distribution of Stories by Major Theme

Theme	Percentage
Politics	43.8
Economics	15.9
Labour	6.5
Crime	4.3
Law	4.0
Disaster	3.9
Human interest	3.8
Energy	3.6
Environment	2.9
Science	2.6
Business	2.5
Religion	1.7
Culture	1.5
Medicine	1.3
Sports	0.8
Education	0.5
Communications	0.4

TABLE 10.4

Distribution of Stories by Minor Theme

Theme	Percentage
Elections/parties	19.4
Foreign relations	13.5
Nuclear arms	12.4
Conflict	8.8
Economic policy	7.8
Legislation	6.3
Human rights	5.7
Scandal	5.1
Domestic policy	4.9
Terrorism	4.7
Military	3.1
Trade	2.9
Defence	2.5
Parliament	2.4
Off-shore policy	0.2
Civil service	0.2

is economics at 15.9 per cent and then come a cluster of categories led by labour and followed by crime, law, disaster, human interest, and energy.

The third point is the shift in frequencies of categories of stories as a function of their location: the national capital, provincial capitals, major cities, rural settings. As Table 10.5 illustrates, some categories – business, the environment, labour, religion, science, and human interest – increase in frequency as the setting shifts from the Canadian centre to the periphery. The most dramatic increases are to be found in the categories of crime and disaster. Others – political and economic stories – decrease. The remaining themes do not change significantly.

The final significant point is the frequency of stories as a function of the province in which they occurred. As Table 10.6 demonstrates, the frequencies almost exactly follow the relative populations of the provinces. Only Newfoundland is out of place. However, one other,

less visible anomaly must be mentioned, the correct ranking of Quebec but the extreme drop in frequency between Ontario and Quebec. While the study did not attempt to calculate what percentage of the Ontario stories were accounted for by the presence of the nation's capital in Ontario (and Table 10.5 suggests that they were considerable), the overall effect appears to downplay the place of Quebec in Canada.

Taken together these four points appear to indicate that the CBC radio news is a counter-force to metropolis-hinterland dynamics as they apply to Canada as a nation. Concentration on Canadian stories in conjunction with an emphasis on politics and economics indicates that the CBC puts forward information about the day-to-day events that keep Canada a stable, economically functional nation. The CBC does not emphasize the kinds of stories, such as crime and disaster, that the wires services tend to emphasize in their coverage of hinterland countries. Nor, more significantly, does it fall prey to accepting stories about the U.S. as superseding Canadian stories in their newsworthiness. Not even in other data we collected on length and placement of story did a secondary rank for Canadian stories occur.

The latter two of the four points, on shifts in frequency of content and on provincial coverage, relate to centre-hinterland dynamics within Canada. In Canadian stories, as we move away from the national capital, political stories become less dominant; in percentage frequency they halve. The percentage frequencies of every other category except communication, the media, and culture increase. The predominant categories at the two levels of major cities and provincial capitals become politics, economics, labour, and to a lesser extent crime, and in major cities but not provincial capitals, human interest. In the rural

TABLE 10.5

Distribution of Canadian Stories by Theme and Locality

Major Theme	National Capital	Provincial Capital	Major City	Rural
Business	2.0%	2.2%	4.6%	12.9%
Communication	.5			
Crime	1.0	7.6	7.3	14.5
Culture	3.0	2.7		
Disaster	.5	1.3	1.8	14.5
Economic	19.0	22.3	20.2	14.5
Energy	2.5	5.4	2.8	3.2
Environment	.5	1.8	4.6	8.1
Labour	4.5	10.3	11.9	8.1
Law	5.0	5.4	6.4	
Media	.5			
Medicine	.5	3.6	1.8	
Political	59.0	27.7	22.0	19.4
Religion	.5	1.3		1.6
Science	.5	3.1	2.8	
Sports	.5	1.3	2.8	
Human Interest	1.0	2.7	10.1	3.2

category we have a further levelling effect with the top five categories in order of frequency being political, a three-way tie with economic, disaster, and crime, and then business. The environment and labour follow not too far behind.

The most dramatic frequency shifts that play into centre-margin dynamics are the increases in the reporting of crime and disaster in rural stories. Other frequency differentials that might have had the same influence – e.g., a great number of science, medicine, and technology stories based in the major cities; a great number of religion and human interest stories with rural settings – do not appear. The only other category to move in the direction that a centre-over-margin bias would suggest was law, a category that appeared constant in all settings except the rural, where it disappeared. To some extent the number of business stories with rural settings could be seen as countervalent to centre-margin pressures.

Overall, it would be difficult to claim that CBC radio news exacerbated centre-margin forces. In fact, the most reasonable interpretation of these data appears to be that they work as a credible contrary force. That contrary force is enhanced by a frequency of stories by province that matches the relative size of provincial populations.

TABLE 10.6

Distribution of Canadian Stories by Province

Province	Percentage
Ontario	50.9
Quebec	11.7
British Columbia	10.5
Alberta	7.3
Manitoba	4.9
Saskatchewan	4.5
Newfoundland	3.6
Nova Scotia	2.6
New Brunswick	1.9
Prince Edward Island	1.5
Yukon and Northwest Territories	0.5

English- versus French-Language Television News Services: The CRTC Study

As Siegel (1983) reports it, the findings of the Boyle Committee of the CRTC into media bias are a "devastating indictment of the state of French-English interaction in the broadcast media: it was almost non-existent" (p. 222). The major findings of Siegel's content analyses, which appear to have been a major part of the research base for the Boyle Committee, are as follows:

1. The differences between French-language and English-language broadcasts far outweighed similarities.

2. Of the 1,785 stories examined, only 259 appeared in both French and English and more than half of those 259 dealt with international issues. Siegel estimates the common ground between French-language and English-language newscasts was about 15 per cent.

3. Differences in viewpoint emerged in the analyses of Canadian events, the international scene, perceptions of newsworthiness, emphasis on personalities, and geographic sources.

4. Half of the French-language television newscasts were devoted to Quebec.

5. English-language services were more broad in their coverage of the national scene although the Maritimes and B.C. received little attention. Seventeen per cent of the stories were Quebec-oriented.

6. Greater emphasis was placed on political personalities by French-language news.

7. English-language news gave more coverage to the U.S. than did French-language news, which gave increased emphasis to western Europe.

8. French-language newscasts had three times as many stories on constitutional issues as did English-language newscasts.

9. Seventy-three per cent of news stories on television and radio together come from four cities: Ottawa, Toronto, Quebec City, and Montreal.

10. In one four-month period only 3 per cent of the French-language news stories in the major national evening newscast dealt with any part of Canada other than Quebec. In the English-language newscasts only 9 per cent originated in Quebec at a time when a general election was bringing the Parti Québécois to power for the first time.

11. In one three-day analysis of 252 stories, only three appeared on all five networks.

Siegel attributes these differences to the structure of the broadcasting system and journalistic norms, an interpretation that seems reasonable enough. But what is relevant to our discussion is the apparent cultural vibrancy evidenced in these findings. Unfortunately, it was a vibrancy centred on a particular point in history when the Quebec French and the Ontario English were having a falling out.

Consider the findings and the political situation at the centre of the study this way. Was not the social movement that brought the Parti Québécois to power newsworthy for Quebecers? Did not the personalities of the political players have a major effect on carrying that social movement? Did the social animation of Quebec not improve conditions for francophones in Canada, and arguably for all provincial interests? Did it not turn out that the anglophones of Canada had really nothing to worry about in terms of a Quebec separation? Is there not a great deal of difference even between various French- and English-language stations in newscasts, not comparing across languages? Is there not a profound cultural difference between the Quebec French and the Ontario English and, for that matter, between the West and the Maritimes in perspectives on Canada?

The answer to all of these questions may well be "yes." If so, perhaps the claim can be made that we should pride ourselves in media so responsive to social movements and viewpoints. We might even claim that we have a rather progressive press that plays to the interests of these movements and not to a more conservative national interest.

One thing the data do make clear: no single metropolitan centre holds sway over the Canadian media and therefore probably the popular "Canadian mind." While 73 per cent of stories at this time period may have emanated from four central Canadian cities (and perhaps that is overplaying their centrality for the rest of Canadians), our radio data show that over the longer term, at least with CBC English-language radio, such findings are not so pernicious. If anything is alarming it is the degree to which the Maritimes and B.C. are underrepresented. But again, the radio data do not support this as a longer-term trend.

AVOIDING HINTERLAND DEPENDENCY: A SHORT COURSE ON RESOURCE-LED DEVELOPMENT

In *Prairie Capitalism*, Larry Pratt and John Richards take on the notion that being a resource hinterland to a manufacturing centre necessarily entails a permanent dependency status. They claim that if the owners of the resource act as passive rentiers, and if the raw materials are exported directly to central markets, then a dependency status is sure to become entrenched. A dependency status is also likely to become built into the system if the resource owners allow the price of a commodity to rise less quickly than prices rise on the various finished products the centre manufactures using the resource base.

These two conditions, however, may not be inevitable. As Pratt and Richards suggest, resource hinterlands can have considerable bargaining power in dealing with large resource-extraction companies. They examine two provinces, Saskatchewan and Alberta, and identify two different strategies for combatting a growing dependency in a resource-based economy. Saskatchewan has made greatest use of the public-sector strategy while Alberta has made greatest use of the public sector for creating manoeuvring room for the private sector.

The general strategy they outline is what they term **resource-** or **staple-led development**. The first aspect of a successful staple-led economy is the appropriate collection of economic rents. They define economic rent as an excess in income arising in any industry above that necessary to generate a normal return to the man-made capital and labour employed. The power to collect rents, just like the power to command profit margins or wage levels, depends on the relative power of the group in society. In an optimistic society where it is assumed that technological progress will overcome any resource scarcities, the power of the resource owner is small. In a pessimistic scenario, for instance when we believe that we may run out of oil or that there may not be enough food to feed the world, the power of the resource owner to command high prices (collect higher rents) is greater. But whether in optimistic or pessimistic times, the possession of an abundance of a resource provides significant cost advantages in certain staple industries. For Alberta these are in petrochemicals and certain types of agriculture. For Saskatchewan they are in petrochemicals, potash, and agriculture.

The key to collecting an appropriate level of economic rents is public entrepreneurship. Especially in pessimistic times, there are considerable opportunities for public entrepreneurship. Such entrepreneurship involves the exercise of the bureaucratic imagination. How might provincial governments step in to accrue maximum rents without facing an uncontrollable backlash or a withdrawal of the companies involved in extracting the resource? What kinds of royalties, taxes, licences can be devised to keep production going while bringing to the owners, the people, a maximum return for their property? In addition, what kinds of tax measures or transportation regulations could be enacted to maximize the development of related or "linked" industries to the resource?

This last consideration leads us to Pratt and Richards' second major point. Forward and backward linkages must be exploited. They define forward linkages as industries that use the region's staples to transform them further, for example, potash into fertilizer. Backward linkages are industries that provide inputs to the staple sector, for example, agricultural machinery manufacture or pipeline manufacture.

Leakages must be counteracted to the maximum degree possible. To explain, any economic activity puts money into the economy in the form of wages, profits, and rents. As this money is spent it sets off another round of spending in the wages, profits, and rents of businesses that depend on the resource-extraction industry for their existence. Leakage occurs in terms of savings, taxes that leave the region, and the purchase of imported goods. The more of these there are, the less is the amplifying effect on the economy.

Pratt and Richards continue their discussion into the various criticisms of staple-led development and counteract those criticisms on the basis of the three points raised here. We should demonstrate the implications of their notions of the power of staple-led development for communications development in Canada.

However, before proceeding to that discussion we should summarize what Pratt and Richards make of the economies of Alberta and Saskatchewan. Both provinces have made good use in recent years of their resource bases. In Saskatchewan, public taxes as well as public companies have been developed to take control of resource development in the province. The people of Saskatchewan have benefited from these measures as a result of their being able to command much higher rents than in previous years.

Two factors have been problematic in Saskatchewan. The first is a conflict between the government of Saskatchewan and the federal government over jurisdictional rights to collect rents in the form of various kinds of royalties and taxes. These differences of opinion have led to lengthy court battles, often to the disadvantage of the province. Also problematic in Saskatchewan has been the lack of the development of a local private entrepreneurial sector to take advantage of the forward and backward linkages to Saskatchewan's three resources.

The authors appear to be more impressed by Alberta. They note that a vibrant local bourgeoisie has developed and that this bourgeoisie is far from being passive in its relations with the big oil companies. The Alberta business community has been very successful in infusing itself into all aspects of the oil industry in full partnership with the big oil interests. Neither has the Alberta government been passive in its actions to garner what rents it could from its ownership of the resources. In fact, as the authors conclude, "In the final analysis it has been the ideas of politicians and the actions of governments that mattered most of all" (p. 329).

AVOIDING HINTERLAND DEPENDENCY: POSSIBILITIES FOR COMMUNICATIONS

An analogy can be drawn between natural resource riches and the resource base for the development of entertainment and information programming. Its basis is the fact, confirmed by the Broadcasting Task Force (1986), that whenever Canadians are given a choice of watching Canadian programming over foreign programming, many choose the Canadian. The second basis upon which Canadians have a comparative advantage in communications is that only Canadians can produce Canadian cultural artifacts.

Cultural Production as a Unique Resource

If we think of Canadian cultural artifacts as the staples to lead linked development we may have a good strategy for Canada's cultural future. Our present cultural policy is to give enormous advantage to imported cultural products and grant to them an even greater competitive advantage than they already have over Canadian cultural producers. We do this in a number of ways. First, because of their large home markets, foreign producers (especially the U.S.) have a competitive edge. What the U.S. producers gain from sales in Canada is gravy on the basic profit they make in their enormous home market. With all development costs recovered in the home market, sales in Canada represent extra profits on a base of only production costs. But that is just the beginning of the competitive edge.

Slitting Our Own Throats

We also provide an expensive infrastructure, which in effect subsidizes the distribution of foreign products. To take a first example, Canada has spent millions of dollars to put up communication satellites. Foreign content producers have equal access (with domestic producers) to this infrastructure. Another example: Canada currently subsidizes the postal rates for books and magazines in Canada *regardless of where they were originally produced* and regardless of their editorial content, i.e., whether it has direct relevance to Canadians. As a result, publications such as *Time* magazine are heftily subsidized by the Canadian taxpayer. The same is true of foreign book clubs that mail to their Canadian members from within Canada.

In the recording industry, when master tapes are imported the tax assessed on them is based on the value of the raw materials upon which the recording is made. Besides the competitive advantage resulting from home market sales, we do not even tax on the value of the imported material.

Canada allows foreign owners to participate also in many businesses oriented to the distribution of cultural products, such as movie theatres. With no base in Canada, little moral suasion can be used to persuade them to insert Canadian cultural products among the mass cultural products that predominate in their distribution system.

Canada has very lax competition laws, too. In the U.S. the movie production houses were forced to divest themselves of their interests in movie theatres on the grounds that such a vertical integration did not allow sufficient competition. In Canada no such requirement has ever come into effect. Only recently have the distributors agreed to give all movie theatres a fair chance to bid on the right to first showings of movies. This they did while never admitting that they hadn't done so all along.

Also, Canada subsidizes foreign book and magazine publishers by forgoing sales taxes on their products. Given that nearly 80 per cent of the market is accounted for by foreign sales in both these areas, this means, as with the postal subsidy, that 80 per cent of the forgone revenue from a sales tax is of benefit to foreign producers.

The list of possible examples is very long. Many of these subsidies that favour foreign producers are historical accidents and will be rectified in time. However, until they are, foreign producers will have a double advantage over Canadian producers. That makes it almost impossible for Canadian cultural industries to survive. When a recording artist gains any kind of world-wide recognition, or even if he or she begins with world market ambitions, that artist looks for a record company that can represent him or her world-wide. Working against the odds in our home market, the likelihood of a Canadian recording company growing big enough to operate on a

world scale is small. Only when the Canadian company has been able to grow, protected by barriers against foreign ownership, has it been able to become a world player.

In terms of Pratt and Richard's model, we have not collected the appropriate economic rents on the sale of Canadian audiences and the sale of the Canadian communications infrastructure to foreign producers and distributors. At the most extreme, the public entrepreneurs could legitimately devise schemes where the costs of Canadian production could provide the basis for pricing (i.e., taxing) imported cultural goods to bring imported material in line with those costs. Also, we have not built up forward and backward linkages nearly enough. (Taking the movie industry as one example, the backward linkages would be to books while the forward linkages would be to broadcast and rebroadcast rights, video shop sales and rentals, and so forth.) Finally, the leakage of money out of the economy in the cultural area through the purchase of foreign cultural materials is astronomical, as Audley's (1983) figures in Chapter 1 show.

Support Programs

The federal government and some provincial governments have begun to realize that the state of cultural production in Canada is counterproductive from both a cultural and a business perspective. A variety of programs have been put in place, some aimed at increasing the opportunities for artists and other cultural workers (e.g., the Canada Council), and other programs are oriented to putting in place stable production houses and facilities to form the foundations of a vibrant cultural industry. Perhaps the best known example is the effort made by the federal government to establish a healthy film production industry. When we realize that in 1980 the estimated wholesale revenue from the sale of films to the Canadian market for both theatre and television was $219 million and that 98.2 per cent and 92.7 per cent respectively of that spending went to foreign producers (Audley, 1983, p. 317), it is easy to understand why the federal government is willing to make a massive investment to try to help Canadians acquire a decent share of that market. It makes eminent sense if only because we cannot afford to lose all these Canadians dollars to foreign producers.

The federal and various provincial governments have taken steps to help Canadian publishers participate in the Canadian book and magazine market. In that industry the schemes have been many and varied, from learning material development plans through outright grants, half-back schemes on lottery tickets, subsidies on sales, subsidies to sell international rights, the development of a copyright act that would favour domestic rather than foreign producers, etc. Each of these plans has had some success, as have many of the plans in other areas, but a striking breakthrough has yet to be achieved.

One of the visible success stories has been the Canadian content regulation on AM radio. Beginning in 1971 all AM stations licensed in Canada were required to devote 30 per cent of their air time to Canadian content. As a result of this single regulation there has sprung up a lively rock music production industry in Canada's major cities. So successful is it that not only is Canada producing international stars but foreign performers of stature are coming to Canada to record. While producer David Foster's attempt to base himself in West Vancouver was short-lived, André Perry's Le Studio in Morin Heights, Quebec, is a mecca for rock-and-roll artists.

Once room is created in the distribution system within Canada for Canadian cultural products, then Canadian audiences apparently will jump at the chance to consume them and secondary linked activities will also grow from that basic market presence. As Pratt and Richards note, the real opportunities will be created by the efforts of politicians and governments. From the early signs of the effects that emerged from a variety of tentative steps, there is little doubt that Canadian artists and entrepreneurs will use the opportunities created by governments to benefit all Canadians.

SUMMARY

The domestic geopolitics of information are not unlike the global geopolitics. Canada suffers, as do non-dominant groups within Canada, from the historical, economic, social, and communications structures that have been built up to serve empire, empire U.S.A., and empire Canada. As a result, in learning materials, broadcasting, the recording industry, writing, theatre, dance, and other modes of cultural expression, one can find the guiding finger of that cultural industry in the content produced. With respect to cultural dominance from outside, Canada worsens her own position with laws and infrastructure and subsidy programs that actually help foreign producers attain a level that exceeds that of domestic producers. In addition, importers are given free reign to bring foreign cultural products into the country to compete with those indigenously produced.*

All, however, is not lost, either in the practi-

*The 10 per cent import tax on books, applied in 1986 in retaliation to a U.S. tariff on shakes and shingles, was rescinded in the 1987 federal budget.

cal world of program production or in a theoretical way of seeing things. As we illustrated, news programming can be designed to counter metropolis-hinterland dynamics, and as Pratt and Richards have demonstrated, a theoretical position can also be introduced to demonstrate the nature of hinterland power. That model can as easily guide cultural industries as it does resource industries.

With regard to policy, four levels of concern must be addressed to improve our domestic status in the cultural industries. (1) Opportunities must be created for Canadians to participate in articulating their own culture. (2) For participation to be significant, steps must be taken to ensure that the incentive structure to produce content does not grossly favour only mass market materials that are going to be oriented to American and world-wide markets to the neglect of the Canadian market. Grade B movies aimed at Home Box Office are not the way to go, although the mass market should not be ignored as a significant market for profit-taking. (3) The various cultural professions must be nurtured from within a national framework so that they develop and maintain a coherence. Out of that coherence will emerge a distinctive Canadian voice. (4) Issues of ownership are also significant. It appears that the various levels of government have realized that importers are not the ones to take on the development of Canadian cultural production. Far more suitable to take on this task for both domestic and international consumption are the small Canadian producers who abound with entrepreneurial energy. The issue of ownership cannot be underestimated. Foreign owners do not have (indeed, cannot have) Canadian interests at heart. Importers are compromised. Programs for the development of Canadian cultural expression need to be directed at Canadian owners whose production is already centred on Canadian cultural expression.

REFERENCES

Althusser, Louis. *Lenin and his Philosophy*. London: New Left Books, 1971.

Audley, Paul. *Canada's Cultural Industries: Broadcasting, Publishing, Records, and Film*. Toronto: James Lorimer, 1983.

Beale, Alison. "The Question of Space," in R. Lorimer and D.C. Wilson, eds., *Communications Canada*. Forthcoming, 1988.

Berger, Thomas. *Northern Frontier, Northern Homeland: Report of the MacKenzie Valley Pipeline Enquiry*. Ottawa: Queen's Printer, 1977.

Canada. *Report of the Task Force on Broadcasting Policy*. Ottawa: Ministry of Supply and Services, 1986.

Canadian Broadcasting Corporation. *Annual Report*, 1981, 1985.

Clymer, T., ed. *Reading 360*. Toronto: Ginn, 1972.

Concordia University, Communication Studies. *Communication and the Canadian North*. Montreal, 1983.

Innis, H.A. *Essays in Canadian Economic History*. Edited by Mary Q. Innis. Toronto: University of Toronto Press, 1956.

Keeney, Patrick. "Deweyan Pedagogy and the Multinational Text," unpublished manuscript, Simon Fraser University, 1984.

Lorimer, Rowland. *The Nation in the Schools*. Toronto: OISE Press, 1984.

Lorimer, Rowland. "An analysis of CBC radio news in English," unpublished paper, Simon Fraser University, 1984.

Lyman, P. *Canada's Video Revolution*. Toronto: James Lorimer, 1983.

McNulty, Jean. "The Political Economy of Canadian Satellite Broadcasting," paper presented at Canadian Communication Association meeting, Montreal, May, 1987.

National Film Board. *Magic in the Sky*, directed by Peter Raymont, produced by Peter Raymont, Arthur Hammond. Ottawa, 1981.

Pratt, Larry, and John Richards. *Prairie Capitalism: Power and Influence in the New West.* Toronto: McClelland and Stewart, 1979.

Rioux, Marcel. *Quebec in Question.* Trans. James Boake. Toronto: James Lorimer, 1973.

Siegel, Arthur. *Politics and the Media in Canada.* Toronto: McGraw-Hill Ryerson, 1973.

Valaskakis, G. "Television and Cultural Integration," in Lorimer and Wilson, eds., *Communications Canada.* Forthcoming, 1988.

von Zur Muehen, Max. "Foreign Academics at Canadian Universities: A Statistical Perspective on New Appointments during the Seventies," mimeo paper, December, 1981.

STUDY QUESTIONS

1. Thomas Berger, in *Northern Frontier, Northern Homeland*, discusses the successive intrusions of white civilization upon Inuit culture. Discuss the role of communications technologies in this vein.

2. Your village on Ellesmere Island has just been offered the opportunity to have a satellite dish and distribution system installed free by a multinational oil company. Until now there has been no television reception in your village. What matters do you think should be considered in deciding whether to accept the company's offer?

3. In the Siegel study of CBC television news, it was found that the French and English services provided different versions of "reality." Discuss the possible benefits and dangers of these differences for Canadians.

4. "A staple-led economy, being necessarily continentalist, is a continual threat not only to Canada's economic and political but also to its cultural sovereignty." Discuss.

CHAPTER

11

New Communications Technologies in a Canadian Context

INTRODUCTION

THE PAST few decades have seen an enormous explosion in our capacity to communicate. This has been brought about largely through the amalgamation of communication with computers. The basis of that amalgamation has been the silicon chip, a device that, as it becomes smaller and smaller, against all initial expectations, becomes more and more sophisticated and efficient as well as inexpensive.

The changes brought about through this tremendous expansion of communicative capacity are legion. A selection of newspaper headlines gives us a sense of the changing environment.

- "New firm cashes in on TV's news boom"
- "Sidewalk summit launched ethnic pay TV pioneers"

- "Pay TV licensees secure top deals as on-air launching draws closer"
- "Telidon adds market zap to Dominion Directory"
- "Cable TV tunes into high-tech wizardry"
- "Satellites: Impinging on North American copyright laws"
- "International copyright agreements and the need for a new legal framework"
- "Electronics revolutionize publishing industry"
- "Computers enable printer to increase flow of black ink"
- "Privacy and the computer state"
- "Terminal man"
- "Videotex net for farmers to be launched by Sasktel"
- "Rogers-Belzberg group granted cellular licence"
- "Home computer David takes aim at Goliaths"
- "Fox defends national jurisdiction"
- "CBC boss eyes two futures"

As the headlines indicate, the changes in the communications environment are of a number of different types. The major changes are in:

1. the technology used to process and shape information;
2. market dynamics, such as economies of scale, or, in other words, national and international dynamics as a result of technological form;
3. the patterns in the content of information that are and will become available (and hence consumed by audiences);
4. the patterns of participation by various types of cultural institutions, for example, large corporations, small entrepreneurial groups, Crown corporations, etc.;
5. the investment patterns in the information sector and, as a result, the emergence of new information services and ownership dynamics;
6. the legal framework appropriate to an enhanced information sector in which more information is packaged many times over but slightly differently for various, narrowly targeted audiences.

In this chapter we will review some of these quite fundamental changes to the global communications infrastructure, discuss their implications for Canada and Canadians, and suggest a strategy for proceeding in this new communications environment.

A TECHNO-INDUSTRIAL EXPLOSION IN COMMUNICATIONS

As Peter Lyman points out in *Canada's Video Revolution*, a book to which we are greatly indebted in this chapter, we have become many times more adept in our use of electricity in recent years. No longer do we simply energize the filament of a light bulb. Now we direct minute amounts of electricity that carry in their patterns all sorts of information. The basic device that has given us this power is the semiconductor, a silicon chip on which is printed more and more complex integrated circuits capable of such functions as information sorting, calculations, and storage.

To digital semiconductor technology is added optical technology, or fibre optics. Whereas electrical pulses have been and still are being used, fibre optics use light pulses. Their major advantage is a 10,000 fold increase in transmission capability over a copper wire of the same bulk. Such a dramatic increase in transmission capability allows for a correspondingly vast increase in the possibilities for two-way as well as one-way communicative exchanges.

The third element of technological development in communications is the satellite. Satellite technology in conjunction with communications technology has led to the communications satellite. Such satellites serve a simple function. They are points to which signals can be sent and from which signals can be received. Being so high in the sky, they can receive and transmit signals from places widely separated by geography. Interlinked with other satellites, they can form a global network for signals to be beamed around the world.

As with practically any technological explosion there is an associated industrial explosion. And as with any recent major industrial explosion or expansion, the large corporations are best positioned not only to benefit from new market possibilities but also to direct technological development in ways that favour their activities. As noted in previous chapters, this comes about not only because of the borrowing power of these businesses but also through economies of scale that allow the expense of new technologies to be paid for by a vast market. As well, large companies control the market to such an extent that they can create markets for the technologies that they wish to introduce. We will bypass this techno-industrial dynamic and concentrate on the evolving forms of communications technology and how they restructure the communications environment of Canada.

THE TECHNOLOGICAL FOUNDATIONS OF TELEVISION BROADCASTING

Historically, television broadcasting has been closely connected to its technological form. Networks were formed on the basis of terrestrial technology, that is, microwave towers that beamed programs across the country. This ability to distribute nationally via a series of microwave-linked stations was basic to the economics of program production as well as the form of programming. For example, the national evening news was made possible because of microwave technology. Until 1958 videotapes were flown out to the regions from the production centre(s) for broadcast.

The commitment to national distribution through microwave-to-local-station technology has created fierce competition at the level of the networks in the U.S. and has removed the local station from the centre of the competition because it has become little more than a carrier of network programming. But in so doing, and because the networks are program producers (usually through contracts to smaller production houses) as well as carriers, this change has concentrated the competition at the level of the networks.

In Canada the competition between two networks, in English the CBC and CTV, in French Radio-Canada and TVA, and among them, the independents, and Global (in Ontario) has been less intense for a number of reasons. The primary one is that all, to a considerable extent, rely on foreign programming, mostly from the three U.S. networks. The French-langauge services, as well, are supplemented by programs from France. They buy such programming off the shelf for prices that hover around 10 per cent of the cost of production. Table 11.1 illustrates a typical week's programming on TVA's Télé-Métropole.

Another reason for less intense competition is that the CBC and CTV, and Radio-Canada and TVA, have different mandates. CTV/TVA rely to a much greater extent than does the CBC on U.S. and French programming. In addition, the cable companies have brought in the three American commercial networks plus PBS (the Public Broadcasting System) on basic service. The possibility of fierce competition between Canadian networks, and indeed the possibility for the American networks to carry on

TABLE 11.1

Télé-Métropole Prime Time Programs for the Week of March 22 - 28, 1986*

7 p.m.	Saturday	Sunday	Monday	Tuesday	Wednesday	Thursday	Friday**
7:30 p.m.	"V"	L'Ile fantastique	L'âme soeur	Peau de banane	Épopée rock	Arnold et Willie	Cinéma du vendredi «Le roi des rois»
8 p.m.	Cinéma du samedi «Valentino»	R.S.V.P.	K-2000	Deux font la paire	Le hockey TVA	Magnum	
8:30 p.m.							
9 p.m.			L'or du temps	Entre chien et loup		Chacun chez soi	
9:30 p.m.		Cinéma «Appelez-moi docteur»	En chanson... Nicole Martin	Made in Quebec		Cinéma du jeudi «Resurection»	
10 p.m.	Justice pour tous						
10:30 p.m.			Dynastie	Pour l'amour du risque	Politique Québec		Contexte
11 p.m.	Sur la colline						

*In this sample week, chosen at random, all of the movies shown were American. This is, of course, not always the case.
**The usual Friday night programming also includes the British series *Arme et charme* from 9 p.m. to 10 p.m.

SOURCE: *Report of the Task Force on Broadcasting Policy*. Ottawa: Supply and Services, 1986.

their intense competition in Canada, is thereby thwarted, and American *ex patria* competition becomes impossible because the Canadian networks can buy programming from any of the U.S. networks on a year-by-year basis.

The new technologies, along with complementary changes in regulation, alter the structure of broadcasting quite fundamentally. The basic component of that alteration is the communications satellite. Communications satellites are used for long-distance transmission and can be joined with local broadcast facilities (on VHF and UHF) or locally distributed by cable. Figures 11.1 and 11.2 describe the coverage of the two satellite series in use in Canada. Table 11.2 lists the services that use each satellite.

Using either of these satellite systems, one television station suddenly can become a network for a great number of Canadians, i.e., those who are either cabled or within reach of the broadcast centre: hence the designation "superstation." Suddenly, technologically, national distribution is at the fingertips of any "broadcaster" or, more accurately, program packager who can assemble the audiences to sell to the advertisers to support a national effort. The vast expense of assembling a network of stations to develop some local programming, but mostly to rebroadcast centrally produced programming, is no longer necessary. Along with the possibility of superstations come special services that have a sufficient national audience to make their operations

FIGURE 11.1
Anik C Footprint

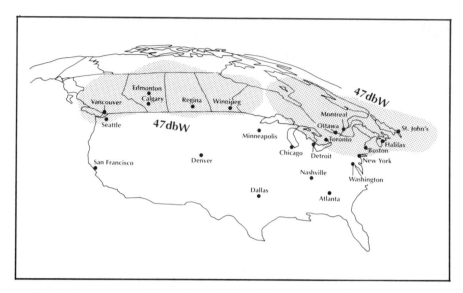

NOTE: This is the area covered by Anik C's half-Canada spotbeams with full-power (47 dbW) radiation. Beyond the footprint, larger-than-standard dish antennas are needed for reception.
SOURCE: Telesat Canada.

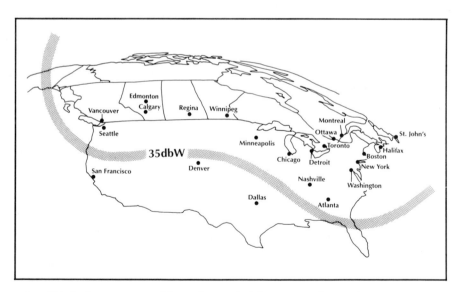

FIGURE 11.2
Anik D Footprint

NOTE: This is the area covered by Anik D with full-power (35dbW) radiation, including all of Canada and part of the U.S.
SOURCE: Telesat Canada.

TABLE 11.2

Optional Television Services Available from Canadian Satellites

	West	East
ANIK C-3 12-14 Ghz.		
First Choice*Superchannel West	X	
First Choice*Superchannel East		X
Super Ecran		X
Knowledge Network	X	
Atlantic Television System Ltd. (ASN)		X
La Sette		X
TVOntario		X
Radio Quebec		X
Access Alberta	X	
ANIK D-1 4-6 Ghz.		
House of Commons	X	X
The Sports Network (TSN)	X	X
MuchMusic	X	X
Cancom*	X	X

*Cancom is composed of: CHCH-TV Hamilton (ind.), TCTV-TV Montreal (TVA), CITV-TV Edmonton (ind.), CHAN-TV Vancouver (CTV), WDIV-TV Detroit (NBC), WTVS-TV Detroit (PBS), WJBK-TV Detroit (CBS), WXYZ-TV Detroit (ABC).

SOURCE: Telesat Canada.

---

economic within this new technological regime.

Recent CRTC decisions have made this all legal. Broadcasters, especially in the already segmented market in Toronto, have been quick to rise to the opportunity. The Global network and Multilingual Television have announced plans to expand nationally and the CRTC has licensed Canadian Satellite Communications Inc., better known as Cancom, a redistribution company that distributes signals via satellite.

The major emergent form in Canada that makes use of satellite-to-cable transmission is pay TV. While, as just about every Canadian knows, pay TV in Canada has experienced economic difficulties, which we will discuss later in this chapter, it is nevertheless opening up the possibilities inherent in satellite-to-cable transmission.

The services that satellite-based distribution makes economically feasible are many and varied. Some, no doubt, will depend on subscriber revenues while others will be advertiser-supported. On the former basis, health information both for the average person as well as for professional development, skills upgrading, or retraining is quite possible. Similarly, business information can be created, packaged, and transmitted easily and quickly to highly specific target audiences. Cultural programming, formerly available in one location, can be transmitted across the country into almost any location where a satellite receiving dish can be erected, or where a cable com-

TABLE 11.3

Current and Alternative Cable Tiering Structure

Current Structure*

Basic Tier (including augmented channel service)

- Canadian channels, public and private, which qualify for priority carriage under CRTC regulations

-Community channel where required

- Parliamentary channel

- Optional channels as permitted by the CRTC, including the American 3 + 1 and, in some cases, independent U.S. stations

- "Barker" channel, which promotes discretionary tier

Discretionary Services

- Canadian movie channel (First Choice/Superchannel/Super Ecran)

- Canadian specialty channels (The Sports Network, MuchMusic, Life Channel)

- American specialty channels approved for carriage by CRTC

Alternative Structure

Alternative Basic Tier

- Canadian channels, public and private, which qualify for priority carriage under CRTC regulations
- Community channel
- The proposed TVCanada services
- Proposed Canadian all-news channel
- Optional conventional Canadian channels, as permitted by CRTC

Second Tier

- Canadian specialty channels (subject to higher Canadian content requirements than at present)
- Optional conventional American signals including 3 + 1 and any additional American signals now carried on basic

Premium Tier

- Canadian movie channels
- Canadian specialty channels (i.e., those that choose not to meet requirements for carriage on second tier)
- American specialty channels that are complementary to licensed Canadian services

SOURCE: *Report of the Task Force on Broadcasting Policy.* Ottawa: Supply and Services, 1986.

pany has set up a dish receiver and offers the programming on its cable system. Premium television (television for which one pays a premium above the basic cable rate) and foreign television services (in addition to American services) are also possible as advertiser-supported systems.

Other services, which require some adaptation of the technology, are also feasible. For example, point-to-point distribution in which signals are sent only to certain addresses is not difficult. The scrambling of signals allows for universal distribution but (theoretically) non-universal reception. Scrambling also provides for security as well as economic return through the control of descramblers.

With the vast increase in channel capability that fibre optics and coaxial cable, as well as

VHF and UHF, make possible, none of these services theoretically need interfere with the other. Part of the challenge is to design and market them for the cultural and economic benefit of Canadians as a whole. If a cable company is involved as a local exhibitor, that challenge can be addressed in part by the tiering of services. Tiering is really an application of the marketer's old standby, packaging. It amounts to including one package of offerings for basic cable service and alternative packages at other levels of service. Table 11.3 describes in general terms the current method of tiering of cable companies alongside a proposal for an alternative put forward by the Broadcasting Task Force (1986).

The socio-cultural implications of tiering are considerable. Certain services of cultural, political, or economic benefit could be linked to popular services so that, in effect, the latter carried the former. To take an obvious example, if all educational and business services were available only to subscribers of a full package of entertainment services, the system designer would, no doubt, become a national villain. However, without local cable control, the potential organizing influence of tiering disappears.

PROGRAMMING IMPLICATIONS OF SATELLITE-BASED TECHNOLOGY

The clearest implication of satellite-based technology and an enabling regulatory framework is an increase in the number of domestic and international buyers of television programming. These buyers will be the new networks or specialty services, i.e., the superstations. In contrast to the networks, which have acted as vertically integrated packagers and programmers, many of the new players will not be in a position to do both, unless, of course, they are merely arms of already existing broadcasters. But even at that, it appears that, following the American example and given CBC cutbacks, Canadian broadcasters are themselves beginning to acquire rather than make programs. This change in function happens partly because a healthy independent producing community is already emerging and partly to stretch programming dollars. This movement could lead to increased opportunities for Canadian independent producers.

A second implication is that, at least in Canada because of the small size of the market, programs will have to be made to appeal to more than one market. This means that what was left of network oligopoly in the U.S. over programming (in Canada, CBC monopoly since CTV has been such an ineffectual program producer) will be weakened by the presence of other major program packagers (for example, Home Box Office). In Canada the added dimension of the CBC's or any other broadcaster's inability to fund programming completely will require independent producers to come up with at least half of their funding in other markets. The implementation of Telefilm Canada's production fund, wherein one-third of the funding is available for assured prime-time broadcast programs, makes independent productions quite feasible. In certain circumstances the Telefilm contribution may be raised to 49 per cent. Up to June 29, 1984, the response of the private stations had not been overwhelming (see Tables 11.4 and 11.5), but predictions are that all broadcasters will make greater use of the fund.

A third implication of satellite-based technology is the challenge the technology presents to regulation. Regulation has an historical base in scarcity of distribution facilities, i.e., the airwaves. With channel scarcity no longer a limiting factor, there are bound to be both

TABLE 11.4

English and French Projects Received for the Canadian Broadcast Program Development Fund by June 29, 1984

	Number of Projects	Total Budget	Telefilm Participation
La Société Radio Canada	33	$37,987,322	$9,292,149
CBC	24	50,104,959	16,555,057
CTV	6	29,653,206	5,632,145
Global	5	3,240,821	954,159
Télé-Métropole	2	741,987	213,207
Independents	18	12,739,046	3,544,941
Total	88	$134,467,341	$36,191,658

SOURCE: *TV World*, April, 1985, p. 32.

TABLE 11.5

Breakdown of Network Participation on Projects Contracted and Accepted by June 29, 1984

	Projects	Budgets	Telefilm Canada
French			
Drama	24	$52,570,672	$10,090,451
Variety	11	4,418,090	1,425,936
Children's	11	7,860,149	2,499,587
Sub-total	46	$64,848,911	$14,015,974
English			
Drama	38	$73,837,574	$23,693,081
Variety	13	9,445,074	2,419,287
Children's	9	10,452,713	3,451,401
Sub-total	60	$93,735,361	$29,563,769
Total	106	$158,584,272	$43,579,743

SOURCE: *TV World*, April, 1985, p. 32.

domestic and international pressures to allow easy access to all manner of programming. These pressures have already been felt, and a general loosening of the regulatory framework occurred in 1985.

A fourth implication derives from the simple mathematics of increasing the number of services. The audience fragments further with the addition of each additional service. The returns to producers are thus fractionalized by the addition of each service. Audience fragmentation increases pressure to operate in the largest possible market.

The corollary to audience fragmentation is that although there will be more program buyers in the market, as the Canadian experience with pay TV has demonstrated, there may be little net increase in the size of the audience. In other words, the money available for programming may not expand appreciably. In fact, if we open the skies to all programmers it may very easily turn out that foreign programmers end up the beneficiaries, as an increased number of foreign program packagers find themselves in a position to exploit Canada as a spill-over market.

A fifth implication is the resequencing of releases to various markets. At the present time feature films are released to theatres, followed closely by release to videocassette distribution, then pay TV, and then broadcast television. Made-for-TV movies are shown first on pay TV and may be followed by other forms of distribution. If pay TV can place itself ahead of videocassette distribution, perhaps by acting as a distributor for home video-recording at times not now used (2:00 to 6:00 a.m., for instance) then its market penetration is bound to be greater than if it is a later element in the release sequence. But if the U.S. feature film industry or its Canadian distribution arm finds itself able to set up distribution to television through totally owned subsidiaries, then pay TV under independent operators may find itself out in the cold.

POSITIONING CANADIAN PROGRAMMING

Regulation of communications has already been loosened considerably as a result of the change in communications technology. The possibility of obtaining increased programming funds for distinctively Canadian, culturally important programming to weather the increased fury of the foreign gale is remote. In the current economic climate a cultural industrial response is more realistic. That response amounts to a determination to seize the opportunity of the flux in programming needs and acquisition structures and use potential market power, Canadian training and experience, and Canadian creativity to become competitive in the domestic and international markets.

Lyman presents a number of ideas on how that cultural industrial response might be made to work. Such ideas, it should be noted, require a high degree of co-operation in the industry. Obtaining that co-operation would be an uphill battle, not particularly because the industry is by nature unco-operative but because the interests of many in the industry are in conflict with Lyman's scenario. In view of these conflicting interests, to bring Lyman's plan into action would require a firmer political will on the part of the government and its regulator than we have seen in all of Canadian history. The point in considering Lyman's plan is to demonstrate the possibilities that do, in fact, exist.

In face of a higher degree of competition, a licence to broadcast will no longer be a licence to print money but a licence to compete, provided that the CRTC does not regulate to protect established interests. That competition is not for what will go down in history as culturally significant but for audiences and, thus, advertising dollars – and profits. In such an atmosphere, Canadian content will suffer increasingly if it cannot hold an audience. Canadian programming of all categories cannot be a continuing net drain on resources because of its failure to draw significantly large audiences. Rather, programming must become competitive in both the domestic and international markets.

Lyman, an economist, claims that the basic variable in becoming competitive is a level of investment more or less equivalent to that spent by others in the marketplace. He may be quite right. If the Americans spend $1 million (Canadian) to compete in the same market, then Canadians, too, must spend money. (The position of the Canadian dollar with respect to that of the U.S. is not insignificant in this regard.) The scheduling, expenditures, packaging, and success of *The National* and *The Journal* tend to support his argument.

Lyman does see a positive role for public bodies and for the private broadcasters. Public corporations such as the CBC and the NFB could make a contribution through providing pre-sale funding for productions. In addition, they and the private broadcasters could use their positions as purchasers of foreign programs to lever Canadian programming they have helped fund into foreign markets. Public and private broadcasters together could argue for a one-for-one trade with all foreign producers except the Americans. In that market it would be more a case of insisting on a less rigid *quid pro quo*. This, by the way, would be an extremely bold step for Canadian broadcasters, one they could have implemented long ago if they had wanted to do so.

Other public measures could also contribute to a cultural industrial response. The capital cost allowance (CCA), the tax deduction individuals can receive for investing in the making of Canadian films, could be expanded to all forms of cultural industrial production. As mentioned above, Telefilm Canada has already been expanded to include made-for-television projects.

A further role for the public sector would be a reconsideration of Canadian content regulations. At the present time these regulations are geared to percentage content, i.e., the number of hours broadcast. Because Canadian programming has been and is now a net drain on resources, broadcasters and now the pay TV operators have the incentive to make as cheap Canadian programming as possible, e.g., game shows and the like. If regulation were to use a different kind of formula where quality and results counted, we might see much improved Canadian programming.

Lyman contends that our best chance is competing not for the blockbuster markets but rather for the specialty markets. In such markets producers work with the kind of budgets to which Canadian producers are accustomed. Also, by a variety of means, we have developed in the country the requisite level of training and professionalism for success in those markets. Those means include individuals working in the U.S., work and training at the CBC and the NFB and, more recently, at the Canada Film Development Corporation (Telefilm Canada).

We are in a good position to take up co-productions with high enough budgets in order to produce programs that will compete with success domestically and internationally. What has been holding us back in both television and feature film production is the difficulty of breaking into the distribution system, the very element that is so much in flux as a result of the new technology. And the distribution system can be entered through a shrewd use of the purchasing power of Canadian program packagers and broadcasters. Here lies the difficulty we spoke of earlier: gaining the co-operation of all parties on the Canadian scene, many of whom have economic interests that actually conflict with building a healthy Canadian production industry, may turn out to be merely a fond dream.

Lyman makes a further point of special relevance to education. Needless duplication of our productions for various segments of our market must be avoided to increase our number of titles. What sense is there to produce five video programs on the same subject? Why compete with ourselves beyond the point of creating good quality and requisite variety? We might also add the possibility of aggregating the acquisition of Canadian programming from foreign sources. There is no value to Canadians in allowing various program purchasers (e.g., CBC and CTV) in Canada to compete, thus driving up the price of foreign programming for use in the Canadian market. It would be far better that they settle their competitive urges behind closed doors and purchase through a central agent. But again, some Canadian distributors of American products benefit more from open competition than from within-Canada bargaining behind closed doors.

Even with this entire system of proposals working we cannot be guaranteed success. It is very difficult to predict the future and for every move of ours there will be counter-moves by others. The best we can expect is to participate in a global industry and perhaps acquire a market position so that we will not have a negative balance of payments in the television programming sector. It would certainly be a boon for us to balance our trade in that sector.

It is also an important planning exercise to think how we might participate in this industry. At present, film and television alone represent a $2-$3 billion drain on our economy. Also, we are not significant participants in the hardware market, a market said to be worth $10,000 million annually in the U.S. alone by 1990. Nearly all of our purchases of television and associated equipment come from foreign sources.

There is a final major point to which we will return. Lyman's scenario contains an implicit definition of Canadian cultural content, for he maintains that a program will sell to audiences around the world if it is done well. If it has distinctive Canadian cultural content it must be presented in a manner that can be universally understood. That content should not make the program any less saleable on either the international or the domestic market.

There is, however, a problem in this notion of the interaction of culture and market. The BBC sells programs internationally that present Britain in the stereotypes foreigners have of the British, e.g., *Upstairs Downstairs*. Similarly, as *The Thornbirds* (especially the movie) and, more recently, *Crocodile Dundee* demonstrate, what succeeds for Australia internationally is based on how outsiders view Australians. The obvious question is for whom are these programs to be made? Will programs about Canada made for foreign consumption be enough for Canadians?

PAY TV AS A KEY COMPONENT OF CULTURAL INDUSTRIAL STRATEGY

Pay TV in Canada has been the biggest disappointment of the decade. It was created in response to political pressure from the Liberal government in the form of a ministerial speech announcing its inevitability (Sauvé,

1976). Before it was approved it was promoted as the great new wonder with sufficient profit to carry along culturally valuable Canadian production with appropriate production values. It was to be a vehicle to allow Canadian production to take its place in domestic and international markets. However, many of the licensed companies have gone under. Those that have not are struggling to stay alive.

The situation was almost entirely predictable. In fact, to a degree it was predicted in a submission to the CRTC by the pay TV applicants on September 8, 1981 (Lyman, p. 83). The CRTC essentially created a situation where national and regional licences were pitted against each other. Because (a) penetration rates were lower than expected, and (b) profitability was dependent on penetration rates, and (c) Canadian program production was contingent on profits, none of the licensees has been in a position to fund appropriately any amount of Canadian production. The sector is falling into the traditional Canadian role, that of being a conduit for American programming.

Lyman argues that pay TV could have been a key sector in providing sufficient budgets to turn Canadian productions into productions of international calibre. Through pay TV Canada had a chance to bring in foreign programming on terms as favourable to Canada as possible. Pay TV was in a good position because it was capable of being regulated and because it could have acted as a central purchasing source rather than a fragmented purchaser.

If one national service had been approved, pay TV could have served these purposes. That service would have then been in a position to pull out all stops to gain market penetration. It could have commissioned Canadian productions at appropriate levels and acted as a pump primer to energize Canadian program pro-

ducers into seeking foreign co-producers. On the basis of its purchasing it could have then acted to find a place for Canadian production in the foreign markets from which it acquired programs.

But in fact pay TV is as weak a link as private broadcasting in the cultural industrial development of Canada. As the situation is, its market penetration is of insufficient size to provide for much bargaining power even within Canada for good rates with the monopoly cable companies, who add on nearly 50 per cent of the price charged by the pay TV companies to distribute the service. It is subject to supplier pressures for up-front payments, for film packages as opposed to individual films (for instance, two losers and two so-so's for every good movie to be purchased), for high prices, and so on. Most importantly, pay TV is losing out to home communication components, unregulated videocassette and videodisc sales, and rental shops that are vulnerable to eventual control by the production majors as well as to satellite receiving dishes. It is to the unregulated sector that we now turn.

HOME COMMUNICATION COMPONENTS: THE CULTURAL JOKER

If desired, the power of a satellite can be increased to the point where the costs of individual receiving dishes are lower than cable redistribution on the ground. At this point the satellite is referred to as a Direct Broadcast Satellite (DBS) and the possibility for regulation weakens, especially in southern Canada where spillover signals from American satellites are certain to be present. However, it is much less costly to the public purse and to business to have a lower-powered satellite that requires a fairly expensive receiving dish and therefore encourages distribution in dense areas by cable. In this case the increased costs of receiving signals are passed on to the consumer.

The cultural significance of a satellite-to-cable system is that it can be licensed and therefore regulated. The licensing and regulatory processes acquire their cultural power by being in a position to demand certain conditions of the licensee, whether the licensee is a broadcaster, cable operator, or pay TV company. Those conditions, if enforced, can aid major program purchasers to negotiate entry of Canadian programming into foreign markets. Obviously the stronger the licensee, given the proper regulatory structure, the more power that licensee has in working to benefit Canadian programming.

The potential cultural (through economic) power, which can be a part of a regulated system, is lost when purchasing power is spread out among many individual buyers. This is exactly what happens with videocassettes, videodiscs, software for personal computers, interactive video games, videotex and teletext, digital audio, and most other home communications components. Take, for example, videocassettes. Videocassettes are now rented or bought through a myriad of video shops equivalent to record and book stores. These stores, unless anti-combines legislation prevents it, will eventually be controlled by the major producers of video materials, probably the major motion picture production and distribution conglomerates.

There is little hope that the proprietors of these stores can be persuaded to stock a certain percentage of Canadian materials. Their position is the same as the chain book stores and record stores, which cannot be persuaded to stock anything but the quick sellers that arrive via the normal American product-dominated distribution channels. Nor does government have any power or the private sector any interest in ensuring exchange arrangements, i.e., Canadian product access to the U.S. or other foreign markets in return for foreign product access to the Canadian market. Government has no basis for bargaining except for last resort non-tariff barriers; the private sector has no interest in the matter since it is unlikely to invest in products competitive to its major line of imports.

What little chance Canadian producers have is in direct competition with all other producers. Given the rigidities of the distribution systems, which have shown themselves to be particularly virulent in the American movie industry, the best chance Canadians have is with newly evolving specialty (i.e., non-theatrical) markets where producer-distributor alignments have yet to solidify. Not only should Canadians be able to play some role in the domestic market but they also may be able to gain a foothold in international markets. The only problem with these pan-national specialty markets is that it is more difficult to produce for them from the Canadian hinterland than from the metropolitan production centres where such opportunities are more easily identified.

Should the major producer-distributors decide to go around Canada's weak pay TV system in favour of the shops, they will be able to consolidate the market position of the shops by vertical integration and by the sequencing of releases. Thereby the shops will be placed far ahead of the pay TV channels. In the Vancouver area one of the factors that contributed to the downfall of the ethnic channel, World View, was the importation by the shops of the very movies that World View announced it would be showing. Similar difficulties have faced the surviving pay TV channels, First Choice and Super Channel.

FRONTIERS OF TECHNOLOGY

The various technologies discussed so far are relatively recent, but they are all in place in Canada or elsewhere. Other technologies are finding their way into business markets and, in some cases, the home market. Before we look at these new frontiers a few words about technology itself are necessary.

Technology is capable of structuring markets on the basis of its power as a tool and also because of its design and its allure. The design aspect can be illustrated with satellites. An investment in DBS satellites of the same power and capacity as what the Americans will use will be bound to keep Canadian communications in an add-on relationship to the American system. The use of a different type of satellite will separate our services from theirs. Presumably that would give us more power to direct our own future. But it might also backfire by encouraging Canadians to purchase equipment to receive only American signals directly.

The allure of technology captures both regulators and individual citizens (McNulty, 1988). We are often in danger of spending more on the delivery system than on the content to make the delivery system justifiable, just in order to have the latest and best technology. For example, the per student (note, not per viewer) costs of the Knowledge Network delivery system in British Columbia are astronomical. Costs of that magnitude would be unthinkable in the province's three universities. Yet the allure of satellite distribution of educational services, services not even available on basic cable in the Vancouver area, is there.

New electronic communications technology also has an anti-democratic element to it. More than its centralizing tendency, the emplacement of technology has the potential for creating information have-nots. For example, at one point Lyman discusses whether the CBC might not abandon its microwave system in favour of a satellite-to-cable or satellite-to-local rebroadcast system (STV or Subscription Television). If basic cable does not come free and if it is not universally available this is untenable. Certainly to proceed without universal free cable or its equivalent in services everywhere in Canada would be socially regressive.

But on to the frontiers. One much discussed frontier is in **interactive services**. There continue to be optimistic forecasts for the development of videotex and teletext in spite of a flat demand for such services. *Videotex* allows interaction with a central database that can be continuously updated. *Teletext* allows the selection of items from a certain number of pages that are being continuously broadcast. Neither has been particularly successful in gaining a market, perhaps because the market is too much in flux. Personal computers can also be hooked up to databases and fully interact with them. If widely purchased they will probably eclipse videotex and teletext.

Videogames are also interactive services and have done very well. As Lyman points out, Pac Man outgrossed the top movie *Star Wars* by a factor of almost 2 to 1. Lyman and others believe that videogames are the thin edge of the wedge that will eventually bring us all to fully interactive banking, shopping, and working on a personal computer.

In an increasingly competitive marketplace, government procurements along with other aggregations of demand can produce players capable of participating in world markets. Just as there is a need for a Canadian presence in other cultural industries, there is also a need for Canadian content and creativity in interactive media.

An equally exciting frontier is in **high definition television** (HDTV) and digitalization. HDTV provides a clearer picture by employing 1,125 as opposed to 525 scanning lines. The picture is sufficiently improved to allow projection on an 8.5 x 11-foot screen. High definition television may completely alter the delivery system of movies to theatres as well as change the viability of the theatre itself. Movies may be delivered by satellite for projection after descrambling or decoding. Together with digitalization of sound the home may become a place of very high-quality entertainment.

A CANADIAN RESPONSE TO NEW COMMUNICATIONS TECHNOLOGIES

The traditional response of Canadians to new technology has been "wait and see." When a new technology comes along we have watched what the Americans have done with it and then once they seem to have mastered it, we include it in our communications environment. The problem with this approach is that it leads to our being a passive market for American cultural products while we attempt, mostly in vain, to secure a place in our own market via protectionist measures.

In the present circumstances, with communications increasingly free to cross borders, we can no longer afford to wait. Lyman asserts that if we were to enter the programming market for any of the new services on a competitive basis we would win our share of the market. We would have to use all our power both as producers and purchasers, as well as our training and understanding of the media and production for the media. However, were we to undertake this with determination we would be in a far better position than if we took our usual "wait-and-see" attitude.

Our combination private/public system places us at considerable advantage. The CBC can be used as an instrument for the development of technology, programming, delivery, co-production, and so forth. We might even set up a high definition television service to transmit by satellite to the U.S. as a pay service for their cable systems. Again, at the least we can expect to improve our balance of payments in entertainment. As a public body the CBC can take on the necessary research and development for all of Canada. The resulting techniques and technology, having been underwritten by the taxpayer, can then be transferred to the private sector (as is customary with these things) for maximum economic if not cultural benefit.

NEW TECHNOLOGIES AROUND THE WORLD: SATELLITES AS A CASE STUDY

Until this point we have explored the significance of new communications technologies from a rather narrow context. First, we have concentrated our attention on Canada. Second, we have examined new technologies from a cultural-industrial context with emphasis on television-based services. In the present section we will look at one central technology, satellite systems as they are being advanced around the world, in an overview largely based on a special issue of *Communication Research Trends*, 4, 2 (1983).

Satellite systems are now being used extensively throughout the developed world and in some parts of the developing world. There are private business satellite systems and national satellite systems sometimes owned by the state, at other times owned jointly by business and the state. Other satellite systems are owned by global consortia and are designed to be used by member nations who pay a fee on the basis of use.

TABLE 11.6

Recent Communications Satellite Launches*

1985

Date	Launcher	Payload	Comments
8 February	Ariane-3(V12)	1 Arabsat-F1 2 Brasilsat-1	Arab States Embratel (Brazil)
March	Atlas	1 Intelsat VA-B	Comsat
7 March	Shuttle/Challenger (51E)	1 Anik-C1 2TDRS-B	Telesat Canada: unsold satellite NASA (US): Tracking and Data Relay Satellite (TDRS): Mission cancelled
19 March	Shuttle/Discovery (51D)	1 Syncom IV-3	NASA (US)/US universities
April	Atlas	1 Intelsat VA-C	Comsat (US)
April	Ariane-3 (V13)	1 G-Star-1B 2 Spacenet-3	GTE (US) GTE (US)
30 April	Shuttle/Challenger (51B)	1 Spacelab-3	European Space Agency (ESA)
30 May	Shuttle/Discovery (51G)	1 Morelos-A 2 Arabsat-A 3 Telstar-3D	Mexico Arab States AT&T (US)
July	Ariane-1 (V14)	1 Giotto	ESA space probe for Halley's Comet
9 July	Shuttle/Challenger (51F)	1 Spacelab-2	ESA (Europe)
August	Ariane-3 (V15)	1 Telecom-1B 2SBTS-2 or ECS-3	DGT/CNES (France) Embratel (Brazil) Eutelsat (Europe)
August	Atlas	1 Intelsat VA-D	Comsat(US)

1986

Date	Launcher	Payload	Comments
January	Ariane-3 (V18)	1 G-Star-1A 2 SBTS or ECS-3	GTE (US) Embratel (Brazil) Eutelsat
16 January	Shuttle/Challenger (61D)	1 Spacelab-4	NASA (US)/ESA (Europe)/European universities
February	Ariane-2 (V19)	1 Intelsat V (F14)	Comsat (US)
February	H-1	1 Experimental Geodetic Satellite	NASDA (Japan): test flight for H-1 launch vehicle
6 March	Shuttle/Columbia (61E)	1 STC-DBS-B	Satellite Telecommunications Company (US)
April	Ariane-2 (V20)	1 Intelsat V (F15) or TV-Sat	Comsat (US) Deutsche Forschungs- und Versuchsanstalt für Luft und Raumfahrt (DFVLR) (Germany FR)
May	Ariane-2 (V21)	1 Intelsat V (F15) or TV-Sat	Comsat (US) DFVLR (Germany FR)
15 May	Shuttle/Challenger (61F)	1 Ulysses	NASA (US)/ESA (Europe)
21 May	Shuttle/Atlantis (61G)	1 Galileo	NASA (US)/BMFT (Germany FR): space probe to Jupiter
June	Ariane-3 (V22)	1 Aussat 2 Flight opportunity	Aussat (Australia)

Date	Launch Vehicle	Satellite(s)	Operator / Notes
August	Atlas	1 NOAA-G	US National Oceanic and Atmospheric Administration (NOAA): meteorology
2 August	Shuttle/Discovery (51I)	1 Aussat-1 / 2 ASC-1 / 3 Syncom IV-4	Aussat (Australia) / American Satellite Corporation / US Navy
September	N-II-7	1 BS-2B	NASDA/NHK (Japan)
September	Ariane-2 (V16)	1 Intelsat V (F13) or Spot-Viking	Comsat (US) / SPOT Image: remote sensing (France)
October	Delta	1 GOES-G	NOAA (US): meteorology
9 October	Shuttle/Columbia (61A)	1 Spacelab-D1	Bundesministerium für Forschung und Technik (BMFT): (Germany FR)
November	Ariane-1 (V17)	1 Intelsat V (F13) or Spot-Viking	Comsat (US) / SPOT Image: remote sensing (France)
1 November	Shuttle/Challenger (61B)	1 Morelos-B / 2 Satcom-Ku-1 / 3 Aussat-2	Mexico / RCA Americom (US) / Aussat (Australia)
27 November	Atlantis (51L)	1 Palapa BR-2 / 2 TDRS-D	Indonesia: relaunch of lost satellite retrieved from useless orbit in November 1984 / NASA (US): TDRS
December	Atlas	1 Fitsatcom	US Navy
20 December	Shuttle/Columbia (61C)	1 Satcom-Ku-2 / 2 Westar-7	RCA Americom (US) / Western Union (US)

Date	Launch Vehicle	Satellite(s)	Operator / Notes
23 June	Shuttle/Columbia (61H)	1 Palapa-B3 / 2 STC-DBS-A / 3 Skynet-4A	Indonesia Satellite Telecommunications Company (US) / Ministry of Defence (UK)
July	Ariane 4 or Ariane 2 (V23)	1 AR-401 / 1 TdF-1	ESA (Europe): test flight / Télédifusion de France (France)
17 July	Shuttle/Challenger (61I)	1 Insat-1C / 2 Intelsat VI-1	India / Comsat (US)
8 August	Shuttle/Atlantis (61J)	1 Hubble Space Telescope	NASA (US)/ESA (Europe)
September	Ariane 4 or Ariane 2 (V24)	1 AR-401 / 1 TdF-1	ESA (Europe): test flight / TdF (France)
September	N-II-8	1 MOS-1	NASDA (Japan): marine observation satellite
3 September	Shuttle/Columbia (61K)	1 Spacelab-1	NASA (US): reflight of technical pallet mission
15 September	Shuttle/Challenger (61L)	1 ASC-2 / 2 A-DOD / 3 Satcom-Ku-3	American Satellite Corporation (US) / Department of Defense (US) / RCA Americom (US)
20 October	Atlas (71A)	1 TDRS-C	NASA (US): TDRS
November	Ariane-3 (V25)	1 SBS-5 / 2 Flight opportunity	Satellite Business Systems (US) / -
4 November	Shuttle/Columbia (71B)	1 G-Star	GTE (US)
15 December	Atlas (71D)	1 DOD / 2 Skynet-4B	Department of Defense (US)

*This table reflects launches anticipated at time of original publication. In fact, many of them did not take place.

SOURCE: *InterMedia*, 13, 2 (March, 1985).

To take some examples, INTELSAT is a global satellite commercial telecommunications network that operates 16 satellites in geostationary orbit above the Atlantic, Pacific, and Indian oceans. These satellites link 375 earth stations in 140 countries. The major investors of the 106 member nations are the U.S., Britain, France, West Germany, Japan, and Canada. Together they hold just over 50 per cent of the shares. The technical success and efficiency of INTELSAT have been based on sticking strictly to its commercial function (Snow, 1980). In spite of this success, Luyken (1984) argues that INTELSAT serves the interest of the developed countries in the design of the pathways while countries in outlying regions are rarely linked to one another. Consistent with the history of the design of international communications systems that we outlined in Chapter 9, INTEL-SAT serves the dominant economic interests. In addition, costs of using the system, although intended to be equitable, are still a major barrier to participation by Third World countries.

The second type of satellite system or network is the national, and in some cases regional, satellite. The U.S. has a bevy of them, Canada has its Aniks, Indonesia has its own (Palapa), and a number of other countries, including Brazil, Australia, and India, are working toward or have recently put in place national satellite systems. (Table 11.6 demonstrates how active various countries are around the world.) In addition, nations in geographic proximity are active in the development of satellite systems. Such regions include Scandinavia, various European countries, the Arab countries, African countries, and so forth. In the case of Europe at least three are under consideration or now launched, based on the differing ambitions and interests of the various European nations.

There are two major international issues in the development and use of satellite systems. Both arise, to some degree, out of the technology. The first is the problem of **signal penetration** into countries without their permission, a broader problem than spillover. Spillover consists of signals not really intended for the receiving country. Following a 1971 resolution of the World Administrative Radio Conference for Space Technology (WARC-ST), in 1982 the UN adopted a resolution requiring a nation's prior consent before signals could be aimed at a country. Prior to this resolution the U.S. had argued that there should be no barriers to the "free flow of information." The Third World and the Communist countries had argued for prior consent. Sweden and Canada had put forward a compromise suggesting that countries of a region agree among themselves (Queeney, 1978). It is interesting to note, incidentally, that spectrum allocation was originally assigned to colonizing countries. When various nations gained independence they found themselves to be inheritors of this colonial legacy, a legacy that existed for the convenience of the colonizer rather than the colonized.

The second major technological issue involves **orbit and spectrum sharing**. The problem here is that while equitable access to geostationary orbits and the radio spectrum should be granted, especially in the case of the latter, many nations are not in a position to use what they might be allotted. Anthony Smith (1980) reports that at the 1977 meeting of WARC on spectrum allocation the United States had a contingent of engineers able to evaluate each decision on the basis of engineering studies already conducted. Clearly, these engineers were in an excellent position to take care of U.S. interests, while many other countries lacked the necessary resources to look out for their own interests.

Rothblatt (1981) argues that an engineering approach ought to be taken to orbit/spectrum resource-sharing. This would allow countries such as the U.S. to use the allotments of other countries until they are in a position to use them. At that time the U.S. would be obligated to come to an agreement on use. It is difficult to see how such a proposal benefits any country other than the developed countries and especially the U.S. Part of Rothblatt's argument is based on the notion that in due course orbit-sharing will be less of a problem. What may ameliorate the scarcity of orbital sites is the presence of geostationary platforms composed of large computer/communications systems capable of providing a multitude of communication and information services simultaneously to a great number of users.

How Is the Development of Satellite Systems Justified?

As mentioned in a previous chapter, communications services are customarily justified in humanitarian terms. In fact, the rhetoric usually expresses a long-rejected view of communications as a strategy for development. That view is the general and vague assumption that modernization on a Western industrialized model will promote economic and social development, a view we found extremely limited if not entirely incorrect in Chapter 9. As a major element of the modern world, the mass media are seen to be strategic in such a modernization program.

One example of such a set of assumptions was in the Satellite Instructional Television Experiment (SITE) undertaken by India, using an American satellite. Some 2,338 rural villages scattered across India received four hours of programming daily. The objectives of SITE were:

- to contribute to family planning,
- to improve agricultural practice,
- to contribute to national integration,
- to contribute to school and adult education and to teacher training,
- to improve occupational skills, health, and hygiene.

As might have been predicted, some success was obtained in achieving the goals that involved the transmission of information. However, little restructuring of social relations or behaviour was observed.

Another example of development rhetoric was found in deliberations over the development of AUSSAT, the Australian national satellite launched in 1985. The major feature of the satellite was to be a "Homestead and Community Broadcast Satellite Service." While that was certainly the justification used for persuading the taxpayers of the value of the satellite, there is little doubt that the major beneficiaries are businesses operating across Australia. Indeed, as launch date approached, benefits to remote homesteads and communities, such as interactive services, seemed to become increasingly problematical because they would be money-losing ventures.

In the case of the Scandinavian satellite NORDSAT, once Nordic electronic and aerospace firms realized that the satellite might become a vehicle for their participation in the space equipment market, the cultural intent of the satellite was eclipsed.

Implications

As noted with SITE, satellites may be used in passing on information to communities in a position to receive them. However, even in that general instance there is a built-in bias. The question rarely asked is what are the information needs of various target populations that satellite systems or any other new technology is supposed to benefit. This question, if asked at all, is usually answered within an ideology of democratic equality and an assumption of upward and geographic mobility, especially for young people. As we argued in Chapter 10, the truth of the matter is that hinterland people are transformed by the information of the centre (rather than having had initial need of it). On the other hand, the businesses of the centre very much do need information about the hinterlands. Satellite systems are just another communications device biased toward the collection of information from the hinterlands for the centre. They certainly are not biased toward serving the limited information needs of the hinterland. When hinterland needs are served, it is often through the indirect route of enabling large metropolitan operators to extend their services to the hinterland.

This bias toward the centre was clearly observable in the operations of PEACESAT, a Pacific Rim satellite experiment reported on in a Master's thesis by Chris Plant at Simon Fraser University. Using an American satellite, 17 countries in and around the Pacific Ocean were linked. One of the founding principles of the experiment was that there would be equal access for member countries. Plant's results show that Honolulu and Wellington (New Zealand) used 54 per cent of the air time, initiated 67 per cent of exchanges, chaired 75 per cent of the exchanges, and accounted for 80 per cent of the messages. U.S. nationals accounted for 40 per cent of the air time. Caucasians dominated over Pacific Islanders by a factor of four to one. The point is that even in this experimental setting, a setting designed to encourage equality and not oriented to business, equality was hardly achieved. Beyond the bias of the technology

(the U.S. and New Zealand were used as bridges), surely its shortfall is attributable to the differing types of information needed by those at the centre and those in the relative hinterlands around the Pacific Rim.

Legal Implications

Not only satellite systems but all new communications technologies present a set of legal problems for the global community. Those problems are centred on the issue and law of **copyright**. They are further enmeshed by such issues as what constitutes sovereignty, and what right nations have to license and regulate communication signals of all types coming into their country.

On the matter of copyright the state of affairs is rather messy. Although there are international copyright conventions to which most nations are signatories, specifically the Berne Convention and the Universal Copyright Convention, there are different levels of these conventions, and the levels agreed to by the U.S. and Canada do not deal at all well with technologies that had yet to be invented at the time of their signing. In Canada, specifically, radio-communication has been given the fairly narrow interpretation in the courts as needing to involve electromagnetic waves. This excludes cable and satellite transmission. Similarly, delivery of signals to a multiplicity of private homes has been interpreted not to be "public display" and is therefore not subject to the copyright owner's permission. In the U.S., although there is a broader definition of public display, cable carriers become exempt if they are passive carriers of signals engaged in secondary transmission (the movement of a signal from point A to point B). Much the same principle holds for satellites. Copyright becomes a consideration only when the satellite is a DBS intended to be used by an audience. If the satellite signals are to be redistributed by a cable company the satellite owner becomes exempt but the cable company pays copyright fees.

As Hylton and Mann (1983) point out, this is hardly satisfactory. They propose a set of general principles that should be used in updating copyright law.

1. As a general rule copyright owners should be entitled to remuneration for any electronic dissemination of their works according to the actual reach of the audience receiving such works. How the public views the material should not matter, nor should the directness of the transmission, the nature of the signal (i.e., broadcast versus cable or satellite signal), or from what source payment is made.

2. Copyright owners should not be entitled to receive duplicate remuneration in respect of the communication of their works to a single audience.

3. The need to avoid duplication liability to copyright owners, and the interest of the public in obtaining access to a wide range of programming, may make it necessary to provide limited exceptions to the right of copyright owners to control satellite communication of their works.

4. The principle relating to copyright liability must be considered in the context of other regulatory issues relating to satellite communications.

Sovereignty, which includes the right of nations to control their own information environment, is also facing a major challenge by new communications technologies. For example, in Europe where there is an extensive spillover of satellite signals, major efforts are being made to conform to the regulations of the various countries. Different countries have different regulations, especially with regard to advertising. Without some kind of accord, "border stations" (i.e., stations set up in one country to take advantage of immunity to the laws of the country in which its target market is located) would abound and introduce international friction. Similarly, difficulties are arising over the flow of data across borders because that flow is transmitted on privately owned satellite networks such as Satellite Business Systems. At both the national and international levels, problems are also being created. With geostationary platforms on the horizon, distinctions that are often the basis of regulation and spectrum allocation – such as between fixed, broadcasting, maritime, common carrier, domestic, international – are becoming next to impossible to make. Such challenges are being addressed daily by the International Telecommunications Union. Canada has a special role to play in these issues because it is a close neighbour to the nation that is most aggressive in pursuing its rights to distribute information broadly and charge for the privilege of receiving it.

COMMUNICATIONS AND CULTURE

We omitted from our discussion of satellite-to-cable distribution in Canada one example of a satellite-based system, Cancom. In a sense, it is the most sensible use of a satellite that has yet emerged. At the same time it is the one system that clearly brings forward cultural considerations that are in conflict with economic considerations.

Cancom, more or less, is cable in the sky. Cancom is licensed to carry four conventional channels and eight radio superstation services to remote and under-served communities and is funded by a basic fee per month. These services are delivered by satellite (Anik D) to local communities. From there they are redistributed to individual households by cable or rebroadcast transmitter. To some degree Cancom was licensed to counteract the illegal reception of U.S. television services. More recently, the CRTC has changed its regulations, which will allow Cancom to participate in the major urban markets in Canada. This ruling will certainly threaten local stations if not all stations for their market share.

The original market for Cancom consisted of approximately 450,000 households scattered across Canada (see Figure 11.3). The Cancom package has a selection of American network programming found on three English-language Canadian stations plus the Canadian programming of these three stations. Cancom has begun to draw away households already receiving programs by American satellite primarily because the American satellite services only include American pay TV services and none of the networks. The licence puts Cancom in a good position to take advantage of new television service directions in Canada, including:

- developing Canadian superstations,
- becoming a major carrier for the U.S. networks,
- becoming a major carrier for pay TV,
- gaining access to the U.S. market by packaging Canadian programming for U.S. audiences,
- developing new Canadian cable-to-satellite services for urban areas.

Lyman looks forward to a rosier future for Canadians as a result of Cancom. It has become even rosier since Lyman wrote his book because of the opening to Cancom of the major urban markets. But it is a rosy *economic* picture, not a rosy *cultural* picture. In Chapters 9 and 10 we discussed at some length the politics of information systems and their bias toward the centre and against the interests of the periphery.

Cancom will bombard rural, semi-rural, and small-town Canada with a plethora of American and Canadian urban-generated programs and advertising that will portray the lives, concerns, dreams, hopes, fears, and products of the city. True, Cancom subscribers will be in touch with "the world" as it is portrayed in the sports, drama, sitcoms, etc. of nightly television fare. But how will that fare actually improve their quality of life? They will identify more closely with the city, but what good will that do them? What good will that do us as a nation? This does not imply that such a service will do them no good, but rather that we do not know how such services will change the orientation of rural and small-town living in Canada. (Laba, 1988, has addressed this issue in a more general context.) Maybe the changes will be insignificant because they will be "more of the same." Maybe not.

The issue becomes slightly more disturbing when we consider native communities. There, as we pointed out in Chapter 10, and as Valaskakis (1988) has documented, the most significant element of enhanced communications services is the transformation of a way of life in conflict with urban, white cultural values. If we consider that small-town and native Canada comprise cultures distinct from urban Canada, and if we value those differences, we must slide past the economic question and ask the more profound cultural question: what will Cancom do for Canada?

TECHNOLOGY AND OTHER CULTURAL INDUSTRIES

This chapter has focused on television-based developments and services. This does not mean that other cultural industries are unaffected by technology. Indeed, in other chapters and in the final chapter of this book that is

FIGURE 11.3 Cancom's Potential Market

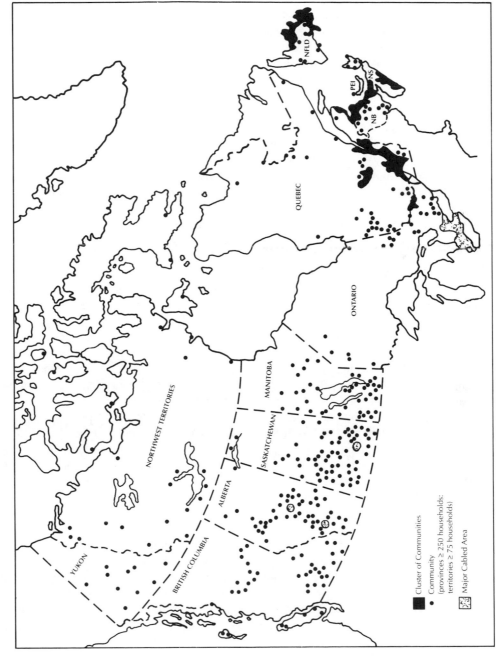

SOURCE: CRTC application by Orbitel Communications Company of Canada Inc. (Cancom).

made apparent. As we noted in the chapters dealing with the geopolitics of communication, technology in general is developed in response to dominant interests and the form of technology that is developed advances those interests. In book publishing, movie production, and even such areas as theatre, dance, opera, and figure skating, technology is pulling continually to the "massification" of markets. As individuals we benefit greatly from a wider distribution of items of quality, but as members of a relatively small and fragile culture we are in danger of becoming extinct.

SUMMARY

This chapter has outlined the dimensions and some of the specifics of change that are being brought about through the development of new communications technologies. New technologies are changing the structure of the communications environment. As that structure changes, old industries and regulations are being placed in jeopardy while new opportunities are emerging. It is important that we understand the nature of these changes so that Canada and Canadians participate as fully as possible in the new communications environment.

On the basis of what we have reviewed here and what has been written more broadly on the subject, a strategy can be developed that would seem capable of working for the benefit of the Canadian industry and Canadians as a whole. The practicality of the matter is another issue. As we mentioned, not only are certain interests within the industry in conflict with such a national strategy, but also foreign producers will be sure to act vigorously to protect their share of the Canadian market.

A parallel exploration of these issues has been created in a set of three papers by Edwards (1988), Strick (1988), and Overduin (1988). Edwards focuses on a national policy for development in telematics or computer communications. Strick analyses the opportunities a free market will present for Canadians in the development of satellites and associated telecommunications technologies. Overduin discusses the interaction between professional roles and technological opportunities. As a group they are a useful supplement to this chapter.

With respect to the material presented in this chapter, in spite of domestic and foreign competition, it would appear that as a result of a number of different developments, there is a very positive outlook for Canadian independent television producers. The emergence of new buyers with limited capital for program production, CBC cutbacks, and expansion of public funding to independent production through Telefilm Canada are all part of that outlook. In the face of spending estimates of Canadians on entertainment, the federal government seems to have a steady resolve not to allow such consumption to be a continuing drain on the economy.

Ultimately, increased production cannot fail to have some positive cultural benefit for Canadians. However, realizing that benefit will be difficult in an environment that requires that foreign sales always be calculated into the profitability formula.

From a cultural and political perspective the international picture is fraught with difficulties. Foreign cultural products from industrial countries threaten to inundate the globe, whether via satellite signals, legitimate distribution, or pirate operations. While international agreements may be signed to stem the tide to some degree, the general movement in trade is in the opposite direction. That movement will continually work against national cultural interests and in favour of the economic interests of producers. In balance, given Canada's capacity for production, we may neither suffer nor gain culturally from such a situation. Economically, we have a better chance to gain. Larger producers have more to gain while smaller producers have much to lose both economically and culturally.

Domestically, as we illustrated with Cancom, the changes now happening are working toward the increased distribution of centre-produced materials to rural hinterlands. The effects of such increases remain to be seen.

REFERENCES

Canada. *Report of the Task Force on Broadcasting Policy*. Ottawa: Ministry of Supply and Services, 1986.

Communication Research Trends, 4, 2 (1983).

Edwards, L. "Telematics in Canada: The Vanishing Opportunity," in R. Lorimer and D.C. Wilson eds., *Communications Canada*. Forthcoming, 1988.

Hylton, John, and J. Fraser Mann. "International Copyright Agreements and the Need for a New Legal Framework," *Broadcaster* (August, 1983).

Laba, M. "Popular Culture as Local Culture: Regions, Limits, and Canadianism," in R. Lorimer and D.C. Wilson, eds., *Communications Canada*. Forthcoming, 1988.

Luyken, Georg-Michael. "New Communications Technology and Global Information Handling," in J. Slack and F. Frejes, eds., *The Ideology of the Information Age*. Norwood, N.J.: Ablex, forthcoming.

Lyman, Peter. *Canada's Video Revolution*. Toronto: James Lorimer, 1983.

McNulty, Jean. "Ideas about Technology and Nation-Building in Canadian Broadcasting," in R. Lorimer and D.C. Wilson, eds., *Communications Canada*. Forthcoming, 1988.

Overduin, H. "Westex News: A Case Study of an Experiment into Journalism of the Future," in R. Lorimer and D.C. Wilson, eds., *Communications Canada*. Forthcoming, 1988.

Plant, Christopher. "PEACESAT and Development in the Pacific Islands" (M.A. thesis, Simon Fraser University, 1980).

Queeney, Kathryn M. *Direct Broadcast Satellites and the United Nations*. Alphen aan den Rijn: Sijthoff and Noordhoff, 1978.

Rothblatt, Martin A. "International Orbit Spectrum/Spectrum Development Policy and the Growth of Geostationary Satellite Communications," *Journal of Media Law and Practice*, 12, 2 (September, 1981).

Sauvé, J. "Notes for a speech to the Canadian Cable Association," Toronto, June 2, 1976.

Smith, Anthony. *The Geopolitics of Information*. London: Faber and Faber, 1980.

Snow, Marcellus S. "INTELSAT: An International Example," *Journal of Communications*, 30, 2 (Spring, 1980).

Strick, J.C. "Socio-Economic Influence of Satellite Communications Technology," in R. Lorimer and D.C. Wilson, eds., *Communications Canada*. Forthcoming, 1988.

Valaskakis, G. "Television and Cultural Integration," in R. Lorimer and D.C. Wilson, eds., *Communications Canada*. Forthcoming, 1988.

STUDY QUESTIONS

1. New communications technologies are continually being developed and introduced. What factors tend to influence their introduction in Canada? Refer to specific technologies in your answer.

2. "Underpinning all the media and communications systems in general is the technological base. The creation of new technology, its management, and its distribution are the ultimate tests of modern power and the ability to dominate." (H. Schiller) Discuss this statement.

3. Does Canada need communications satellites?

CHAPTER

12

Canada in an Information Age

INTRODUCTION

THROUGHOUT this book we have outlined how communication, information, and the media play a major role in contemporary society. Communication is infused in every aspect of our lives, technological forms pattern society, the mass media exist within formal and informal social and legal structures, and the media are a crucial part of the national fabric. In this chapter we turn to a final major question. What is the position of Canada to be as information becomes much more sophisticated, manipulable, and easily distributed? In other words, what is to become of Canada in an information age?

We will address this question by taking up five major areas of debate that bring into play much of the discussion of the previous chapters. These are:

1. Public versus private control in a technologically changing environment;
2. Foreign versus domestic control and production;
3. Industry versus culture as basic to policy;

4. Participation versus professionalization;
5. Education.

PUBLIC VERSUS PRIVATE SECTOR: INFORMATION AS COLLECTIVE PROPERTY

For a very long time, information has had a special status in society. That special status has taken material form in the library. Libraries, as Basil Stuart-Stubbs (1981) has pointed out, are ownership collectives. They are ancient institutions that have been in existence ever since information has been recorded, whether on clay tablets, papyrus, paper, or film. Their collective nature arises from their function: to acquire information that they then lend to others. Libraries are based on the dual notion that an individual cannot own all the information to which he or she may want or need access and that one's access to wealth should not determine one's access to information.

Industrial society carried forward this approach to information. Works that explained technology and industry of the industrial period were written and published. Many found their homes in libraries of workers' organizations. The value of information and of the collective organization necessary for a reasonable level of access by a social group was established.

Public Electronic Information

The public element of information access was carried through to the electronic age, although with some difficulty. Marconi, through patent law, attempted to control the development of radio communication. He leased his radio sets, along with his employees as operators, and refused to let his employees communicate with those using non-Marconi equipment. Only by governments declaring the airwaves to be a public resource was Marconi's grip on radio communication broken. Once this attempted monopoly was broken, and as Fessenden's invention for carrying voice communication was taken up, governments found themselves getting into the business of broadcasting. Only a very few countries, including the United States, decided to let private enterprise rule the airwaves. State-owned radio and television are much more common around the world, even in Western capitalist countries.

Today, however, we are determinedly imposing a monetary value on information, especially when it is in electronic form. Thus, we are placing it much more fully into the hands of private entrepreneurs. The development and employment of electronic communications technology have required vast research and development funds, and the hardware and software, for the most part, are now controlled by private corporations whose reason for existence is profit.

Because of these material realities we are seeing a shift away from the possibility of maintaining public and collective participation in dealing with information. Primarily, this is because producers or their representatives are gaining control over information access (through the creation of databases) rather than users or their representatives (libraries and other social governmental agencies).

Information as a Commodity

It is not that information corporations are pushing their interests on an objecting society. As both Audley's *Canada's Cultural Industries* and Lyman's *Canada's Video Revolution* point out, economists have discovered their oversight of information and culture as economic activities. Governments, too, have initially encouraged this whole sector to expand through their willingness to fund technological research and development in the area.

To the list of those who are promoting the economic recognition of information, i.e., information corporations, economists, and governments, we must also add information workers. Such workers include those on the creative side – artists, singers, composers, writers – and also those on the manipulation or recording side – secretaries, librarians, computer programmers, database managers. These information workers are emerging as a powerful vested interest with a stake in the full economic recognition of information products.

As the full economic value of information is recognized, a public presence becomes increasingly difficult to maintain. This is not just on account of the cries of the private sector to be left to accrue their profits. It arises also from the desire and need to exhaust every market to cover the increased costs of information production. In addition, private control is related to a change in the dominant technology used for the transmission of information.

Technological and Industrial Influences: Print

The difference between working with an older industrial and technological system, i.e., print, and a newer one, film and video, can be illustrated by referring to the development of this book and other material associated with it. In drawing out this contrast we should point out that it would seem that the technologies and the practices surrounding film and video are more attuned to capturing returns in the form of fees and royalties from original production than are the technologies and practices associated with print.

Two chapters of this book were developed primarily from other books on the subjects of those chapters. Chapter 9 was developed from *The Geopolitics of Information* by Anthony Smith just as Chapter 11 was based on Peter Lyman's *Canada's Video Revolution*. In both those chapters the original authors' words were changed but to a great extent the meaning was, and was intended to be, the same. In certain instances new information was added; in other instances ideas were reformulated and changed intentionally.

The work became ours essentially because as an author one of us put the matter in his own words. It became ours as a result of the foundation of copyright law wherein the expression of an idea can be protected but the idea itself cannot. (Copyright law differs from patent law, in which the exact composition of, say, a chemical compound can be protected.) Consequently, had we summarized their work by using the topic sentence of every paragraph, we would have been guilty of plagiarism. We would have infringed on their copyright. On a related point, we need not have made our debt to these authors so obvious. We could have neglected the notes in each chapter acknowledging our debt and only cited them when directly quoting. However, because part of the job of this book is to open the field of communications to those unfamiliar with it we emphasized the contributions of those authors.

Techno-Industrial Influences: Video

Quite a different situation presents itself in the video materials available to complement this book. There is no way we could have reconstructed programs such as *The Press and the Prime Minister*, *Inside TV News*, and *Magic in the Sky*. First, there are the economic and creative realities of video production. To match the production values and the treatment provided in these programs was beyond our budget and certainly would have taxed our every creative ability. Second, each of these programs has captured footage now impossible to obtain for which we would have had to purchase rights, presuming that those rights would have been purchaseable. Consequently, we purchased the rights to broadcast these whole programs in British Columbia, the first province in which the book and video materials were used together. The original "authors," that is, the copyright holders, maintained the copyright and collected the royalties.

We, in turn, made several programs, mostly composed of original footage but also containing clips from other sources, for which we acquired rights. In some cases our requests were denied or the fees were too high and we found ourselves having to overlook certain examples that were historically salient. Such a situation is anathema to print scholarship but is a market reality in electronic communications. One can only compensate by inserting verbal descriptions to replace graphic examples. But that is rather like trying to appreciate the *Mona Lisa* without ever having seen it or any reproduction of it.

One other problem arose both with the programs we attempted to acquire and with the clips we acquired for use in our programs. This problem would not have arisen had we been dealing with print materials. In asking for permission to broadcast some of the above-mentioned whole programs, we were at first stymied by the inability of the producers to grant us those rights. In each case this difficulty arose from the fact that they had used footage from other sources to construct their programs. In obtaining that footage they had not made clear their intent to sell the program to other broadcasters for use. Thus, they were forced to go back to the contributors and get permis-

sions. In our own case, in numerous instances involving commercial material, we were granted permission for use only if we restricted our distribution to the educational sector in Canada. Therefore, we ended up in a position where we could not sell the programs to the CBC or PBS unless we were to return to the source of the materials and to the original artists, unions, etc. to pay them in order to gain a higher level of clearance. The contract on the following page (Figure 12.1) illustrates the nature of the agreement we entered into to gain access to certain material.

Very easily, the usefulness of the programs others had made and the feasibility of our program could have been spoiled by the inability to gain permissions or to pay the requisite fees, not to mention lawyers' charges for tracking down the people involved. As it was, we had to delete one sequence in *Magic in the Sky* that contained the standard introductory segment to the Sunday night Disney television program because someone did not or could not obtain permission for it to be used. (The segment has Tinkerbell flitting around the Disney castle lighting it up with glints. See how print works in contrast to video!)

The Implications of Original Ownership

The ownership of original material is more significant than it might at first seem. Today, much of the international footage used by the CBC and CTV is fed from the American networks. It is based on an exchange with the condition that what is collected by the Americans cannot be released for use by the Canadians to others, and vice versa. This means that any program that is a commentary on Canadian news, which uses footage from Canadian news programs, for example on how the CBC covers

FIGURE 12.1

FILM FOOTAGE/CLIP AGREEMENT

Date: May 3, 1985

Licensor: The Collection Administrators ^C/o Eagle/Cine-Circle Prods.
                         2230 Hillsboro Avenue, Los Angeles, CA 90034

Licensee: Simon Fraser University ^C/o Dr. Martin Laba + Dr. R. Lorimer
                         Dept. of Communications, Burnaby, Brit. Col. V5A1S6
                         Western Video Co. 30 E 6th Ave, Vancouver, B.C. V5T164(David Baker)
Footage/Clip Description:

                               One clip of Chuck Berry singing "Maybellene"
                               from Hollywood A Go Go #16.
Name of Production:

                         SFU ROCKS
Permitted Use of Footage/Clip:
                               To be used only in the academic video course
                         of study which will be carried by The Knowledge Network,
                         a non-profit, gov't and/or public funded cable TV station.

Permitted Term of Use: 10 years

License Fee: Twenty-Five Dollars ($25.00) U.S.
(All reproduction, handling and shipping charges will be paid by Licensee.)

   Subject to the provisions hereof, Licensor hereby grants to Licensee, without warranty,
a non-exclusive and non-transferable license to use said footage/clip in the production
described above, but only for the purposes hereinabove set forth. This license is granted
on the following terms and conditions:

   1. Licensee will not make any reproduction of or from the footage/clip whatsoever, in
whole or in part, except for the use in connection with the production herein described.

   2. Licensee represents, warrants and agrees that it will obtain all required author-
izations, consents and releases and pay all re-use fees necessary for the use of the footage/
clip hereunder, including, but not limited to, consents from any copyright owners and from
all guilds and unions to the extent required under applicable collective bargaining agreements; and that if any music is included in the footage/clip, as used hereunder, Licensee
will obtain all necessary music synchronization, mechanical and performing rights from the
copyright proprietors of such music and such other persons, firms, associations, societies,
corporations and/or record companies as may own or control any rights and/or recordings hereto.

   3. Licensee will indemnify Licensor, and its agents, employees and representatives, and
save and hold them harmless of and from any and all loss, cost, damage, liability and expense
including attorneys' fees, arising out of any claim whatsoever which may be brought based
upon Licensee's use of said footage/clip hereunder. Licensee further acknowladges that a
breach by Licensee of any of its representations, warranties or undertakings hereunder will
cause Licensor irreparable damage, which cannot be readily remedied in damages in an action
at law, and may, in addition thereto, entitle Licensor to equitable remedies, costs and
attorney's fees.

                                        The Collection Administrators

                                        By _____

Agreed to and Accepted

By _____

international events, must obtain permission from the U.S. networks to use that material. Indeed, this is just what we had to do. Of the three U.S. networks only CBS would give us that permission for a fee we could afford – not what one would call a terribly free flow!

In addition, what Canadians can reliably export in terms of television material is only that which they collect themselves, unless, of course, they receive permission from the original producers to use their material as part of a Canadian product. While such permission might be forthcoming, in some cases this cannot be relied on, and in many cases it might be in the interest of the original producers to try to sell their own product in the same market in which the Canadian product was being offered.

But why worry about exports? And how do these developments jeopardize the public involvement in information dissemination? On exports, as Chapter 11 points out, one reasonable strategy for the survival of a Canadian production industry is to sell to more than one market. Without sales to multiple markets the production values of domestic programming will be insufficient to command audiences and therefore advertisers or subscribers. Without advertisers or subscribers there will not be enough money to produce good programs. It is a vicious circle broken only by operating in anticipation of sales outside the domestic market.

Public Involvement in Production

With increasing pressure on program producers to exploit all markets, the distinctive, national cultural orientation of programming, which forms the basis of public subsidy, becomes difficult to maintain. Once markets are exploited after the fact of production, potential sales to known markets soon become a consideration in the conception of what should be produced. When subsidiary markets are vastly larger than domestic, primary markets, productions must be oriented as much to subsidiary markets as to primary domestic markets. Over the past several years we have seen this phenomenon in action in Canada's feature film industry. Canadian producers cannot seem to find a way to serve the cultural interests of the Canadian market and at the same time economically exploit the U.S. and other foreign markets.

In the face of these changing realities the justification for public support of such productions must inevitably shift. It can no longer be found solely in the content because the content must be attractive to foreign audiences. Why should Canadian taxpayers be supporting an effort designed, at least in part, to please foreign audiences? The justification must therefore be found in the notion of supporting a growing industry that will develop Canadian talent, bring in needed foreign currency, and prevent Canadians from spending all their entertainment dollars on foreign products.

Once the major justification for public support has shifted to industrial support, one must then wonder why a public corporation, i.e., the CBC, should be involved in this enterprise as a major player. Since the central concern is industrial development, surely, the argument goes, private enterprise should be the key player. Because the economics of survival require taking advantage of every possible sales opportunity, not a cultural concern at all, surely, the argument goes, the action should be in the hands of the private entrepreneurial sector. Perhaps a much more limited role should be assumed by the CBC, somewhat along the lines of a research and development organ as was proposed by the Applebaum-Hébert

Report (1982). Or maybe CBC should be sent along the same path as the National Film Board (NFB) to become a research and training institution.

Public Involvement in Consumption

Public involvement in consumption is also threatened. The ease of transforming a printed work from one form into another through reading and rewriting means that the library is only mildly threatening to author/producers. True, it means that the author does not receive the same level of royalties. But it is almost as if the power of the author is to be found in the extent to which his or her ideas are used and transformed by readers. There is also the tradition of the industry and associated information institutions, which stands in the way of a more assiduous accounting in payments to authors. To some extent these issues have been addressed in other countries and are currently being addressed in Canada through legislation giving recognition to "public lending right." Such payment is a form of royalty, which goes to authors for allowing their books to be lent out by the library.

However, when material can be easily copied virtually in its original form, and very cheaply, as with software, videotapes, audiotapes, etc., and when that material comes from an industry accustomed to a high level of return for its products and with a tradition wherein its products have been deemed non-essential, producers are going to be much more reluctant to see public institutions lending out materials for multiple public use and probable copying. There is little doubt that items such as records are copied on home recorders when they are borrowed from libraries. Producers may well ask why this should be allowed to happen and why they and the general public should subsidize this activity, especially when there is no disincentive to copy as there is with the book (photocopies cannot be bound very handsomely).

At some point, as the variety of communications items expands, the public role in the consumption process should come up for review. However, if television sets can be declared necessities of life, as they are in the U.S. where they are unremovable by bailiffs, then what items of information could be said to be "entertainment" (implying that they are frills) as opposed to "necessary information"? To deprive members of a society of universal access to their symbols may be a self-destructive step. It may even contravene the Universal Declaration of Human Rights.

Neither should the technology factor be underplayed. While technology cannot be said to be entirely responsible for a change in the structure of the use and exploitation of information, it does make a major contribution to the way information is used and distributed. Thus, when the use of new technologies is considered for recording and disseminating information not created for profit but for audiences who can use and transform it, e.g., scholarly information, we must be very wary of shifts in the technology. (See Lorimer, 1985; Stuart-Stubbs, 1981.) Were academics working in the public sector and public institutions, foundations, and the like and attempting to gain maximum payment for information they contribute to producing, we might easily see science, technology, and social organization grind to halt.

FOREIGN VERSUS DOMESTIC CONTROL

In a world where every possible ounce of profit is wrung out of every piece of information, the issues of foreign versus domestic *con-*

trol of information and foreign versus domestic *production* of information are pressing economic concerns. They are even more pressing as cultural concerns because, in the competitive struggle of the marketplace, the images and symbols available for consumption, e.g., the golden arches of McDonald's, or the moral superiority of this or that empire, are those that have won out in a mighty economic battle for domination. They are not dominant for political or cultural reasons.

In such a world, for the most part, considerations of the public good disappear. Gone with them, for instance, is the gentlemanly patronage of the publisher, the willingness to undertake a project destined to lose money but somehow seen to be a major contribution to culture and civilization. In its place are innumerable devices, formulae, and vast amounts of money whose primary purpose is to capture large audiences so that, in the case of television, for example, they can be sold to advertisers. The purpose of such sales is to accumulate even vaster amounts of money to be combined with more formulae and devices so that more audiences can be assembled and sold to other advertisers. And when spending money on productions ceases to be a challenge, the accumulated wealth can be used to buy whole media and related companies to capture the dollars of book and newspaper reading audiences, sports fans, department store shoppers, and so the list goes on.

Free Flows, Freely Flowing Information, and Censorship

In earlier chapters we mentioned the notion of free flows of information. As we pointed out, the rhetoric behind the notion sounds noble and fine. All individuals should be free to communicate with all other individuals the world over. It is implicitly or explicitly claimed that in such a way we can achieve a universal brother and sisterhood and thereby world peace. The actualities of free flows are quite different. As we illustrated in Chapter 9, free flows of information mean the right of those who dominate the world information system to continue to dominate that system. This certainly does not mean that information flows freely among all who may want to use it for whatever purpose.

Canada has a certain level of and capacity for media production. But when it comes to the crunch, we are able to do no more than put together a program that concentrates on Canadian-only phenomena as does *The Press and the Prime Minister.* Once we attempt to portray an element of our lives not totally encompassed by our national boundaries, our ability to portray such a reality becomes problematical. For example, with the portrayal of the interaction between the Inuit and the media in *Magic in the Sky* we begin to run into trouble because the Inuit watch American TV. In *Inside TV News,* when we attempt to portray how Canadian news services are designed and operated and what Canadians see, whether on Canadian or American stations, we are muted by our dependency on the American feeds. When such a program as *The Fashionable Image* portrays the craft and activity of Canadian photographer Howard Fry, we are not hampered. But when we attempt to portray the information environment of Canadians, as in *Media Information Canada,* or media-audience interactions, as in *Video, Vinyl & Culture,* we run up against problems of access to illustrative material.

Free flows allow the copyright holder of the material to maintain control over his or her piece of communication and to exploit every possible use and every possible market. What this means is that there is not a free flow of information at all, as we saw with our attempts to acquire programs and bits of material. Rather, those who control information are free to operate solely to their advantage and no one else's. Not everyone in such a position behaves in that way, but they have the legal power to do so, and it is important to remember this.

Alternative Information Management

Matters need not be this way at all. Another system that would respect property rights would be to require that all copyright materials enter the public domain after a specified number of years or showings. A set of compulsory licence fees (fees to be paid to copyright holders that would compel them to make the material available) could be developed for various categories of use. In addition, once a piece of communications material entered a country it could be required that its copyright be held in that country by nationals, thus preventing foreign nationals from controlling what we are able to produce about ourselves.

Bill C-58: Sovereignty or Unfair Dealing?

These issues of foreign control over domestic information are focused, between Canada and the U.S., on Bill C-58. As we noted earlier, Bill C-58 disallows tax deductions of Canadian companies for advertising carried on U.S. border stations. Similarly, it disallows deductions for advertising in U.S. magazines sold in Canada.

Put this way, Canada does appear to be acting unfairly. We seem to be not allowing the American border stations to carry on their business. But the other side of the coin is this: Canada has the right, as does every sovereign nation, to control broadcasting within its

boundaries; all Canadian stations require licences to operate; yet the border stations can operate in complete disregard of Canadian law and regulatory procedure. These border stations are absolutely free, for example, to ignore completely the Broadcasting Code in Canada.

One of the few actions open to Canada in the case of the border stations is to take retaliatory measures by disallowing advertising deductions and retaining the right to interfere with the signals as we so choose once they have been beamed into Canada. The present practice is called **simultaneous program deletion and substitution**. When two identical programs are being broadcast on the same cable system, one originating from a Canadian station and one from a border station, the Canadian station can request that its signal with its advertising be substituted for that of the border station. The idea is to take what Canadians want but to protect Canadian stations from direct competition. Beyond the matter of national sovereignty, the penetration of Canada by foreign television signals and programs is taking away the opportunities from Canadians to make a living from providing similar services.

Now we have both sides of the story. But the matter does not end there. As a May 6, 1985, story in *The Globe and Mail* pointed out in quoting from a participant at the annual meeting of the Association of American Broadcasters, these stations provide a service for advertisers in their attempts to reach Canadian audiences. The article does not carry on to raise another point the border station owners might also want to argue. How can the CRTC on the one hand claim the right to interfere with the signals of the border stations when it licenses cable companies on the other to distribute these signals in Canada? When the signals of the border stations are the basis for the economic health of a key sector of the Canadian communications industry it is a little inconsistent to deny them some right to do business on a footing that takes into account the service they are providing to Canadians and Canadian advertisers. Nonetheless, the principle of sovereignty must be maintained.

Added Complications in New Technologies

With Direct Broadcast Satellites broadcasters need be nowhere near the border to beam their signals into Canada, as we discussed in Chapter 10. Transborder flows are going to become more, rather than less, problematic. As the novelty of satellite communications wears off we can expect to see increasingly persistent attempts to collect royalties from all who receive signals from the satellite even when the signals are "spill-overs." Perhaps broadcasters will follow the lead of PBS and use moral suasion directly on their audiences.

A slightly different but equally perplexing problem is arising in computer communications. When we purchase foreign computer equipment or store our own information in databases outside our country we export jobs and move into a position where the survival of foreign companies that maintain the equipment and those databases becomes part of our interest. Especially with databases, once we have such interests in the survival of foreign companies, supporting a realignment of information management along national lines becomes quite problematic.

Political Ramifications

Such considerations are based in economics. The political ramifications are more crucial. In a time when economic sanctions are frequently used to bring pressure to bear on other countries and when access to information is an integral part of economics, one must be very careful in putting one's own data in the hands of foreign-based companies. American companies may be and often are prevented from trading with certain other nations. Canada may wish and often has wished to remain a trading partner with both the U.S. and a third nation that is out of favour with the American government (Nicaragua is a good case in point). Were there a greater consensus in American opinion, no doubt there would be some harassment of Canadian companies using American databases, even if it were done on the basis of a misunderstanding.

Economic Considerations

Just as there are both economic and cultural issues involved in control, so both types of issues are involved in considerations of foreign versus domestic production. The economic issues are simpler and more straightforward and we have discussed them to some degree in previous chapters.

All predictions suggest that the information economy will expand considerably over the next years. Further, it appears that there will be as large an expansion in business information flows as in flows of entertainment products. Business information will include hardware, software, and database markets while the entertainment side will include hardware and content. The expected Canadian market for hardware alone in 1990 is predicted to be $1,000 million annually. In 1980, Canadian consumers, producers, advertisers, and governments spent $5.4 billion in the publishing, broadcasting, recording, and film markets (Audley, 1983).

With domestic production having a domestic market share in books of 20 per cent, records, 6.8 per cent, theatrical films, 1.8 per cent, and television drama, 4 per cent, obviously such large expenditures on foreign-produced materials are a considerable drain on the economy. With a very minuscule participation in computer hardware and a limited participation in software and databases, the situation cannot get much better. The dramatic possibilities for profit and expansion, the other side of the coin, can be seen in the success of such companies as Northern Telecom and Rogers Cablesystems Inc., both large and successful international companies.

Cultural Implications

The cultural implications are considerably more subtle and complex. The debate over Canadian content in learning materials, radio and television programming, films, books, libraries, and so on has been raging ever since the advent of these technologies and institutions. As the media come to play a greater social and cultural role in our lives, the degree to which Canadian realities are reflected in those media will become ever more important. The matter is simple: the more we consume media images the greater is the importance of those images.

A Crucial Issue: The Culture of Business

The emerging issue is where culture and business intersect, in business communication. If Canadian businesses, unions, professionals, in fact, if Canadians in all walks of life become members of North American (which is to say American) and global (which is, as often as not, to say American) information networks, three problems will emerge.

First, it will be difficult to maintain any distinctiveness at a national cultural level. Such information networks will allow businesses and individuals to distinguish themselves and specialize and operate successfully in a larger market or environment. But they will become distinctive and specialize within the context of the information network as a whole. Providing we do not cripple ourselves with an inadequate education system, as British Columbia is doing currently, the future looks bright, economically, for many Canadians. But within such information networks culture becomes incidental. Culture will be what happens to fall out of the sum total of the choices that Canadians make in the context of the international information networks.

As these information networks produce opportunities for businesses and individuals, an increasing momentum in their use will occur. Their users will see themselves in terms of the organization of information basic to the network. This will result in an increasing difficulty in organizing nationally integrated markets among nationally based producers. That difficulty will arise from a self-vision of individuals and businesses following database structures. It will also arise from a lack of economically viable databases organized on nationally oriented criteria. This, then, is the second problem.

A third problem will be increasing governmental difficulty in serving the interests of Canadians. Because of a government's geographically constrained legitimacy, if it must deal with a majority of individuals and companies whose operations are only fractionally oriented to Canada then its power is that much lessened. The legitimacy of government will be further undermined should a majority of individuals and business be oriented internationally. The thinking and policy of the government, being nationally oriented, will be out of step with that of the majority. Attempts to preserve some national integrity, such as setting up nationally organized databases, will be seen as uneconomic rearguard actions intended to save the politicians' own skins at the ballot box.

Art, Culture, Industry, and Policy

Three bases might be considered for founding communications policy. They are art, culture, and industry. The fact that we tend to emphasize only culture and industry, as George Woodcock, author of *Strange Bedfellows: The State and the Arts in Canada,* might say, shows how far the situation has deteriorated. But he has a rather special notion of culture, as we shall see.

We opened the discussion of a policy base in the first section of this chapter. Here we will start with a consideration of art as a basis for policy. Woodcock's anti-statist quarrel with the involvement of the Canadian state in the arts is one of design and extent. He makes the case that state support in Canada has become politicized. It is no longer arm's-length funding of art for its extrinsic value. All funding to artists outside that given to the Canada Council (and even within the Council there is some difficulty) is now being given for the intrinsic value of art, to achieve the ends of the state through artistic means. Those ends may be to lend a sense of grace to national life or they may be an attempt to extend the power of a party or even a particular minister, set of ministers, bureaucrats, or set of bureaucrats. But whether one or the other, the funding is conceived in a political framework. In his view, art should be for art's sake. (See Mitchell, 1988, for a particularly lucid discussion of these points.)

This issue may seem a little beyond our concerns, but it leads us to a broad consideration of culture as opposed to industry in communications and requires a bit more introduction. Art in nearly anyone's view is both universal and particular. It develops out of the particular situation of a particular artist. It gains its universal quality from the ability of the artist to capture the universal condition in particular material. In pre-historic times, in societies such as the Amerindian prior to white contact, and in Western society even up to the previous century, the artist was a central figure. The artist expressed the fundamentals of life and created the central icons, which were totems to members of one society but which could be appreciated by other cultures for their universal expressive or artistic qualities.

Gradually, during the period of the Renaissance, a change occurred in the role of the artist. In very general terms, the integration of the artist with the community through craft guilds and major church projects became far less common, and art was more affected by a new individualism. That individualism was expressed in the emergence of both individual patrons, such as the Medicis, and individual artists, such as Michelangelo and Rubens.

After a period associated with the beginnings of capitalism, when artists, like other people, were left to drift with the market, the state, as one concentration of wealth, emerged as a new patron of the arts. (In Canada it has been nearly the only generous patron.) Early forms of state patronage assumed a welfarist role in the sense of looking to (but not completely after, by any means) the welfare of artists. Such programs were providers. Then the state set up cultural institutions such as the CBC and became employer. But the Royal Commission on National Development in the Arts, Letters and Sciences (1952), the Massey Commission, moved the Canadian government into a genuine role of patron. Through the Massey Commission's concept of an arm's-length council for the support of the arts, letters, and sciences and by means of an initial endowment from the estates of two very rich men, Sir James Dunn and Isaak Walton Killam, the Canada Council was born, on March 28, 1957.

Government at Arm's Length

A scant 25 years later the arm's-length relationship between the government and the Council was under major attack on two flanks from the government. Economically, the Council was not long in outgrowing its original endowment of $53 million. It thus entered an anomalous position of going to Parliament for annual funds, but according to its founding act of 1957 being independent of government influence. While this grating relationship has not been allowed to undermine the original arm's-length relationship (although there have been some close calls), the government has found other means to lead the Council into what it has seen as priority areas. The most direct method has been to increase funding to the Council by creating special funds earmarked for certain purposes.

The Council has also been under attack philosophically since Pierre Trudeau first became Prime Minister (see Mitchell, 1988). Woodcock names Trudeau and his early culture minister, Gérard Pelletier, as leaders of the attack. He characterizes Trudeau's view as stemming from the notion that the arts add "an essential grace in the life of civilized people" (p. 108) and that the role of government should be as follows:

> I do not think that modern society, or the artist as a member of that society, need fear a generous policy of subsidy to the arts by

governments as long as those governments have the courage to permit free expression and experimentation – and, for that matter, to take it in good part if the mirror held up to their faces is not a flattering one.

But beneath this aesthetic surface Woodcock sees an illegitimate guiding hand of the state. He quotes Trudeau as saying that government should "set a general course for development" in its aid for the arts.

His conception of Pelletier's desire to democratize the arts through opening doors to much larger numbers of people, thus inducing them to enter, and by conceiving of culture differently, as something for all rather than for a middle-class-based elite, is that it was "frankly philistine." Although the word "philistine" has a negative connotation, one dictionary definition is "common." To democratize culture is certainly to make it more accessible to common people. Most importantly, Woodcock sees the entry of the notion of culture into the funding of the arts as an intermediate step toward an inevitable industrially based and conceived support program.

Such a development is not inevitable, however, unless government sets an industrial priority. While that is just what Canadian governments have done recently, it is not necessarily inevitable that the arts, or for that matter culture, be brought to heel under an industrial regimen. If one is moderately sympathetic to state intervention, the political realm and art can easily be seen as a basis for a reintegration of the individual artist with the community over a concern for culture.

CULTURE VERSUS INDUSTRY AS A BASIS FOR POLICY

When we consider a cultural orientation within a communication framework it provides a way of bringing aesthetic and artistic value to the concern of community. A cultural approach assesses expression within any medium for its ability to generate social, cultural, or even spiritual value. Just as with any piece of art, a judgement must be made on that contribution. The difference between an artistic and a cultural approach is the element of community. In making a judgement of an item of culture, artistic values come together with the nature of the community in which they are created. On the other hand, as Rotstein (1988) points out, an industrial or economic approach examines these activities in particular terms such as *merit goods, market failure*, and *infant industries*. Such terms allow a certain flexibility, but in the end cultural and artistic activities are examined in terms of their ability to generate material wealth.

Industrial Considerations

Government involvement in communications for economic or industrial purposes leads to the kinds of considerations we stressed in Chapter 11 when discussing new technologies. As we said, new communications technologies will create new forms of expression with which we must become familiar in order not to lose our abilities to speak among ourselves.

Must we use these new forms at all? Of course we must, because all the market organizing power of vast American, European, and Japanese conglomerates will be mustered to persuade all people with disposable income to receive cultural products through these new media forms.

As a nation we ride a technological juggernaut created by large foreign conglomerates who have a clear idea of what products can be brought forward, at what pace, at what price, with which capacities in order that they may make huge profits and thereby grow. We are by no means innocent of fuelling that juggernaut. We do so through research and development programs in communications hardware, such as Telidon and communications satellites. We supercharge that research and development by creating industrial opportunities through the transfer of that technology to private enterprise, by creating industrial opportunities, and through regulation for such large companies as Northern Telecom and Rogers Cablesystems. In participating in these technological and industrial activities, and Canada has done so with enthusiasm over the years, we take what might be termed a hardware high road.

However, a hardware high road presents us with the rather onerous task of organizing our cultural production so that we are not silenced by this technological wizardry. In addressing that task we must realize (and authors such as Audley and Lyman help us in this) that to keep our expressive capacity abreast of technological developments is not an economic cost but is rather a way of guarding against a vast drain of money out of the country. The important question is not whether we should have an industrially based communications policy. We must, in order to survive economically, let alone politically or culturally. The important question involves understanding the consequences of an industrial-based policy in order to plan a complementary culture-based policy.

The Consequences of an Industrially Based Communications Policy

One of the first consequences of industrial development in communications is the necessity to participate in creating the databases, software, and content in all the requisite formats these technologies demand. Necessarily that will take money away from new productions as it is gobbled up by production in multiple formats.

Second, industrial development in communications compels us to encourage the development of "world class" (meaning internationally active) corporations. They are required as earners of foreign currency, as a stable element in the industry, and as potential implementers of the latest and best technology. Allowing tax deductions for takeover expenses is one policy that encourages the emergence of large players. Rewarding high sales (as distinct from quality programming) is another. And there are many more, both direct and indirect.

However, the emergence of large players further accentuates the centralizing bias of the technologies that the large conglomerates create and market and exploit. In communications not only does this centralization introduce an homogenizing influence. It also discourages the vast majority of Canadians from participation in creating cultural products. The distance between us and the cultural products we consume increases.

Third, as we discussed briefly in the first section of this chapter, emphasis on industrial development requires an assessment of the potentiality of public versus private players. It does not mean that the public sector should be slashed back. Public companies can be used for all sorts of purposes. Petro-Canada was created so that the government would have a window on the industry, so that it could understand the dealings of the industry from the point of view of a participant. When the industry was effectively owned by seven large petrochemical companies, having that window seemed a necessary step. Moreover, it gave Canadians a chance, as the ads say, to pump

money back into Canada. Public companies can also be used to provide social services. Again, as the ads say, "We know who you are in business for, CN."

Public companies can also be used as chosen vehicles to bring technology to the marketplace or to market Canadian technology abroad. Public companies are free to undertake risks private companies might not. Public companies as political or cultural vehicles can also operate according to broader concerns than the bottom line. Private companies are beholden to their shareholders and are responsible to earn as much as they can for those shareholders. Public companies can be used to provide services, say to distant, small communities, which are uneconomic, exactly the role of the CBC over the years. Public companies can be used to foster the development of infant industries. Without the NFB it is doubtful that we would have an independent film-making industry in Canada. In short, the roles for public companies are determined by the imagination of those who create and run them. (A fine discussion of the role and potential of public companies can be found in Herschel Hardin's A Nation Unaware, 1974.)

The major problem with public companies is that they must change as they either succeed or fail in their goals. The failures of Canadair may suggest that it should be sold off to the private sector or closed down; the successes of the CBC and NFB and the changing communications environment may suggest that they take on new roles and challenges. The difficulty with public companies is that they pose a politically ticklish question because, inevitably, people are displaced. The problem, unfortunately, is often tackled in a manner that rejects the value of the public sector in total.

A Culturally Based Communications Policy

In a sense, it would seem that the whole point of an industrially based communications policy is to provide the infrastructure for cultural expression. After all, what is the point of being able to talk to anyone anywhere in the world if you have nothing to say to them? The key question to ask is how cultural goals are to be achieved within the predictable emerging technological and industrial environment.

One of the major advantages of participating in an ever-changing communications environment is that there is always considerable demand for content for evolving technological forms. One of the weakest aspects of the federal government's attempts to promote Telidon technology was that there was no exciting, up-to-date content once the hardware was set up for demonstration (see Overduin, 1988). Indeed, often the connections could not be made and the whole exercise had to be simulated.

New technologies usually provide new opportunities. Once a technology has been introduced – e.g., videocassette recorders, video-game machines, videodiscs, compact discs, multiple television channels, communications satellites – opportunities arise very quickly as the machine takes hold in the marketplace. At first these opportunities are seized by producers for other technologies. Thus movies are now distributed on videocassette just as they were and are on television. Books have been made into movies ever since the early days of film. Music was made over into music videos. Films are placed on videodiscs. And so forth.

But each new technology has the capacity to encourage production for itself. Numbers of movies are now being distributed through videocassettes and never shown in theatres. Television programming took its place alongside movies reshown on television. In a kind of reverse action some successful movies have created books rather than the other way around. Videos are now almost a necessity in launching new music and packages of music videos are being created and marketed.

The cultural advantage of all this activity is that it can create innumerable opportunities for cultural production. As long as restrictive practices are not allowed to interfere with opportunities for Canadians, this environment of opportunities can create a culture out of which will grow exciting creative expression. There is nothing magical in the production of culturally valuable works or even in the production of works of art. As with creation in any other field, the creator must have outstanding talent and must be surrounded by the elements essential to his or her craft.

The only thing that might be considered magical in producing works of art is that we do not know what the essential elements of historically significant works of art are. They probably have as much to do with a social integrity, which can be as present in times of social upheaval (consider Beckett's *Waiting for Godot*) as in times of tranquility, as they do with a plenitude of cultural work.

A culturally based communications policy must strive for both these ends. It must create possibilities of entry for cultural producers, not just for marketable products. It must create opportunities for culturally sensitive expression, whether these forms of expression have a predictably sizable market or might not even be later sold in the marketplace. At the same time it must, through the encouragement of cultural activity, foster the emergence of, in the case of Canada, and the maintenance of, in the case of some other cultures, a cultural integrity. That latter task is well beyond the purview of this book. Full discussion of it would entail a discussion of history, political ideology, social structure, and so on. In fact, it would be difficult to say what would be left out of such a discussion. But we can deal with the emergence of cultural integrity by way of illustration.

Before we do, however, consider this. Could it be that we Canadians have created for ourselves a cultural identity we cannot sustain? That is, perhaps our struggle to prevent ourselves from being silenced by the technological juggernaut prevents us from giving due recognition to those elements we hold dear, such as bilingualism, regionalism, heterogeneity, and so on. Again the question arises, if we cannot say what we want to say, what is the use of speaking?

Cultural and Industrial Support Structures in Publishing

As of 1985 there were, at the federal level, two major programs of support for Canada's book publishers. The more generous of the two was run by the Department of Communications. The less generous, not through any design of the funding agency, was that run by the Canada Council.

The program run by the Department of Communications was an industrially inspired program. It subsidized publishers based on one major criterion, sales. Thus the more successful the publisher in the marketplace the greater the rewards from the DOC. Such a subsidy program allowed the commercially successful to grow. It was argued by some in the industry that the program was key to the takeover by one very large (for Canadian companies) publisher, Gage, of another somewhat large operation that was floundering, Macmillan. While policy statements from the DOC have not been entirely clear on the intent of the program, de facto it has contributed to the further success of the commercially successful.

The Canada Council program was, and will undoubtedly continue to be, a culturally inspired program. Its aim is to "offset publication deficits on books which make an original contribution to Canadian literature or identify and address public concerns in Canada." It consists, at the time of this writing, of several parts. On the one hand are **block grants**. These are given to publishers with 16 or more eligible titles in print and on their active backlist and who are publishing in areas considered by the Council to have cultural significance in a broadly defined sense, such as poetry, drama, fiction, non-fiction, and children's literature. For smaller publishers manuscripts may be submitted and funded on a project-by-project basis as long as they have four eligible titles in print. In addition, the Canada Council funds a National Book Festival, translations, and a considerable number of initiatives designed to help promote and distribute Canadian books to Canadians and to foreign markets. As a general caveat, the Canada Council's review process "is determined by an assessment of the publisher's program as a whole. This process takes into account both the quantity and the quality of the titles published."

The presence of these two programs demonstrates the dual priorities that must be considered in all the media. Because the publishing of most original works of cultural value to Canadians can never be a profitable enterprise, the government must have in place a policy to ensure the publication of such titles. At the same time it would be folly not to reward those in the industry who are able to contribute to the publication of good Canadian books and who are able as well to be moderately successful commercially. Co-ordination of these programs is undoubtedly desirable. Indeed, both the Canada Council and the Applebaum-Hébert Report recommended administrative co-ordination and integration. But such an integration would need to preserve the two principles upon which the programs are based, cultural value and business success.*

Designing support programs that reflect both cultural and industrial principles is no mean feat. One of the problems with the support programs of the Canadian Film Development Corporation, now Telefilm Canada, was that they led to the making of culturally useless films because these were supposed to be commercially successful. Few were. The exceptions were such memorable masterpieces as *Meatballs*.

PARTICIPATION VERSUS PROFESSIONALIZATION

The next dimension of mass communication we will explore in the context of an expanding communications sector derives from

---

*In late 1986 the Mulroney government introduced a replacement for these publishing support programs. It targeted cultural publishing and a profitable and culturally sensitive publishing sector, educational publishing. It increased support to cultural publishing by increasing funding to the Canada Council for this purpose. It then created the Book Publishing Industry Development Program to be administered by the federal Department of Communications. Under the latter program publishers qualify for funds to undertake projects which are aimed at the educational market. This combination of programs is intended to respect both the cultural and industrial side of publishing in a manner which is designed to lead to a culturally vibrant and economically healthy industry able to be independent from government assistance.

the sensitivity of the media to the social and cultural milieu within which they exist. A few years back one of the rallying cries against the media was that they were one-way rather than two-way flows of information. They are no less so today although, as we have illustrated in various chapters, we are beginning to understand the nature of the very muted return flow of information from the media consumer to the media producer. This issue has been taken up both domestically, by the Kent Royal Commission on Newspapers, and internationally in the MacBride Report. Thelma McCormack (1983) has compared the approaches of these two reports and we have used her ideas as a starting place for this discussion.

The Modernization Paradigm of the Kent Commission

Tom Kent sees the major problem of newspapers in Canada to be the increasing concentration of ownership. His notion is that increased concentration of ownership has led to what he terms a "rationalization," which also might be termed a centralization of expenditures. In turn, this has led to a centralization of content development, budgetary procedures that ensure profit to the neglect of news, and generally a denigration of the historical function of newspapers, which is to inform readers of important events and to provide a range of interpretation of those events.

Kent introduces a modernization paradigm by arguing for the development of professional qualifications and ethos. He believes that by increasing their professionalism through training, continuing education, self-policing, and the like, journalists can increase their power essentially by exercising their professional autonomy in a manner similar to doctors.

McCormack's analysis is that on the one

hand owners seek economies of scale in expanding their production. On the other hand, journalists seek protection from the increased power of the owners through professionalism. This counter-move is designed to make journalists responsible not to the owners but rather to their own ethics and their interpretation of "social responsibility."

The major drawback of this scenario is that it increases the isolation of both the owners and the journalists from the audience. McCormack considers that if the journalists were to participate in owning newspapers they would be accountable economically for their ideals and might, via this accountability, tailor their ideals to meet the needs, as expressed through subscriptions, of their readers. (The troubled record of *Le Monde*, a French newspaper owned by journalists, suggests otherwise. Opportunities for stock ownership by employees provided for by the Maclean Hunter-owned *Sun* newspaper chain is a less radical model of journalistic participation in and resultant accountability through ownership. As much as anything it probably demonstrates the lack of control journalists have over the content of the newspaper for which they work.)

The Participation Paradigm of the MacBride Report

In contrast to Kent, the MacBride Report focuses on inequality, power, and technology. Following the reasoning of the MacBride Report, professionalism contributes to inequality and the dependency of the audience on elites. Professionalism increases the sophistication of a one-way flow. It confirms the right of the audience to receive information. At the same time it eclipses the goal of access and participation. It denies the public a role in agenda-building.

In McCormack's and MacBride's view, media power derives from the media being part of the social process, not part of a semi-autonomous elite. Yet, unless media are part of the social process, as Desbarats (1985) points out, they will be distrusted as much as big government and big business. Professionalism cuts off active consultation. Without that consultation what the media produce may be true but it may not be authentic. Remember Trudeau's "Where's Biafra?" Truth is derived from a logical, literate analysis. Authenticity is derived from the nature of community.

Within the Canadian context, both Kent's concern for professionalism and MacBride's concern for participation have their place. The increased power of owners must be matched by a power over content. As we discussed in the previous section, there must be a balance between industrial and economic concerns on the one hand and cultural concerns on the other, here represented by owners and journalists respectively. In broadcasting, that balance is attempted by regulation. In the book publishing industry it is done by means of variously designed support programs. With newspapers, the acceptance by both owners and journalists of state interference as infringing the freedom (and power) of the press makes difficult the marrying of cultural interests with those of business. Liberal government inaction on the Kent Report and the rescinding by the Conservative government of an order-in-council preventing greater cross-ownership in the media of any particular place have made it abundantly clear that the power to enforce business priorities rests firmly in the hands of the present contingent of large owners.

Professionalism, however, may be more appropriate to Canada than McCormack believes. In the Third World, where the professional class is very small in comparison with the peasant class, increased professionalism would indeed lead to the inequalities and lack of participation that MacBride suggests. But in Canada, where the professional class is extremely large in comparison to Third World nations, where there is no peasant class, where the poor are a much smaller percentage of the population, and where the class of journalists can produce both the tabloids and the broadsheets that typify our newspaper environment, it is dubious whether newspapers isolate the audience from participation in agenda-building. It may even be that newspapers are not a major factor in Canada in the agenda-building process.

McCormack no doubt is right in her belief that newspapers are no longer aligned with their traditional readership. But whether that audience needs or wants a daily newspaper in the modern age is a question she appears reluctant to consider.

EDUCATION

We cannot end without a few more words on education. Education, according to the Canadian constitution, is a provincial responsibility. The provinces have been very protective of their responsibility for education and this protectionism has led to a severe restriction of the market power of educators in the learning materials marketplace. The producers, operating in a transnational market, have greater power than the consumers, who are limited in their bargaining power to the size of their provincial population of students.

With broadcasting satellites in place, educational programming will be created for purchase by anyone who cares to receive it. The CRTC decision to allow cable companies to offer a U.S.-based service, The Learning Channel, despite the objection of a consortium of provincial education television producers, demonstrates that the educational market is as open as the home entertainment audience.

Given these technological developments, the provinces must consider their insistence on autonomy, which has led to each making its own bargain on how to homogenize its interests with those in the U.S. The foundation of that reconsideration needs to be the development of production consortia, the materials of which must be as widely used as possible in Canada.

The implication of such a development is a reconsideration of curricula, but without a view to homogeneity across the land. As we have said before, there is no use in speaking if one cannot say what one wishes. The implications are that a culturally based heterogeneity must be preserved alongside an appropriate homogeneity in those areas of the curriculum where it is warranted. To do otherwise will severely jeopardize the future of the country.

SUMMARY

The implications of the five major points discussed in this chapter are wide-ranging. As information and its creation, dissemination, manipulation, and ownership become increasingly important, the ramifications of domestic versus foreign control, public versus private control, an industrial versus a cultural policy, a grassroots, particular perspective versus a more elite stance all become increasingly important in regards to education and culture. These elements will also have profound implications for the wealth and existence of nations.

We cannot design ourselves a future devoid of difficulties; at our peril we blithely follow the priorities of powerful nations. For if we can be sure of anything, it is that the powerful will consider their own interests and do their very best to ensure that these interests are protected regardless of others.

The situation is exactly parallel inside Canada. If we are lax we will find increasing concentration of energy at the centre. By neglect we can certainly let the forces of the metropolis run their course. Or we may choose another route. Yet, in choosing to follow a route that helps to equalize development opportunities everywhere and for everyone, we must be aware that we are making a cultural and political decision, not an economic one.

The "information age" may not represent a change of the same order of magnitude as did the "industrial age." Nonetheless, information and its manipulation are changing our world, and far from being a victim of such change, Canada is one of the few nations of the world in a position to guide and design these changes.

REFERENCES

Canada. "The Federal Cultural Review Committee" (Applebaum-Hébert Report). Ottawa: Minister of Supply and Services, 1982.

Canada. *Royal Commission on National Development in the Arts, Letters and Sciences* (Massey Report). Ottawa: Queen's Printer, 1952.

Canada. *Royal Commission on Newspapers* (Kent Report). Hull: Canadian Government Publishing Centre, 1981.

Canadian Broadcasting Corporation. *The Press and the Prime Minister*. Toronto, 1977.

Canadian Broadcasting Corporation. *Inside TV News*. Montreal, 1982.

Desbarats, Peter. "Watchdog of Others Shrinks from its own Accountability" (and other articles in "Eye on the Media" column), *The Financial Post*, 1985.

Globe and Mail, May 6, 1985.

Hardin, Herschel. *A Nation Unaware*. Vancouver: J.J. Douglas Ltd., 1974.

Lorimer, Rowland. "Implications of New Technologies of Information," *Scholarly Publishing* (April, 1985).

McCormack, Thelma. "The Political Culture and the Press in Canada," *The Canadian Journal of Political Science* (September, 1983).

Mitchell, D. "Culture as Political Discourse in Canada," in R. Lorimer and D.C. Wilson, eds., *Communications Canada*. Forthcoming, 1988.

National Film Board. *Magic in the Sky*, directed by P. Raymont, produced by P. Raymont and A. Hammond. January, 1981.

Overduin, H. "Westex News: A Case Study of an Experiment into Journalism of the Future," in R. Lorimer and D.C. Wilson, eds., *Communications Canada*. Forthcoming, 1988.

Rotstein, A. "The Use and Misuse of Economics in Cultural Policy," in R. Lorimer and D.C. Wilson, eds., *Communications Canada*. Forthcoming, 1988.

Simon Fraser University. *Media Information Canada*, Part 1 of a 5-part series, *Mass Communication in Canada*. Burnaby, B.C., 1985.

Simon Fraser University. *The Fashionable Image*, Part 2 of a 5-part series, *Mass Communication in Canada*. Burnaby, B.C., 1985.

Simon Fraser University. *Video, Vinyl and Culture*, Part 3 of a 5-part series, *Mass Communication in Canada*. Burnaby, B.C., 1985.

Stuart-Stubbs, Basil. "Scholarly Communication and the New Information Order," *Canadian Journal of Information Science* (1981).

UNESCO, International Commission on Communications Problems (MacBride Commission). *Many Voices, One World*. Paris: Unipub, 1980.

Woodcock, George. *Strange Bedfellows: The State and the Arts in Canada*. Vancouver: Douglas & McIntyre, 1985.

STUDY QUESTIONS

1. Contrast the perspective of the Kent Com-

mission to that of the MacBride Report. Is each appropriate to its venue, or does the MacBride Report have some relevance to Canada?

2. Do you think Canada is in a position to play any unique role in the international communications order, given our status as a rich but underdeveloped country?

3. What is the future of public-sector broadcasting?

4. What is the future of Canada in an information age?

Index

ABC network, 238
ACCESS Alberta, 213
Access to information, 80, 86; *see also* Freedom of information
Access to Information Act (1983), 75, 187
ADN news agency (East Germany), 232
Advertising: advertorial, 110-11; advocacy, 110; corporate image, 110; economic influence of, on private media corporations, 55, 58; by governments, 15, 58, 76; lifestyle-image, 27, 108; political, during elections, 76; in print, 27; semiotic analysis of, 95-102; survey, 27; on television, 27; *see also* specific products and advertisers
Advertising industry, 105-10
Affiliates, privately owned, of CBC, 55, 196
Agence France Presse (AFP), 232, 242
Aird Commission (1929), 158
Alberta economy, 269-71
Allen, Woody, 133
Anderson, Peter S., 175
Andrews, Cecil, suicide attempt on television, 135, 136, 191
Anik satellites, 280, 294, 297
Annie Hall, influence on fashion, 133

Antithesis, 115
Applebaum-Hébert Report (1982), 307-08, 319
ASIN news exchange pool (Latin American and Caribbean), 232
Associated Press (AP), 232, 236, 237, 238, 242
Association of American Broadcasters, 310
Audience fragmentation, 285
Audley, Paul, 33-34, 37, 219n, 220, 303
AUSSAT, 295
Australian Broadcasting Tribunal, 161, 196
Australian television: Special Broadcasting Service, 26

Babe, Robert, 34, 37
Barber, Bruce, 110
Barrett, Dave, 79
Barthes, Roland, 95
Bartók, Béla, 133
Baton Broadcasting, 167
BBC, 238
Beachcombers, The, 256
Beale, Alison, 34, 37
Beatles, 119
Beats system of information-gathering, 82, 94, 191, 192
Beer, advertising of, 27, 108-09, 110, 122, 123
Bell Canada, 210, 211, 224
Berger, Thomas, 253
Berger Report, 253-55
Berne Convention, 296
Bias, media, 196-97, 268-69
Bilingualism, influence on policy, 31, 34, 201, 216, 268-69, 278
Bill C-58, 153, 247, 310-11
Bird, Chris, 187-88
Black, Conrad, 157
Black, Edwin, 67, 69, 87
Black, Montegu, 197
Blackburn family, 165
Block grants, Canada Council, 318
Blumer, H., 62
Board of Broadcast Governors, 214
Book Publishing Industry Development Program, 319n
Bookstores, chain vs. independent, 164
Border stations, U.S.-Canada, 261, 262, 297, 310

Bourassa, Robert, 84

Boyle Committee, 268-69

British Columbia Telephone, 210

British influence on Canadian culture, 201

Broadcasting, participation in, *see* Participation in broadcasting

Broadcasting, provincial educational organizations, 213

Broadcasting Act (1968), 52-54, 151-53, 213, 215, 216

Broadcasting Code in Canada, 310

Broadcasting institutions, 213

Broadcasting statutes, 213

Broadcasting Task Force (1985-86), 197, 204, 219, 271

Broadcast licences, 52, 211, 214, 215, 310

Broadcast News, 175

Broadcast Program Development Fund, 221

Broadsheets, *see* Newspapers, broadsheet vs. tabloid

Bronfman family, 167

Cable television: as multicultural service, 31; outlet for movie chains, 157; regulations regarding, 158, 207-08, 215, 218; technological aspects, 46, 204, 261, 281-82; tiering by, 283; *see also* Pay television; Premium television

Caesar, Julius, 25

Canada Council, 221-22, 272, 313, 314, 318-19

Canada Elections Act, 52

Canadair, 316

Canada's Cultural Industries, 33-34, 303

Canada's Video Revolution, 303, 304

Canadian Bill of Rights (1960), 180

Canadian Broadcasting Act (1936), 213

Canadian Broadcasting Corporation (CBC): as cultural and regulatory agency, 214-15, 247; cutbacks, effects of, 283; emphasis on spoken word, 85; foreign correspondents, 185, 246-47; mandate of, 53, 216-19; news and current affairs programming, 185-86; vs. private, profit-making corporations, 151, 159, 160; vs. provincial educational broadcasters, 55; *see also* Extension of service

Canadian Broadcast Program Development Fund, 219

Canadian Charter of Rights and Freedoms (1982), 180-81

Canadian Constitution, 201

Canadian content: debate over, 224-25, 312; regulations, 48, 77, 217-19, 243, 273

Canadian Film Development Corporation, *see* Telefilm Canada

Canadian Institute for Economic Policy, 33

Canadian National Railways, 209

Canadian Pacific Air Lines advertising, semiotic analysis of, 95-102

Canadian Pacific Railway (CPR), building of, 14-15, 30, 253

Canadian Press (CP), 76, 175; *see also* Broadcast News

Canadian Radio Broadcasting Commission (1932), 53, 213, 214, 217

Canadian Radio Television Commission (1968-74), 53

Canadian Radio-television and Telecommunications Commission (CRTC): border stations vs. cable companies regulations, 310; broadcast licensing, 211, 214, 215; cable subscriber rates, 158; Canadian content regulations, 298; free flow of information, interference with, 247; history and purpose of, 53-54, 151, 214, 215; pay television approval given, 19; public hearings, 59, 202, 215; refused purchase of Télé-Métropole by Power, 156; restriction of foreign ownership, 214; satellite systems licensing, 281; study of media political bias, 196-97; telecommunications rates, 211

Canadian Radio-television and Telecommunications Commission Act (1976), 213

Canadian Security Intelligence Service, 89

Cancom (Canadian Satellite Communications Inc.), 212, 281, 297-98

Cantel, 209

Capital Cost Allowance, 221, 286

Capitalism, 149-50, 233

Caplan, Gerald, 219

Censorship of press, 70, 80

Centre-hinterland theory, *see* Metropolis-hinterland theory

Chain journalism, 163-64

Chains, newspaper, 154, 163-65; *see also* Southam chain; Thomson chain
Challenger explosion, news coverage of (1986), 143
Channel Ten 10 (Australia), 161, 196
Chernobyl meltdown, news coverage of (1986), 143
Choice, consumer, in broadcasting, 224-25
Cicero, 25
Cineplex Odeon chain, 221
Cité du Cinéma, 221
CKO radio network, 217
Closed-caption service, 216
Clyne Committee Report (1979), 204
CNCP Telecommunications, 208, 209, 210, 224
Coaxial cables, 282-83
Cohen, Dian, 27
Cohen, Leonard, 119
Colonial Advocate, 15
Comeau, Paul-André, 175
Commercials, *see* Advertising, on television
Common carriers, 208-09
Communication, effect on dimensions of society: cultural, 18-19, 255-57; economic, 15-18, 255-57; educational, 18, 255-57; familial, 20, 255-57; individual, 20-21, 255-57; political, 15; social, 14-15, 255-57; technological, 19, 28-30
Communications, Department of: establishment of, in 1969, 204; functions of, 205-07; policies, 202, 218-19, 222, 318-19; technical licensing, 214; telecommunication systems standards, 210
Communications policy, *see* Communications, Department of; Policies, Canadian
Community ownership, 177
Compact discs, 317
Competition, in telecommunications, 223-24
Computers, 18, 204, 281, 290
Conglomerates, 162-63
Content, in communications, 91-92
Content analysis, 102-05, 116, 141-42
Co-operative ownership, 177
Copyright, 220, 296-97, 304-05, 309-10
Corporations, Crown, 159-60; *see also* specific Crown corporations
Corporations, private, 47, 48, 150-51, 160-176; *see also* Ownership types
Corporations, private vs. public compared, 48-49, 260-61, 269-71, 291, 303-08, 316

Corporations, public, 158-60
CP, *see* Canadian Press
CP Air, *see* Canadian Pacific Air Lines
CPR, *see* Canadian Pacific Railway
Criminal Libel Act, 187
Crocodile Dundee, 287
Cross-ownership, 154, 165-66
Crown corporations, *see* Corporations, Crown
CRTC, *see* Canadian Radio-television and Telecommunications Commission
CTV network, 154, 164, 217, 262
Cultural industries policy, 219-23
Cunningham, Lynn, 129

Dallas, 117, 247
DBS, *see* Direct Broadcast Satellites
de Kerckhove, Derrick, 21-22, 92
Democracy, rise of, 67-69
Department of Communications Act, 213
Desbarats, Peter, 320
Desmarais, Paul, 156, 167
Developmental journalism, 73
Devoir, Le, 175-76
Dewey, John, 240
Dialogue on Drinking (government health program), 108-09, 120-24
Diefenbaker, John, 180
Digital data system, first nation-wide (1973), 30
Digitalization, 290-91
Digital semiconductor technology, 277
Direct Broadcast Satellites (DBS), 288-89, 290, 296-97, 311
Donald Duck comics, American ideology in, 240-42
DPA news agency (West Germany), 232
Dryden, Ken, study of hockey analogous to study of communications, 13-14
Dumont, Gabriel, 252
Duplessis, Maurice, era of, 75
Dunn, Sir James, 314
Dvorak, Anton, 133
Dwyer, R. Budd, suicide of, on television, 136
Dyad, 95
Dylan, Bob, 24, 133

Eaton's, 154
Eco, Umberto, 63, 93, 105, 128

Economies of scale, 164
Editorial construction function, 189-92
Editorial page editor, 190
Editor-in-chief, 190
Editors: function of, 187; types of, 190
Edmonton Sun, 85, 154
Education, spread of, 18
Educational television, 321
EFE news agency (Spain), 232
Effective monopolies, 165
Effects analysis, 126-27, 130-31
Elections, coverage of, 76-77, 87
Encoding, 92-94
Enlightened action, principle of, 32-33
Enright, Michael, 110
Entertainment, definition of, in mass media, 61
Erotica, 145
Eslin, Martin, 27
Ethnic broadcasting, *see* Multiculturalism
Executive editor, 190
Extension of service: effect on northern native tradi-
    tional culture, 255-57; government commitment
    to, 30, 33, 34, 159, 202; inaccurate predictions
    of consumers' wishes, 213; mandate of and ser-
    vices offered by CBC, 216; use of satellites, 212,
    281-82, 297-98

Fair access, in telecommunications, 223
Falklands War, 238
Famous Players chain, 157, 221
Federal Combines Investigation (Canada), 158
Federal-provincial disputes, 207-08
Fibre optics, 204, 277, 282-83
fifth estate, the, 144
Film industry, Canadian, 153, 221-22, 272-73
Financial Post, 154
First Choice network, 196
Flashdance, 120
Fletcher, Fred, 75-76
Food and Drug Act, 52
Foreign correspondents, Canadian, 185, 246-47
Foreign ownership: of broadcasting stations, 214;
    in cultural industries, 226; of publishing houses,
    220, 222-23, 259
Foster, David, 273
Fotheringham, Allan, 187

Four Theories of the Press, 70-73
Fourth Estate, 69, 72
Fox, Bill, 186
Frankfurt School, 62-63, 127
Freedom: of access to information (right to know),
    231-32, 242; to distribute information, 231, 242;
    of enterprise, 33; of expression, 180, 231, 242; of
    the individual (U.S.), 38; of information, 15, 76,
    231; of media to create meaning, 140-42; of na-
    tional collectivity, 244-45; of the press, 32; to
    publish, 231
Freedom of Information Act (U.S.), 75
Free flow of information, 231-32, 309
French-language programming, *see* Bilingualism
Front de Libération du Québec (FLQ), 77, 137
Fry, Howard, 195, 309
Frye, Northrop, 93

Gage, 318
Garneau, Marc, interviewed by news agencies, 236
Gatekeeping, 188, 190, 191-92, 236-37
Geography, Canadian, influence of, 30, 33-34;
    see also Extension of service
Gerbner, George, 144
Gershwin, George, 133
Ginn, 257
Glasgow Media Group, 193
Global TV network, 262, 281
Global village, concept of, 26-27
Globe and Mail, 21, 67, 83, 85, 102, 103,
    141-42, 164
Gossage, Patrick, 87
Gould, Glenn, 23
Government: advertising by, 15, 58, 76; agendas of,
    88; manipulation of public opinion, 89; policy
    development by, 88; as source of information for
    mass media, 58, 76, 77, 82-83, 186-87; support
    programs for cultural industries, 272-73; *see also*
    Canada Council; Politics
Grant, George, 28-29, 33
Grants, Canada Council, 318
Green Papers, 202, 207
Grenada, U.S. invasion of, 138-40, 230
Grierson, John, 190
Group ownership, 177
Gulf Canada advertising, 110

Gunsmoke, 130
Gwyn, Richard, 133-34, 192

Hackett, Robert A., 102-05
Halton, David, 246, 247
Hardin, Herschel, 156, 158
Harris, Michael, 67
Hatter, D., 166
Havas, Charles, 233
Health and Welfare Canada advertising, 108-09,
    120-24; *see also* Advertising, by governments
Hedley, Tom, 120
Hester, Al, 188
Heterogeneity, *see* Multiculturalism
High definition television (HDTV), 290-91
Hinterland, 252-53; *see also* Extension of service;
    Metropolis-hinterland theory
History of Journalism in Canada, A, 31
Hockey Night in Canada, 261
Home Box Office, 283
Honderich, Beland H., 183
Horizontal link, 161
House of Commons proceedings, televising of, 216
Hsin Hua news agency (China), 236
Hudson's Bay Company, 252, 254
Hume, David, 72
Hutchins Commission on the Freedom of the Press
    (1947), 72

I am a Hotel, 119
Images, definition of, in mass media, 61-62
Import tax, on books, 273n
Indeterminate systems, 92-94
Infant industries, protection of, 220, 315
Informatics policy, national, need for, 39
Information, definition of, in mass media, 61
Information networks, Canadian involvement in,
    312-13
Information officer, 186-87
Innis, Harold, 14, 21, 22, 39, 251, 257; *see also*
    Toronto School
Inside TV News, 185, 304, 309
INTELSAT, 209, 211, 294
Interactive services, 290
International Telecommunications Union, 297
International Thomson, *see* Thomson chain

Inukshuk, Inuit television service, 30, 212;
    see also Extension of service
Inverted pyramid, 111, 112
Invisible hand theory, 152, 160
Iran, news coverage of, 238
Irving family, 165, 166
Isolated areas, service to, *see* Extension of service
Issacs, Jeremy, 140
Isvestia, 71

Jackman, Hal, 167
Jackson, Michael, 119
Jolt cola, advertising of, 106
Journal, The, 137, 186, 190, 286
Journalism, 179-97; chain, 163-64; ideals of,
    180-81; realities of, 183-85; television, 185-86;
    see also Press
Journalists: personal values of, 193; self-perceived
    role of, 181-83
Juneau, Pierre, realignment of CBC under, 197
Jurisdictions, *see* Federal-provincial disputes

Kent, Tom, 78, 181, 319, 320
Kent Commission, studies and findings: concentra-
    tion of ownership, 78, 158, 175, 319-20; press
    gallery, 75; social responsibility of press, 58, 72-
    73, 163, 183
Kesterson, W.H., 31-32
Khomeini, Ayatollah, 21, 238
Killam, Isaak Walton, 314
Knelman, Martin, 19, 190
Knowledge Network of the West (KNOW), 213, 290
Knowles, Henry, 166
Korean Airlines Flight 007, media coverage of crash,
    102-05
Korporaal, Glenda, 182
Kyodo news agency (Japan), 232

Labatt's advertising, 27, 108, 110
LaMarsh, Judy, 260
Lauren, Ralph, 133
Lazowski, Jan, 246
Learning Channel, The (U.S.), 321
Lekich, John, 128-31, 145
Lennon, Julian, 119
Lester, Richard, 119

Lévesque, René, 87, 185, 186
Lewis, Jerry Lee, 133
Lewis, Stephen, 67
Libel law, 74, 187-88, 194
Liberal-pluralist perspective, 69, 165
Libraries, 303
Licences: broadcast, 52, 211, 214, 215, 310; satellite systems, 281; technical, 214
Linked companies, 154
Locke, John, 72
Lord, Albert, 23
Lunn, Richard, 71
Luther, Martin, 68
Lyman, Peter, 285-87, 291, 298, 303, 304

MacBride Report (UNESCO, 1980), 14-20, 39, 244-47, 319, 320-21
MacDonald, Flora, 219
Macdonald, Sir John A., 14, 253
MacGregor, Roy, 186
Mackenzie, William Lyon, 15, 252
Mackenzie River Valley Pipeline Inquiry, 253
Maclean Hunter, 154, 155, 158, 166
Maclean's, 89, 98, 100, 154
Macmillan, 318
Magic in the Sky, 255-57, 304, 305, 309
Magna International, 67
Marconi, Guglielmo, 152, 303
Market failure, 315
Mass audience, definition of, 62-63
Mass communication, forms of, 43-45
Masse, Marcel, 219
Massey Commission (1952), 313-14
Mass media: biases created by technology: print, 83, 94, 105; radio, 84; television, 84, 94, 105; definition of, 42-43; in developing nations, 46-47; elections coverage, 76-77, 87; forms of: institutional, 47-49, 86; technical, 43; function of, 45; and government: liberal-pluralist perspective, 69; neo-Marxist perspective, 69-70; governmental regulation of, 50, 58-59; influences on: audience, 59-60; business, 55, 58; governmental, 58-59; legal system, 59; media professionals, 60; owners, 60-61; private ownership of: liberal-pluralist perspective, 69; neo-Marxist perspective, 69; role in Canadian society, 50-52, 80-82;

role of technology in, 45-46; as a social structure, 50, 82
McCormack, Thelma, comparison of Kent Commission and MacBride Report, 319-21
McCuaig, Bruce, 27, 110
McGraw-Hill Ryerson, 258
McLuhan, Marshall, 14, 21, 22, 26-27, 39, 69; see also Toronto School
McPhail, Tom, 247
McQuail, Denis, 42, 59-60, 62
Meaning, connotative and denotative, 93
Meaning-generative systems, 127, 131
Meatballs, 319
Media-advertising interaction, 132, 195
Media-audience interaction, 127-28, 131, 140-45
Media bias, 84-85
Media-business interaction, 194-95
Media-culture interaction, 130-40
Media-fashion (clothing) interaction, 133-35
Media-government interaction, 194
Media logic, 85
Media-politics interaction, 135-40
Merit goods, 315
Metropolis-hinterland theory, 251-73; Canada as hinterland of U.S., 257, 260, 261-65, 271-73
Miami Vice, influence on fashion, 135
Microwave towers, 278
Mill, John Stuart, 72
Mintzberg, Henry, 190
Monde, Le, 139, 320
Monopolies, 165-66
Mosco, Vincent, 203
Mulroney, Brian, 67, 84, 186
Multiculturalism, 31, 33-34, 51, 77, 201, 318; see also Broadcasting Act; Cable television
Multilingual Television, 281
Murdoch, Rupert, 157, 161, 163, 183, 196
Murray, Don, 246-47
Music, popular, 24, 262; see also Rock videos

Name of the Rose, The, 93
NANAP news agency, 232
Nash, Knowlton, 246
National, The, 286
National Book Festival, 318
National Film and Video Policy (1984), 221

National Film Board (NFB), 153, 190, 221, 247, 286, 308, 316
National interest, invoked by government to control press, 80
Natural monopolies, 165
Neo-Marxist perspective, 69-70
Nestlé, 184, 247
Networks, television, 164
News agencies, 232-38
News and information programming, Canadian, 48, 262-69
News director, 185
News editor, 190
News events, presentation of, 27
News management, by government, 80, 82-83
Newspapers, broadsheet vs. tabloid, 112-14, 140-42, 171
Newspapers, history of, in Canada, 31-32
News stories, newspaper, structure and elements, 111-14
News stories, television, vs. print journalism, 114-16; structure and elements, 115
Newsweek, 102, 103
New world information order, 243-48; opinions on, of CBC foreign correspondents, 246-47; see also World information order
NFB, see National Film Board
Nicaragua, 311; information war with U.S., 140
Nickel, Herman, 184
Nielsen, Erik, 67
Nielsen Task Force on Program Review, 220, 223
Non-Aligned News Agency Pool, 232
NORDSAT, 295
North, Canadian, acculturation process in, 253-56
North, Canadian, service to, see Extension of service; Inukshuk; Northern Television Service
Northern Frontier: Northern Homeland, see Berger Report
Northern Telecom, 315
Northern Television Service (CBC), 212

October Crisis (1970), 77, 137
Official Secrets Act, 52
Optical fibre networks, see Fibre optics
Orbit and spectrum sharing, 294
Ortega, Daniel, 140

Orwell, George, 94
Osborne, Ronald, 155
Ostry, Sylvia, 112
Ottawa Citizen, 183-84
Ottawa Journal, closure of (1980), 76, 78
Outlying areas, service to, see Extension of service
Overdrinking, government program against, 108-09, 120-24
Ownership types: community, 177; co-operative, 177; group, 177; history of, 151-52; linked company, 154; chain, 154; conglomerate, 154; cross-ownership, 154; vertical integration, 154; single enterprise, 153

Pack journalism, 75
Pahlavi dynasty, 238
Paisley, Ian, 21
Parliamentary press gallery, see Press gallery
Participation in broadcasting, 225; see also Co-operative television; Community television; Extension of service; Inukshuk; Northern Television Service; Multiculturalism
Patent law vs. copyright law, 304; see also Copyright
Patronage, 70
Pay television, 54, 196, 204, 225, 281; failure to meet expectations, 19-20, 218, 285, 287-89; see also Cable television
PEACESAT, 296
Pekinpah, Sam, 119
Peladeau, Pierre, 112, 154
Pelletier, Gérard, 207, 314
Perkins, Carl, 133
Perry, André, 273
Perry Mason, 130-31
Petro-Canada, 316
Photocopying, by public, ethics of, 308
Pitfield, Michael, 112
Plagiarism, definition of, 304
Plant, Chris, 296
Plato, 24-25
Policies, Canadian: broadcasting, 213-19, 224-26; cultural industries, 219-23, 226; federal-provincial disputes, 207-08; film and video, 221-22; influences on and formulation of, 201; publishing (book and periodical), 222-23; telecommunications, 208-13, 223-24

Politics and mass media, relationship between, 66-90; early history, 68-69; *see also* Elections, coverage of; Government
Politics and the News, 67
Polls, public opinion, 89
Popular programming, 46, 54
Population, scattered, influence of, 201; *see also* Extension of service
Pornography, 145
Postal subsidies, 223, 271
Powell, Enoch, 71, 140-41, 163
Power Corporation, 154, 156, 175
Pratt, Larry, 269-71
Premium television, 282
Presley, Elvis, 119, 133
Press: government regulation of, 70-71; and government, relative powers, 79-80; *see also* Mass media
Press and the Prime Minister, The, 77, 137, 138, 187, 304-05, 309
Presse, La, 154, 175
Press gallery, 15, 73-74, 75-76, 186
Press systems, theories of: authoritarian, 70; libertarian, 72; social responsibilty, 69, 72-73; Soviet Communist, 70-71
Primary definers, 94, 193
Private broadcasters, *see* Corporations, private
Professional standards: in broadcasting, 50; in print journalism, 50; *see also* Broadcasting Act
Promise of performance, regulations, 76-77, 166
Province, The, 112, 141, 171
Public affairs programming, Canadian, 48
Public Broadcasting System (PBS), 278, 311
Public enterprise, *see* Corporations, public
Public Lending Right legislation, 308
Public service, central ethic of public corporations, 159
Publishing, Canadian, 151, 153; book, government support for, 318-19; educational, 259; industry policy: books, 222; periodicals, 222-23; *see also* School textbooks

Quebec, demand for autonomy in communications, 201, 207-08, 211
Quebecor, 154
Quest, reasons for failure of, 129

Radio, transatlantic link (1901), 30
Radio Act, 205-06, 208
Radio broadcasting in Canada, 202
Radio-Canada (French-language CBC), 278
Radio Canada International, 55, 217, 244
Radio network, trans-Canada (1927), 30
Radio Québec, 54-55, 213
Radio Reference case (1932), 213
Ramone, Phil, 119
RCMP, 15
Reagan, Ronald, 84, 104, 138
Reality vs. idealized portrayal, 142-45
Red River Rebellion, 251
Regionalism, 30-31, 33-34, 77, 216, 318
Reichmann brothers, 167
Reporters, *see* Journalists; Press; Press gallery
Representation, 92-94
Resource-led development, 269-71
Restrictive Trade Practices Act, 165-66
Reuter, Paul Julius, 233
Reuters news agency, 232, 233, 242
Richards, John, 269-71
Riel, Louis, 252
Right of free speech, 75
Right to individual privacy, 73
Right to know, *see* Access to information; Freedom of information
Right to own property, 150
Rock videos, 24, 118-20
Rogers Cablesystems, 158, 315
Rothblatt, M.A., 295
Royal Commission on National Development in the Arts, Letters and Sciences (1952), 313-14
Royal Commission on Newspapers (1981), *see* Kent Commission
Royalties, from library use, 308

Saskatchewan economy, 269-71
Saskatoon Star-Phoenix, 184
Satellite Business Systems, 184
Satellite dishes, 19-20, 281, 288-89
Satellite Instructional Television Experiment, 295
Satellites: cultural effects of, 256-57; economic and political effects of, 204; history, 30, 211-13, 256; policies and regulations, 211-13, 224; technological aspects, 277-78, 279; for distance

education, 18; regulatory challenge, 283, 285; and right-to-privacy concerns, 15; systems, 291-96; licensing by CRTC, 281; see also Direct Broadcast Satellites; Telesat

Satellite-to-cable transmission, 204, 216, 281-82; vs. Direct Broadcast Satellites (DBS), 279, 288-89, 290, 296-97

Saturday Night, 61, 98, 100

Sauvageau, Florian, 219

Sawatsky, John, 184-85, 187

Schiller, Herbert, 203

Schlesinger, Joe, 247

School textbooks, American content in, 240, 257-58

Scrambling/descrambling, 282, 291

Selkirk Communications, 154

Semiconductor, 277

Semiology, 95

Semiotic analysis of news, 116

Semiotics, 95-102, 104-05

Separatist movement, Quebec, 52

Siegel, Arthur, 268

Sign, 95

Signal penetration, 294

Signification, 45, 94; see also Semiotics

Signified, 95

Signifier, 95

Silicon chip, 276, 277

Simultaneous program deletion and substitution, 310

Singer of Tales, The, 23

Single enterprise, 153-54

SITE, 295

60 Minutes, 144

Smith, Adam, 152, 160

Smith, Anthony, 229-47 passim, 294, 304

Soap operas: effect on audience, 143; role, structure, and techniques, 116-18

Social responsibility of journalism, 180

Societies, effect of principal means of communication on: electronic, 26-27, 29-30; literate, 24-26; oral (ancient), 22-23; oral (modern), 23-24

Sony, 17

Southam, R.W., 183-84

Southam chain, 78, 158, 166, 167, 171, 175

Southam-Selkirk, see Southam chain

Sovereignty, national, in international communications, 297, 310

Special Broadcasting Service (Australia), 26

Specialty television, 54, 225, 281, 283

Spillover, 294, 311

Sports programming, Canadian, 48, 261

"Squamish 5," news coverage of, 181-82

Stanfield, Robert, 87

Stanley, H.M., 229

Staple-led development, 269-71

Starowicz, Mark, 190

Stevens, Sinclair, conflict-of-interest inquiry, 67

Stewart, Walter, 183

Stewart-Patterson, David, 67

Stock trading in media companies, 166-67

Structural functionalism, 80-82

Stuart-Stubbs, Basil, 303

Studio, Le, 273

Subscription Television (STV), 290

Sullivan, Edmund, 141-42

Superstations, 279, 283

Surinam independence, limited coverage of, 236

Symbols, definition of, in mass media, 61-62

Synthesis, 115

System interconnection, in telecommunications, 224

Tabloids, see Newspapers, broadsheet vs. tabloid

Tanjug news agency (Yugoslavia), 232, 238

Task Force on Broadcasting Policy (1986), 151

Task Force on Government Information (1969), 74

TASS news agency, 71, 232

Tax benefits, to foreign companies, 272

Tax deductions, for film investors, 286

Teacher education in Canada, 258-59

Technical licences, issuing of, 214

Technics, 17

Technological compatibility, Canadian-U.S., 46

Technological forms, social influence of, 45-47, 288-91

Technology, influence on communications, 203-05

Technology and Empire, 28

Télécable Vidéotron, 156

Telecom Canada, 208-09, 210, 211, 224

Telecommission (task force of Communications Canada), 206-07

Telecommunications: policy, 208-13, 223-24; regulation of, 210-11

Telefilm Canada, 219, 221, 247, 283, 286, 319
Teleglobe Canada, 209
Telegraph, as unifying factor, 253
Telegraph industry, regulation of, 210
Telemedia, 155
Telemedicine, 18, 281
Télé-Métropole, 156, 167, 175, 278
Telephone companies, regulation of, 210
Telephone systems: mobile, paging, and cellular, 209; municipal, 210
Telesat Canada, 210, 211-12, 214
Telesat Canada Act, 211, 213
Teletext, 290
Television: culture of the 1950s, 130-31; presentation of news stories, 27; transcontinental service (1958), 30; see also Cable television; Pay television
Telidon, 315, 317
Terrorists, media coverage of, 137-38, 182
Thatcher, Ross, 184
Thesis, 115
Third World, news coverage of, 236-38, 242-44
This Hour Has Seven Days, 144
Thomson, Ken, 167
Thomson, Roy, 154, 157, 261
Thomson chain, 78, 161-62, 164, 167, 175
Thornbirds, The, 287
Tiering, 283
Time, 102, 103, 138
Times, The, 233
Toronto School, theories of, 21-27
Toronto Star, 183
Toronto Stock Exchange, 27, 167
Toronto Sun, 141, 154
Toronto Telegram, 141
Towards a New National Broadcasting Policy, 218-19
TransCanada Telephone System, see Telecom Canada
Trudeau, Pierre, 77, 87, 115, 136-38, 314, 320
Tuchman, Gaye, 192, 193
Turner, John, 83, 238
TVA (French-language CTV), 278
TVOntario, 54-55, 213
TWA jet, coverage of hijacking (1985), 182

UHF broadcasting, 279, 283
UNESCO, 14, 39, 236, 244-47; see also MacBride Report
United Press International (UPI), 232, 233, 236, 242
United States: influence on Canadian business, 262; influence on Canadian culture, 31, 33-34, 37-38, 130-31, 201; influence on Canadian education, 257-58; influence on Canadian television production, 260-62; influence on Cancom programming activities, 298; influence on world culture, 38; news clips used on Canadian news, copyright of, 305-07; program purchase for Canadian market, 48, 132, 218, 243; proximity to Canada, 54, 201-02, 260; see also Border stations
United Technologies advertising, 110
Universal Copyright Convention, 296
Universal Declaration of Human Rights, 245, 308
Upstairs Downstairs, 287

Vancouver Province, see Province, The
Vancouver Sun, 171
van der Hoop, Peter, 182
Vander Zalm, Bill, 83
VCRs, see Videocassette recorders
Vertical integration, 154
Vertical link, 161
VHF broadcasting, 279, 283
Videocassette recorders, 19-20, 204, 317
Videodiscs, 317
Videogames, 290, 317
Video programs, copyright of, 304-05
Videorecording, by public, ethics of, 308
Video rental industry, 19-20, 157, 225, 285, 289
Videos, rock, see Rock videos
Videotex, 204, 290
Violence: on CTV programs, 196; portrayal of, in media, 144; on television news, 27, 71
Vogel, Richard, 187
Voice of America, 236

Wallace, Mike, 144
War Measures Act, 77, 137
War of the Worlds, The (1939), 143
Watchdogs: of business, 194-95; of government, 194

Welles, Orson, 143
Western Broadcasting, 154, 167
Western values, dominance of, 18-19
Weston, Galen, 167
White Papers, 207, 211, 212-13
Williams, Raymond, 45
Wilson, James R., 133
Winner, Langdon, 203
Winnipeg Free Press, 175
Winnipeg Sun, 112, 141
Winnipeg Tribune, closure of (1980), 78, 141, 175
Wolff, Bernard, 233
Woodcock, George, 313, 314
Woodsworth, Charles, 183-84
Woodsworth, J.S., 183
Woollacott, Janet, 94
World Administrative Radio Conference for Space
    Technology, 294
World Information order, 242-43; *see also* New
    world information order
World View channel, 289

ZZTop, 119